RESEARCH METHODOLOGY

This book must be returned on or before
the last date stamped below

RESEARCH METHODOLOGY

in the Life, Behavioural and Social Sciences

Edited by
Herman J. Adèr and Gideon J. Mellenbergh

SAGE Publications
London • Thousand Oaks • New Delhi

SAGE Publications Ltd
6 Bonhill Street
London EC2A 4PU

SAGE Publications Inc
2455 Teller Road
Thousand Oaks, California 91320

SAGE Publications India Pvt Ltd
32, M-Block Market
Greater Kailash - I
New Delhi 110 048

British Library Cataloguing in Publication data

A catalogue record for this book is
available from the British Library

ISBN 0-7619-5883-5
ISBN 0-7619-5884-3 (pbk)

Library of Congress catalog record available

Printed and bound in Great Britain
by Athenaeum Press, Gateshead

Contents

List of Figures

List of Contributors

Herman J. Adèr is a senior staff member of the department of Clinical Epidemiology and Biostatistics at Free University, Amsterdam. He studied Mathematics and Social Science Methodology at the University of Amsterdam. He has been a statistical advisor for many years, first at the psychology department, later at the faculty of Medicine of Free University. In these functions he contributed to numerous research articles and several PhD theses.

In his PhD thesis a formal system to represent methodological knowledge is proposed. Current research interests include graphical knowledge representation, model search methods and neural network modelling in which fields he published several papers and articles.

Gideon J. Mellenbergh (1938) studied psychology at the University of Amsterdam. He received his Masters Degree in 1965 and his PhD Degree in 1971 (English translation of the Dutch dissertation title: 'Studies in achievement testing'; chairman of the dissertation committee: Prof. Dr Adriaan D. de Groot). Since 1982 he is professor of Psychological Methods at the University of Amsterdam. Moreover, he is director of the Interuniversity Graduate School of Psychometrics and Sociometrics (IOPS), associate editor of Psychometrika, and member of the editorial board of Psychological Methods. His scientific interests are in fundamental and applied psychometrics, especially construction and analysis of psychological and educational measurement instruments, differential item functioning, psychometric decision-making, and theoretical analysis of psychometrical concepts and models.

Jaap van Heerden is Associate Professor in Methodology and the Foundations of Psychology at the University of Amsterdam. He contributed as author and co-author to the Journal of Mathematical Psychology, Inquiry, the Journal for the Theory of Social Behaviour, and New Ideas in Psychology. His scientific interest at the moment concerns consciousness studies.

H.P. (Paul) de Greef studied psychology at the University of Amsterdam. In 1984 he joined the department 'SWI' of the University of Amsterdam. This department provided a meeting ground for computer science, social science and behavioural sciences. In the group of Prof. Wielinga he worked in various European research projects on knowledge acquisition and representation. In 1989 he was appointed lecturer in human-computer interaction at a similar SWI department of the University of Leiden. There he obtained a number of large research grants. In 1991 the SWI department in Leiden was terminated and he returned to Amsterdam. His current interests are in representation, modelling and cognitive engineering. In 1999 he was awarded a PhD on a thesis entitled: 'Computer support by knowledge enhancement: constraints and methodology'.

Paul Darius studied mathematics at the Katholieke Universiteit Leuven, where he obtained his doctorate in 1982. He teaches statistics at the K.U. Leuven faculty of agricultural and applied biological sciences, and is currently director of the International Study Program in Statistics there. His research interests include mixed model methodology, meta data, statistical expert systems, visual software for experimental design and software for teaching statistics.

Kenneth M. Portier is an Associate Professor of Statistics and Agricultural Experiment Station Statistician at the University of Florida in Gainesville Florida. A 1979 graduate of the Biostatistics program at the University of North Carolina at Chapel Hill, Dr Portier has worked as a statistical consultant on agricultural, ecological and environmental research projects in the Southern United States, Central and South America. He has taught courses in statistical methods for research, natural resource sampling and advanced statistics for environmental biologists. His publications cover a wide range of statistical applications with more recent work on computational methods in statistics.

Stuart J. Pocock has been a Professor of Medical Statistics at the Medical Statistics Unit at the London School of Hygiene and Tropical Medicine since 1989. He received his MSc at Imperial College of Science, Technology and Medicine in 1968 and his PhD at the London School of Hygiene and Tropical Medicine in 1972. He is the author of the well-known textbook 'Clinical Trials, a practical approach' published by Wiley. His present interests are in standards for reporting on randomized controlled trials, statistical consultation, stopping rules for clinical trials, and Meta-analysis.

Jelke G. Bethlehem studied mathematical statistics at the University of Amsterdam. After obtaining his pre-doctoral degree he was employed as Research Worker at the Statistical Department of the Mathematical Centre in Amsterdam. His work concentrated on multivariate statistical analysis and development of statistical software.

In 1978 he joined the Department for Statistical Methods of Statistics Netherlands, first as Research Worker and later as Senior Statistician. His main topics were the treatment of non-response in sample surveys, in which he obtained his PhD, and disclosure control of published survey data.

From 1987 to 1996 he was head of the Statistical Informatics Department. The work of this department concentrated on the development of standard software for processing survey data. Important projects were the

Blaise System for computer-assisted survey data collection, the StatLine system for the electronic dissemination of statistical publications, and the Bascula package for weighting sample survey data.

Now he is senior methodogical adviser of the the Statistical Methods Department. He is involved in several research projects in the field of survey methodology. He is also part-time professor in Statistical Information Processing at the University of Amsterdam.

Peter C.M. Molenaar's areas of statistical experience include dynamic factor analysis, applied non-linear dynamics, adaptive filtering techniques, spectrum analysis, psychophysiological signal analysis, artificial neural network modelling, covariance structure modelling and behaviour genetical modelling. He is a Professor of Psychology at the University of Amsterdam. He published widely in the above mentioned areas, emphasizing applications to cognitive development (stochastic catastrophe analysis of stage transitions), brain-behavior relationships (real-time artificial neural network simulation of cognitive information processing), brain-maturation and cognition (equivalent dipole modelling of longitudinal registrations of electrocortical fields), genetical influences on EEG during the life span, and optimal control of psychotherapeutic processes. He teaches courses on covariance structure modelling, dynamical factor analysis and state-space modelling, psychophysiological signal analysis, and artificial neural network modelling. He has been and is the Principal Investigator of 21 grants focusing on methodological issues from the Dutch Scientific Organization, the Royal Dutch Academy of Sciences, and the University of Amsterdam.

Joe Whittaker is a Senior Lecturer in the Department of Mathematics and Statistics, Lancaster University. He is a Fellow of the Royal Statistical Society, past member of its Council, Research and chairperson of its Multivariate Study Group. He has been an elected member to the Board of Directors of the European Region of the International Association for Statistical Computing. He has held visiting Professorships in the Department of Statistics at Colorado State University, University of Chicago, and Paul Sabatier University, Toulouse. He is the author of over 60 articles in the open research literature. His research interests lie in graphical modelling, transport models and credit scoring.

Whittaker's contributions include his international best selling graduate text on graphical models. He has given numerous short courses on graphical models some sponsored by the Economic and Social Research Council, U.K. and have been given in Europe and America. He was co-organizer of the conference on Probabilistic Graphical Models, held at the Isaac Newton Institute, Cambridge, part of the Neural Networks 1997 Program in which he was a Visiting Fellow. He was the Program Chair for Uncertainty99, the Seventh International Workshop on Artificial Intelligence and Statistics, held in Florida 1999.

Pete Sewart obtained his first degree in Mathematics and Operational Research from Lancaster University. He continued his studies at Lancaster for his PhD which was supervised by Joe Whittaker, concentrating his research on graphical and longitudinal data models relevant to the area of finance and credit scoring. He has now taken his research and analytical skills into the business world and is currently employed by Marks & Spencer Financial Services in their Credit Development Department where he assists in the analysis and modelling relevant to their credit lending decisions.

Willem E.Saris is full professor in Methodology at the Social, Cultural and Political Sciences faculty of the University of Amsterdam. He has worked in the field of Structural equation models, especially with respect to models for evaluation of quality of survey questions. He has published papers and a book on this topic and has done substantive research in the field of Political decision-making and life satisfaction.

Judea Pearl is a Professor of Computer Science and Statistics at the University of California Los-Angeles, where he is the Director of the Cognitive Systems Laboratory. His areas of research include heuristic reasoning, probabilistic networks, causal discovery, and theories of actions and counterfactuals.

Professor Pearl is the author of 'Heuristics' (Addison-Wesley, 1984), 'Probabilistic Reasoning in Intelligent Systems' (Morgan Kaufmann, 1988) and 'Causality' (forthcoming, 1999). He has published close to 200 research articles, and is serving on the editorial boards of Artificial Intelligence, Annals of Mathematics and AI, and the Encyclopedia of AI.

Professor Pearl is a recipient of the RCA Laboratories Achievement Award (1965), NATO Senior Fellowship in Science (1975), UCLA 81st Faculty Research Lecturership (1996) and IJCAI Research Excellence Award (1999). He is a Fellow of the IEEE, a Founding Fellow of the American Association of Artificial Intelligence, and a member of the National Academy of Engineering.

John E. Cornell received his PhD in psychology from the University of Southern Mississippi, and he completed two years of postdoctoral training in behavioral statistics under the direction of Roger Kirk at Baylor University. He is an Associate Professor in the Department of Medicine at the University of Texas Health Science Center at San Antonio and he is the chief biostatistician for the Geriatric Research, Education and Clinical Center within the South Texas Veterans Health Care Center, Audie L. Murphy Division, in San Antonio, Texas. He also serves as the resident meta-analyst for the VA Cochrane Center at San Antonio. His primary research interests are in the design and analysis of studies involving longitudinal data. Within meta-analysis, he invests time in statistical models to assess and account for heterogeneity — including hierarchical Bayesian models — and in statistical models for combining information from correlated observations (multivariate, time-to-event, and repeated measures).

Cynthia D. Mulrow received her medical degree, residency training, and chief resident experience at the Baylor School of Medicine, Houston, Texas. She completed a General Medicine Fellowship as a Mellon Fellow at Duke University Medical Center, Durham, North Carolina. She was then awarded a Milbank Research Scholar award and received a MSc in Epidemiology from the London School of Hygiene and Tropical Medicine.

Dr Mulrow currently is the Chief of General Internal Medicine at the Audie Murphy Veterans Affairs (VA) Hospital, and a Professor of Medicine at the University of Texas Health Science Center at San Antonio. She is a graduating Senior Career Scientist in the VA Health Services Research and Development Program and is currently Director of the Agency for Health Care Policy and Research-sponsored San Antonio Evidence-based Practice Center and the Cochrane Center at San Antonio.

Dr Mulrow's special areas of interest are systematic reviews and guidelines, primary care, hypertension, and depression. She was co-editor of a special ten-part series and book on systematic reviews produced for the Annals of Internal Medicine. Currently, she is an associate editor for the Journal of General Internal Medicine for the 'From Research to Practice', an editorial board member of the British Medical Journal and ACP Journal Club, and a member of the US Preventive Services Task Force.

Chapter 1

Introduction

How this book was born... The idea for this book originates from a study on statistical expert systems that centered around the question why such systems are hardly ever used. One of the answers to that question was: the conceptual level at which such a system should function is *not* of a statistical nature but of a higher, more methodological one.

To put it in a more popular way: if you want a computer to act like a statistical expert, it should learn not only how to handle Statistics but also how to handle high-level methodological issues.

Of course, a computer is much more stupid than a human being and it requires very strict instructions as to what it has to do. On the other hand, if one can formulate rules for a computer, humans can certainly understand and apply them.

The research mentioned above forms only a slight pretense to write this book. To find out the fundamental rules that underlie the activity called 'scientific research' seems a worthwhile undertaking in itself.

Someone may argue that it is not so obvious that there is some underlying method to all empirical research. We think there is. And one of the aims of this book is to show there is. In the discussion at the end of the book we tried to dig out a general framework that encompasses the essential similarities and the obvious points of difference in the fields covered.

Thus, the point of departure of the book is the view that the Methodology of quantitative research is a discipline of its own, of which the basic notions, procedures and ways of reasoning can be precisely described.

About the title. By 'Research' we do not mean qualitative research, although we recognize that the approaches are closely related. Furthermore, the subtitle mentions a broad range of disciplines. One may ask whether it is too broad. Which fields of empirical research are *not* included? Essentially, none of the 'classical' empirical sciences is intended, like Physics or Astronomy.

To whom is the book addressed? Researchers involved in practical research tend not to make use of the methodological attainments of the last

1

decade (which, by the way, are overwhelmingly many, as you will notice while reading through this book). This is not only because they are not aware of this progression but also since they perceive Statistics as a separate discipline with no obvious relationship to the solution of the problems they are facing. Since they approach their work in a practical way, their approach of statistical applications is practical, often resulting in a data analytical, technique-driven view.

It is easy to understand why the ongoing statistical discourse is of no direct consequence to the 'researcher in the field': It is often theoretical and not even methodological oriented.

This book may serve to bridge the gap between those two distinct points of view: the practical one directed towards doing practical research in a specific area like Experimental Psychology or Radiology. And, on the other hand, the point of view of the methodologist or the statistical advisor who is interested in responsive application of newly developed techniques.

For the researcher in the field, it describes the basic methods he or she can apply. Since the viewpoint is methodological, no deep statistical knowledge is required and, indeed, the contents are mostly closer to the actual research problems than a standard statistical text would be.

The book also provides a useful text for students of methodology and statistical consultation, since it describes in a unified way how to design and analyse research in various fields of the social and behavioral sciences and in Medicine. The student may learn what he can expect when he gives actual advice and which issues deserve special attention.

We would be very satisfied when the reader of this book would react somewhat like: "I got a better idea of what is available in this field, I learned something that I can use in my own research. If something is not in the book and I want to know more, I can consult the state-of-the-art references of the 'Further reading' sections the chapters provide".

Basic Idea.   The informal title we used between us was: 'Methodology as a discipline' (In Dutch: 'Methodologie als vak'). This may seem amazing, considering the fact that we both call ourselves 'methodologists'. The reason was that when you call Methodology a discipline, it must be possible to indicate basic notions and ways of reasoning used by everyone who does research. When we tried to indicate what these basics might be, this turned out not to be straightforward at all.

We suspected there exist research paradigms, deeply anchored in the philosophy of science on which researchers subconsciously are oriented when they do their work. Therefore, our main question was

> *'What are the basic elements, the basic lines of reasoning and the paradigms underlying research methods?'*

The book is an attempt to discover these basic notions and to describe them. We do not deny that their development closely corresponds to, even coincides with developments in Applied Statistics and to research methods in all those specific areas of empirical research that use statistics during design and analysis.

We are well aware that in most disciplines a substantial literature on research methods exists that in some cases is rapidly expanding. But we also noticed that much less has been published on differences and similarities between the methods used in those application fields. The aim of the book is to do just that: to give the reader an impression of what methods are used in those fields and how they correspond or differ.

How did we proceed? As you can see, a considerable number of authors were asked to contribute a chapter to this book, each with his own views and expertise. This has pros and cons. Of course, it is downright unique to have contributions of people that have been working in their field for a long time and that have a lot of specialized knowledge, and on top of that can write comprehensively on the subject they love.

On the other hand, we ran the risk of getting a heterogeneous whole with contributions of different level and style. Also, from the point of view of the authors it is difficult to lay links to other subjects outside their field.

For the editors this resulted in a decision problem: to choose between readability on the one side and depth and personal style on the other.

We solved this in two ways. First of all, we discussed at length the contents and the structure of the book and decided how links between chapters should be established. We discussed this with the authors and tried to have them discuss the relevance of their field to the outside world, and, more particular, to the contents of the other chapters. In fact, the authors were supplied with some basic questions that could serve as a guideline during writing:

o *What are the basic notions and ways of reasoning in your field?* This, in a nutshell, is what the book is about.

o *What is your own position in your field?* This question was included since we thought it much more interesting to read about the specific themes an author is working on than about well-known principles that can be found in any textbook. It also took away the obligation for the authors to give a full account of their field in an insufficient number of pages.

o *Can other fields benefit from the findings in your field and are methods from other fields applicable in your own field?* This question was meant to offer the possibility to indicate links to and from other disciplines.

General structure. Apart from a historical introduction (Chapter 2) and one on meta-analysis at the end (Chapter 13), three parts may be discerned.

o In the first part *REPRESENTATION* is at the center. Various graphical representation methods are discussed in Chapter 3 and high level representations of data in Chapter 4 on meta data.

o The second part concerns *DESIGN* and describes a number of fundamental research designs: Experimental Design, Clinical Trials, Cross-sectional designs and Longitudinal Designs.

o The third part focuses on *MODELLING*. Like the part on Design, it has also four chapters, discussing respectively (a) Measurement models, (b) Graphical models, (c) Structural Equation models and, (d) Causal models.

Care has been taken to make the second part of the title '... in the Behavioural, Life, and Social Science' credible by taking examples from different subject matter fields. Of course, there is an end to this: most authors are familiar with one of those fields only and it would turn out unnatural to ask them to describe research outside their field of application. But most authors were quite able to illustrate the line of thought with a small sample from another field.

Are we satisfied with the result?   The writing of the book went off unexpectedly well considering the many people that participated. Working on the project has been very rewarding both for the authors and the editors.

If we have in fact been able to point out what the foundations of this new, unified field called 'Research Methodology' should look like, remains to be seen. We undoubtedly produced a worthwhile overview over what is going on in various subfields. And this is the texture that the more fundamental stuff should be made of.

Acknowledgements.   Special thanks go to David Hand who not only has been very stimulating during the whole project but who did carefully read all material and provided us with his sound and often very fundamental commentary.

All chapters have been reviewed by especially selected reviewers who, like the authors of the chapters, are specialists in the field covered by the chapter. Their comments have been invaluable. There is no way in which we could have done our job if the reviewers had not first commented on the abstracts and drafts, since it would have been virtually impossible to properly judge and value the importance of all the specific issues the chapters deal with. More importantly, not being an expert in the field, we would have been unable to spot which important topics had been left out.

Only the amount of space available and the emphasis the author of the respective chapter wanted to put on particular issues made us depart from reviewers' advice. Thus, the final responsibility for the contents of the chapters is the authors' and our own.

Amsterdam, May 31, 1999
Herman J. Adèr
Gideon J. Mellenbergh

Chapter 2

Some Remarks on the History of Method

Jaap van Heerden

It is interesting to note that a successful scientific achievement in the past is by historians of science appreciated for quite different reasons. Sometimes this appreciation differs considerably from the appreciation the scientist concerned originally wanted to attain. The reputable historian of psychology, E. C. Boring, cites Pascal's experiment in 1648 with Torricellian tubes at the Puy-de-Dôme as an early example of the use of control observations as a standard of comparison for the principal observations. "In 1648 the Torricellian vacuum was known to physics in general and to Pascal in particular. This is the vacuum formed at the upper closed end of a tube which first has been filled with mercury and then inverted with its lower open end in a disk of mercury (...). Pascal was of the opinion that the column is supported by the weight of the air that presses upon the mercury in the disk (he was right: the Torricellian tube is a barometer) and that the column should be shorter at higher altitudes where the weight of the atmosphere would be less" (Boring, 1954, p. 577). By measuring the height of the column at the foot of the Puy-de Dôme, at the top and at intermediate altitude one could collect evidence for the correctness of the hypothesis involved. It should, however, be noted that it was not Pascal's exclusive aim to prove that the Torricellian tube was a barometer. His aim was to prove in this way that the alleged horror vacui in nature does not exist. That was his principal purpose.

The horror vacui thesis stems from Aristotle. It says with so many words that nature does not tolerate and even abhors a vacuum. The actual Latin phrase was coined by Johannes Canonicus in the Thirteenth century. The thesis was still a matter in dispute in Pascal's days. In a letter to his brother-in-law, Monsieur Périer, he wrote "j'ai peine à croire que la nature, qui n'est point animée, ni sensible, soit susceptible d'horreur [du vide], puisque les passions présupposent une âme capable de les ressentir, et j'incline bien plus à imputer tous ces effets à la pesanteur et pression de l'air ..." (Pascal, 1954, 393) (I find it hard to believe that nature, not being animated nor sensitive, should be susceptible of horror [vacui], because passions presuppose a soul capable of feeling them and I rather incline to attribute all these effects to atmospheric weight and pressure). He then asked his brother-in-law, living in Clermont near the mountain Puy-de-Dôme, to perform an experiment, in the sense described above. It is Monsieur Périer who can take the credits for the well-balanced experimental design. He set up two tubes at the foot of the mountain, found that the columns were equal in length, left one at the base watched by an assistant in order to register possible changes during the time of the experiment, carried the disassembled other one to the top where it was put together. In fact, Périer ascertained in this way the indispensable control observations. "How important (...), How wise (...), How intelligent (...)", comments Boring (op.cit. p. 578). He obviously appreciated Périer's methodological sophistication. Pascal, on the other hand, explicated another methodological principle: an experiment should be decisive between two hypotheses. "vous voyez déjà sans doute, que cette expérience est decisive de la question, et que, s'il arrive que la hauteur du vif-argent soit moindre au haut qu'au bas de la montagne (...), il s'ensuivra nécessairement que la pesanteur et pression de l'air est la seule cause de cette suspension du vif-argent et non pas l'horreur du vide ..." (op.cit. p. 394) (You see for sure that this experience is decisive as to the question and that if it turns out that the height of mercury is less at the top of the mountain than at the foot (...) it necessarily follows that the atmospheric weight and pressure is the sole cause of that suspension of the mercury and not the horror vacui). In Pascal's opinion it was a crucial experiment. Dijksterhuis (1961) argues that Pascal's expectation as to the status of this experiment is unfounded, because other interpretations are not completely excluded and Copi (1953) has convincingly shown that the consequences of a crucial experiment can in principle always be undone by changing one of the auxiliary premises or by introducing an ad hoc hypothesis that explains the unfavourable outcome away. The term *crucial experiment* is not a useless one, however, says Copi "Within the framework of accepted scientific theory which we are not concerned to question, a hypothesis can be subjected to a crucial experiment. But there is nothing absolute about such procedure, for even well-accepted scientific theories tend to be challenged" (Copi, 1953, p. 425).

There is one other lesson to be learnt from Pascal. He attempted to decide this question by quantitative measurement in an experimental setting. The essence of quantitative measurement is the production of numbers as Kuhn (1977) says. These numbers indicate a position on a scale and the difference between the numbers record a difference in reality. But one of the significant functions of measurement is, according to Kuhn, "that measurement can be an immensely powerful weapon in the battle between two theories (...)" and: "In scientific practice the real information questions always involve the comparison of two theories with each other and with the world, not the comparison of a single theory with the world. In these three-way comparisons, measurement has a particular advantage." (op.cit. p. 211). That was exactly Pascal's strategy.

As said above, Boring appreciated this experiment for its methodological finesse, "195 years too soon for the experimenters to have read John Stuart Mill's Logic." (op.cit. p. 572). He obviously had in mind that Pascal and Périer are to be admired for this experimental design long before the methodological rules of experimentation were explicitly and systematically formulated. That was done by John Stuart Mill. As to experimental inquiry, his aim was to give a complete "enumeration of the means which mankind possess for exploring the laws of nature by specific observation and experience" (Mill, 1862, p. 436).

Laws of nature stipulate causal relations between phenomena or events. The inquiry into lawlike relations has a two-fold character: one either tries to find the cause of a given effect or the effects of a given cause. In fact mankind possesses four means or methods to find the causal connection between events. Mill's exposition has become classical and nowadays every textbook of Methodology gives a concise survey of his findings. Also Boring's article on the history and nature of control contains a fine summary. But we will turn to the original text because of the illuminating examples Mill provides each method with and because of the fact that the original text contains modifications of methods obviously of some historical importance, but rarely mentioned in contemporary overviews.

Mill denotes antecedents by large letters of the alphabet and consequences by small letters. "Suppose, for example, that A is tried along with B and C and that the effect is abc; and suppose that A is next tried with D and E, but without B and C and that the effect is ade. Then we may reason thus: b and c are not effects of A, for they are not produced by it in the second experiment, nor are d and e, for they were not produced in the first. Whatever is really the effect of A must have been produced in both instances; now this condition is fulfilled by no circumstance except a." Mill coins this way of experimentation the *method of Agreement*, essentially consisting in comparing different instances in which the phenomenon occurs. Under all possible circumstances A is followed by a. So we conclude that A in all probability is the cause of a. Mill's example is the production of soap (a). When we bring an alkaline substance into contact with an oil (A) under a variety of circumstances, the result is "a greasy and detersive or saponaceous substance" (op.cit. p. 426). The method of Agreement is never conclusive. Mill considered his second method, the *method of Difference*, as more potent. The procedure is: "If the effect of ABC is abc and the effect of BC is bc, it is evident that the effect of A is a" (op.cit. p. 428). It is evident that the joint methods of Agreement and Difference make a strong case. In a variety of circumstances A is always followed by a and in a variety of circumstances not-A is never followed by a. Mill noticed that both methods are methods of *elimination*. "The Method of Agreement stands on the ground that whatever can be eliminated, is not connected with the phenomenon by law. The method of Difference has for its foundation, that whatever cannot be eliminated, is connected with the phenomenon by law." The method of Difference can not always be employed as in history or astronomy. It requires *manipulation*. The method of Agreement is the justification of painstaking observation. Mill's third method is the *method of Residues*. If we know that the effect of ABC is abc and the effect of A is a and the effect of B is b, the method of Residues implies that "subtracting the sum of these effects from the total phenomenon, there remains c, which now, without any fresh experiment, we may know to be the effect of C" (op.cit. p. 436). This method is of special importance in cases where the effect of c cannot independently be established or measured, but only indirectly as part of the effect of another phenomenon.

I know of at least one example in the history of psychology wherein this method of Residues is applied. It concerns the subtraction method as developed by the Dutch physiologist F. C. Donders (1818–1889). It was widely used in the field of mental chronometry. How much time do mental processes take? One can register the reaction time of a subject, asked to press as quickly as possible a button as soon he sees the flickering of a light. One can refine the experiment by introducing three lights of a different colour with three corresponding buttons to be pressed as soon as one of the lights flashes. Now the reaction time is longer. By subtracting the first reaction time from the second one gets, approximately, the time it takes to discriminate and to make the proper movement. This is essentially Mill's method of Residues applied to measurement. By introducing one button only to be pressed at the flashing of one specific colour out of three or more, a task which takes less time than the previous one, because the subject has not to choose between different movements, one can now by subtracting the first reaction time from the last, find out how much time it takes to discriminate (see for more details Kolk, 1994).

A special difficulty is constituted by causes "which we can neither hinder from being present, nor contrive that they shall be present alone" (op.cit. p. 437). A good example of this difficulty is the relation between body and temperature or heat. "We are unable to exhaust any body of the whole of its heat. It is equally certain that no one ever perceived heat not emanating from a body. Being unable, then, to separate Body and Heat, we cannot effect such a variation of circumstances as the foregoing three methods require" (op.cit. p. 438). But there is still a resource, because we can study the effect of *modification* of the phenomena under consideration. We can try to change or modify or vary the impact of the alleged cause and effect. We can do so by careful observation as nature happens to bring about a change, or experimentally if the circumstances allow such an intervention. "If some modification in the antecedent A is always followed by a change in the consequent a, the other consequences b and c remaining the same, or vice versa, if every change in a is found to have been preceded by some modification in A, none being observable in any of the other antecedents, we may safely conclude that a is, wholly or in part, an effect traceable to *A...* " (op.cit. p. 439). In case of heat we can attain the conclusion that an increase or diminution of the temperature leads to an enlargement or contraction of the body. This fourth method is termed by Mill as the *method of Concomitant Variation*. But Concomitant Variation is in itself not sufficient to establish which of the two varying phenomena is the cause and which the effect, and it cannot be excluded either that the two modifications are due to a common cause. "The only way to solve the doubt would be (...) by endeavouring to ascertain whether we can produce the one set of variations by means of the other. In case of heat, for example, by increasing the temperature of a body we increase its bulk, but by increasing its bulk we do not increase its temperature; on the contrary, we generally diminish it: therefore heat is not an effect, but a cause, of increase of bulk" (op.cit. p. 442).

Reading Mill one is struck by the elegance of exposition and the clarity of thought. But his was not the last word in Methodology. He was even sometimes a bit naive in his practical strategy how to compare the experimental and control condition. Take for example how he conceived of an experiment in which one could establish the deadly effect of carbonic acid gas. "If a bird is taken from a cage, and instantly plunged into carbonic acid gas, the experimentalist may be fully assured (at all events after one or two repetitions) that no circumstance capable of causing suffocation has supervened in the interim, except the change from immersion in the atmosphere to immersion in carbonic acid gas" (op.cit. p. 431). The previous state is the control condition and Mill has to warn the would-be experimentalist to act "as rapidly as possible". It did not occur to him to form two groups of birds and to give one of them the required treatment. (If one accepts this sacrifice as justifiable for the sake of science. But that is another question.) In Methodology it took some time before the *Experimental Design* was developed and valued of drawing randomly a sample from the population and assigning randomly subjects to the experimental and control conditions. That in itself was a great innovation (See Dehue, 1997). The random assignment of subjects to conditions meant, properly understood, an optimal realization that individual characteristics of subjects were equally distributed over the experimental and control group. The same could be realized by matching. This kind of experimental design was in psychology not realized until around 1900, partly because mainstream psychology was primarily interested in individual achievements of well-trained subjects, reporting by introspection on the performance of mental tasks, and partly because the statistical means were not yet fully developed to properly deal with group-differences.

Aristotle adhered to the rule that everything goes in sevens. This rule had to be considered as self-evident. Moreover, it was a useful device for analysing scientific problems. It revealed, for instance, that man has seven ages, each seven years long. This fundamental insight made it possible to deduce and prove all kinds of interesting theorems.

One could say that this septuple or hebdominal rule, although essentially dogmatic, was an early attempt to use an *algorithm* in matters of science.

In a primitive way it involves the assignment of numbers to phenomena, and the application of simple arithmetics warrants a fruitful continuation of empirical research. Aristotle's approach is a methodological innovation that deserves the requisite attention in the history of ideas but at the same time it shows that not all methodological innovations contribute to the advancement of science. It refutes the myth that the enhancement of scientific knowledge exclusively depends on the developments of methods. What the growth of knowledge requires is an *independent analysis* and *justification of scientific methods* (as Mill did), free from metaphysical assumptions as to the dominant place of one number or another. Bear in mind that the same metaphysical assumption about the pre-eminence of the number seven prevents regarding Aristotle's rule as a primitive form of measurement. It is impossible to see it as such, not only because of the queer consequence that all measures would yield the number seven as a result, but also because of the fact that the outcome of any measurement whatsoever precedes the factual process of measuring. The outcome is fixed and reality has to obey or to be accommodated. The best one can say of Aristotle's rule is that it is a heuristic advice: it may be profitable to view any phenomenon as consisting of seven parts. But that is more a form of modelling than a form of measuring.

Beginning with classification, i.e. ordering by comparison, Science step by step developed quantitative measuring in the sense that each item falling under a certain concept, occupies one and only one place on a numerical scale although more than one item could occupy the same place.

Francis Galton (1822–1911) has to be remembered for several outstanding contributions to the methodology of the life sciences.

In the first place he observed that eminent mental ability frequently goes by descent and seems to run in certain families. By studying family-histories he found that the proportion of highly talented relatives exceeded the proportion to be expected by chance. Being a cousin of Charles Darwin and probably strongly influenced by his cousin's 'Origin of Species', Galton became a strong believer in the heredity of intelligence, talent and character. Mental characteristics could in principle to the same extent be measured as physical ones. Galton adopted Quetelet's method of fitting normal curves to data. As Stigler (1985) says: "He was fascinated by the appearance of the 'very curious theoretical law of deviation from an average' in so many different cases, for heights and chest measurements and even such measures of talent as examination scores. Following Quetelet, he proposed that the conformity of the data to this characteristic curve was to be a sort of test of the appropriateness of classifying the data together in one group; or rather the non-appearance of this curve was indicative that the data should not be treated together".

In a way one could also regard Galton as the inventor of the mental test. He took measurements for association, by registering the reaction times needed to respond to a target word. But more important still is his invention of the measure of *correlation*, for which he gave a calculation instruction. He applied his method to variations in measurements of diverse parts of the human body: tallness and long head length, for instance, go together. The upshot of his scientific endeavours was a political manifesto. He wrote "What an extraordinary effect might be produced on our race, if its object was to unite in marriage those who possessed the finest and most suitable natures, mental, moral and physical" (Galton, 1865). He became the founder of eugenics and the eugenic movement. In this he was followed by his disciple Karl Pearson (1857–1936), who also improved on his calculation of the correlation coefficient, the well-known Pearson's product moment estimate of the correlation coefficient. Given the deplorable state of the British Empire, Pearson formulates the remedy: "getting the intellectual section of our nation to realise that intelligence can be aided and be trained, but no training can *create* it. You must breed it, that is the broad result for statecraft which flows from the equality in inheritance of the psychical and physical characters in man" (Pearson, 1903). The debate on this issue is still with us.

Chapter 3

Graphical Representation of Methodological Concepts

Herman J. Adèr

What may be the reason for representing methodological concepts in a formal way? It is not difficult to think of situations in which a reliable and easy-to-use formal representation could be beneficial. For instance, since *Planning* largely determines the research design and thus the data analysis and the interpretation of the results, an unambiguous representation of the research plan could help to avoid design flaws.

As an example, think of Computer Assisted Interviewing (CAI). Assume we were able to represent the order in which the questions have to be put to the interviewee as a decision tree. The very activity of drawing such a tree will uncover any omission.

Another example is the design of a protocol for a Clinical Trial in Medicine. Here also, a formal description could help to spot ambiguous points in the whole procedure during the trial and specify it in complete detail.

Now an obvious next question is: *What exactly should be imagined by 'Representation'?*

In Artificial Intelligence the term 'Knowledge Representation' is used to indicate formal ways to lay down knowledge of experts in a specific domain. Starting from this representation more or less intelligent computer software can be built that mimics the approaches of these experts. Many methods to describe high level concepts have been proposed in this field, several of which will be considered in the next sections.

. Some notions are too frequently used in Artificial Intelligence not to briefly mention them here. The set of entities composing the knowledge of concern is called *universe of discourse*. A distinction is made between *declarative* and *procedural* knowledge. The first kind refers to the plain definition of the objects in the universe and the relations between them. The second kind refers to the actions that may be taken upon the defined objects and their relations. *Strategic* knowledge is a special kind of procedural knowledge, concerning the way to use declarative and procedural knowledge to attain some predefined *goal*. An example is the way the data analyst goes about in the series of analyses he or she performs (Oldford, 1990). Genesereth & Nilsson (1987, Chapter 12) explain the theoretical side of the representation of strategies in their chapter on Planning. Strategic knowledge will be discussed in Section 3.5.1.

With the representation of methodological knowledge two concepts play a key role: *Context* and *Time*. Of course, the notion of Context is important in many other fields. What makes this case a special one is that we can indicate what the context consists of. Apart from ideas and notions from applied statistics, many elements of the context originate from the research field ('the subject matter field') in which the basic research question was posed.

As to the notion of Time, for many study designs temporal issues are essential, be it to study variability over time (in reproducibility studies and studies on responsiveness) or to study development of a phenomenon over time. This may be on a per person basis as occurs in a repeated measurement design or in a more epidemiological sense in a cohort study. A host of statistical methods is available to appropriately handle the resulting data: The analysis of repeated measurements, Trend analysis, Time series analysis, Longitudinal analysis, and the analysis of survival data are all well-studied statistical techniques, specially devised to analyse temporal data.

Therefore, both Context and Time are notions that should be expressible in any representation system. In this chapter, this will be touched upon in Section 3.3 on Time and Section 3.5 on Context.

Although the chapter discusses a formal subject, the approach will be rather informal. The reason is that I will concentrate on *graphical* representation methods that invite a casual discussion. I even restrict myself to a particular kind of diagram, called *planar graph*. This is a graph placed in the two-dimensional plane that has as its building stones *nodes* and *edges* between nodes.

In Section 3.1 different ways to graphically represent statistical and methodological concepts will be staged. We will try to find out what their respective merits are in provisions to the express methodological notions and activities. In Section 3.1.1 some general requirements will be formulated that seem essential. In Section 3.2 basic ideas of so-called *Functional notation* (Adèr, 1995, Chapter 5 and 6) will be given. In the subsequent sections, this notation is used for the representation of temporal notions (in Section 3.3), reasoning (in Section 3.4), strategy (in Section 3.5.1) and context (in Section 3.5.2).

This introduction ends with a word of warning: Diagrams are often supposed to be self-explanatory and easy-to-comprehend while implicitly it is assumed that all elements shown as well as their interrelations are well-defined. But very often the formal correspondence between a diagram and its meaning is not trivial at all. One of the aims of this chapter is to clarify where and when graphical representation methods can be usefully applied without leaving much room for ambiguity.

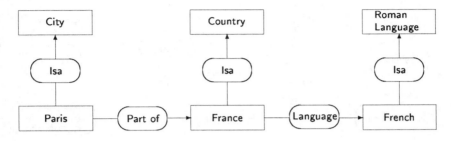

Figure 3.1: Example of a semantic net.

3.1   Common approaches in various fields

In artificial intelligence, a variety of graphical representation styles of conceptual data models have been proposed, many of them derived from so-called *semantic nets* which will be discussed hereafter. Other approaches have been developed in the realm of social science research: I will comment on graphical methods to represent experimental design, on structural equation models and graphical models. At the end of this section the usual graphical representation of Artificial Neural Networks are considered.

Semantic Nets, Conceptual Graphs and Concept Mapping. Figure 3.1 gives an example of a semantic net[1]. The boxes (City, Paris, French ...) contain Concepts, while the arrows are labelled to indicate relationships between concepts: Isa, Part of and so on.

The idea of semantic nets go back to the work by Peirce (See Peirce (1933)). Being a logician, Peirce constructed a graphical notation for predicate calculus. Other graphical systems for general knowledge representation have developed from this. Quillian (1968) was first to formulate a symbolism in connection to cognitive models for memory organization. This forms the basis of later knowledge representation methods. Other areas of application are language research (for a recent review, see Willems (1993)).

Although the representation differs slightly, *conceptual graphs* are similar to semantic nets. Sowa (1984) formulated the syntax and semantics that can be used to build such graphs. In the conceptual graph representation all important facts are grouped around nodes, so that a two dimensional

---

[1] I preferably adhere to the way graphs are usually drawn in the field they are taken from. If no particular conventions seem to exist, I will use *Functional notation* as described in Adèr (1995). A succinct description of this formalism will be given in Section 3.2.

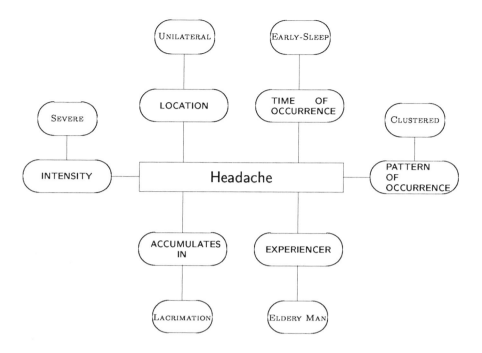

Figure 3.2: Conceptual graph, describing headache complaints. Source: Clancey (1985).

structure arises. There are two basic elements: *notions* and *relations* between notions, which are both labelled. In Figure 3.2 the notion 'Headache' is depicted in the middle of a net of related predicates ('severe', 'unilateral' 'early-sleep' and so forth). Relations have uppercase labels like 'intensity', 'location', 'time of occurrence', respectively). In the figure, relations are indicated by undirectional edges with a label inside an oval, while the predicates are indicated by ovals with small caps as a type font. Note that what is depicted here is the data of a single patient. Substituting other values for the predicates gives the representation of another patient suffering from the same disease. Putting variables over a set of predicates in place of the present values would extend the present representation to indicate a group of patients and would make it *generic*.

Conceptual graphs may well be used to describe subject matter concepts previous to the formulation of an empirical research design. Thus, a generic version of Figure 3.2 could be interpreted as a formal description of the complex structure of headache complaints previous to the formulation of the design of a clinical trial to investigate the disease[2]. Although this graphical formalism is effective as a means to depict complex phenom-

---

[2] Clancey (1985) introduces conceptual graphs as a formal specification after which to construct diagnostic computer software.

ena, some aspects are difficult to express. In particular, logic operations like negation and disjunction and procedural knowledge can not easily be incorporated.

As stated in the introduction, any representation of methodological knowledge, be it graphical or not, should have provisions to represent objects placed in time. Conceptual graphs have only imperfect provisions for this, since time is handled like any other attribute and thus it is difficult to indicate how more complicated structures behave in time.

Authors like Novak (1990) have extended the idea to a related representation called *Concept maps*. It was used to describe the knowledge context of learning. In this area a lot of effort has been invested in developing computer programs with which these kinds of graphs can easily be constructed (See Lanzing, 1996, for an evaluation of existing software). In Figure 3.3, a screen dump is given of one of these programs: again a concept (the starlike figure) is surrounded by a net of connected notions. Note that in contrast to the conceptual graph of Figure 3.2, directional arrows are used instead of links.

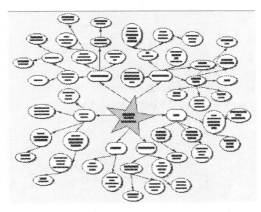

Figure 3.3: Screen dump of Inspiration©, a program to construct concept maps.

Experimental Design. Figure 3.4 shows the way Cook & Campbell (1979) indicate the designs of (quasi-)experiments. (a) indicates the basic experiment: Observation followed by treatment, followed by another observation. In (b) a control group is present, on which the same observations are done, but no treatment is given. The dashed line indicates that the experimental groups are not randomly formed. In picture (c) the precondition is observed in a different (but comparable) population. Note that the figure differs from other figures in this section in that it is not built from nodes with interconnecting edges.

A modern graphical representation of an experiment is given in Figure 3.5. This representation gives an impression of the general structure of

$$O_1 \quad X \quad O_2$$

$$
\begin{array}{ccc}
O_1 & X & O_2 \\
\hline
O_1 & & O_2
\end{array}
$$

$$
\begin{array}{cc}
O_1 & \\
& \\
X & O_1
\end{array}
$$

(a)   (b)   (c)

Figure 3.4: Notation to indicate quasi-experimental designs.
Legend: O: Observation, X: Treatment. (a) Observation, treatment, observation; (b) Non-randomized design with a control group; (c) Design in which the precondition is observed in a different (but comparable) population. Source: Cook & Campbell (1979).

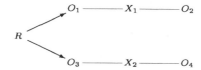

Figure 3.5: Experimental design: before–after two-group design. R: Randomly assigned subjects; O_i: Observation; X_i: Treatment (original caption).

a randomized clinical trial (See Judd, Smith, & Kidder (1991) for several alternative designs.) After randomization, subjects are assigned to either one of two treatment arms.

Both Figure 3.4 and 3.5 are ambiguous (although they may be effective if benevolently interpreted). In particular, in Figure 3.4, information on the structure of the experiment is intermingled with information on experimental units: in Figure 3.4 dashed and wavy lines indicate population characteristics, while the figure itself describes the temporal arrangement of the observations.

In Figure 3.5, R represents a group of subjects that have been already randomly assigned while O_i and X_i are activities *one* patient is subjected to. Note that this makes the meaning of the arrows unclear: The group of randomly assigned subjects cannot possibly *produce* observations O_1 and O_3. The figure would be more comprehensible if we were allowed to read R as 'one subject to be randomly assigned'. R and the two arrows originating from R could then be interpreted as representing the randomization procedure and the subsequent assignment to either of two arms. In this case we are left with the interpretation of the links between observation and treatment and vice versa: we would have been happier when arrows had

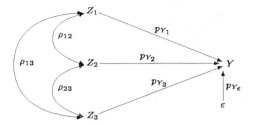

Figure 3.6: Example of a path diagram of a regression model. Y: dependent variable; z_i: independent variables (predictors); ρ_{ij}: correlation coefficients; p_{Y_i}, p_{Y_ϵ}: path coefficients.

been used here, since now the reading order in the figure implicitly indicate the arrangement in time. Admittedly, this is also indicated by the indices of observations and treatments: odd indices indicate the first administration while even ones indicate the second administration. But when we compare this to Figure 3.4 in which comparable observations have the same index, it is no longer clear whether O_1 and O_3 indicate the same kind of observation (this also holds for O_2 and O_4).

Finally, to end this niggling discussion, note that the nodes in this figure do not refer to objects but rather to activities, R being the act of randomization, O that of observing and X of giving treatment. Later on, in Section 3.2, a detailed representation of this design is given.

Path diagrams and Structural Modelling. Wright (1934) introduced so-called *path diagrams*, to visualize regression models. In Figure 3.6 an example is given. The objects that occur in this particular figure are variables Z_i and Y and the error term ε. The ρ_{ij}s labelling the bidirectional arrows are product-moment correlation coefficients indicating the strength of association between covariates Z_i. The path coefficients p_{Y_i} and p_{Y_ϵ} indicate the strength of the influences of the covariates and unsystematic error on the dependent. Thus, if we have to formulate what meaning should be attached to the arrows in the figure, we could read the bidirectional arrows as 'is associated with' and the directional arrows as 'is influencing'.

Wright's work led to the introduction of 'Structural Equation Modelling' (SEM by abbreviation) in which similar graphical representations are used (See Chapter 11 and 12 for a more extensive account of the historical background of path diagrams and Structural Equation Modelling).

SEM offers a wide variety of modelling possibilities. Confirmatory factor analysis, regression analysis and perhaps most importantly, models with latent parameters, can all easily be represented. It is a way of analysing in which both methodological and statistical considerations play an important part. As such, this field has much potential when it comes to the formulation of the basics of research methodology. Initial interest in the technique was raised when some authors tried to assess causal relationships and used

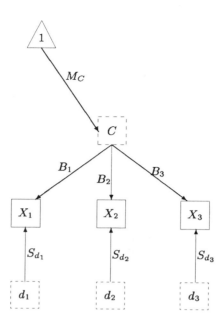

Figure 3.7: Structure diagram for a CURVE factor model. 1: constant; C: latent factor, X_1, X_2 and X_3: manifest variables, d_1, d_2 and d_3: measurements at time $t = 1, 2, 3$. B_i, S_{d_i}: parameters to be estimated. Source: McArdle & Epstein (1987).

structural equation modelling for it. This direction is now usually called *causal modelling*. Much more on the subject is discussed in Chapter 12.

As argued before, it is important that a representation method allows to express temporal notions. The following example, taken from McArdle & Epstein (1987), demonstrates the usual approach to model temporal aspects in SEM. It is an application of structural models in the field of child development research. Figure 3.7 gives what they call the 'CURVE' model that assumes a latent factor C, with manifest variables X_1, X_2 and X_3, measured by d_1, d_2 and d_3 on three occasions ($t = 1, 2, 3$).

Note the way in which time-related aspects are modelled: by duplicating objects and indexing for time. The notation is not different from a model with three observed variables without repeated observations. In Section 3.3 an alternative representation method will be given in which temporal aspects can be indicated more clearly.

Graphical modelling.   Whittaker (1990) discusses statistical models that use a graphical representation of the (in)dependence structure of the variables. This will also be the subject of Chapter 10. A variety of statistical models can be represented this way including Markov chains. Structural equation models may be interpreted as a special case.

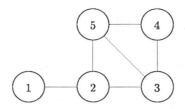

Figure 3.8: Dependence diagram of the logit model: $\log p_{12345} = u_\phi + u_1 + u_2 + u_3 + u_4 + u_5 + u_{12} + u_{23} + u_{25} + u_{34} + u_{35} + u_{45} + u_{235} + u_{345}$.

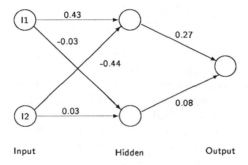

Figure 3.9: Neural network implementing the XOR-function.

In Figure 3.8 an example is given of a logit model with five main effects. The objects are variables indicated by a number placed in a circle. The links (undirectional arrows) between nodes should be interpreted as 'are interdependent'. Note that the term u_{24} is not present in the model, according to the absence of a link from node 2 to node 4. It is not possible to distinguish in this way between the model shown and a model from which third order terms are left out.

Artificial Neural Networks (ANNs). Since applications of neural networks in statistics are not uncommon any longer, we consider their graphical representation here, too. Hassoun (1995), who gives a thorough mathematical treatment of this kind of computational structure, characterizes artificial neural networks in the following way: ... *"parallel computational models comprised of densely interconnected adaptive processing units."* Applications of neural networks in Statistics and pros and cons thereof are discussed in Ripley (1993). Adèr & Bramsen (1998) discusses connections between neural networks and structural equation models.

Usually, a distinction is made between *feed-forward* and *interactive* networks. Both kinds can be represented as a directed graph. An interactive network may have bidirectional arrows, while in a feed-forward network only arrows in one direction occur and cycles are not allowed. Figure 3.9 gives an example in the usual graphical representation. Note that a feedforward network has at least an input and an output layer. Often, there are also one or more hidden layers. The nodes of the same layer are not interconnected.

In many cases, three phases can be discerned in the use of the network: a *training* phase in which network weights are calculated using a training set consisting of input patterns and corresponding target patterns that should be delivered as output; a *testing* or *generalization* phase in which new patterns including the desired output are processed without adapting the network weights but calculating some error function to assess the adequacy of the already trained network; and an *application* phase in which the optimally trained network functions as a device to calculate output patterns from new input patterns without providing target patterns. In Figure 3.9, the arrows of the network have weights attached that have been calculated during training.

During application, information flows through the network in 'waves': when an input pattern comes in, the input layer is activated which passes on information to the hidden layer. When all processing in the input nodes is finished, the hidden layer takes over and information passes to the output layer which produces the desired output pattern.

In Figure 3.9 a network that functions as the XOR-function (exclusive OR) is shown. This network has one hidden layer. The arrows are validated by weights. It is easy to see that the network functions as a XOR operator: for instance, when the input is $(I_1, I_2) = (1, 1)$, the upper hidden node receives $0.43 + (-0.44) = -0.01 < 0$ and therefore does not pass on information. The input to the lower hidden node is $-0.03 + 0.03 = 0$. Since both hidden nodes do not produce output, the output node is not activated and the network yields 0.

The term 'parallel' in Hassoun's formulation refers to the possibility that nodes of one layer process (or are processed) in parallel. Parallel execution is possible since in all phases layers are processed sequentially and nodes of one layer are not interconnected.

It may be clear from the above description that function and meaning of the nodes and arrows in the graphical representation of a neural network differ between phases. Generally speaking, one may say that:

o each node is able to perform a distinct action which may be different between layers or modules. For instance, a node in the hidden layer should be able to sum the weights of the incoming edges multiplying them by the value of the corresponding input nodes (typically: 0 or 1).

   During training, the computed output pattern as a whole has to be compared to the target pattern and weights of the network have to be adapted to decrease the value of the error function.

o The arrows of the graphical network representation are unlabelled. They have, however, an attached weight. During training, some operation on the arrow sets between layers should be available to minimalize this error function. The operation changes the weights of the arrows accordingly.

The meaning of both nodes and arrows of a neural network cannot be understood by reading the graph: one needs to know the phase the network is in and even then the meaning of the nodes may differs from layer to layer and between arrows. In the training and evaluation phase, operations occur that are applied on layers or even on the whole network.

3.1.1 What requirements should an ideal graphical representation fulfill?

As we saw in the previous section the basic elements of most graphical representations are objects and edges between objects. Sometimes these objects are indicated by letters in a box or a circle (as in the case of graphical modelling), sometimes only letters are used. As we saw in the discussion of Figure 3.5, sometimes nodes do not indicate static entities (objects) but *activities* (like 'randomize' or 'observe'). Since directed edges (arrows) are commonly used to indicate activities, it follows that the distinction between objects and arrows is not strict. Several kinds of edges are used: unidirectional, bidirectional and undirectional. Relations are usually represented by undirectional edges (links).

When figures are ambiguous, this is often caused by the *meaning* the reader has to attach to the edges. Sometimes they should simply be understood to mean 'produces', 'go to the next step' or 'pass on information', but sometimes, completely different interpretations are needed like 'influences', 'is dependent on' or in the training phase of a neural network, something like 'change the attached weights and pass on the result'. Usually, this meaning is not explicitly given with the figure and, for some dark reason, assumed self evident.

In Adèr (1995, Chapter 5) requirements are formulated to make any formalism to express methodological concepts more effective. Although the approach there is more general, it applies to graphical representations, too. We mention these requirements here without elaborating much on the rationale behind them: Several of them do not require much explanation, others will be highlighted in the rest of the chapter.

Recognizability. A representation should look familiar to those who use it. In particular, it should not deviate to much from existing formalisms.

Rough descriptions. A representation should stay meaningful even if the user doesn't care to specify the notions in full detail. In this way, rough indications can be given that are eventually completely specified at a later stage.

Handling complex pieces of information. It should be possible to label pieces of information of high complexity without requiring to completely specify the complex internal structure.

Adaptability. It must be straightforward to adapt a representation to a specific research domain.

Temporal notions. As has been stressed in the introduction, a representation should allow to express, eventually complex, temporal notions.

Context. Furthermore, a notation should have provisions to express contextual information.

Strategic Knowledge. Likewise, a notation should have provisions to represent *strategies*. (This also was indicated in the introduction).

Logical inference. Finally, a notation should allow to indicate *logical inference* processes.

It may be clear from the previous section, that none of the formalisms reviewed answer all of the above requirements, although path diagrams as used in structural equation modelling come close to what a notation should look like. They suggest a kind of causality that is relevant for the formulation of research design. However, from the CURVE factor model in Figure 3.7, it may be concluded that descriptions of time-dependency are not altogether adequate.

In the next section, a notational system is sketched that improves on many of these points and that allows to represent most of the formalisms considered in Section 3.1.

3.2   Functional notation

In Adèr (1995, Chapter 5) so-called *Functional notation* (or *F-notation* for short) is developed. It has a well-defined graphical variant. The graphs drawn under this regime are called *F-graphs*. The principles of these F-graphs are briefly described here. For a more principled discussion the reader is referred to the original source or to Adèr (1998).

Like other representations we saw in section 3.1, F-graphs are built from two classes of building stones: *objects* and *arrows*.

Two basic points of the definitional framework of F-notation should be particularly brought forward. First, *All sets are assumed to be finite.* This has to do with the discrete nature of graphical representations and can be shown to be no severe restriction. Secondly, all kind of mappings are allowed between sets of these building stones. In particular, *Arrows having as a domain a set of arrows and arrows that are mapped on arrows, are allowed.* This unusual kind of mapping is needed since, as we saw before, arrows are often used to indicate *activities* and we should be able to handle both objects and activities in the same way.

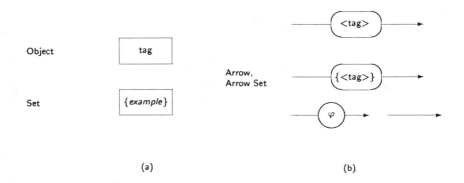

Figure 3.10: Basic elements of F-graphs. (a) Objects and Sets; (b) Arrows and Arrow Sets.

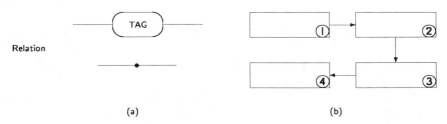

Figure 3.11: Basic elements of F-graphs. (a) Relations; (b) Indication of Time dependence.

Basic elements of F-graphs.   Figure 3.10(a) shows how objects and sets are represented. An object is indicated by a box with 'tag' (label) placed inside. A set is indicated by a box with curly brackets ({}) around the tag. The tag in this case is called an *example*[3], an element of the set to which the other elements are alike. Objects are always boxed.

Figure 3.10(b) shows various representations of arrows. Like an object, an arrow may be equipped with a tag placed in an oval or a circle. Tags of arrows are surrounded by angled brackets: <tag>. These tags can be used to indicate the operation the arrow represents ('produce', 'go to next' and so forth). To indicate a set of arrows (or: an *Arrow Set*), curly brackets are used like in the set denotation.

Since a function corresponds to a special arrow set, functions may be indicated either this way or by an arrow with a Greek letter tag. Arrows can also be untagged.

Figure 3.11(a) gives examples of the way relation is indicated: by tagged or untagged *links*[4]. When a link is untagged, it is marked with a dot. This

---

[3]This convention is due to Sowa (1984).

[4]One may wonder what happened to the two classes of building stones I announced above: links seem to be neither objects nor arrows. Frederiks, Hofstede, & Lippe (1994)

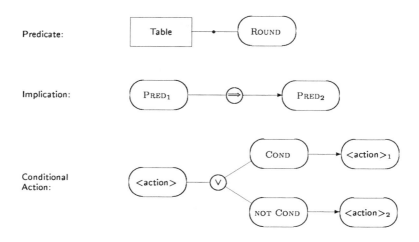

Figure 3.12: Predicates, Implications and Choosers.

is needed to distinguish it from parts of arrows. Tags of relations are in capitals (compare Figure 3.2).

To indicate that an object is time-dependent it is provided with an index indicating the time point to which it is related (see Figure 3.11(b)). Thus, only distinct time points can be indicated (The possibility to use time intervals is not considered in this chapter, although this extension is easily made.). When objects are connected to the same time point, they have the same index. In the figure, the arrows indicate the transition from one time point to the next. It is well possible that more than one set of time points is used in a figure. To indicate this, a different set of indices is used, for instance ❶, ❷ ... or ①, ② .... Instead of numbers in circles, we often use boxed numbers in the sequel.

Figure 3.12 indicates how some logical connections are represented. The top diagram shows an object that has a predicate attached to it as an attribute. Predicates also function in implications which are simply indicated by an arrow with a $\Longrightarrow$ tag.

In many situations one has to indicate that choices have to be made between objects or activities, for instance while drawing a flow chart. Here, this is done by allowing operations on arrow sets.

The bottom diagram of Figure 3.12 gives the representation of an action that is followed by one of two alternative actions, dependent on the value of two conditions that exclude each other. In this case the arrow set consists of two arrows, labelled COND and NOT COND. A ∨-symbol indicates that a choice has to be made between the arrows in the arrow set. The arrow set together with the ∨-operation is called a *Chooser*. When no ambiguity can arise the ∨-symbol is left out.

explain how relations and links can be represented using arrows. For the moment the reader is asked to accept that there is this extra class of connections consisting of links.

3.2.1   Example: Design of a clinical trial

In Figure 3.13 an alternative representation of a clinical trial is given (Compare Figure 3.5). The upper panel of the figure indicates the inclusion procedure. According to inclusion- and exclusion criteria {crit.} patients are included in or excluded from the trial. $< i >$ and $< ic >$ are Choosers. Since this is the first step, an index 1 is appended.

The next panel indicates the randomization procedure. $< r >$ is a (tagged) Chooser: it assigns an included patient to either one of two mutual exclusive alternative treatment arms. The lower two parts of the figure indicate the study design for one subject. As before, the small indices in boxes indicate subsequent points in time. Note that all these figures describe the situation *for one subject only*. Usually time points differ between subjects when considered in 'absolute' time since in most clinical trials patients are included one after another and consequently time points differ between treatment arms. If we need to express this, each time index can be provided with a subject index to indicate that the time sets are different. In most analysis techniques, it is implicitly assumed that the time sets of different patients can be identified. If time points between treatment arms are different, for instance while inter-observation times differ, this should be accounted for at the analysis phase and the indices between treatment arms in the lower two figures should be chosen differently.

3.3   Representation of Time

The idea behind the following formal characterization of the manipulation of time-related objects is to define finite sets of time points to which objects or arrow are 'hooked'. New time sets may be introduced into the graphs whenever needed. For instance, in the 'clinical trial' example of the previous section, each patient could have his own time set which for analysis purposes can be identified during analysis.

Definition 3.1 (Time Sets) *Let T be a strictly ordered finite set with ordering relation $\prec$ and let t be a variable over T. Then $\mathcal{T} = (t, T)$ defines a* Time Set. *The variable t is called the* current time point *and T, the set of time points.*

Any particular value t_0 of t divides $\mathcal{T}$ in three sets: $Pa_0 = \{x | x \in T, x \prec t_0\}$, $Pr_0 = \{[t_0]\}$ and $Fu_0 = \{x | x \in T, t_0 \prec x\}$. Since T is finite, Pa_0 and Fu_0 are finite. If t_0 equals an end point of T, either Pa_0 or Fu_0 is empty. The set Pr_0 can be thought of as representing 'the Present'. Therefore, t_0 is called *the present time point*, or briefly *Present*. Similarly, Pa_0 is called *Past*, Fu_0 is called *Future*. Since we can also use time sets to describe for instance, hypothesis testing or the events in a dialogue, in some cases these labels are less meaningful.

We can now define objects placed in time by defining sets of arrows which point into a time set:

<Inclusion>:

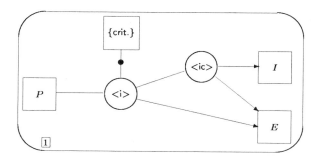

<Randomization>:

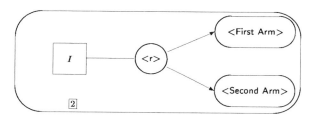

<First Arm>

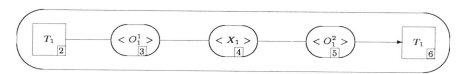

<Second Arm>

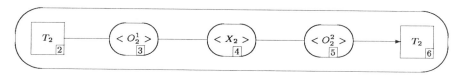

Figure 3.13: F-graph of a clinical trial design. P: Patient. $<i>$: Inclusion Procedure. $<ic>$: Ask for Informed Consent. I, E: Included or excluded patient. $<r>$: Randomization Procedure. T_i: Subject assigned to treatment group. O_i: Observation in group i. X_i: Treatment in group i.

Definition 3.2 (States) *Let be given time set* $\mathcal{T} = (t, T)$ *and an object* $[a]$. *The arrow set* $\{[a] \longrightarrow t | t \in T\}$ *is called the set of* $\mathcal{T}$-*states of the object* $[a]$.

We use the following notation:

$$\widehat{[a]} \stackrel{\text{def}}{::=} \{[a] \longrightarrow t\}$$

$\widehat{[a]}$ in this expression is called a $\mathcal{T}$-*connected object*.

EXAMPLE 1

F-notation provides a more or less literal translation of path diagrams. In the example presented in Figure 3.7 on page 20, we can use a mapping on a set of time points $T = \{t_1, t_2, t_3\}$ that corresponds to different occasions. Figure 3.14 gives a version of the same problem as a F-graph. Note that the parameters $B_i (i = 1, 2, 3)$ in the original figure have been replaced by a function β. m is depicted as a $\mathcal{T}$-related object.

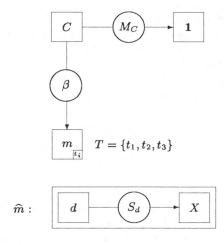

Figure 3.14: F-graph of the chronometric factor model (compare Figure 3.7). C: latent factor; 1: constant; T: set of time points; d: measurement; X: manifest variable. M_C, β, S_d: parameters to be estimated.

The three arrows of which β consist, may be related. To describe the associations between them in detail, a separate figure could be drawn.

The real-valued mappings indicating error-terms are separately shown in Figure 3.15: a difference is being made between error assumed in the observed variables and parameters of the model. The estimation process is aimed at finding mappings ϵ and π.

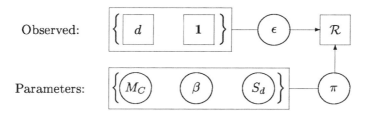

Figure 3.15: Estimation functions for the chronometric factor model. ϵ, π: error functions to be estimated; $\mathcal{R}$: real numbers; M_C, β, S_d: parameters.

3.4 Representation of Reasoning

F-notation offers ways to indicate logical inference steps (See Figure 3.12): Relations between objects may be given a $\vee$ or & label to indicate 'or' and 'and' relationships. Similarly, by labelling a Chooser, an arrow set can be provided with a logical operator that indicates which arrows should be applied. Thus, Reasoning by graphical means is well possible and eventually instructive. To express complicated logic relationships, the language of logic is preferable. It is specifically developed for this and provides efficient and parsimonious ways to express whatever complicated train of thought. A lot of research has been done and is still going on, on the applicability of different logics for knowledge representation. Throughout their book, Genesereth & Nilsson (1987) discuss the many aspects and possibilities.

Inference Mechanisms. How can inference steps that play a role in Reasoning about methodological matters be formally handled? To keep things simple, let us assume that logical inference in this field obeys 'at most' first order predicate logic.

Logical inference on a set of statements S may then be described using rules of the form if T_1 then T_2 (or as implications of the form $T_1 \Rightarrow T_2$). In this, T_1 and T_2 are sets of predicates that can be attached to S.

Such rules indicate that if the *antecedent* T_1 is true, then it follows that the *consequent* T_2 is also true(In Adèr (1995, Section 5.5) a precise formal definition in terms of statements with attached predicates is given.)

Using the implication operation repeatedly, a series of inference steps can be indicated:

$$T_1 \Longrightarrow T_2 \Longrightarrow T_3 \ldots$$

If special sets of predicates T_{start} and T_{goal} are defined, the inference process aims to find a series of steps that can connect the two.

In view of Section 3.3, it seems natural to also consider $\widehat{\{T_i\}}$, in other words, to make $\{T_i\}$ $\mathcal{T}$-connected. This corresponds to the idea that inferential reasoning proceeds in steps, put one after another, leading to some pre-defined target statement.

The time points of $\mathcal{T}$ then correspond to the states $\{T_i\}$ assumes during the inference process.

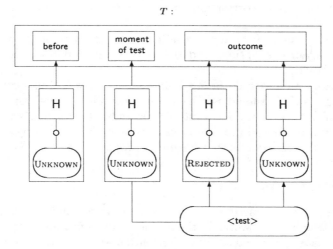

Figure 3.16: Hypothesis testing.

EXAMPLE 2

Hypothesis Testing. An example of a short chain of inference steps occurs in hypothesis testing: the underlying set of statements $\{H\}$ corresponds to the hypotheses formulated. Attributes chosen from the set $\{Unknown, Rejected\}$ may be attached to each H (See Figure 3.16).

The testing procedure <test> consist in a Chooser that either maps on a rejected, or an unknown hypothesis. The time set $\mathcal{T}$ that is used here, contains three points: $T = \{$before, moment of test, outcome$\}$. Hypotheses that, after the test, have still an attribute $Unknown$, cannot be rejected, in the other case they are falsified.

3.5   Strategies and Context

The line of thought in this section is as follows. We start off by assuming that in any field of interest, notions and reasoning about notions can be formulated in terms of arrows and objects. We then show that, under this condition, to represent concepts like 'Strategy' or 'Context' boils down to finding the proper set of arrows that can indicate strategic steps or contextual inclusion.

We first introduce two new notions: *Description* and *Domain*.

Definition 3.3 (Description) *A Description S is a pair (O, A) consisting of a set of objects O and a set of arrows A. O is called the* Object List *and A the* Arrow List *of S.*

Note that the above definition does not prescribe anything on the specific nature of the objects and the arrows in the description.

A description may correspond to any aspect of the field we want to describe.

A *Domain* can now be defined as a special description of which the objects are again descriptions and the arrows are mappings between the composing descriptions.

Two observations should be made in connection with this definition of a domain D: (a) D should not itself be a member of the object list of any of its members, or an unacceptable recursive structure arises. (b) An arrow between two descriptions induces a mapping between object lists and between arrow lists. Arrows that have this property are called *functors*.

3.5.1   Strategies

Dube & Weiss (1989) describe an expert system for maintenance of message trunks in a telephone network. In their article, strategic knowledge is represented by means of a so-called 'State Transition Model'. States of a system are represented as nodes in a directed graph. Obviously, this approach is quite general and may be easily transmitted to, for instance, the planning of the data analysis phase of a research project.

Figure 3.17 gives an example (the F-graph is constructed after Figure 4 of Dube an Weiss). Each node may refer to a complicated procedure in which several steps are taken. For instance, in Figure 3.17, S_{start} and S_{goal} may stand for 'data cleaning' and 'report writing', respectively. Likewise, the choice between subsequent nodes (here indicated by a chooser) may involve complicated considerations.

A strategy is now defined as a path in this graph from start to goal. Some alternative strategies are $S_{start}, S_{11}, S_{43}, S_{75}, S_{86}, S_{goal}$ and $S_{start}, S_{32}, S_{64}, S_{goal}$ (Note that the second index indicates the time point at which the activity takes place.)

Test Construction.   As an example of some steps in a methodological analysis strategy, let us assume that a questionnaire has been administered in two groups of subjects. The questionnaire consists of several tests, some of which have been validated before, while others have been constructed anew.

In this case, different research questions may lead to different analysis strategies. For example,

o when the main interest is in the development of a new measurement instrument, emphasis should be on item analysis, but

o when the interest is in the differences between subgroups those tests of the questionnaire that have already been validated can be compared using a t-test or a non-parametric test.

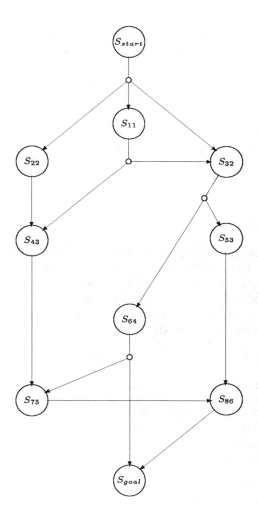

Figure 3.17: Representation of strategy as a transition network. The goal S_{goal} may be reached via different paths. The second index indicates the time point.

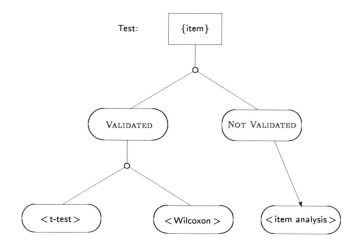

Figure 3.18: Strategic choices between validation of a test or using test scores as a measurement instrument.

In the graphical representation given in Figure 3.18, a particular test (Test) consists of items ({item}). The test is item analysed in case a new instrument has to be developed. When a validated test is used, the groups can be compared using a test for mean differences.

Note that the figure does not express anything about the actual data analysis procedure, which in both cases may involve elaborate methodological considerations.

3.5.2 Context

We start this section with an example (See Figure 3.19).

To arrive at a statistical model, a research question is reformulated in methodological terms and the specification of a statistical model is based on that. In the process, the context of each step is in the context of the previous ones:

1. The research question is formulated in terms of the research domain;

2. The methodological reformulation has this question as its context and thus the research domain;

3. The context of the statistical formulation and the subsequent data analysis includes both methodological and research domain considerations.

4. And finally, to interpret the results, all of the above contexts play a more or less important role.

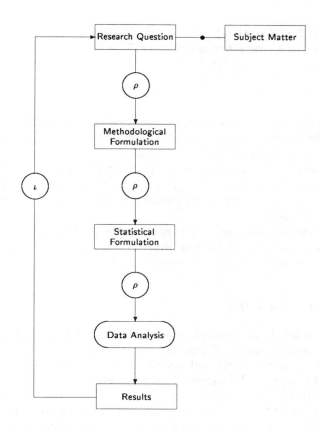

Figure 3.19: Subject matter knowledge, research question, methodological and statistical formulation form each others contexts. ρ: Reformulation; ι: Interpretation.

Generally speaking, any (methodological) structure S_0 receives a particular meaning stemming from its context. The question how to represent this embedding, is a question after the best way to *import* elements of the context C_{S_0} into the structure we want to describe. To do that, it is necessary to first be able to describe both S_0 and its context in some elementary way.

As we did at the beginning of this section, we assume that aspects of any domain (in our case: a research domain) can be described using objects and arrows, so that we can think of it in the way we defined it in Section 3.5: as a finite collection of descriptions, each determined by an object list and an arrow list. For convenience, assume that S_0 can be specified as a description (otherwise, we have only to look for a description of which S_0 is a member). The idea of the following definition is that when S_0 is one of the descriptions of a domain $\mathcal{M}$, then its context is the complement relative to $\mathcal{M}$.

Definition 3.4 (Context) *The context C_{S_0} of a description S_0 in domain $\mathcal{M}$ is the union of the other descriptions S in $\mathcal{M}$:*

$$C_{S_0} = \bigcup_{S \in \mathcal{M} \setminus S_0} S \qquad\qquad (3.1)$$

Thus, descriptions constitute each others context. Since C_{S_0} consists in a union of descriptions, we may consider the unions of the object lists and arrow lists, too. Let's call them $O_{C_{S_0}}$ and $A_{C_{S_0}}$, respectively.

The operation of importing elements from C_{S_0} now consists in finding a proper mapping of $(O_{C_{S_0}}, A_{C_{S_0}})$ into (O_{S_0}, A_{S_0}). (Note that when the context of S_0 is not particularly influential, only a few elements of $O_{C_{S_0}}$ need to be imported.)

In this way the relatively vague notion of context may be represented in a formal way. In Figure 3.19 these mappings are indicated by the arrows ρ and ι (ρ for reformulation; ι for interpretation.)

Further reading

In a book called 'Diagrammatic reasoning' (1995), Chandrasekaran and his co-authors give a wealth of material on the way concepts and reasoning on concepts can be stored and manipulated using figures and diagrams. Biennial 'Thinking with Diagrams' conferences are held on this theme (See also Adèr, 1998).

Lanzing (1996)'s web-side[5] contains several links to commercial and freely available software to construct and handle concept maps.

Oldford (1990) considers statistical strategies in relation to statistical software. Recently, Duchateau (1995) discussed applications of strategic knowledge in connection to the analysis of the results of experiments.

The idea to use objects and arrows originates from Category theory. Category Theory can be considered an extension of mathematical Set Theory. That is why Goldblatt's fundamental introduction starts with a discussion of the roots of Set Theory (Goldblatt, 1986). Category theory is an extensive field in which a wealth of literature exists. A good introduction can be found in Pierce (1991), while general coverage is given in Rydeheard & Burstall (1988) and Barr & Wells (1990). Frederiks et al. (1994) give an introduction to a categorical treatment of conceptual data modelling with an up-to-date literature list.

On the representation of temporal notions Van Benthem's study on 'The Logic of Time' is relevant (Van Benthem, 1991). It discusses different models that may be used to describe temporal processes. Models that are infinite are emphasized. In the realm of Artificial Intelligence Allen's work on time interval logic is mentionable (Allen, 1983). Recently, renewed interest in this area lead to several other publications: see, for instance, Boddy (1993),

---

[5]http://utto1031.to.utwente.nl/

Yampratoom & Allen (1993). Finally, Berzuini should be mentioned, who uses belief networks to represent temporal knowledge (Berzuini, 1990).

3.6   Discussion

In the introduction it was argued that graphical knowledge representation is worthwhile while planning a research design. There are several other instances in which graphical representation methods could be useful. In the context of this book *Meta data modelling* and *Meta research* should be mentioned in particular:

Meta data models. Lately, much work has been done to develop methods to formally represent data that describe the structure of a research data set. More of this will be said in the Chapter 4 on Meta data models.

> These models are particularly useful when part of the analysis phase has to be done routinely or even automatically, and are essential when data sets have to be reused or combined, since they contain information on the precise structure of the data set described.

> This is an area where the graphical methods discussed in this chapter could be fruitfully applied to represent not only the formal structure but also the operations applied to the meta data models.

Meta research. In this field, data often results from written research reports. In many cases, it is difficult to demonstrate that procedures applied in the studies are comparable. If precise scripts of the experiments or trials were available, a responsible combination of results could be made based on appropriate statistical procedures. (In contrast to research planning and meta data modelling, as yet not much work has been done in this area at the point of formalization.)

Chapter 4

Meta data: well-defined models of data sets

H. Paul de Greef

4.1 Introduction

Statistical analysis works with data. Most of the work is not in data analysis, but in planning, collecting, cleaning, combining and manipulating data sets, and producing the report. In practice this is no trivial affair. Various directions have been pursued to provide computer support beyond data storage and statistical analysis: statistical expert systems, computerized questionnaires, generation of experimental designs to name a few. Support of isolated activities is of little practical help; integration is important.

All activities around data consume or produce information about the data. Aiming at computer support, the question is which information about the data is needed and in which manner this data about the data[1] can be formalized (De Feber & De Greef, 1992; Van den Berg, De Feber, & De Greef, 1992; Darius, Boucneau, De Greef, De Feber, & Froeschl, 1993; Adèr, 1995; Froeschl, 1997). An important type of meta data is *methodological knowledge* (Adèr, 1995).

This chapter presents an approach for the representation of methodological knowledge, based on modelling principles similar to those in statistical analysis: information in a data set can often be briefly summarized using a model. There are many readily available languages for models of data sets. A language provides *sentences* that can be used to make statements about data sets. Figure 4.1 shows several examples. These models of the data set do not present anything new that is not already present in the data set, but they provide a concise summary of structural characteristics of the data. The data set itself can be regarded as a formal object and there is a formal relation between the language in which a model is expressed, and the data

---

[1] Hence the term 'meta data'.

set as a formal object. Models of the data set can be computed from the data set, provided the data is available.

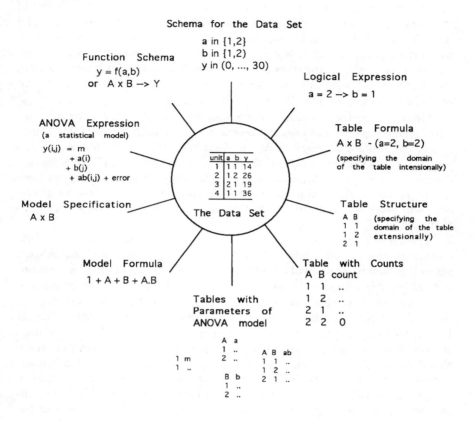

Figure 4.1: Samples of languages for models of data sets.

Models can provide a selection of information relevant for a particular activity[2] by a human or a program. The information needs of the interviewer are different from those of the statistical analyst, and those are different from the needs of the interview program running in the interviewers laptop.

Models can also provide abstraction from operational details. In planning and design, hierarchies of models can be used to facilitate successive refinement. Models at a more abstract level can be used to formulate requirements and global design decisions. Operational details can be filled in using models at a more detailed level.

Models of data can provide compressed storage of information present in the data. With *lossless compression* no information is lost by the compression[3]. In this way, models can even replace (part of) the data and be

---

[2] Often called *User views*.

[3] There is an *isomorphism*, as will be explained below.

used to store data efficiently. For example, if all cases in a data set are male, then the data set may contain a variable 'gender' that has the value 'male' for each unit. Instead of this the variable 'gender' can be left out of the data set (the entire column can be deleted), and be replaced by a model for this part of the data, for example the expression 'gender = male'. This saves storage space and it is a form of lossless data compression. Special attention is needed if the data set is modified. If data of women is added, the model is not valid any more and the variable 'gender' has to be stored explicitly into the data set itself.

Models of methodological aspects can be defined in a similar manner. The usual concept of data set can be extended, to include more information about methodological aspects in the data set itself. For example, it can be extended with the notion of time, as in Langefors's (1977) elementary datum: $(object, property, value, time)$. The data for such extensions need not be stored in any real data set; models may be used to efficiently represent and store the additional information about the data in a compressed manner.

The term *data set* is usually associated with the concrete result of data collection: the file with data to be subjected to statistical analysis. A data set in this chapter is more of a theoretical object. Most, if not all, extensions are not intended for use in real data sets, but to provide a basis for models.

A data set may also serve as a representation that can be used in planning. To understand this, imagine that a researcher and a methodologist have a meeting to discuss plans for a future investigation. There is no data set yet, but they are already talking about a data set. In a *platonic* sense this data set already exists: this is what researcher and methodologist apparently assume to be there. It is only that the thing, or a sample thereof, has yet to be collected. If this conversation between researcher and methodologist establishes a list of variables and a sample size, the contours of the data set have already become established.

During the discussion, in an iterative design process, the plan or the platonic data set can be changed repeatedly. In information systems that support such work processes, such modifications are difficult. If the problem representation is changed in one place, for example, the value set of a variable is modified, then the problem representation may need to be changed in other places as well. The issue is that a modification involves much more than just editing. Compare this to changing a text. If all occurrences of 'he' are changed to 'they', then many other changes (*e.g.*, the verbs), must be made to keep the text consistent. There is a need for a knowledge representation that supports such changes and helps to maintain consistency. This is a general requirement for all computer support: meta data, including the representation of methodological knowledge, should be *adaptable* (Adèr, 1995).

This chapter presents *well-defined models* as basis for representations that can be modified in a consistent way. There is a central, platonic data set; all objects in statistical tasks are elements of models of this central data set. Modifications in the problem representation are modifications of these models, and, if we take care that all models are well-defined, then an entire collection of models (*i.e.*, the problem representation in its entirety), can always be modified in a consistent way.

The use of well-defined models of data provides a framework for meta data with many desirable features. It provides an unambiguous meaning to meta data. It facilitates the expression of structure in the data. It makes interrelationships among various meta data elements explicit, and it allows for consistent modifications of meta data.

Section 4.2 introduces models. Section 4.3 defines a language for classical data sets: $\{(unit, variable, value)\}$. Section 4.4 presents the idea of well-definedness in an informal manner. Section 4.4.1 defines well-definedness in a mathematical framework, that is, as a homomorphism from data set language to model language. Properties of homomorphisms provide a general solution for consistent modifications. Section 4.5 investigates interrelations among well-defined models of a common data set. It provides glimpses of the structure that exists among homomorphic images of a common data set. Then an example is given of language design using the well-defined models concept in the design of representations for data collection plans. Section 4.6 extends the data set concept with time (4.6.1), and operational definition (4.6.2). Then examples are given of well-defined models for the temporal aspects of the data collection process (4.6.3). The final section (4.7) can only conclude that well-defined models provide a firm and indeed *well-defined* basis for meta data languages. They can be consistently modified, are defined over the entire domain of data sets, and seem to have many more desirable properties.

4.2   Models

All important theories of models have in common that there are two worlds between which there is a correspondence that is not so much in the elements — the worlds are different, the elements are not identical — but that is in the structure, allowing one to say something about the other. The book *Modeling Theory* by Rosen (1991) provides a concise and elegant definition.

A model requires two systems, interrelationships among these, and three criteria to be met. The first criterion is that each system has elements and relations and an entailment function. Entailment means that there are laws governing the system. Events or situations in the system have a necessary consequence or correlate. To give an example, in a formal logical system the proof procedure and proof rules provides entailment:

> *Socrates being human, and humans being mortal, entails Socrates being mortal, using the modus ponens rule.*

In a physical system causation, for example, may be taken as entailment.

The second criterion is that there are encoding and decoding functions between these systems. Elements and relations in one system can be mapped

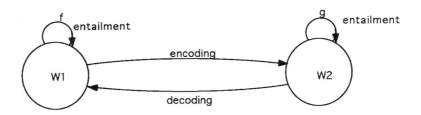

W2 is a model for W1 if for all w1 in W1
f(w1) = decoding(g(encoding(w1)))

Figure 4.2: Modelling theory.

to the other system, and back. The context so far is illustrated in Figure 4.2. This figure also shows the third criterion. The diagram of functions is a commutative diagram. Starting from a w_1 in W_1, there are two paths to get at w'_1. Both paths lead to the same result.

If this third criterion is fulfilled, the second system can be said to be a model of the first. I find this formulation from *modelling theory* a simple and precise formulation of the essence of *model theory* as can be found in, for example, Genesereth & Nilsson (1987), and mathematical modelling as described by Maki & Thompson (1973). Below such view on what a model is will be used, but impregnating it with concepts from statistics (Table 4.1), and making it more precise using the concept of homomorphism rather than isomorphism.

System 1:	The data set as a formal object (e.g., equation 4.1).
System 2:	A model for the data set stated in a particular language
Entailment 1 (f):	An operation on the data set
Entailment 2 (g):	An operation on the model statement
Encoding:	Computational methods of a wider class than, but including those as provided by statistical packages
Decoding:	Generation of a data set that satisfies the model

Table 4.1: Introduction to the well-defined model concept.

4.3   The data set

The data set is the central object in a statistical investigation. A data set is a record of data collection in a sample of units. It may be a record produced by interviewers going door to door with a questionnaire obtaining answers from respondents. Or it may be the result of different groups of patients being treated with different combinations of drugs and their progress being monitored. Both statistics and data base theory provide formalizations for storing the information.

unit	gender	marital status	age
person 1	female	married	29
person 2	female	unmarried	36
person 3	female	married	28
person 4	male	married	35
person 5	female	unmarried	33

Table 4.2: Example of a complete rectangular data set of 5 units by 3 variables.

(unit, variable, value). Let us start from the data set that is most often used in statistical investigations: a rectangular array (matrix, table, spreadsheet) with rows for Units (*i.e.*, Cases), and columns for Variables. A complete rectangular data set contains a value for all pairs (*unit, variable*) in *Units × Variables*. Table 4.2 provides an example of such a data set. But, in a data set, not all units need to have values for all variables. Reasons for that may differ, for example, the data has not yet been completely collected, or not all variables are defined for all units, or data collection happens in a non-systematic way. In the framework above, we cannot describe this situation, unless we introduce special values. For example '...?' for a value not yet known, and '-not applicable-' if the variable is not defined for the unit. Table 4.3 provides an example.

unit	gender	beard	# of pregnancies
person 1	female	-not applicable-	2
person 2	male	yes	-not applicable-
person 3	female	-not applicable-	...?

Table 4.3: Example of an incomplete rectangular data set.

To decrease the tension between a rectangular format and a possibly arbitrarily shaped data set, we rather use the following formalization: an *elementary datum* is a tuple (*unit, variable, value*). A Data Set is a set of such elementary datums. This provides a simple formalization of the data set:

$$\text{Data Set} = \{(unit, variable, value)\} \qquad (4.1)$$

Because variables are functions (See, e.g. Hays, 1974), there is a constraint upon Data Set: there is not more than one tuple for each (*unit, variable*).

$$\text{Data Set} \subseteq (Units \times Variables \rightarrow Values) \qquad (4.2)$$

The subset relation indicates that not every data set must be a full cross product of Units and Variables. The cross product establishes the maximal domain for the Data Set. The domain of an actual data set is either this cross product or a subset.

Table 4.4 shows a data set structured according to this format. Data that are missing or not applicable are simply left out. This formalization is attractive, because the elementary datum can be extended with additional information about the valuation.

unit	variable	value
person 1	gender	female
person 1	# of pregnancies	2
person 2	gender	male
person 2	beard	yes
person 3	gender	female

Table 4.4: Example of a data set in (unit, variable, value) format.

Operations on Data Set. The Data Set is a dynamic object, not only because new data can be inserted, but also because it can be modified. The formalization chosen makes it simple to define operations that change the Data Set. Set theory provides two basic operations on a data set: inserting and deleting an elementary datum. Using these, it is not difficult to define more complex operations. For example: delete variable or delete units that satisfy a certain criterion.

4.4   Well-defined models of a central data set

Models of the data set are descriptions, representations, summaries, or specifications of some property of some part of the Data Set, as defined in equations (4.1) and (4.2), or according to the more extensive definitions to follow.

There are numerous languages for such models available (*e.g.*, Figure 4.1). These languages have a formal semantics, that is, there are clear formal criteria to establish correspondence between the data set and a model expressed in the language. For these models, correspondence can simply be based on a function from data sets to models.

This is not to say that such a model always will be the result of a computation on a data set. Like the drawing of a house, the model may precede the thing being modelled (design of a new house) rather than the other way around (drawing of an existing house). The function is just a convenient way of expressing the relation between data set and models. This function may have an inverse: the data set can be computed or generated from the model. If it does not have an inverse, there can still be a function or procedure that generates data sets that are in the relationship.

Corresponding operations. In the world of data sets, it is possible to define a small set of basic operators that can be used, in composition, to transform any data set into any other data set.

Using the terminology of software packages for statistical analysis, the most important operations are:

o Deleting certain variables (columns).

o Inserting a new variable (column). This can be a completely new variable or a new variable as a function (*i.e.*, computation) of existing variables. Important examples of the latter are recoding of a variable or summation of a number of variables to obtain a total score.

o Deleting or selecting units (rows) using a certain criterion that can be applied to each unit (row).

These operations are similar to Codd's (1979), projection (delete variable), extension (insert variable) and restriction (select units) operators. Such an operator transforms a data set to a new data set:

If such an operation is performed on the data set, then it may be that a corresponding operation has to be performed on various models of this data set. Similarly, if an operation is performed on a model, then it may be that a corresponding operation should be applied to the data set as well (or to other models).

Well-defined Models of Data Sets. A model of the data set is well-defined if and only if the following commutative diagram holds:

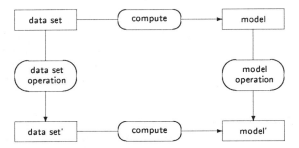

By defining for each operation on data sets the corresponding operation on a model, the entire system of the data set and the entire system of the model are brought to a correspondence relation.

Consistency Between Well-defined Models. If there are different models for the data set, we can define corresponding operations for each different model. For example, if we have two different well-defined models, we can, for each, separately predict what they would be like after a certain operation on the data set.

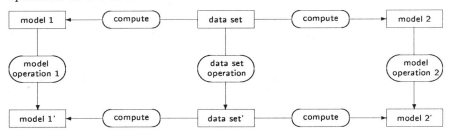

If the data set is not available, consistency between well-defined models can be maintained, provided the models are consistent to begin with. Once all models have been defined in relation to the data set, the actual data set is not needed:

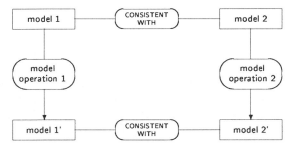

By adhering to strict criteria for a well-defined model of the data set, the interrelations between different models in different languages are (made) tractable. The data set itself need not to be available and the corresponding operations can be trusted to maintain correspondence between models under various operations.

Schemata for Data Sets. An example of a model of the data set is its schema. Figure 4.3 shows specimens of four different schema specification techniques all applied to the same data set in the middle of Figure 4.3. The examples illustrate how various schema languages may be regarded as functions from a common domain of data sets. Secondly, with this example it is easy to see how various operations on data sets have their counterparts in each schema language.

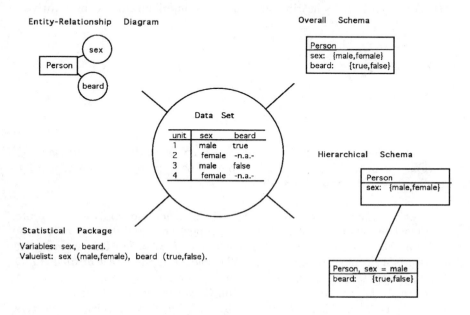

Figure 4.3: Schema specification techniques.

In the writing above, in the examples, and in the diagrams, no distinction was made between a pair (data set, sentence-in-a-language), and the general case. For example, the distinction between a specific table with counts and the general concept of tables with counts. The general case concerns all data sets in the domain or universe of data sets D, and all sentences in the domain of sentences M. The general case is: all pairs (d, m) in $D \times M$.

The story of this section can be retold with greater precision, using mathematical language, and with greater impact, by addressing the general case, having recognized that mathematical concepts such as isomorphism and homomorphism can be used.

4.4.1 Structure-preserving functions

The idea of a mapping $A \to B$ from one set to another is very general. If A and B have some internal structure, defined by operations upon them so that they can be indicated by $[A, \Diamond]$ and $[B, \Box]$, then the interesting

functions are the ones that preserve that structure. Functions that do so
are homomorphisms.

Homomorphism. When $A \to B$ is a homomorphism, the effect of operations on A is preserved in the operations on B. More specifically, first
applying the operation $\diamond$ on A and then f on the result gives the same
final result as first applying f and then $\square$ to B. This can be expressed as
$f(\diamond a) = \square f(a)$, or by stating that the following diagram is commutative:

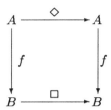

Similar definitions can be given for binary operations, for external operations (presented below), and for operations in many-sorted algebras (cf.
Dougherty & Giardina, 1988; Vickers, 1989).

Surjective Homomorphism. A surjective homomorphism is an onto
function (*i.e.*, a *surjection*). The onto property ensures that for all $b \in B$,
one can choose an element $a \in A$ such that $f(a) = b$. This means that
if there is a problem of the type: *'What would be the effect of applying* $\square$
to an element $b \in B$?', the answer can be obtained by choosing an $a \in A$
with $f(a) = b$. To this a the operation $\square$ can be applied to give a'. The
required answer in B is then obtained by applying f to a'. With a surjective
homomorphism, A can be said to *simulate B*.

In addition to the commutative diagram of the homomorphism, the following diagram also holds:

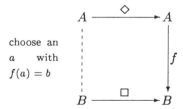

Isomorphism. When a (surjective) homomorphism is isomorphic, A and
B can simulate each other. The success of the two-way simulation depends
on an additional property of the isomorphism: f is a bijection (an onto
function that is one-to-one). Then, f has an inverse $f^{-1} : B \to A$ that is
also an isomorphism. When A and B are isomorphic, the diagram of the
homomorphism holds, and the following two commutative diagrams hold as
well:

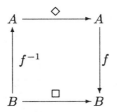 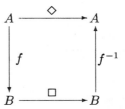

If there is a surjective homomorphism but not an isomorphism from A onto B (the function is many-to-one), then A simulates B, but B only imperfectly simulates A; that is, B is isomorphic to a structure composed of classes of A. Each class is the inverse image of an element of B.

Homomorphism with respect to two external operations. Among definitions of several different homomorphisms provided by Bouvier & George (1983), there is one that matches the definition of well-definedness of models of data sets. It is the definition of a homomorphism with respect to two external operations: Let $[D, \Diamond]$ and $[M, \Box]$ be sets with an external operation of which the common domain of the operators is Ω. The operation $\Diamond$ applies an element of Ω to an element of D and returns an element in D. The operation $\Box$ applies an element of Ω to an element of M and returns an element in M.

A function $f : D \to M$ is a homomorphism from $[D, \Diamond]$ to $[M, \Box]$ if for all pairs $(\alpha, d) \in \Omega \times D, f(\alpha \Diamond d) = \alpha \Box f(d)$. That is, the following diagram commutes:

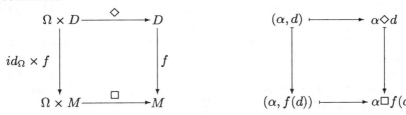

This is a more precise version of the diagram used in the definition of a well-defined model. Now let D be a set of data sets (*i.e.*, the powerset of *DataSet*), and M a model language, *e.g.*, tables with counts. The set of common operators, Ω, contains a few basic operators, for example 'delete variable', with the name of a variable as parameter. The operation $\Diamond$ applies it to the data set. In a data set with rows for units and columns for variables, an entire column is deleted. The operation $\Box$ applies 'delete variable' to the table of counts. The table is collapsed over that variable, and numbers of units are added to produce the counts in the collapsed table.

More models can be introduced, for example, let $[M_2, \Box_2]$ be a language for schemas for the data set. The operation $\Box_2$ applies the common operators to a schema. Limiting oneself to models that are homomorphisms of a central data set brings the advantage that entire sets of different models $[M_i, \Box_i]$ can be modified in a consistent way, using the common set

Ω of basic operators. Implementation of more complex operators using Ω operators *just once* then provides an overall implementation in all models available and in those yet to come.

D	data set language (powerset of Data Set)
M	model language
Ω	a set of operators such as 'deletevariable(*variable*)'
$d \in D$	a data set
$\Diamond : \Omega \times D \to D$	external operation on data set language
$(\alpha, d) \mapsto \Diamond d$	
$m \in M$	a sentence or statement —'a model'— in the model language
$\Box : \Omega \times M \to M$	external operation on model language
$(\alpha, m) \mapsto \Box m$	
$f : D \to M$	a homomorphism:
	for all pairs $(\alpha, d) \in \Omega \times D, f(\alpha \Diamond d) = \alpha \Box f(x)$

Table 4.5: Summary of the well-defined model concept.

Summarizing, well-defined models for data sets are obtained by using homomorphisms to map on model languages. This guarantees preservation of the effect of data set operators in operations on models in the model language. Therefore, the operators preserve consistency under modifications.

This well-defined models concept provides a solution to the problem of consistent modifications of representations. Everything that is contained in a well-defined model is also contained in the data set. As long as we limit ourselves to well-defined models, an entire set of statements about a data set can be consistently modified using the common operators. A summary of this concept is provided in Table 4.5. Note that an individual sentence m, (*i.e.*, a specific instance of a table with counts or an ANOVA expression), is often referred to as a 'model', also in the introduction of this chapter. There is nothing wrong with that, as long as the entire context (Table 4.5) is kept in mind.

4.5   Interrelationships among models

The previous section defined the meaning of language expressions in relation to a data set. Using this we can study the interrelationships between different languages, that is, different well-defined models. First the concepts of homomorphism and isomorphism are used to analyse this structure. Second, models are compared on the basis of their extension in the universe of data sets.

Homomorphic and Isomorphic Functions Between Models. Even with a simple data set concept, there are many languages that can serve to formulate a well-defined model. Between these, many functions may exist, and some of these functions may be homomorphic and even isomorphic. The properties of these functions can be used for a classification in three categories: isomorphic, homomorphic but not isomorphic, and non-homomorphic.

Among the schema languages indicated in Figure 4.3 there seem to exist a few homomorphisms, but on closer inspection, and trying to generalize from statements to languages, they appear to be 'almost homomorphic' more often than not.

The classification based on isomorphism and homomorphism has a disadvantage: Models that are very similar and models that appear totally unrelated, end up on the same pile of non-homomorphic pairs of models. Below we indicate means to analyse this pile in more detail.

When the purpose is not to analyse a set of existing languages, but when it is possible to design or select one's own, care can be taken to select a set of homomorph model languages. One may start from a data set concept that contains the information of interest, and then define a cascade (or a tree) of homomorphisms: Data Set $\to M_1 \to M_2 \to M_3 \ldots$, that filter and select the information in steps.

The composition of two homomorphisms is also homomorphic. Therefore, when introducing a new model, instead of showing there is a homomorphism from data set to new model, it is sufficient to show that there is a homomorphism from one of the previously established models to the new model. Such a chain of levels of specificity can be useful in planning and design of a data set. Such tasks may traverse the cascade in the inverse direction, starting with models of low specificity, which are refined to models of higher specificity. Along the way, according to the previous section, the set of models may be modified repeatedly, using the common operators.

Figure 4.6 presents an example of a diagram of homomorphisms and isomorphisms. Homomorphisms and isomorphisms can be composed and the composite function is again a homomorphism or isomorphism. In all cases the composition can be seen in the diagram by tracing the arrows. The composition laws thus help to keep the diagram simple. The composition of two isomorphisms is isomorphic: Let $f : M_1 \to M_2$ and $g : M_2 \to M_3$ be two isomorphisms. Then there exists an isomorphism $h : M_1 \to M_3$, formed by the composition $h = g \circ f$. If the diagram contains arrows for f and g, the arrow for h can be omitted. The composition of an isomorphism and a homomorphism or two homomorphisms is always homomorphic.

The approach based on homomorphisms starts from the data set. Models can be computed, from this central data set, using a homomorphic function, and sometimes one model can be computed from another, using a homomorphism between models. Starting from the data set as the most specific model, there can be a cascade of homomorphic functions providing a chain of models of decreasing specificity.

Equivalence and Specificity. A sentence m in a model language M is a statement about a data set. A data set satisfies the statement or does not satisfy the statement. The statement m thus partitions any 'universe' of data sets, that is, D, into data sets that satisfy (the extension), and data sets that don't. To give a simple example, the language statement: 'number of units $= 100$' may be regarded as a well-defined model. It can be defined as a function from data sets, and it is clear that it is simple to assess for any data set how many units it has. The set of all data sets with 100 units is the extension of the statement.

The relationships between models can be studied as relationships between extensions. If we compare the extensions of a pair of statements in different languages there are four possible outcomes (Figure 4.4).

m1 and m2 are equivalent

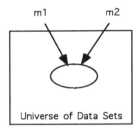

m1 is more specific than m2

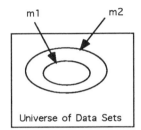

m2 and m2 cannot be compared

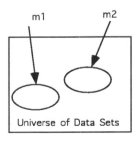

m1 and m2 cannot be compared, but their conjunction is more specific than either one of them.

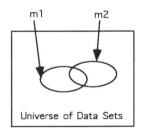

Figure 4.4: Comparing extensions. Each subfigure shows for two statements (*i.e.*, 'models') their extensions in the domain of data sets.

Two statements m_1, m_2 in different languages are *equivalent* if and only if their extensions are identical. Then they state exactly the same about the data. The languages M_1 and M_2 in which they are expressed are different, but if their extensions are identical, the models are interchangeable. If this can be generalized, the languages can be said to be equivalent. In that case there exists an isomorphism between the languages.

In a pair of statements m_1 and m_2 in different languages the first is *more specific* than the other if the extension of the first is a subset of the extension of second. If this can be generalized over data sets and all pairs of statements, the two languages M_1 and M_2 are in a specificity relation. If M_1 is more specific than M_2, there is a homomorphism $M_1 \to M_2$. The data set itself (or a copy thereof), may be regarded as the most specific model of itself. If a data set satisfies the most specific statement of a pair, it also satisfies the less specific statement. There can be series of models of increasing specificity, that is, a cascade of homomorphic functions.

In the two other cases (see the lower part of Figure 4.4), the two extensions cannot be compared. If any function exists at all between these model languages, it certainly isn't homomorphic. When the extensions do not overlap (the third case in Figure 4.4), there is no data set that satisfies both. The statements are incompatible or inconsistent. When the extensions overlap (the fourth case in Figure 4.4), it is always possible to construct a compound statement of greater specificity by taking the conjunction of two intersecting models.

Using conjunction, one can engineer levels of increasing specificity by starting with a model that will have the role of least specific model, and introduce other models only in conjunction with the least specific model.

Introducing models in conjunction with another model can also help to smooth out differences between languages that are almost equivalent. The most obvious candidate for M_0 is the overall schema, that is, the variables and their domains. That is, when m_1 and m_2 are not equivalent, $m_0 \wedge m_1$ may be equivalent to $m_0 \wedge m_2$, and it may be possible to generalize this over the languages. The schema defines a more local 'universe' in which the similar models/languages are in a homomorphic or even isomorphic functional relation. Since in any practical application there will be a schema, no harm is done to general applicability.

The concepts of equivalence and specificity (in analogy with isomorphism and homomorphism), and the possibility of taking the conjunction of two models provide us with the means to battle the chaos of potentially available languages for models of data sets. We can now put models in equivalence classes that are ordered with respect to specificity.

To give an example of statements in different languages that are equivalent when each is taken in conjunction with the schema as a third model, the following schema for the data set is assumed:

Person	
Gender	{male, female}
Marital status	{unmarried, married}
Age	N

The following four statements in different languages all have the same meaning in terms of the data set, provided they are taken in conjunction with the above schema. They all express the same aspect of the data set; they are equivalent. The first is a *table with counts* with the cell count in one cell set to 0:

Age	Marital status	count
< 16	unmarried	. . .
< 16	married	0
≥ 16	unmarried	. . .
≥ 16	married	. . .

The second is a *table structure*, that is, an enumeration of the cells not set to 0:

Age	Marital status
< 16	unmarried
≥ 16	unmarried
≥ 16	married

The third is a *table formula* defining a cross product with one element deleted:

$$\text{Age} \times \text{Marital Status} - (\text{age} < 16, \text{Marital Status} = \text{married})$$

The fourth is a *logical expression*:

$$\text{age} < 16 \rightarrow \text{Marital Status} = \text{unmarried}$$

The most striking difference is the difference in size or sheer volume occupied by the language expression.

Level of Compression. If two statements are equivalent they express the same information. If one of the two is smaller, it can be said to provide a compressed representation. Among equivalent statements, compression is lossless. At each level of specificity the equivalent statements, and perhaps the languages, can be (partially) ordered according to size or compression level. This gives a 'two-dimensional' classification. In Figure 4.5 it is used for the examples above.

Generally speaking, the compression dimension may be problematic. For instance, with compression methods used in computer graphics (Gomes & Velho, 1997) there are conditions or situations in which the more compressed language is not defined. This can not happen with well-defined models. This is guaranteed since well-defined models are defined over the entire domain of data sets.

There are conditions in which there is no reduction in size or where the compressed version is even larger than the original. That this can happen is caused by the fact that the length of a language expression depends on what is being expressed.

Generalizing the 'more compressed' relation from statements to languages can be difficult. It will seldomly be the case that one language

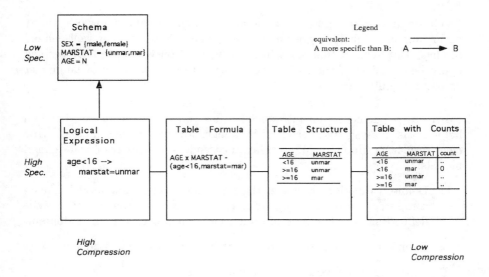

Figure 4.5: Languages cross-classified by levels of specificity and compression.

is consistently better for all data sets. Compressed languages are often designed with a particular situation in mind, (*i.e.*, certain symmetries or certain invariants in the data set), and provide good compression in this situation. Otherwise they may fail to provide size reduction.

Bearing these limitations in mind, the two-dimensional lay-out is useful in clarifying the interrelations among languages.

Presentation. There is still variation among languages that are equally specific (*i.e.*, equivalent), and that are of the same level of compression. Even these may look remarkably different. For example, a table with counts may be presented in a cross-tabular format:

Age	Marital status	count
< 16	unmarried	. . .
< 16	married	0
≥ 16	unmarried	. . .
≥ 16	married	. . .

or

	Marital status	
	unmarried	mar
Age < 16	. . .	0
≥ 16	. . .	. . .

These statements are equivalent and, approximately, of the same size. The remaining difference can be characterized as one in presentation.

In fact, the example of the cross-table is not a very good example. The cross-table is simply not defined on the entire domain of data sets, and therefore it cannot act as a language for well-defined models. For instance, consider the operation of adding a variable: This operation is impossible

(excluding tables of higher dimensional lay-out). There are however, many
other languages, including graphical languages, that allow for well-defined
models. But even at this point in the classification where we have defined
equivalent models of the same level of compression, the pile of languages
can still be quite large.

Summary. This section introduced a few concepts and means that can
help in the analysis and design of languages for well-defined models. One
clear result is a simple recipe to create a cascade or hierarchy of well-defined
models:

1. Define a function by which the statement of the new model can be
   computed, either directly from the data set or from another well-
   defined model. The function must be defined over the entire domain.

2. Define the application of the Ω operations in the new model.

3. Show that the function is a homomorphism.

The result from the previous section still stands. Even if the inter-
relationships between model languages can be hard to characterize, models
can always be consistently updated using Ω operations.

The next sections will explore this well-defined models concept in the
design of representations for statistical and methodological knowledge.

4.6   Extending the elementary datum

By enlarging the concept of data set, more information about the data collection process, for example Adèr's (1995) methodological knowledge, can
be stored in the data set itself. This extended data set concept can then
serve as a common basis for various well-defined models that represent statistical and methodological knowledge. In everyday data-analysis practice
the extra properties of the elementary datum need not be included in the
real data sets. They serve a theoretical purpose, to provide a basis for
well-defined models.

Potentially there are many properties one could add to the elementary
datum. Here we concentrate on a representation of the *data collection process*. That is, the data set is to be extended to capture a trace of the data
collection actions. Each datum represents an action in the real world involving a unit and the researcher. When we extend the elementary datum
with time, the data set will contain the timing and ordering of all the actions. When we also add the operational definition, the elementary datum
will contain a precise action specification.

With these extensions, the data set itself contains a trace of the actions
of the researcher, and can serve as a base language for the data collection
process. If data is collected in a systematic way, according to a plan or
design, there will be many invariants and symmetries in the extended data

set. In this situation, the structure of data collection can be expressed in
a more succinct fashion using a few well-defined models. If data is collected in a haphazard, chaotic fashion, most models will fail to provide any
compression. Then one can always use the data set as a base language.

4.6.1   Time

Values for variables of units may change in time and there are data sets
where time is an integral part, as shown in the example of Table 4.6. In this
example, each variable is observed at two time points. This is an example

	GNP		Unemployment	
Nation	1997	1998	1997	1998
Country 1	88	99	9	11
Country 2	44	52	11	16

Table 4.6: Example of a data set that explicitly takes the time of observation
into account.

of a data set in which time is very prominent. In many investigations and
data sets time is not prominent, but time or time order is always of great
importance in research design. First of all, the ordering of observations of an
individual unit is considered important for causal reasoning. For example,
the meaning of a variable (*e.g.*, the state of the patient), measured before
or after an experimental treatment (*e.g.*, the drugs given to the patient) is
often the central measurement in a clinical trial.

In a survey with a questionnaire ordering is also important. The interviewer must know in which order to put the questions to the interviewee. In
general one has to know the order in which different variables are observed
with each individual unit.

The elementary datum can be extended with a time aspect. We adopt
Langefors's (1977) definition of an elementary datum as a tuple:

$$(object, property, value, time)$$

In statistical parlance, a property is called 'variable' and an object is called
'unit'. This motivates the following definition of a Data Set:

$$\text{Data Set} = \{(unit, variable, value, time)\} \tag{4.3}$$

To express the constraint that each unit can at most have one value for each
variable at each time, the definition can be narrowed down to:

$$\text{Data Set} \subseteq (\text{Units} \times \text{Variables} \times \text{Times} \to \text{Values}) \tag{4.4}$$

The subset relation indicates that not every data set must be a full
cross-product of Units, Variables and Times, The cross-product establishes

| Unit | Variable | Value | Time | | | |
			Date	Clock	Rank	rel. Rank
1	gender	male	July 4 2003	9.03 am	1	1
1	drug A	yes	July 4 2003	9.05 am	2	2
1	drug B	yes	July 4 2003	9.05 am	2	2
1	bloodpressure H	120	July 4 2003	9.35 am	3	3
1	bloodpressure L	80	July 4 2003	9.35 am	3	3
2	gender	female	July 4 2003	9.15 am	4	1
2	drug A	yes	July 4 2003	9.21 am	2	2
2	drug B	yes	July 4 2003	9.21 am	2	2
2	bloodpressure H	104	July 4 2003	9.55 am	3	3
2	bloodpressure L	78	July 4 2003	9.55 am	3	3
3	cue	nocue	July 4 2003	9.21 am	5	2
and so on						

Table 4.7: Example of a data set with timestamps.

the maximal domain for the Data Set. The domain of an actual data set is either this cross-product or a subset.

There are choices to be made in what we take as a domain for time. Table 4.7 shows three options. One option is time as measured on clock and calendar. Then the time entry becomes a time stamp for the elementary datum the moment it is observed and recorded in Data Set, assuming observing and recording takes place at the same time. However, when duration is irrelevant and only the sequence of time points is important, we may simply use rank numbers. If we only need to express the sequence for each unit separately, we may start for each *unit* with time is 1 (cf. Adèr, 1995). The exact time when a unit is engaged can be expressed at the level of the unit, that is, as another variable in the data set.

Since Data Set will serve as the central, most specific, model, the time scale should be at the most specific level. Data sets in which this time scale is mapped onto a less specific timescale may be regarded as a well-defined model of the central data set.

In the elementary datum, time is the time when the elementary datum is observed and inserted into the Data Set:

$$\text{Data Set}_{time} = \text{Data Set}_{time-1} \cup \{(unit, variable, value, time)\} \qquad (4.5)$$

First of all there is a concern that such valuation is true to reality. The valuation provided by the elementary datum must correspond to the valuation in reality at time. Having a tuple such as: (patient 23, bloodpressure H, 112, 17) in a data set means that it has been observed that patient number 23, for the function bloodpressure H, maps to a value of 112, at $time = 17$. To ensure this the researcher, or one of his helpers, must operate or interact with the unit in the real world at time. Therefore, the meaning of the elementary datum is two-fold: a certain valuation at time and a certain action at time.

With a so-called retrospective measurement (*e.g.*, a question to the respondent in a survey about events in the respondent's past), the time of the observation and the time of the valuation are different. For example, in an interview, it is asked whether the respondent was subjected to a tonsillectomy, and, if appliccable, some questions around this event are asked. The sequence of events (*i.e.*, birth, tonsillectomy), and the sequence of questions do not need to be the same. Both sequences may be important, and, if so, two time recordings are needed. Since in this chapter the emphasis is on the process of data collection we take time to be the time of the action by the researcher or one of his helpers.

If existing data sets or archives are being used in an investigation, the time of the original collection and the time of the action by the current researcher are different. Since in this chapter the emphasis is on the process of data collection viewed as actions or interactions with the unit, we only use the timepoint at which the original observation was made.

4.6.2   Operationalization

The time property adds an important aspect of data collection to the data set itself: the temporal order in which the lab assistant or the laptop must collect the data. To provide a more complete instruction for the data collection, the actions and instruments involved must be specified.

Given an elementary datum, for example:

(patient 23, bloodpressure H, 112, 17)

someone could ask serious questions about the 'bloodpressure' function and one would want transparency regarding the method of establishing the value (questions about the scale, the manufacturer of the instrument, the tolerances, and so on). According to scientific standards, the method by which the value is observed should be described in sufficient detail such that others (or at least investigator's peers) can *replicate* it in their laboratories. This is referred to as the *operational definition* or *operationalization*: the meaning of a value is in the details of the procedure by which it is obtained.

The operationalization gives information about the action the researcher or his helper must perform. Therefore, it ought to be included in the elementary datum, providing a more complete representation of the plan or process of data collection in the data set itself:

$$\text{Data Set} = \{(unit, variable, value, time, operationalization)\} \qquad (4.6)$$

Information about the operationalization also contributes to the meaning of the valuation (unit, variable, value). The domain of operational definitions

Time Point	Action by Researcher	Insertions in Data Set
1	sample a unit (unit 63) with gender = male	(unit 63,gender,male,1,sampling/selection)
2	treat unit 63 with drug A = yes with drug B = yes	(unit 63,drug A,yes,2,treatment) (unit 63,drug B,yes,2,treatment)
3	measure unit 63 bloodpressure H = ... bloodpressure L = ...	(unit 63,bloodpressure 1,x_1,3,measurement) (unit 63,bloodpressure 2,x_2,3,measurement)

Table 4.8: Example of a data set as a trace of the data collection process.

cannot be defined in advance. It is up to the creativity of the researcher and the customs in the research area. However, it is possible to use a global classification. Just like the time scale may be abstracted to simple time ranks, the domain of operationalization may be abstracted to three types. Following the distinctions made in the theory of block designs, and in the GENSTAT system (Nelder, 1974), there are three types of action that can ensure that an individual unit has a certain value for a variable at time.

These can be introduced by example: With *measurement*, patient 23 arrives, the measurement device is applied, and its value is read. It reads 112. The researcher can look at the clock, and insert the datum with the right timestamp in the data set.

With *treatment*, patient 23 arrives, is hooked-up to a measurement device, and is given some drug until the device reads 112. Then, after consulting the clock, the researcher can insert the datum with the right timestamp in the data set. The unit, the variables and their specific values are all determined beforehand, but the researcher must go through the motions to make them true.

With *sampling/selection*, the investigator walks around, measuring different patients, until one is found that gives a reading of 112. This one is selected, this one will serve as patient 23. The researcher can look at the clock, and insert the datum with the right timestamp in the data set. Variables and specific values for the selection are determined in advance.

These examples show that the same elementary datum can have very different meanings indeed. It can be a value that has been measured, freely allowed to take any value that it might take, or it can be an action specification for selecting or treating a unit as to make it have a certain value. The three categories are assumed to be exhaustive, that is, there is no other action or method to obtain an elementary datum through interaction in the real world with a unit. However, in a data set one may find elementary data of a different origin. For example, an elementary datum may be computed from others. In that case the the new datum may inherit the classification of its sources, provided it is the same category for each of the original data. The timestamp of the computed variable is the same as the most recent one among the original data.

Summary. The elementary datum with time and operationalization provides us with a data set that represents the data collection process. The data set becomes a trace of the actions of the researcher. Table 4.8 gives an example, showing how operations in the real world may correspond to operations on the data set. More concise or less specific languages for the data collection process can now be studied as well-defined models of the data set in equation 4.6 above.

Extending the data with time, and having well-defined models thereof, warrants an extension of the set of Ω operators. The operators for adding or deleting a variable will have a version that takes a pair *variable* and time as parameter. The effect of add variable is that *variable* is inserted at time. The effect of delete variable is that *variable* at time is deleted.

4.6.3 Well-defined models for the process structure

If the data set language can describe a trace, it can also describe a plan for a certain trace in the future. In this plan one may use timestamps in the future, and use placeholders for the values to be measured in the future. Well-defined models can then be used as more concise representations of this plan. Examples of this dual usage can also be found among the classical statistical models. For example, a table with counts may be used to describe the statistical design before data collection and it may be used in statistical analysis, where the counts are computed from the data set as collected. Below we discuss a few well-defined models for the time extension.

The *process structure* describes the timing of the actions in data collection and this temporal structure can be discussed at different levels of specificity. The data set with time on a date and clock scale serves as the most specific level. Using this as a basis, we can define homomorphic functions that hide unnecessary details and concentrate on the information that is relevant. This provides a number of levels of decreasing specificity. Figure 4.6 shows a diagram. The data set is shown at the bottom, to the right.

Starting from the data set, each abstraction step is based upon an assumption.

First it is assumed that *value* and operationalization are not important in the temporal structure: therefore these aspects of the elementary datum can be ignored. Then to provide a more compressed representation, for each unit the pairs (*variable, time*) are collected in a set.

Next it is assumed that only ordering is important: therefore, one may use ranks or timepoints instead of timestamps.

In addition it is assumed that units are independent and that only the temporal ordering within a unit is important. Therefore the time property can be mapped to *unitrank*. This leaves us with

$$\{(unit, [(variable, unitrank)])\}$$

as a more abstract language.

For each unit, the set $[(variable, unitrank)]$ shows one or more variables at each timepoint *unitrank*, and the set can be compressed to a sequence. Using the example data in Table 4.8, the sequence of unit 63 is the following:

gender < (drug A, drug B) < (bloodpressure H, bloodpressure L)

Determining the sequence for all units gives a set $\{(unit, sequence)\}$. Sequences can be counted, showing the number of units following the different sequences. When the focus is not on the numbers of units, but on the set of sequences that exist in the data, the counts can be ignored. This gives the set of sequences $\{(sequence)\}$. It contains the sequences present in the data.

If the sequence is invariant over units (*e.g.*, all units go through the same sequence), as it will usually be the case in a well-designed investigation, this 'set-of-sequences' language provides a rather good compression: a set with one sequence. When the invariant is not perfect, when there are different sequences for different units, the set will contain all these sequences. All the variants (*i.e.*, the second sequence, and more if there are more), are reported. There is less compression, but no information is lost.

Abstraction and compression can be carried a little further. For example, by simplifying to $\{(variable, unitrank)\}$, showing the timepoints of each variable. The timepoints of each variable can be collected in a set: $\{(variable, [unitrank])\}$. As soon as there appear two rank numbers or time points for one variable, it is a sign that one may need a more specific language. There are different situations that can give rise to a variable occurring at two time positions: multiple instance of the same variable in a single sequence, or different sequences among units. To differentiate, one needs a more specific language, and that would be the 'set-of-sequences' language. There is nothing wrong with the ranks language, it is still well-defined, but for tasks that need detailed temporal information, it lacks specificity when the process structure is complex.

Summary. In the design of languages for well-defined models, one can build a cascade or tree of homomorphisms, with decreasing level of specificity, for a particular property of the data set. There is another characteristic of well-defined models of which the importance is becoming more and more recognized: Well-defined models are defined for the entire domain of data sets, meaning that they can always be computed. They are simple and robust, they will always do their job, and always have a clear and unambiguous meaning. When there are imperfections of the invariance

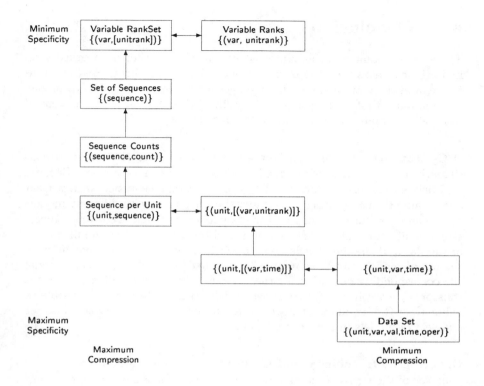

Figure 4.6: Well-defined models for the process structure. Languages are ordered by specificity and level of compression. Arrows represent homomorphisms, double arrows isomorphisms.

or symmetry (asumptions are violated, lack of fit), they are still defined, they are defined over the entire domain of data set, but they provide less compression, and relevant information may be lost. Then a more specific model in the cascade or tree may provide the specificity needed. If all fails, there is always the data set itself, as the most specific language.

Complex operations example. Having these abstractions of the temporal structure may suggest certain complex operations on the data set. For example, a swap operator might be considered useful. It swaps timepoints of two variables, and its action can be defined using the common operators. Having done that, the swap operator can be effectively applied to the data set with time stamps, and to any other well-defined model in which time is present. This example is to show that models may suggest more complex operators, that the set Ω of common operators is in no way limiting, these common operators can be used to define the complex operator, and, having done that, the complex operator can be applied to all well-defined models.

4.7   Conclusion

The starting point of this chapter is that all objects that are worked with
in statistical tasks are models of data sets. A model is formulated in a language, and there are many such languages for models of data sets available,
to an amount that is confusing. The result of this chapter is the concept of
well-defined model. It has great advantages to use well-defined models.

Ω-**Operations.**   If one needs representations that can be modified consistently at any time, well-defined models provide the solution. Because
well-defined models are formal, they provide a representation with a clear
and unambiguous meaning. The interrelationships among different models
and languages can be traced and made explicit through the data. Consistent modifications of models can be based on corresponding modifications
of the data. If the data set is being described by a set of different models,
the set of models can be consistently modified by applying to each model
the corresponding operation for that model. The corresponding operations
thus provide a solution for consistent modifications. It appears possible to
define a set Ω of common operators that can be used to modify the data set
and sets of models in a consistent manner.

Ordering by Specificity and Compression.   Furthermore, we can see
glimpses of the structure among well-defined models of a common data set.
This brings some order in the confusing multitude of languages available.
With well-defined models we can order models on specificity, and, for equivalent models, we can order languages on degree of compression. Operators
such as conjunction can help to make interrelations among models that are
similar, but not equivalent, more explicit.

We may want to minimize the number of different languages, and pick
just one. For example, from the most specific languages one may choose the
one that is most compressed. Nevertheless, we may still want to use more
than just one language, because languages may differ in level of complexity
for the user, or for other reasons as mentioned in the introduction of this
chapter. The concept of well-defined models does not prescribe the selection criteria, but it greatly facilitates selection, because it provides a sorted
overview of options.

It is also possible to simultaneously use a number of different models
that address the same aspect of the data at different levels of specificity.
The common operators will take care of consistent modifications of any set
of models.

Extensibility.   The concept of well-defined models of data sets is exten-
sible. A larger data set concept allows a richer set of well-defined models.
One example was given of an extended data set concept and a model that
adresses time and data operations: the process structure. Other exten-

sions of the data set and other models can be introduced when a particular application requires them.

Well-defined models provide a radically general and robust solution for consistent modifications at a fundamental level, and there are, I expect, many more interesting properties and implications of well-defined models. Being fundamental, well-defined models do not provide all the answers to the questions of design and implementation of systems that use meta data. A few adjoining issues are briefly mentioned below.

Meta Classes. A theme that recurs again and again is that a formalism in itself does not tell enough. Even though the sentences of well-defined models have a clear meaning, namely that the data set has a certain property, the meaning of this clear 'fact' is not clear, it is not given in the formalism itself. The same model of the data set (*e.g.*, identical formulae or expressions), may have different meanings, depending on the role in the task. An example for statisticians is statistical analysis. The same ANOVA formula or expression can have the role of Maximal Model, Alternative Model, or Best Model (Wolstenholme & Nelder, 1986).

Another example can be found in statistical design. The same formula or expression or table can have the role of Requirements, Design Solution, or Constraints. Think of the example, presented earlier, in which a zero occurred in a table with counts. This could be caused by the legislation of the land, and then it is impossible to have units in that cell. Thus, in a design task, the table or expression would have the role of Constraints. The zero could also have been the result of design decisions of the researcher. Then it belongs to the Design Solution. Alternatively, it might be part of the Requirements, as a Maximal Model for the statistical analysis.

The knowledge-engineering approach KADS (Schreiber, Wielinga, & Breuker, 1993), stresses the importance of meta-logical classifications based on the role in the task or in the problem solving process. This concept of meta class is also applicable to well-defined models. In models of statistical problem solving, these meta-classifications can be made explicit — each statement is associated with its role, or statements in different roles are stored separately — and be used to control the problem solving process.

The extension of the elementary datum with operationalization can also be thought of as providing a meta-classification. The elementary datum with time can have different roles in the data collection process, and the extension with operationalization tells which role.

Meta Data Management. Well-defined models are relevant for data/meta data management systems. The project 'Modelling Meta Data' (Darius et al., 1993), was based on pairing a data set with its 'meta data set'. The project investigated the use of binary operations to merge and align data/meta data sets. A full functional prototype demonstrated the feasibility of this approach. A recent thesis on meta data management is provided by Froeschl (1997), and it contains many pointers to ongoing meta data research.

User-Interface Design. Well-defined models are important for user interface design. The selection of representations to be used in the interaction with the user can be made with more deliberation, to allow ease of learning and ease of use. The availability of operations is a good basis for a more flexible dialogue in which the user does not have to redo previous work, or make errors in editing, whenever a change is made.

Inter-operability. Well-defined models also provide a basis for inter-operability of different software systems. Many investigators today have to use at least two or three software systems in their work, and any modification that is desired may force the investigator to go back to each of the three systems. Sharing a common set of operators Ω would provide integration and reduce a change to a single operation that updates all well-defined models.

In conclusion, well-defined models provide a firm and indeed *well-defined* basis for meta data languages. They can be consistenly modified, are defined over the entire domain of data sets, have a clear meaning, and seem to have many more desirable properties and open up a whole new universe for further study.

Acknowledgements. Many thanks are due to Joachim Mowitz and David Hand who provided valuable comments on an earlier version of this chapter. This research was partly performed within DOSES project B 41: 'Modelling Metadata', funded by EUROSTAT.

Chapter 5

Experimental Design

Paul Darius and Kenneth Portier

We live in an age where data is all about us. We hear of government agencies, corporations and others collecting data to address one question or another. Often the how and why these data are collected is not clearly described. It might look as if there is no underlying design to these studies. Yet, the ability to answer specific questions critically depends on how the data are obtained.

Data represent measurements on characteristics of individuals. Since these characteristics vary from individual-to-individual they are often referred to as variables. Most studies involve comparing the average value of one or more variables referred to as responses, for two or more groups differentiated by other variables or characteristics referred to as factors. A factor is simply a characteristic which is assumed to affect, in some way, the average response observed.

Comparison is the key activity of the scientific method. Any research study in which the researcher deliberately changes or assigns values (levels) to one factor in order to determine its effect by comparing the groups created by this factor is called an experimental study or experiment. On the other hand, in an observational study, the researcher who sets up the study cannot, for whatever reason, control or assign the levels of the factor of interest. In general, experimental design is concerned with setting up studies such that the comparisons made directly address the study questions at the same time requiring the minimal amount of data necessary to be confident in the results of the comparison.

In all studies, there are factors which are directly related to the questions of interest. We call these the treatment factors. There are factors which we know will affect the responses of interest but which we are not directly interested in. If these factors are incorporated into the study design they are called *control* or *blocking* factors since their major reason for being in the study is to control for these extraneous sources of variation in the response. Finally, there are factors which we know will affect the response but which we either choose not to incorporate into the study design or cannot incorporate into the study design. The effects of these factors are mitigated by the use of randomization in the design.

The research literature is full of methods and examples of good and bad study designs (see Section 14.1.1). Statisticians and others, working from a set of basic concepts and tools have developed a vast literature of different approaches to study design. Most of this literature deals with the experimental study, since it is in these studies that the ability to control and assign factors allows efficient designs to be developed. These same concepts and tools are applicable to observational studies and special situations such as clinical trials, but with less control there are fewer optional approaches.

In this chapter we will discuss the questions a researcher must answer as he/she proceeds to design a research study. If the researcher has control, the questions asked include: Where and how should it be exercised? What are the best design approaches? and Which designs allow us to make the important comparisons while also minimizing resources and time?

5.1   Concepts

5.1.1   The experimental process and experimental design

Designing experiments is an integral part of the experimental process. Experimentation is a multi-step, iterative process (Figure 5.1) consisting of discrete activities. Each step in the process depends on the decisions made in the previous steps. Often the researcher will have to return to earlier steps to reconsider the choices made because of findings at later steps. In this way, experimentation is a feed-forward process with feedback loops at each step.

Experimental design starts with a research question. Clearly stating the research question is critical, since all subsequent decisions flow from the research question. In this way, the quality of the experimental design also depends on a clear research question. A vague statement of the research question can lead to a poor experimental design, which in turn will result in the failure of the whole study. No matter how complex the statistical analysis of the resulting data, starting with a poor design will result in weak or inadequate conclusions. The quality of the design is measured by how well the study objective is addressed. A good experimental design will answer the key study questions using the least amount of resources.

EXAMPLE 1
A large food distribution chain explores the possibilities of marketing a new apple variety. After harvest, apples are stored under controlled temperature and atmospheric conditions for up to several months, before being offered to the consumer (for simplicity reasons, we assume that it is technically possible

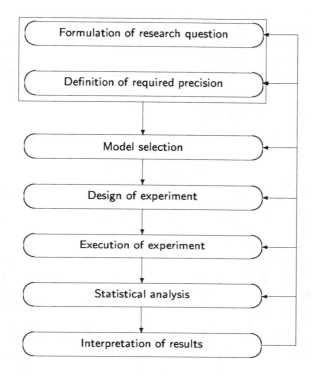

Figure 5.1: A schematic overview of the experimental process.

to apply these conditions in a perfectly repeatable way, without any errors involved). The question is:

> 'How should storage conditions be adapted for this new variety, so that each arrives at the store in optimal condition?'

It is clear that this question needs considerable refining before an experiment designed to answer it can be set up. The end result of the refinement process may be a research question like

> 'What setting of constant temperature and oxygen concentration results in maximum hardness (as measured by a standard compression test) after 6 months of storage?'.

but also

> 'After how much time under the storage conditions used for the other apple varieties is the consumer acceptability (as measured by a tasting panel's mean score on a standard questionnaire), maximal?'.

These two questions will lead to two very differently designed experiments[1].

---

[1] We will use this example throughout the chapter to clarify various key points in experimental design.

It is not uncommon to find that a considerable part of the total design effort has to be spent on refining the research question. This stage can pose difficult problems, and little formal work has been done in developing paradigms for successful research question formulation (see Hand, 1994).

5.1.2   Some basic terms

Any feature of a process or individual item is referred to as a characteristic. A variable is a measurable characteristic which may change or vary over time, space or from individual-to-individual. When discussing experimental designs, a number of different types of variables are of interest (see Kish, 1987). *Explanatory variables* relate directly to the objectives of the research. The response or responses to be measured are sometimes called the *predicted variables, response variables* or even *dependent variables.* Those characteristics which are assumed to be associated or cause changes in the response variable and in which we are directly interested are called *predictor variables, stimulus variables, treatment factors* or *covariates.* Finally, there are other characteristics which may be associated or cause changes in the response variable but which are not directly related to the research questions. The effect of these *extraneous variables, control factors* or *blocking factors* must be accounted for in the experimental design and in the statistical analysis if the effects of the treatment factors are to be examined. It is assumed that the researcher in an experimental study has some choice in which treatment factors and control factors will be included in the design, and to some extent which levels of these factors will be used.

We used the term *treatment* to describe conditions or manipulations which must be compared in order to answer the study questions. The choice of treatments and treatment factor levels is critical to an effective experimental study. Thus, for example, if the study question addresses the effectiveness of a new drug over the standard drug in treating a medical condition, the two treatments will be the new drug and the standard drug. When we talk about a *treatment effect*, we refer to the differences in effect among the levels of a treatment factor.

Often the research questions may require examination of the effects of more than one treatment factor. In these studies, the actual treatments applied are defined by some or all of the combinations of these treatment factor levels. These treatments are referred to as *factorial treatments*, and the experiment as a *factorial experiment.*

An *experimental unit* is the smallest quantity of experimental material to which a treatment factor level can be allocated independently of other units. Thus, for example, in the new drug/standard drug treatments study, the experimental unit might be a mouse. The *sampling unit* or *measurement unit* is that material or quantity on which measurements are taken. In many experiments, the experimental unit and the sampling unit are one and the same. In other experiments, the sampling unit will be some piece of the experimental unit, usually selected at random. In other experiments, the

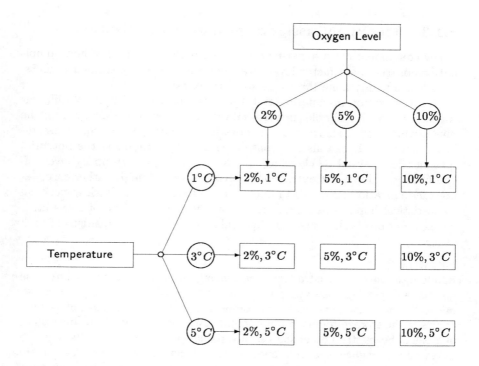

Figure 5.2: Example of a factorial experiment. The boxes represent the treatment combinations used.

sampling unit may represent measurement of the experimental unit at one point in time. In general, measurements on sampling units may or may not be assumed to be independent. Also, in some experiments, different treatment factors may have different sizes of experimental units (see Section 5.3.2).

EXAMPLE 2

Using the first research question proposed previously, the treatment factors might be temperature and oxygen concentration, the experimental unit the apple, and the response variable the hardness. We should then decide on what levels of the treatment factors will be used, e.g. 2%, 5% and 10% for the oxygen concentration, and $1°C$, $3°C$ and $5°C$ temperature. To make this a factorial experiment, a number of apples should be subjected to each of the nine treatments defined by the combinations of treatment factor levels: 2% and $1°C$, 2% and $3°C$,... up to 10% and $5°C$ (See Figure 5.2). If we choose to take two samples out of each apple to determine the hardness on, then the sample becomes the measurement unit.

5.1.3   Treatment assignment and randomization

A key component of an experimental design is the definition of how combinations of treatment factor levels are to be assigned to experimental units. This is commonly done through some form of randomization.

Randomization in experimental design can be viewed in many different ways. First, it is a simple, impersonal or 'blind' technique for evading the biases which can arise from other more judgemental or systematic assignment methods. It can also be considered a tool for reducing the potential biasing effect caused by choosing not to control for, i.e. group by levels of, one or more known but extraneous sources of variation. In either case, using randomization allows us to make certain assumptions which are critical to statistical hypothesis testing at the analysis phase. One of these critical assumptions is that the experimental errors will be independent of each other.

EXAMPLE 3
Randomization can be introduced by dividing the apples randomly into nine groups, and putting each group in a storage room with an atmosphere determined by one of the nine treatment combinations. If we would have placed the apples in the storage rooms in a non-random way, e.g. according to their place in a pile of boxes, then other sources of variability may bias our results: e.g. the boxes on top might come from another part of the orchard or be picked more recently. If these are placed in the low temperature storage rooms, we have no way of telling whether differences between low and high storage rooms are due to a temperature effect, or are simply caused by differences in time since picking (See also the discussion on internal validity and causality in Chapter 14 in Sections 14.1.1 and 14.2.3).

In general, as many aspects of the experimental procedure as possible should be randomized. Sometimes however randomization is very costly and/or highly impractical. Then a reasonable compromise must be sought, and the randomization restrictions taken into account in the analysis (see Section 5.3.2–5.3.4).

5.1.4   Experimental error, blocking and balance

Experimental material (units) are inherently variable. This inherent variability is reflected in the differences of measurements on experimental units which have been treated similarly. That is, if two experimental units receive the same treatment, one would expect the response measured to be the same. The failure to obtain similar responses is sometimes called the *experimental error*. Large amounts of experimental error increase the difficulty of determining whether treatments produce different effects. Hence another design goal is the reduction of experimental error.

Blocking refers to the allocation of experimental units into groups, called blocks, in such a manner that the experimental units within a block are relatively homogeneous while the greater part of the predictable variation among units is now associated with the variation among blocks. That is, the experimenter uses knowledge of the variability among units to group them in such a way that most of the unwanted experimental error will be removed in this block effect. In many cases, one or more of the extraneous variables is used as a guide to the grouping of experimental units. The blocking factor levels are the names given to the different block units created.

Balancing refers to the assignment of experimental units into blocks, groups and treatments in such a way that a balanced configuration occurs. Statistically, balancing refers to the situation where comparison of factor levels is performed with equal precision. This can be achieved by allocating (a) equal numbers of units in each block, and (b) equal number of units receiving each treatment. Often, full balance in an experimental design cannot be achieved due to resource constraints. In this case partial balance may be achieved by defining sets of treatments to be compared at different levels of precision.

EXAMPLE 4
Balance can be achieved by storing the same number of apples under the nine atmospheric conditions. We would use blocking if there are known sources of heterogeneity that may affect the response. If e.g. the apples come from two suppliers, we could use supplier as a block variable and still achieve balance by using the same number of apples from both suppliers under each atmospheric condition.

5.1.5 Replication and pseudo-replication

Replication refers to the application of the same treatment to several experimental units. Primarily we replicate treatments to provide the information needed to estimate inherent variability in the experimental material, i.e. the experimental error. The more replicates we use, the more precise the estimate of treatment effects and hence smaller differences in treatment effects can be declared statistically different. More experimental units can result in greater experimental error through the inclusion of units with different values for uncontrolled sources of variation.

A common problem in experimental design is to confuse multiple measurements or observations on the same experimental unit (i.e. sampling unit responses) with true replication. True replication involves, at a minimum, randomly applying the treatment to a number of different (independent) experimental units. When multiple values from the same experimental unit are used to estimate experimental error, we commit the error of *pseudo-replication*. Making measurements on sampling units is, in itself, not incorrect. It is the incorrect use of the variability among sample unit measurements to estimate underlying experimental error which creates the pseudo-replication mistake. For this reason it is very important to establish at the design phase exactly what constitutes true replication for each comparison of interest.

EXAMPLE 5

Replication can be increased by using a larger number of apples for each treatment. This requires more storage space and measurement effort, but will make treatment comparisons more precise. Increasing the number of samples per apple however, will not increase the precision of treatment comparisons. Dealing with the sample measurements as if they were independent measurements of apple response to a treatment would be a case of pseudo-replication.

5.1.6 Characteristics of a good experimental design

The mathematician R. A. Fisher initiated the modern study of experimental designs by defining what must be present in a research study in order for fair comparisons to be possible. The main features of a good design are as follows.

- o The experimental design should allow for unbiased estimation and comparison of the treatment effects. In this way the key study questions can be answered.

- o The experiment must facilitate meaningful estimation of the underlying variability (experimental error) in experimental units, assuming treatment factor and control factor effects have been accounted for.

- o Adequate numbers of replicates should be used in order that effects can be estimated with sufficient precision to detect the smallest differences of practical importance.

- o Experimental units should be grouped or blocked in order to control for or balance out known sources of extraneous variation. That is, blocking factors should be used when necessary to explain away part of the total variation in the responses. Where possible, all treatment factor combinations should be accounted for in each block unit.

- o Treatments should be randomized to experimental units so that the treatment effects are all equally affected by uncontrolled sources of extraneous variation.

- o The simplest design possible to accomplish the objectives of the study should be used.

- o The experiment should make efficient and effective use of available resources. In general, Fisher suggested that a single complex factorial experiment is often more efficient and effective in investigating the effects of multiple treatments than devoting a separate experiment to each treatment factor.

Finally, for all experimental studies, the method used to analyse experimentally derived data must reflect the relationships among the experimental units and the conditions imposed in the randomization of treatments to these experimental units.

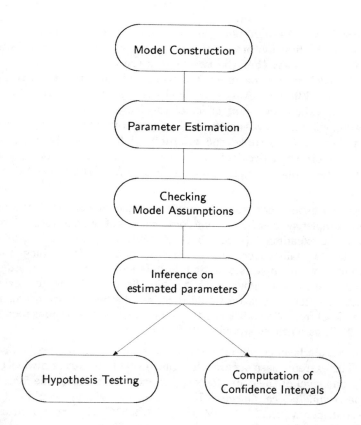

Figure 5.3: Statistical analysis of a designed experiment.

5.2   Analysis

Statistical analysis of a designed experiment proceeds as follows (see Figure 5.3):

1. Construction of a model.

2. Estimation of the parameters of the model.

3. Checking of the model assumptions.

4. Inference on the estimated parameters. This can take the form of hypothesis testing or the construction of confidence intervals.

5.2.1   Relation between factors

To explain how a model is constructed, it is necessary first to explore the possible relationships between two factors in an experiment. If we look at two factors from an experiment with at least two factors, it may be that every level of the first factor occurs with every level of the other factor. If this is the case, we say that the two factors are *completely crossed*. Then we may, for each factor, be interested to see whether the main responses are different at different levels (averaged over the levels of the other factors). This is called the *main effect* of the factor. We may also, instead of averaging, examine how the effect of a factor differs at different levels of another factor. This is called the *interaction effect*. The concept can be extended to more than two factors, in which case we can explore a *higher order interaction* (one for each subset of factors from the crossed factors).

EXAMPLE 6

In the factorial experiment from the apple example, temperature and oxygen levels were completely crossed: all nine combinations of temperature and oxygen occurred in the experiment (Figure 5.2). A model to analyse this experiment would contain a main effect term for the temperature (describing how the mean hardness of the apples stored at $1°C$ differed from the mean hardness of all the apples in the experiment,...), a main effect for the oxygen level, and an interaction effect. The latter would describe whether for instance changing the oxygen level from 2% to 5% has the same effect on the response for apples stored at $1°C$, as on those stored at $3°C$ or $5°C$.

When certain level combinations are not present, the factors can still be crossed. The extreme case occurs when one level of one factor always occurs with only one level of the other factor, and vice versa. Then the factors are said to be *completely confounded*. If the apple experiment would only contain the treatments $(2\%,1°C)$, $(5\%,3°C)$, $(10\%,5°C)$ then temperature and oxygen level would be completely confounded. Such an experiment would only require three storage rooms, but the resulting data would be inadequate to examine (test) the effect of temperature or oxygen level alone on hardness. Since any change in temperature is accompanied by a corresponding change in oxygen level, it is impossible to decide which part of the difference has to be attributed to temperature, and which part to oxygen levels. We can only know the joint effect of changing both. If we are interested in the effect of temperature as such and also in the effect of oxygen level, it would be disastrous to embark on such an experiment. It would also be disastrous if some extraneous factor, not considered in the experiment, was completely confounded with a factor used in the experiment. Randomization can be considered an effective technique for avoiding such confoundings.

However, when carefully used, confounding is also a useful tool to reduce the size of an experiment. If we are willing to assume that some effects are far less important than others, we can control the confounding pattern in such a way that effects considered important do not get confounded with each other, but only with effects considered less important (usually higher order interactions). The risk of making the assumptions is often more than compensated by the reduction in experimental units. This is the idea underlying fractional and related types of experiments (see e.g. Box, Hunter, & Hunter, 1978).

Sometimes, the nature of the factors prevents them from being completely crossed. When each level of one factor does not occur together with more than one level of another factor, we say that the first factor is *nested* in the second. Designs with nested factors are called *hierarchical*.

EXAMPLE 7

Suppose that we selected our apples from five trees in each of two orchards, and we want to know the extent to which the apple's behaviour under the conservation treatment depends on the tree it comes from. Then orchard and tree will be factors, but they cannot be crossed: a tree can only belong to one orchard. We say that the factor tree is nested in the factor orchard.

When one factor is nested in another, a two-factor interaction between the two is meaningless: interaction describes how the effect of a factor differs at different levels of the other factor, but now those factor levels cannot occur at different levels of the other factor. In general, a model will never contain an interaction term in which one of the constituting factors nests one or more of the other factors.

EXAMPLE 8

In our example, there will be an orchard and a tree (within orchard) effect, but no orchard-tree interaction. The orchard term is the usual main effect. The tree (within orchard) term describes how each tree is different from the mean of the trees from that orchard. An orchard-tree interaction would describe whether e.g. the difference between tree 1 and tree 2 is the same in the two orchards. This has no interpretation in the context of the experiment, since tree 1 of the first orchard is not the same as tree 1 in the second orchard — their common label is just a coincidence.

Although not explicitly acknowledged, nesting is present in every design. The experimental unit can always be considered as nested in any factor. In the factorial apple experiment, any apple can receive only one treatment combination, hence apple is nested in any treatment factor. However, since an experimental unit is usually not considered as a factor, the resulting design is not called hierarchical.

5.2.2 Fixed and random factors

There is another factor property that plays a crucial role in the analysis. When the levels of a factor were chosen because of intrinsic interest in them, we call the factor *fixed*. When the levels of a factor were sampled from a distribution of levels, and we are interested in the properties of the distribution rather than in the levels actually sampled, we call the factor *random*.

Every random factor defines a source of randomness which the analysis must identify and estimate. As a result, the analysis will be more complicated, even more so when the design was not balanced or there were missing observations.

Whether a factor is fixed or random determines the type of questions the analysis will typically have to answer: for fixed factors, we will want to compare particular levels, for random factors we will typically want to estimate the variability of the distribution of levels.

EXAMPLE 9
The temperature factor would typically be considered fixed since we are interested in the properties of storing at the temperature levels chosen. The factor tree would typically be considered random, again since we are not interested in the trees that happened to be chosen, but rather in the amount of variability caused by tree-to-tree differences (i.e. the variance of the distribution of tree means).

5.2.3 The model

A model basically has the form:

$$\texttt{Response} = \texttt{effects} + \texttt{experimental error}$$

The model tries to explain the response measured on a unit as a function of known factors and a random variable that models the experimental error.

Several notations can be used to describe models for experiments. A very general notation is the *general linear model*, which is written as follows, using matrix notation:

$$Y = X\beta + \varepsilon$$

Here Y is a vector of responses, X a matrix of known quantities and β a vector of parameters to estimate. In the general linear model the response is explained as a linear combination of effects (the columns of X) plus an experimental error. The latter is represented by ε, a vector of random variables with assumptions about their distribution, mean and variance-covariance matrix.

The general linear model uses a rather abstract notation, and is not necessarily unique for a given experimental situation (categorical variables can be represented in X in several ways). On the other hand, it can deal in a uniform way with a vast array of experimental situations, ranging from observational studies with multiple regression to complex designed experiments.

The general linear model assumes that the random variables in ε have a normal distribution. A still more general model, the generalized linear model, can deal with other error distributions (see McCullough & Nelder, 1989).

For comparative experiments, a more explicit notation is commonly used. A model for a factorial experiment with two factors will be written as:

$$Y_{ijk} = \mu + \alpha_i + \beta_j + (\alpha\beta)_{ij} + \varepsilon_{ijk}$$

Here μ is usually interpreted as the population overall mean, α_i as the deviation from the overall mean of the i-th level of factor A (the A main effect). The β_j form the B main effect, and the $(\alpha\beta)_{ij}$ describe how the response deviates from the sum of the overall mean and the main effects (the AB-interaction effect). If the interaction effects are zero, the effect of changing the level of A is the same at any level of B (and vice versa).

In the simplest case, it is assumed that the ε_{ijk} are independent and have an identical distribution: a normal distribution with mean zero and a certain variance.

The choice of a model (including the assumptions) for a given experimental situation will be based partly on the nesting/crossing relationships of the factors, their interpretation as random or fixed, and partly on the interests and the assumptions the experimenter is willing to make (e.g. about the covariance pattern, or the negligibility of certain effects). It follows that different analysts may use slightly different models to analyse the same experiment. Nevertheless, many of the standard designs (see Section 5.3) will almost always be analysed with their usual model.

5.2.4   Inference

Once the model has been constructed, its parameters can be estimated. This is done by fitting the model: finding those values of the parameters for which the model 'fits' the observed data best, according to some criterion. For most experiments the least squares criterion is used, for more complex experiments (random factors with missing values, unusual assumptions, ...) it may be necessary to use maximum likelihood.

The estimated values of the parameters can then be used for making statistical inferences. In particular, hypotheses can be tested (e.g. that a given effect is zero), or confidence intervals can be constructed (e.g. for the difference in response between two levels of a factor). The results of the major hypothesis tests are usually summarized in an Anova-table (see the end of this section for an example). This table shows, for each effect in the model, an SS (sum of squares) which represents the contribution of that effect to the total variability in the data. This SS becomes, after division by the number of degrees of freedom, an MS (mean square). The MS for each effect is then compared with another MS, which plays the role of the 'yardstick' for that effect. The test that each effect is zero, is based on this comparison.

When the experiment is balanced, the Anova-table has a direct interpretation as the unique decomposition of the total variation in the data into a sum of variations, one for each effect. That variation for each effect is then the sum of the squared deviations of the group means of that effect with regard to the overall mean. When the experiment is not balanced, there are generally many possible decompositions. The SS that are then shown in the Anova-table (and which are called type III SS), cannot be interpreted as sums of squared deviations like in the balanced case, and do not sum up to the total variation. When the pattern of missing values is such that some treatment combinations have no observations at all, further analysis complications may arise (Neter, Kutner, Nachtsheim, & Wasserman, 1996).

Analysis through an Anova-table is standard in all textbooks and software packages. The only tests available from the table are tests that a given effect is zero. In almost all practical situations, this is not enough to answer all questions of interest. After inspection of the Anova-table, the analysis usually proceeds with further tests and the computation of confidence intervals, e.g. to compare specific groups of treatment combinations.

A further complication arises when a substantial number of comparisons are made, either explicitly or implicitly. A situation where a large number of explicit comparisons are made arises when every level of a factor is compared with every other level (when there are L levels, there are $L(L-1)/2$ such comparisons). Another situation where a large number of comparisons is made is called *data snooping*. This refers to making a comparison inspired by the results of the experiment (which seemed of little interest before the data were gathered). An example would be to compare the level that had the best results in the experiment, with the level with the worst results. Then there is only one explicit comparison, but it is based on a lot of implicit comparisons (to see which ones were the best and worst). Such comparisons should only be made under protection of the methods described in the following paragraph.

Each comparison has an error rate which is under the control of the user (and is typically taken to be 1% or 5%). However, the joint error rate of a family of comparisons, explicit or implicit (i.e. the probability that the family contains at least one error) can be much larger than the comparisonwise error rate. When it is desired to control the error rate over a family of comparisons, specific techniques should be used. They are called *multiple comparison methods*. There is a substantial number of these methods, each with slightly different properties. An overview can be found in Hsu (1996).

Finally, it should be stressed that the whole analysis is based on the assumptions that have been made about the model, and as such, is only valid when the assumptions are not violated. Hence, a check of the model assumptions is a necessary part of any analysis. The checking is usually done by inspection of the residuals through specific types of plots.

EXAMPLE 10

We conclude this section with an example analysis of data resulting from the factorial experiment described earlier (see Figure 5.3). Assume that 27 apples were randomly allocated to the nine temperature-oxygen combinations (three apples for each treatment combination). The response measured was the rupture force in a compression test after three months of storage. An appropriate model would then be:

$$Y_{ijk} = \mu + \alpha_i + \beta_j + (\alpha\beta)_{ij} + \varepsilon_{ijk}$$

where μ is the overall mean , α_i the temperature main effect ($i = 1, .., 3$), β_j the

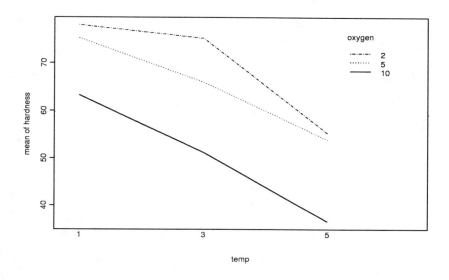

Figure 5.4: Analysis example. Plot of the estimated treatment means.

oxygen main effect ($j = 1, .., 3$) and $(\alpha\beta)_{ij}$ the temperature-oxygen interaction. k refers to the replication within each treatment combination ($k = 1, .., 3$). Results of fitting this model are shown in Figures 5.4–5.6. Figure 5.4 is a plot of the estimated treatment means. Figure 5.5 is a plot of the residuals versus the fitted values, and Figure 5.6 is a normal probability plot of the residuals. Neither 5.5 nor 5.6 reveal substantial problems with the model assumptions (independent, normally distributed errors).

We can now proceed with an examination of the inferences in the Anova-table:

```
             Df  Sum of Sq  Mean Sq   F Value       Pr(F)
      temp    2   2585.530  1292.765  690.2491  0.00000000000
    oxygen    2   1803.477   901.738  481.4673  0.00000000000
temp:oxygen   4     93.294    23.324   12.4532  0.00004978412
  Residuals  18     33.712     1.873
```

Figure 5.7 is a Granova plot, a graphical representation of the information in the Anova-table (Darius, Coucke, & Portier, 1998). The plot shows the error sums of squares and the degrees of freedom for error for several possible models, displayed in such a way that the slopes of the lines on the plot are the mean squares of the corresponding effects in the Anova-table. The Anova-table and plot teach us that there is a rather weak interaction (although significant at the 0.01 level). This implies that the effect of temperature is not the same at the different oxygen levels. In Figure 5.4 we see that increasing the temperature

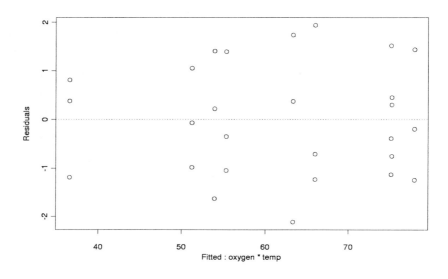

Figure 5.5: Analysis example. Plot of residuals versus fitted values.

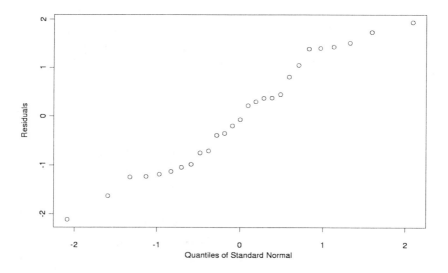

Figure 5.6: Analysis example. Normal probability plot of the residuals.

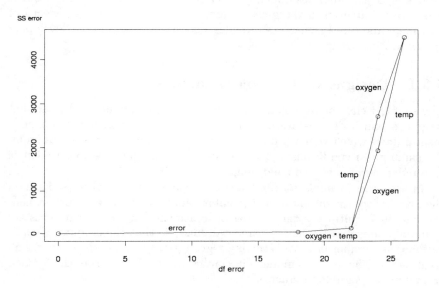

Figure 5.7: Analysis example. Granova plot.

leads to a substantial reduction in hardness, although the pattern is somewhat different at oxygen level 2. Similarly, increasing the oxygen level generally leads to a decrease in hardness. This is confirmed by the very low p-values for the main effects in the table.

We can now proceed with more detailed questions. For instance a pairwise comparison of all nine treatment combinations, using Tukey's multiple comparison method (with a joint error rate of 0.05 over the family of all pairwise comparisons) shows that the treatment combinations $(2\%, 1°C), (2\%, 3°C)$ and $(5\%, 1°C)$ are not significantly different from each other, but significantly better (higher hardness) than the others.

5.3 An Overview of Study Designs

This section gives an overview of the more well-known, classical designs. These designs should be seen as prototypes — each highlights a solution to a particular design problem. In practice, study designs are often used which combine the features of several classical designs. A convenient way to think about designs is by characterizing their *design* and *treatment structures*. The design structure describes the number, crossing/nesting relationship and replication pattern of the block factors. The treatment structure similarly describes these components for the treatment factors. In real life problems, it is sometimes difficult to classify a factor as either a treatment or a block, but even in these cases, adopting the description by means of treatment and block structures provides a good starting point to developing an appropriate design.

5.3.1   Designs with no block factors

The simplest class of designs has no block factors, and a factorial treatment structure. Such designs are best used when the experimenter has experimental units which would produce relatively homogeneous responses under the same given conditions. This is often the case when the experiment is run under very controlled conditions.

In a *balanced completely randomized design*, the treatments used are all the possible treatment factor level combinations, the number of experimental units is a multiple of the number of treatments, and the treatments are randomly allocated to the experimental units, so that the amount of replication (the number of units receiving a given treatment) is the same for all treatments. The analysis model will contain main effects for all the factors, as well as all possible interactions.

This design is also quite useful when there is a high probability that some experimental units may not survive to be measured. In this case the experiment may start as a balanced design, but through attrition end up providing data on only some of the original units, and hence present an unbalanced design for analysis. As long as the attrition of experimental units is not a response to the treatment, the data from an unbalanced completely randomized design poses no problems in statistical analysis.

When there are not enough experimental units to allow replication, the design can also be run without replication (each treatment combination used once). In the resulting *unreplicated* completely factorial design, there will be no degrees of freedom left for estimating the error term. If however, we make the assumption that the highest order interaction does not exist, it can be shown that the MS computed for this effect can be used as the yardstick to compare the other MS against. Hence, under the assumption, we can still test and estimate all the other effects, and the savings in experimental units are substantial. If the assumption is wrong, it will be harder to detect effects which should be significant, but at the same time spurious effects will be detected less frequently.

When experimental units are in such short supply (or are so expensive) that even an unreplicated factorial cannot be done, another type of design is needed. In such a situation, one will first try to reduce the number of treatment combinations by reducing the number of levels for each factor to the absolute minimum necessary to answer the research questions. Then, designs are considered where only a fraction of the factor level combinations are used. This causes effects to get confounded, but the fraction is chosen in such a way that the confounding pattern has some specific properties, such as low-order effects not being confounded with each other, but only with high-order interactions.

Fractional designs work well if there are a large number of factors, the response behaves smoothly, and only a limited number of factors really influence the response. They result in huge savings, compared to the complete factorial design. The research question should not ask for detailed effects of all the factors, but rather to isolate (using a small number of experimental units) the few factors that are most important. These *screening designs* are widely used, especially in industrial settings. Often, they are used in the initial stages of investigation to identify the most important factors, which are then used to set up a follow-up full factorial design.

Fractional factorial designs are only one type of screening designs. Designs with nice properties can be found when all factors have two levels, and for some situations in which one or more factors have a slightly higher number of levels. The fractions used are based on the powers of 2: one half, one quarter .... The confounding pattern of a fractional design is summarized in its *resolution* value, with designs of higher resolution having better statistical properties (Montgomery, 1991).

A completely different situation arises when the factors are continuous. Then the experimenter has to choose numerical values for each factor to define the treatments to be used rather than just using all the possible combinations as is done in the categorical case. For continuous factors, the model has to assume a functional relationship between the factor(s) and the response. This can take the form of a linear, polynomial, or non-linear relationship in the parameters. When the relationship is linear, the most convenient design points are the minimal and the maximal feasible values. The situation is then not fundamentally different from designs using categorical factors. But when there are several factors and the research question asks e.g. for the location of the maximal (or minimal) response, the model must assume at least a second degree polynomial relationship in several variables. Designs that allow one to estimate those polynomials and locate the maximum efficiently are called *response surface designs*. The desirable properties used for constructing these designs are different from those used in designs for categorical factors. An overview of this area can be found in Khuri & Cornell (1987).

When the model contains a functional relationship that is intrinsically non-linear in the parameters, a major design problem arises. In this case it has been shown that the location of the most efficient design points depends on the values of the parameters, which are of course unknown. For this type of problem, no simple prototype designs exist, and the experimenter must construct his/her own design based on an 'educated guess' of the unknown parameter values. The effectiveness of the design will depend on the correctness of this initial guess.

5.3.2   Designs with one block factor

Grouping the experimental units in an experiment according to one of their characteristics is called blocking, and the factor expressing that grouping is called a block variable. Blocking is often initiated to account for expected differences in the average response of untreated experimental units in each group. The grouping may be the natural consequence of not being able to find sufficient homogeneous experimental units to handle all treatments and their replications in one group. Sometimes the objectives of the study require examination of the consistency of treatment effects over a broad range of conditions defined by the grouping factor. Finally, the grouping may be required for implementation or administrative purposes, as would happen where there is just not sufficient time or personnel to do the full set of treatments and replicates at one time. In this case, the ability to include a block factor into the experimental design allows for more flexibility in experimental layout.

Deciding on which factors to include as block factors, and how to group the units into blocks is not always obvious. Including a block factor which turns out not to be a major source of heterogeneity may have made the experiment unnecessarily large. Ignoring a major source of heterogeneity in the experimental units makes the experimental error larger, and hence the comparisons less sensitive. Moreover, the ignored source might get confounded with a factor of interest if randomization was not performed thoroughly. For some blocking factors (e.g. batch of material, observer) the choice of levels is obvious. For others (e.g. age or weight of the subjects) the experimenter will have to decide on the intervals used to generate the blocks. As will be discussed next, the size of the blocks determines the type of design. It is also possible not to categorize continuous nuisance factors, and use an analysis method that can deal with both categorical and continuous factors (analysis of covariance). This is however not often a preferred alternative to blocking.

The best known type of block design is the *randomized complete block design*. Here all blocks have the same number of experimental units as there are treatments. The treatment combinations are randomly allocated to the experimental units, but in such a way that each treatment combination occurs once in each block (note that this places a constraint on the allocation scheme). The model contains the treatment effects, a block effect, but no block-treatment interaction.

When the blocks contain sufficient experimental units that each treatment combination can be replicated a number of times, the design is called a *generalized block design*. Such a design facilitates examination of a block-treatment interaction.

The situation where the blocks are too small to contain all the treatment combinations is more common and hence of more practical importance. For this case, designs with good statistical properties exist in which the missing treatments are evenly spread out over the blocks. In such a *balanced incomplete block design*, any two treatments appear together (i.e. in the same block) an equal number of times. These designs use additional constraints on the allocation to ensure that every pair of treatments is compared with the same precision.

Balanced incomplete block designs exist for any combination of block size and number of treatments, but the number of blocks required may be prohibitively large. In these cases, a *partially balanced incomplete block design* may be used. These designs allow for similar precision only between treatments within a given group of treatments (called an association class), but different precision between treatments belonging to different treatment groups. Lattice designs are special cases of incomplete block designs, frequently used when the number of treatments is very large (e.g. in agricultural variety trials). The analysis of incomplete block designs is somewhat more complicated, and consists of an intrablock and an interblock analysis.

EXAMPLE 11

If there were known sources of heterogeneity among the apples, blocking should be considered. This would be the case if, e.g. the apple supply came from different orchards or was harvested on different days, and we had reason to believe that the hardness of apples having received the same treatment but coming from different orchards (or days) was more dissimilar than that of apples from the same orchard (or day). Orchard would then be used as a block variable, with levels e.g. 1 for the first orchard, 2 for the second, etc. ... If it is desired to use harvesting day, we might use a similar coding for each day, or group the apples into e.g. harvesting weeks. If there are nine treatments, a randomized complete block design would consist of nine apples taken from each orchard, assigning the treatments randomly to the nine apples from the first orchard (one apple for each treatment), and repeat the process with an independent randomization for each orchard in turn. If more apples are available, a better design would be to use a multiple of nine apples from each orchard, and set up a generalized block design. If less than nine apples from each orchard are available, an incomplete block design might be used. In this way, the conclusions from the experiment would not be restricted to the behaviour of apples from one orchard, or just to those harvested at one particular time.

5.3.3   Designs with two or more block factors

Often, the constraints associated with a research project and the material available for experimentation require the use of two or more blocking factors. Multiple blocking factors can increase the complexity of an experimental design, primarily through the restrictions placed on the randomization of the treatments to experimental units.

In a two blocking factor design, each experimental unit is assumed to belong simultaneously to two groups. One group is defined by the levels of one of the blocking factors, and the other group is defined by the levels from the second blocking factor. The difficulty in designing multiple blocking factor experiments is assigning treatment factor levels to experimental units in such a way that both treatment effects and blocking factor effects can be estimated while also providing adequate replication (Section 5.1.5).

Multiple blocking factor designs can lead to very efficient experimental

```
A  B  C  D  E  F  G  H  I
B  C  D  E  F  G  H  I  A
C  D  E  F  G  H  I  A  B
D  E  F  G  H  I  A  B  C
E  F  G  H  I  A  B  C  D
F  G  H  I  A  B  C  D  E
G  H  I  A  B  C  D  E  F
H  I  A  B  C  D  E  F  G
I  A  B  C  D  E  F  G  H
```

Figure 5.8: Latin square design for the apple example.

studies. One class of designs, called *Latin Square designs* (see e.g. Montgomery, 1991), allows for two blocking factors and one treatment factor to be examined with a minimal number of experimental units. The major requirement of this design specifies that if there are t treatment levels to be examined, then $t \times t$ experimental units must be available, each block factor has t levels and each experimental unit belongs simultaneously to one level of block factor 1 and one level of block factor 2.

Related designs are *Graeco Latin Squares*, allowing blocking in three directions, and *Youden Squares* with properties similar to a Latin Square, but where one of the block factors may have a smaller number of levels than the other blocking factor and the treatment factor.

EXAMPLE 12

The need for a Latin Square may arise if e.g. it is known that the hardness measurement is influenced by the person who cuts the sample out of the apple, and also by the person who places the sample in the pressure apparatus. An experiment to compare the treatments from the factorial example may then be set up according to the scheme shown in Figure 5.8.

Here the row represents the person who cuts the sample (persons are randomly assigned to rows), the column represents the person who installs the sample in the apparatus (these may or may not be the same persons as those in the rows), and the letters A to I represent the nine treatments (randomly assigned to the letters). Note that each treatment letter occurs exactly once in each row and in each column. With this design, only 81 apples are needed to compare nine treatments, while simultaneously controlling for two sources of heterogeneity.

5.3.4   More complex designs

Cost and/or feasibility constraints associated with the experimental situation may make it necessary to use a design that is even more complex than the ones described in the previous sections. Such designs may have a combination of nested and crossed factors, as well as both fixed and random factors. We briefly describe some well-known designs in this class, and the type of situation that commonly leads to their use.

It often occurs in practice that observations of the response variable are made on samples selected from the experimental unit (i.e. the measurement unit is a random sample from the experimental unit). This makes the experimental unit into a random factor, nesting the measurement unit. Such designs are said to have *subsampling*. This can occur at several levels (samples from samples from experimental units), and it can be combined with any of the treatment structures described in the previous sections. In the apple example, we would have subsampling if from each apple several samples were cut, and hardness was measured from a compression test on each sample.

Another type of experimental situation that leads to nesting occurs, when one factor requires larger experimental units than another. The resulting designs are of the *split-plot* type. A well-known example is an investigation to study the effects of irrigation methods and fertilizers on yield of a crop. Irrigation methods can, by their nature, only be applied to large areas of land (here called *whole plots*), while fertilizers can be applied to much smaller areas (here called *split-plots*). Although the whole plots could be used for both factors, the use of the split-plots will generally make the fertilizer comparisons much more precise. A wide variety of split-plot designs has been developed.

In a third type of situation each experimental unit is, after being given its treatment, observed repeatedly in time. The design is then called a *repeated measures* design. Such a design makes it possible to compare response trends over time. Their analysis can be approached from different angles: as separate experiments at each time point (this rarely answers the questions about trends), with the responses at the different time points for a given experimental unit considered as a multivariate observation (this leads to the use of multivariate analysis methods), or with time considered as a factor. The last approach leads to problems, since it is likely that one of the basic linear model assumptions (uncorrelated errors) will be violated. Methods have been developed to deal specifically with the problems associated with repeated measures designs (Crowder & Hand, 1990; Diggle, Liang, & Zeger, 1994).

EXAMPLE 13
We can only have a repeated measures study if the hardness measurement is non-destructive. For example, if we would use an acoustic measurement method, we would have a repeated measures study if every apple was taken out of storage at several time points (for instance, after 1, 2 and 3 months of storage), a measurement taken and the apple placed back.

A last type of situation discussed here occurs when each experimental unit receives several different treatments in time (and the response is observed after each treatment). Such designs are *crossover* designs. They can be quite cost-effective (e.g. if we let wine-experts judge several wines, it would be unwise not to let each expert taste several wines) and precise (the treatments can be compared on the same experimental unit, not influenced by between-unit variation). Their biggest problem is the occurrence of *carry-over effects* (effects of a treatment that continues into the next treatment period). An overview can be found in Jones & Kenward (1989).

EXAMPLE 14
A crossover design would probably not be a good idea, since a storage period under specific circumstances will clearly continue to have a profound effect on the apple ever after.

The greater complexity of designs with both crossed and nested factors as well as random factors causes, in general, the analysis to be more complex. Most experimental design textbooks contain a set of rules that can be used to find appropriate inference formula's for any balanced situation with uncorrelated errors. If the data is not balanced, even when the errors are uncorrelated the analysis must be based on the mixed model approach, which is a general approach for dealing with correlated data (Searle, Casella, & McCulloch, 1992; Littell, Milliken, Stroup, & Wolfinger, 1996; Verbeke & Molenberghs, 1997). Care must be taken in using software (see Section 5.6).

5.3.5   Other types of designs

In this section we have tried to provide some idea of the more classical approaches to experimental design. There are, of course, other approaches which have been developed in recent years, many of these being created to handle specific constraints of the experiment. Two of these are briefly discussed below.

There are situations where the factorial approach (combining every level of one factor with every other level of the other factors) cannot be used in practice, usually because some of the resulting combinations are infeasible, impractical or unsafe. Ad hoc designs can be constructed, using computer search algorithms, which optimize general goodness criteria, such as the overall variance of treatment contrasts or pooled parameter precision (see Snee (1985), Atkinson & Donev (1992) or Pukelsheim (1993)). These designs will rarely display nice balance properties for example.

The factorial concept also breaks down in experiments with *mixture treatments*. Here the factors are components or ingredients of a mixture. In a mixture, the proportions of the components must always add up to one, hence a change in the proportion of one component (a factor level) results in necessary changes in the levels of one or more of the other components. For mixture experiments special designs, called *simplex designs*, have been developed to exploit the special geometry of this situation (see Cornell, 1990).

5.3.6   Amount of replication

Once an experimenter has decided on the type of design, the next decision must be on the number of experimental units to be used (i.e. the amount of replication) for each factor level combination in the design. This is a very important decision since choosing the wrong amount of replication can render the experiment either useless or much too costly. Methods to help the experimenter decide on an appropriate level of replication are also found under the labels *sample size planning* or *power analysis*.

5.4   Errors in inference

Sample size planning is based on control of the risks involved in statistical inference. In Section 5.1.1 we argued that experimentation should be based on a research question. Research questions get translated into hypothesis statements which specify the behaviour or pattern one expects to find. These general hypotheses are further refined into statistical hypotheses in which the study hypotheses are stated in terms of unknown parameters which usually describe average responses expected under the conditions defined by the treatments. These general hypotheses can each be written as a pair of hypotheses. The *Null Hypothesis* (H_0) is a statement concerning the expected condition of the parameters of interest when the status quo is maintained, i.e. there are no treatment effects. The *Alternative Hypothesis* (H_a) is a statement which contradicts the null hypothesis. That is, if H_0 is rejected in the inference test, the alternative hypothesis, H_a, will be considered the new null hypothesis. An *implicit alternative hypothesis* simply states the negative of the null hypothesis. Hence, if the null hypothesis states that there is no difference between treatment factor level effects, then the alternative simply states that for some comparisons of the factor level effects, the differences are indeed not zero. An *explicit alternative hypothesis* will specify the size of the differences in factor level effects which must be observed before the null hypothesis should be rejected.

Statistical tests are based on quantities defined as *test statistics*. The test statistics are functions of data which measure the effect of the treatments being compared relative to the underlying experimental error. Because the data are realizations of variables, the test statistics are realizations of variables as well. The conclusion drawn using the observed value of the test statistic is subject to error due to experimental error. Two types of error are possible. A *Type I* error is made when we incorrectly reject H_0 when in fact H_0 is the true underlying condition (i.e. when we find a difference that is not there). The probability of a Type I error can be specified by the researcher. It is typically designated by the Greek letter α. Convention usually has this value at 0.05 (i.e. 1 in 20 chance) or 0.01 (a 1 in 100 chance). A more risk-averse researcher would set α at a smaller level, whereas a less risk-averse researcher would set α at a higher level.

A *Type II error* is made when we incorrectly do not reject H_0 when in fact H_0 should be rejected, that is, H_a described the true condition (i.e. when there is a difference, but we fail to detect it). The probability of a Type II error is typically designated by the Greek letter β. The probability of a Type II error however, cannot be specified by the researcher. It can only be computed for an explicit alternative hypothesis. In fact, it becomes smaller when the explicit alternative hypothesis is further away from H_0 (it is harder to fail to detect a large difference, while a small difference can easily be overlooked). It can be shown (when α is considered constant) to be a function of the distance between the alternative and the null hypothesis, the size of the experimental error, and the amount of replication. To quantify the probability of a Type II error (or one minus that probability, which is called the *power*), the researcher has to specify values for the three quantities it is a function of. Alternatively the researcher can specify the power and two of the other quantities, to derive the value of the third — usually the amount of replication (Neter et al., 1996).

5.5   Power and amount of replication

Sample size planning works in the following way: the researcher must specify:

1. The minimum differences in treatment which would be considered important to be detected (the *critical effect*).

2. An 'educated guess' (probably based on previous experience) of the size of the experimental error.

3. The risks (α and β) he/she is willing to accept.

It is not always easy to come up with reasonable values for the error variance and the critical difference. Nevertheless it is a necessary exercise: when the sample size is such that the power is too low (it can easily become much smaller than, say 50%) there is only a small chance that the experiment will actually detect the kind of differences it is looking for. When the power is too high, we could have detected what we wanted with a much smaller (and probably cheaper) experiment.

EXAMPLE 15
Consider the following simplification of the apple experiment (sample size determination becomes quite involved when there are many levels and/or factors). We usually store apples at (3°C, 2% Relative Humidity), and would be willing to consider storing the new variety at (1°C, 2% Relative Humidity), but only if it makes the hardness increase with at least 5 Newton. We want to set up an experiment to compare the two storage conditions for the new variety. How many apples for each condition should we use?
Here the critical difference is 5 Newton. We need a guess for the variance of the experimental error. This is difficult, since after all we have not experimented yet with the new variety. Assume that in the past, experiments with other varieties resulted in hardness variances for apples receiving the same treatment ranging from 12.4 to 17.9 Newton^2. Here, 12 may be used as an 'optimistic' guess for the error variance of the new variety, and 18 as a 'pessimistic' guess. Let us

take α to be 0.05, and the required power to be 0.80 ($\beta = 0.20$). Consulting an appropriate table (they can be found, in some form, in all standard statistical design textbooks) or appropriate software, we learn that to satisfy these risks, the sample size must be 13 or 14 for the pessimistic scenario, and nine or 10 for the optimistic one. Unless the cost per experimental unit is very low, 12 apples per treatment group would be a reasonable choice.

5.6   Software for experimental design

There are two main areas where computer software can assist the experimenter with the statistical aspects of his/her experimentation: by helping to find an appropriate design, and by providing a correct analysis of the results. Software for analysis is far more available than software for design. Still, many separate programs have been developed that deal specifically with design problems, and many of the well-known statistical packages have added modules for experimental design. A comparative overview of a substantial number of these programs can be found in Rasch & Darius (1994). Recently, many new programs have been introduced. After a general overview, we will discuss some of the problems experimenters may (and frequently do) have with using these statistical procedures.

  Software to support research designs can be broadly classified into the following four groups.

1. *Administrative support programs.* This software provides help in randomizing treatments to subjects and hiding subject identity (in blinded trials for example), especially when the number of subjects is large.

2. *Design constructors.* Programs in this group range from software which allows choice from a catalog of classical designs, to software which lead the user in the construction of complex classical layouts, such as balanced incomplete block designs or layouts for large variety trials. Another set of programs in this group facilitates finding designs which meet user-specified optimality criteria and layout constraints (Section 5.3.5).

3. *Integrated design and analysis support.* For certain typical but highly limited situations, such as factorial experimentation in industrial settings and general response surface designs, software is available which leads the user through the complete design and analysis process. Some general guidance (expert advice) is available in many of the larger statistical analysis packages.

4. *Sample size determination.* A number of software packages are available which lead the user through the sample size estimation process via menus and dialogs. These often only address the simplest of research designs. More recently, programs have become available for a

broader class of designs but even this cannot address size issues in the more complex designs typically encountered in practice.

In general, design software is often found as a late add-on to a statistical analysis package, usually marketed as a separate product. In addition, sample size determination programs are found separate from the other three types. This has lead to many of these valuable design tools being overlooked by researchers and statisticians and hence underutilized.

The major problem with all of these design programs is the general lack of integration among the tasks of problem formulation, experimental layout, sample size determination, randomization, analysis model specification and final statistical testing. Rarely can the original study problem and hypotheses be stored with the chosen research design. While the research design is of necessity linked with the final measurements, the model used to analyse the final data may not reflect properly the study design nor reflect the hypotheses of importance. The output from most study design software is a dataset containing values for factors but empty values for the responses. No arrangements have been made to store with the design dataset the *meta data* (see Chapter 4), such as factor names, level definitions, research objectives, hypotheses, etc, which really describe the project.

Without meta data, the design dataset may be inadequate to determine key analysis components, such as whether two factors are crossed or nested, or whether a factor should represent a fixed or random component in the final analysis model. The burden of correct analysis model determination falls entirely on the user, the same individual who looked for help from the design software in the first place. Because a number of models may be syntactically correct for a situation but only one of these will actually reflect correctly the experimental protocol, the chances for mistakes at the analysis stage is high. Better integration of software should reduce the problem of this type of error (misspecified model) from occurring.

Even when the analysis model correctly reflects the research design, the analysis software may not correctly compute the appropriate test statistics. This is particularly a problem with unbalanced designs (whether deliberate or undeliberate) and designs which incorporate many random effect factors (split-plot and repeated measures studies particularly). Incorporating checks in the software to identify these problems is very difficult but we hope to see progress on this in the future. Advice to the user on follow-up analyses (multiple comparisons or contrasts) is also needed to avoid conclusions being based entirely on the overall analysis of variance.

Finally, we would like to see integrated design software which facilitates evaluation and comparison of alternative designs. This is particularly needed if statistical and economical research designs are to be found for complex study situations. The user should be able to see the good and bad points of a proposed design very quickly and be able to easily compare the characteristics across alternatives. Modern computer hardware can easily support such computations, it falls to methodologists to develop such software to accomplish these tasks.

In conclusion, we find that experimental design is a difficult process with many opportunities for developing ineffective and inefficient study protocols. Basic tools for designing experiments have been available for decades but only recently has computer software been available to aid this design process and analyse the subsequent data. The main burden of experimental design will always lie with the researcher. We hope that as time goes on, he/she will learn more about these basic tools and will use the computer software available to support these tasks.

Chapter 6

Clinical Trials: A Statistician's Perspective[1]

Stuart J. Pocock

In this chapter, I will attempt a perspective on those methodological and practical developments in clinical trials that have made notable contributions to biostatistical and medical/public health knowledge.

My approach is non-technical and through themes of design, conduct, analysis, reporting, and interpretation I intend to guide the reader through a series of specific topics concentrating on the current state and future needs, with some historical reference. The list of topics is not comprehensive nor is the list of references intended as particularly full, but I have attempted to present a personal view and to indicate some of the current areas of controversy.

6.1   Randomization

The one key issue that has transformed clinical research into potential treatment advances has been the random assignment of patients in comparative (controlled) trials. Sir Austin Bradford Hill in a series of UK Medical Research Council Trial conceived in the late 1940s is generally recognized as the one most significant pioneer in persuading clinical investigators to accept random assignment as the only reliable means of achieving unbiased treatment comparisons (see Hill, 1990; Armitage, 1992). However, continual reinforcement has been needed over the decades to persuade skeptics (e.g., Hellman & Hellman, 1991) that there is no alternative worth considering and that the randomized design has been underutilized in many areas of health service research (Cochrane, 1972).

[1]Based on Chapter 20 with the same title in *Advances in Biometry*, Edited by Peter Armitage & Herbert A. David. ISBN 0-471-16018-0. 1996 John Wiley & Sons, Inc.

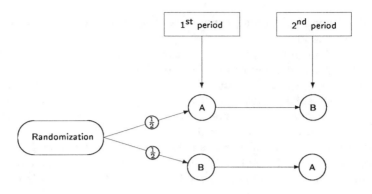

Figure 6.1: Diagram of the design of a two-period crossover trial. A, B: treatment.

The statistical methods for implementing randomization with appropriate restrictions to achieve good balance have been well established for many years. More elaborate methods exist for achieving balance across many baseline factors (see e.g., Taves, 1974), though in practice few trialists consider such efforts worthwhile. However, there remain doubts about whether lack of bias in performing randomization is genuinely achieved in many trials (cf. Schulz, Chalmers, Grimes, & Altman, 1994) so that one has greater concern about practical implementation of the randomization process rather than statistical details of balancing and stratification.

6.2 Alternative trial designs

Within the broad umbrella of randomized trials many alternative designs have been used and contemplated, and four topics in particular are worth brief mention: crossover trials, factorial trials, cluster randomization, and adaptive allocation.

The two-period randomized crossover trial (See Figure 6.1), and various extensions to more than two periods/treatments have had a controversial history with various concerns about their misuse (Brown, 1980). While appropriate statistical design and analysis remain well documented, the main concern is to ensure that the crossover design and its associated within-patient short-term comparisons is kept in its rightful place, usually at the early (Phase 2) stages of any treatment's evolving clinical trials program.

The factorial design has been less frequently employed, but since some major factorial trials have made such marked impact (e.g., ISIS-2 Collaborative Group, 1988) their pros and cons deserve some note (Byar & Piantadosi, 1985). Under the strong assumption of no interaction, the opportunity of being able to investigate more than one treatment idea within the same trial (without any apparent need to increase sample size) is very appealing, with the added bonus of gaining experience of a treatment combination should more than one idea actually work.

The obvious difficulty is that skepticism about a true lack of interaction is inevitably aroused and cannot be ruled out by a non-significant (usually underpowered) interaction test. Also the dual presentation of the 2×2 factorial trial's results as both two 'factor contrasts' and $2 \times 2 = 4$ 'treatment groups', can generate confusion. Thus, one might argue that the factorial design has been underutilized in clinical research but that it requires especially large studies if disputes in interpretation are to be defused.

The term *clinical* trial implies that the subjects are *patients*, but important applications of the randomized design have also occurred in evaluating disease prevention, and screening policies. Here especially an attractive option may be cluster (or group) randomization whereby natural groupings of individuals, e.g., factories (WHO European Collaborative Group, 1986) or general practices (Family Heart Study Group, 1994), become the units of randomization. This may be more organizationally efficient and avoids the 'contamination' of controls with awareness of intervention that might occur with individual randomization. However, analysis needs to take account of the clustering with recognition of cluster and individual components of variance, and one therefore needs adequate replication of groups to avoid serious loss of statistical power. With the increasing use of cluster randomization, especially in developing country intervention trials, there is a need for their methodological foundation to be more thoroughly understood.

In the search for more ethical adaptations of randomization, the principle of data-dependent allocation has provoked considerable creative effort (Armitage, 1985; Ware, 1989). Sometimes known as 'play the winner rule' (Zelen, 1969) the intention is that on the basis of ongoing trial results one biases the randomization to allow a higher proportion of future allocations to the treatment with better observed outcome. Statistical ingenuity and debate in design specifics and also in statistical inference (Begg, 1990) has stimulated methodologists, but there have been very few clinical trials that have actually used data-dependent allocation. One extreme example (Bartlett et al., 1985) ended up with treatment failure rates of 0/11 and 1/1 but even with more modest adaptations to the 'biased coin' the impracticality of its implementation (early results usually arrive too late) and the suspicions of bias in allocations (e.g., secular trends in the type of patient recruited) have in my view rightly kept this approach as a statistical curiosity rather than a serious contender for clinical application.

6.3   Size of trials

This is just a small section for a hugely important topic! One could argue that all the principles of how to do good randomized trials are well established. Biases still do often occur and the wrong questions are frequently studied, but the one single issue that gets in the way of really serious progress is that the great majority of clinical trials are too small. Inadequate sample size leads to a high Type II error rate (Freiman, Chalmers, Smith, & Kuebler, 1978) and a subsequent literature-based survey by the same group indicates little improvement over the years. Furthermore, when combined with publication bias (Simes, 1986) and the fact that most true treatment advantages are either modest or non-existent, the end result is a high proportion of false positives in the medical literature (Peto et al., 1976).

The case for large simple trials ('mega-trials') has been effectively made (Yusuf, Collins, & Peto, 1984) and backed up by some outstandingly important achievements, especially in cardiovascular disease, e.g., the ISIS and GISSI series, and it remains a prime matter of motivation, organization, and collaborative spirit to get major clinical issues resolved by more widespread use of large multicentre (and multinational) randomized trials.

By comparison with these practicalities, the statistical techniques of determining sample size need not be explored in depth. Power calculations are commonly used (Campbell, Julious, & Altman, 1995) and rightly receive criticism for their arbitrariness and misuse (a 'game' that can produce any number you wish with manipulative juggling of the parameter values!). While alternative Bayesian approaches may have philosophical advantages (Spiegelhalter, Freedman, & Parmar, 1994), I believe that the end result, a sensible order-of-magnitude plus an attitude of 'get as many patients as you can afford', is not much dependent on the statistical method as such.

One particular problem with conventional sample size estimation is its lack of flexibility given the uncertainties in parameter values, e.g., variance of quantitative outcome or control group event rate. Having 'got it wrong', say with a healthier patient selection than envisaged, there is a need to adapt without any accusations of statistical manipulation. The term 'internal pilot study' has been adopted in early proposals for solving this problem (Wittes & Brittain, 1990), which I see needing more widespread and routine consideration in ongoing trials.

6.4   Data monitoring

Since much has been written on this topic in the past, I will confine myself to just a few essentials. Clinical trials more than any other type of biomedical experiment accumulate data slowly so that for reasons of ethics and efficiency there is usually a need to monitor comparative results in interim analyses.

Much creative effort has gone into defining appropriate statistical stopping rules. From early sequential analysis methods outside medicine (Wald, 1947) grew a variety of sequential plans (Armitage, 1975) mostly based on the principle of continuous data analysis for patient pairs (one on each treatment). In practice, interim analyses were often done at fixed intervals and group sequential methods were developed accordingly, the most commonly still used being that of O'Brien & Fleming (1979). Within the same general ground rules (stopping early in the face of strong evidence of a treatment difference while controlling Type I error and preserving power), more flexible plans have subsequently been developed which allow variable gaps of accumulating patient data between analyses (see e.g., Whitehead, 1992). In recognition of the ethical asymmetry of treatment comparison, whereby 'new treatment better' requires stronger evidence than 'new treatment worse', methods of early termination for lack of efficacy (sometimes termed futility or stochastic curtailment) have been developed (Fleming & Watelet, 1989).

Alongside these methodological developments, there has been an increasing use of independent data monitoring committees for major trials to ensure responsible handling of interim data in ongoing decision-making, but one suspects that still for all too many trials the process is more chaotic, with insufficient formalization of procedures and consequent risk of inappropriate (premature) actions.

In my experience the practical and ethical functioning of data monitoring committees is such that statistical stopping guidelines can rarely act as precise rules, but are one, often quite small, component of the decision-making process (Pocock, 1992). The situation is virtually always more complex than can be encapsulated by a definable statistical guideline: there are multiple outcome measures, patient subgroups, external evidence from other trials, balances between individual ethics and collective ethics, and clinical judgments on benefits versus adverse events and costs, all of which make for lively debate. Thus the actual membership of the committee and their judgment based on experience is often more important than the formal statistical guidelines.

More attention needs to be given to the practical and statistical consequences of stopping a trial early. The ethical issues are quite complex, since even highly significant evidence of treatment benefit in a trial (whether it stopped early or not) does not by any means assure its widespread use. My exposure to the data monitoring process and awareness of particular prematurely stopped and published trials lead me to agree with Doll (1991) that the 'ethical responsibility is to report the results when they would be likely to change normal practice in the future' and in this respect the term 'proof beyond reasonable doubt' evokes the right spirit.

A more statistical problem in stopping early relates to the tendency for both point and interval estimates of treatment effect to exaggerate beyond the true effect. One is inevitably prone to stop on a 'random high' and so, were further data to be collected either from within the same trial or in others, one can expect some 'regression to the truth' to occur, whereby estimates of treatment difference on larger data shrink back to more realistic values and maybe even no effect. This phenomenon requires wider recognition and further methodological inquiry.

6.5   Regulatory issues

Of all randomized clinical trials undertaken worldwide, probably a majority are of drug treatments sponsored by the pharmaceutical industry, with the view to obtaining or extending regulatory authorities' approval for marketing. One could therefore argue that the biggest single influence on clinical trials practice is from these national authorities, of which the US Food and Drug Administration (FDA) is the most powerful. It was following the thalidomide disaster in the early 1960s (Sjöstrom & Nilsson, 1972) that current trial methodology began to be introduced into pharmaceutical research, but not until 1969 did evidence from randomized trials become mandatory for getting FDA approval.

From a statistical perspective what are the main current concerns in drug regulation? I think one major problem is the conflict between the very detailed, unduly mechanical use of statistics in regulatory submissions (and indeed in study protocols) and the thoughtful and concise reporting of trials that goes along with good statistical science and effective communication. For instance, the inappropriate dichotomous interpretation of significance testing and its excessive use in drug company trial reports, plus the sheer volume of boring tables required in documentation, all seem to have got out of hand. Specifically, the reporting and analysis of adverse event data seem prone to excessive mandatory tabulations from which often little insight is gained. Of course, one needs statistical rigor and safeguards against data manipulation, but surely there are better ways to achieve this, e.g., by focusing more on quality data for specific plausible prior hypotheses.

On the design aspects of pharmaceutical trials research programs the crucial issue is whether the right studies are being done for any particular drug's development. I suspect insufficient research effort is put into determining the most appropriate dose schedules, and also the inappropriate use of placebo controls may be falsely encouraged by regulatory requirements.

In Europe there have been some interesting recent developments in regulatory statistics. While pharmaceutical companies have employed appropriately substantial numbers of statisticians, there was until recently a woeful underutilization of statisticians by the various European regulatory authorities but this appears to be improving with experienced biostatisticians now employed in the German, Swedish, and UK authorities. The progression towards a single European Community authority, the Committee for Proprietary Medicinal Products, is still being worked through. It has already stimulated European biostatistical guidelines for clinical trial methodology (Lewis, Jones, & Rohmel, 1995) and has the scope to enhance the quality of clinical trials research throughout Europe.

6.6   Intention to treat and non-compliance

The distinction between explanatory and pragmatic attitudes in therapeutic trials was first made clear by Schwartz & Lellouch (1967), and for most major trials it is the pragmatic interpretation that really matters, i.e., the overall effects of the treatment policies as implemented rather than idealized intentions under full compliance. Hence analysis by intention to treat, pioneered by Hill (1977), has become the accepted primary presentation of trial results, in which all patient follow-up in each randomized group is included regardless of the treatment actually received.

However, it would be oversimplistic to suggest that the story ends there, and there remains substantial interest in whether analyses taking account of treatment actually received are a valuable supplementary option, and various statistical approaches, some quite complex, have been proposed in endeavours to tease out the 'true treatment effect' for any level of compliance (Efron & Feldman, 1991). The fundamental problem is that selection biases inherent in any inference not based on randomized groups can only be accounted for by quite strong modelling assumptions, and no amount of statistical ingenuity can really compensate for this justifiable lack of credibility. On the other hand, must the extrapolation of trial findings depend solely on the intention to treat analysis when heavy non-compliance can result in very substantial dilution bias? From a patient perspective it seems a valid question to ask, 'How well will the treatment work if I take it properly?' and perhaps it is relevant to distinguish between non-compliance by personal choice and non-compliance by necessity, e.g., side-effects. This intriguing dilemma seems intrinsic to much of clinical trials research and doubtless more debate will follow.

For trials with data obtained at planned visits, non-compliance and lack of follow-up data are often linked, so that analysis by intention to treat is impossible. There remains considerable doubt as to how best to handle such missing data. Gould (1980) proposed rank-based methods based on an ability to classify reasons for drop-out into cure, intolerance, no therapeutic effect, and unrelated to treatment, but usually there is too much uncertainty to allow such a classification. One popular approach is to carry the last observation forward, but it is doubtful whether this actually answers a scientifically relevant question. What is crucial is whether data are missing at random or arise from informative censoring. In most instances one must suspect the latter to be inevitable, in which case the problem is intractable. Of course this will not stop statisticians trying to solve it in the years ahead![2]   In the last few years intensive work has been done in this area, in particular to find methods to account for missing observations that can not be assumed to be missing at random (See, e.g., Little & Rubin (1990) and Little & Yau (1996)).

---

[2]Compare Section 7.4.2, where something more is said about various categories of missing observations and methods to account for them either by estimate a (more) complete data set or by estimating them during analysis.

6.7 Outcome assessment

In recent years there have rightly been increased concern and effort regarding the wider and more appropriate choice of patient outcomes in randomized trials, so that fully informed judgments can be made on future health care policy. Here, I tackle three topical issues: surrogate endpoints, quality of life assessment, and economic analysis.

The use of *surrogate endpoints* (short-term measures of response to treatment) rather than major long-term indicators of patient outcome (e.g., survival, disease events) has been a deceptively attractive pursuit for far too long in many areas of clinical trials research. The ethics and efficiency of being able to use short-term outcome measures are reflected in the trial program's smaller size and far more rapid completion, but the huge assumption that these really are surrogates for the unobserved longer term responses that truly matter is difficult to check and in some fields found to be invalid.

The statistical methodology needed to explore surrogate endpoints has undergone considerable development in recent years, both in conceptualizing the issues (Prentice, 1989) and in defining the statistical techniques needed to explore surrogacy (Fleming, Prentice, Pepe, & Glidden, 1994). Such advances need taking further, preferably backed up by application to large-scale examples from major trials.

In several areas of cardiovascular disease presumed surrogates have been found to be quite misleading, e.g., anti-arrhythmic treatment (suppression of arrhythmias but higher mortality), treatment of heart failure (short-term improvements but higher mortality), while in lipid-lowering the surrogate marker (LDL cholesterol) really does seem to fully encapsulate the longer term benefits. Similarly in HIV research much hope was invested in CD4 count as a potential surrogate that could shortcut the need for longer term follow-up trials, but the Concorde trial's negative outcome (Concorde Coordinating Committee, 1994) has shown the oversimplicity of that view. The biggest current controversy is in hypertension, where evidence from observational studies (quite convincing but fraught with potential biases) suggests that calcium antagonists, though effective in lowering blood pressure, may actually be harmful in increasing risk of coronary events (Psaty et al., 1995). One may well ask why new anti-hypertensive treatments have been allowed into routine use without direct evidence from randomized trials that they achieve the prime aim of reducing risk of cardiovascular events. Such trials are now underway but several years will elapse before results are known.

The principle that patient perceptions of health-related *quality of life* should receive a higher priority in clinical trials is widely accepted. However, the use of appropriate quality of life measures in any specific trial requires considerable care in planning and interpretation (Fletcher, Gore, Jones, Fitzpatrick, & Cox, 1992), and the need to maintain simplicity has perhaps not received sufficient attention by quality of life enthusiasts. There are still relatively few examples of trials that have explored the merit of alternative quality of life assessment in any depth, but there is still much continued effort to generate appropriate new scales, both disease-specific and generic. Perhaps what trialists need to do is to cut through the jargon-ridden pretentiousness that can bedevil this topic, and get on with applying simple, relevant measures in trials large enough to provide clear answers. Presentation of quality of life results is an additional problem, with multidimensional scales and statistical sophistication making the plethora of tables and figures somewhat indigestible to the non-specialist reader.

Economic analysis is also becoming an increasingly important component of clinical trials research (Drummond & Davies, 1991; Drummond, O'Brien, Stoddart, & Torrance, 1997), though again there is more debate about what should be done rather than widespread experience in publications. However, this may well change rapidly over the next few years as more trials collect data on individual patient use of health care resources. There is a danger that superficial attempts at economic analysis may become fashionable, whereas in many instances it may be the long-term health economic consequences that need exploring alongside clinical outcomes. For instance, studies of bypass surgery versus angioplasty as initial interventional policies in angina show a short-term cost advantage to the latter which has substantially narrowed after two years (Sculpher et al., 1994) and only after say ten years' follow-up will we fully know the economic picture. Setting that against the clinical outcome differences raises important cost-effectiveness questions which require further methodological development.

One note of caution here is that both quality of life and economic analysis may often not matter if the new treatment does not improve the clinical outcome. This can pose a dilemma in that one needs to leave the door open by having relevant data collection, but not invest too much intellectual effort until one knows that clinically relevant differences justify exploring issues of economics and patient perception.

6.8   Statistical analysis and reporting

It has often been pointed out that the quality of clinical trial reports in medical journals often falls short of desired standards without much enhancement over the years, and recent proposals have been made for improvement (Standards of Reporting Trials Group, 1994). Much inadequacy relates to design and its documentation, conduct, and follow-up, but here I will dwell on statistical analysis and its interpretation.

One particularly worthwhile trend in the last decade has been the less obsessive and dogmatic use of significance testing and the greater emphasis on statistical estimation and confidence intervals. For clinical trials this has a particular value in deterring the tendency to extrapolate from evidence (data) to decisions (apparent proof), but still I think we need to beware of overusing confidence intervals in the way that we previously used p-values. The former occupy more space on the page, and there is a danger of cluttered tables (too many numbers) unless we preserve confidence intervals for only the major trial results.

The statistical content of clinical trial abstracts (summaries) has also improved in recent years with the introduction of structured abstracts. On the whole, I think biostatisticians could give greater attention to concise communication: the statistical one-liner in an abstract can be as crucial as the whole results section because the former is read by far more people.

Many of the interesting statistical issues in clinical trials arise because of their multiplicity of data (Cook & Farewell, 1995). Subgroup analysis, multiple outcomes, repeated measures, multiple treatments, and alternative analytical approaches all give ample scope for data manipulation and misleading promotion of apparently positive findings, often out of a sea of random noise. This might seem unduly cynical but is my way of expressing just how serious is the problem of exaggerated interpretation out of complex data sets.

Subgroup analysis remains a particularly common problem. Of course, we can hypothesize that treatment effects will depend on patient factors, but rarely do we have sufficient data to explore this reliably, nor can we resist the temptation to interpret once an apparent subgroup finding appears. All too often statistical tests of interaction are not used, and even if they are, the problems of multiple testing and selective reporting are insufficiently addressed. Perhaps the biggest educational impact can be made by reporting nonsense subgroups, e.g., astrological signs in ISIS-2 Collaborative Group (1988), but even then an astrologer has been known to come up with 'sensible' explanations!

Selective emphasis across several measures of patient response can also lead to distorted reporting. There have been some useful statistical developments for handling multiple outcomes (cf. O'Brien (1984) and more recently, Läuter, Glimm, & Kropf (1996)), but still for most trials the pre-declaration of priorities amongst outcomes (usually a single primary endpoint) is the most ready safeguard against post hoc emphasis. While this has become increasingly common practice, the excitement of a positive result can still blow away the prior restraint, as with the Physicians' Health Study Research Group (1989) who emphasized aspirin's risk reduction for myocardial infarction when the primary outcome, cardiovascular death, showed no difference.

The analysis of repeated measurements over time has a long and none too happy history in clinical trials. There have been many and at times very complex proposals for analysis, but the quality of repeated measures analysis in clinical trial publications has remained poor. Common problems include repeated significance testing across time points, misuse of baseline data and uninformative (often wrong) use of repeated measures ANOVA. For instance, mistakenly using baseline measures as an outcome rather than as a covariate.

The appropriate use of analysis of covariance for handling baseline data is still insufficiently recognized and also the use of summary statistics could valuably simplify the key findings in many repeated measures trials. However, I think the most important development is in multi-level modelling

(Goldstein, Healy, & Rasbash, 1994) in which patient effects, time effects, treatment effects, appropriate correlation structures, covariates, and unequal follow-up can all be cohesively held in a single model, with newly developed software (e.g., the MLn package) making such analyses feasible. Even so, such efforts may best be saved for more substantial repeated measures trials with sufficient data to explore the validity of any chosen model. The level of sophistication in repeated measures analysis is part of a broader dilemma faced in every trial's statistical analysis and reporting: how to balance the conflicting needs for (a) effective communication of statistical findings to non-specialists in medical journals and (b) the most appropriate (often complex) analyses which provide the inferential basis for the conclusions drawn. Presentational skill is undoubtedly the key, an art which I think is a sadly neglected profession.

Bayesian approaches to the design, monitoring, and analysis of clinical trials (and indeed other medical and biological research) have been proposed and debated for many years. However, practical applications have been very few, perhaps because in the past too much Bayesian activity has been theoretical and philosophical rather than in day-to-day statistical analysis. I think this situation is now changing as more Bayesian authors grapple with clinical trial practicalities and accept such design principles as randomization. The consequent Bayesian insights rightly challenge the established frequentist approach (Spiegelhalter et al., 1994), and I believe should be seen as complementary rather than in opposition to conventional trial planning and reporting. On the positive side, Bayesian conceptualization in trial design could often be very useful and Bayesian interpretations in data monitoring and in the discussion sections of trial reports could be informative, especially when applying cautious (commonsense) priors to surprisingly large treatment differences in order to achieve realistic shrinkage of point and interval estimates. The problems are lack of objectivity and reproducibility, difficulty in choice of prior, philosophical differences when doing repeated data analyses over time, insufficient time to explore and space to report Bayesian analyses, and some computational difficulties (which are being overcome). What we now need is more active implementation of Bayesian methods in the design and reporting of some major trials.

6.9   Meta-analysis

In the past two decades we have seen a remarkable transformation in the way that evidence is combined across related studies: essentially a new 'science of reviewing research' has developed (Light & Pillemer, 1984). Meta-analyses (systematic reviews, overviews) have become a dominant feature of the medical literature, and the best can get close to encapsulating all the essential findings of a whole worldwide research endeavour in the way that no other approach can achieve (e.g., Fibrinolytic Therapy Trialists Collaborative Group, 1994). While sometimes applicable to other fields such as

observational epidemiology, meta-analysis has made its most powerful contributions in clinical trials, the two most notable driving forces being Tom
Chalmers and Richard Peto; see Chalmers et al. (1987) and Peto (1987) for
their philosophical positions.

There has been much discussion of statistical issues in meta-analyses
(see below), but these are secondary to the main issue: which studies to
include. There are three determining factors in any specific meta-analysis:
problem definition (how broad is the topic under investigation and consequently which studies are relevant to include), quality (which studies are
good enough) and comprehensiveness (are some eligible studies left out?).
Here a thoroughness of approach, preferably with a collaborative spirit felt
by all the contributing trialists, has been crucial in achieving success. This
has now been greatly enhanced by formation of the Cochrane Collaboration
which has immense international potential for the preparation, maintenance,
and dissemination of systematic reviews of clinical trials (Chalmers, 1993).

Another valuable development has been the increased use of individual
patient data for meta-analyses. Published data has limitations of inflexi-
bility, inconsistency, and sometimes errors, and clearly more reliability and
insight can be gleaned by using the raw data files of all the trials. This
requires even greater collaborative will, effort and concern over detail, and
as a study of human relationships within science it will be fascinating to see
whether striving towards common goals can win over competitive, parochial
instincts.

The statistical basis of meta-analysis is now well established, (Fleiss,
1993), the main controversy being over the choice between fixed and random effects models, the essentials of which have long been known. At times
I have found such debate frustrating since (a) if there is no serious heterogeneity, then the difference is negligible and (b) if substantial statistical
heterogeneity does exist, then both approaches require rather peculiar assumptions for valid interpretation of the estimated treatment effects. What
is really needed, and tends to get neglected, is serious investigation into the
sources of heterogeneity (Thompson, 1994).

6.10   Future needs

Today there are probably more randomized trials taking place and more
patients entered into them than ever before, and similarly there has been
a continuing growth in the numbers of biostatisticians engaged in clinical
trials research. However, this apparent success story is not without flaws
and I would like to finish with brief comments on the major practical and
biostatistical needs of the future.

Overall, I think there are three main concerns: quality, size, and relevance. The regulatory concern with 'good clinical practice' for pharmaceutical industry trials is enhancing organizational standards, but I suspect
much still needs to be done to achieve comparable high administrative qual-

ity across all trials research. There are major international variations in both the scale and quality of clinical trials endeavour, and one can anticipate a considerable growth of activity and experience in many parts of the world so far not so familiar with randomized trials, e.g., Eastern Europe, China, and developing countries generally. Scientific quality is also crucial, and whereas the input of biostatisticians is increasingly valued in major trials, I am doubtful that in less fashionable research areas (and also in the smaller-scale phases of drug development) the impact of statistical science on research quality has been sufficient.

Concern about relevance has two aspects: are the right trials being done and are their results being appropriately absorbed into improving clinical practice? The biggest funder of clinical trials is the pharmaceutical industry, and perhaps the bottom line is how can we best balance their profit motivation with the health care needs of society? While regulatory authorities control quality and application of new drugs research, I wonder if enough is done to influence which drug trial programs are pursued, and our biggest ethical contribution in future might be to suppress more heavily clinical trials that have little public health merit, of which I suspect there are many. On the other hand, there are many aspects of health care (surgery and medical devices, patient management issues, screening and prevention policies) where there is a gross underutilization of randomized trials. Reasons for this include lack of resources, insufficient awareness of the validity problems in more observational research, ad hoc introduction of new therapeutic ideas, resistance to randomization often on pseudo-ethical grounds, inadequate leadership, absence of any collaborative track record, and lack of training to health care providers.

As mentioned earlier, most clinical trials are too small (and follow-up often too short) to properly resolve the issues they tackle and hence we need better collaborative efforts, more focus on essentials (collect less data per patient often) and again improved education to get investigators and health institutions truly motivated to achieve scientifically realistic targets for sample size (and length of follow-up).

For biostatisticians, clinical trials will continue to offer a rich source of creative methodology and collaborative application. Sadly, there are too many instances still where the statistician functions as routine data analyst or, at the other extreme, pursues abstruse methodology of little relevance to actual clinical trials (though perhaps neither are likely to read this chapter!). However, in general I think clinical trials are one of the most notable success stories for our profession in which our philosophy and concrete ideas have been truly integrated into major achievements of benefit to society.

Acknowledgment

I am grateful to Simon Thompson for many discussions and also helpful comments on the draft manuscript.

Chapter 7

Cross-sectional Research

Jelke Bethlehem

7.1 Cross-sectional surveys

7.1.1 About sample surveys

Studies can be carried out in several ways. On the one hand, you have experimental studies, in which you have control over some of the variables to be observed. This makes it possible to detect and check relationships between variables. There are also study designs in which control over variables is not required or not possible. This is the area of *observational studies*. The aim of this type of study is to explore and establish possibly existing relationships between variables by systematically measuring the same set of variables for all elements (or a subset of elements) in a population. When measuring variables is carried by means of asking questions of persons, we call the observational study a *survey*.

The target population of survey need not necessarily consist of persons. It could, for example, also consist of households, farms, or companies. Typically, in surveys information is collected by means of questionnaire forms. The questions on the form are presented to and answered by representatives of the elements in the population in a systematic way.

A *cross-sectional survey* investigates the state of affairs in a population at a certain point in time. To study changes over time, the survey must be repeated at a number of different points in time. This is the area of *longitudinal surveys*, and it is treated in the next chapter. This chapter concentrates on methodological and practical aspects of cross-sectional surveys.

One way to carry out a survey is to collect information on all elements in the target population. Such a survey is called a *census* or a *complete enumeration*. This approach has a number of disadvantages. In the first place, collecting information about a large population is very expensive. In the second place, the survey is very time-consuming, and this affects the timeliness of the survey results. Last but not least, there is a heavy response burden. We live in a society experiencing an increasing demand for information. Consequently, more and more people are asked to participate in surveys, and more and more they see this as a burden and an intrusion of their privacy. Therefore, they are less and less inclined to cooperate.

The sample survey is a solution to many of the problems of a census. In a *sample survey*, information is collected on only a small part of the population. This small part is called the *sample*. In principle, the sample only provides information about the sampled elements of the population. Nevertheless, if the sample is selected in a proper way, you can make inference about the population as a whole. 'Proper' means in this context that elements in the sample are selected at random. If you know how the selection mechanism works, and you are able to compute the probabilities of being selected in the sample, you can use the results for making inference about the non-sampled elements. This may seem odd at first glance: by introducing an element of uncertainty in his investigation, the survey researcher is able to draw conclusions about a population without having examined every element of it. Still, survey sampling theory shows that this 'man-made randomization' works.

This chapter is about the theoretical and practical issues of cross-sectional surveys, and more in particular, sample surveys. The remainder of this section is devoted to a summary of the history of sample surveys, and an overview of the various steps you have to take in order to carry out a sample survey. Section 7.2 describes the basic methodological framework for selecting samples and making proper inference on the population using sample data. It is shown how use of specific sample designs and estimation techniques can improve the accuracy of estimates of population characteristics.

Sampling theory and practice shows that sample surveys work. However, you do not have everything under control. In the course of the survey process, you may be confronted with many practical problems. Section 7.3 describes these problems. One of the most important problems of survey sampling is non-response. This is the phenomenon that it may not be possible to obtain the required information about the sampled elements. If a sample survey is affected by non-response, it may result in invalid estimates of population characteristics. Section 7.4 describes the non-response problem in more detail, and discusses two methods for reducing the negative impact of this phenomenon.

Section 7.5 is about the analysis of data collected by means of a sample survey. It describes two types of analysis: exploratory analysis and inductive analysis. Furthermore, attention is paid to data mining as a new approach to the analysis of large quantities of data.

Section 7.6 draws some conclusions, lists some of the future challenges, and makes some suggestions for further reading.

7.1.2   Some history of survey sampling

Survey sampling does not have a very long history. Although it is generally not very easy to determine a starting point in time of a new development, the year 1895 seems a reasonable one for sampling theory. Up until that moment there had been no attempts to create a well founded theory of survey sampling and estimation. Investigators engaged in population surveys rejected the idea of sampling. They had two reasons not to carry out surveys: (1) If it is possible to observe all elements in a population, nothing else will suffice, and (2) it is not appropriate to substitute mathematical methods for real observations.

In 1895, at a meeting of the ISI (the International Statistical Institute), A. N. Kiaer, the director of Norwegian Statistical Institute, presented a report on his experiences with his 'Representative Method' (see Kiaer, 1895). He argued that good quality population estimates could be obtained on the basis of a partial survey in which observations were made on a large number of elements distributed through the population so that this sample would form a miniature of the population. Selection had to take place according to some scheme guaranteeing the distribution of a number of characteristics to be in agreement with the known population distribution (e.g. the distribution of the population over the regions of the country).

Kiaer's method had two disadvantages. In the first place, implementation of a selection scheme satisfying the condition of representativity turned out not to be so easy. In the second place, it was difficult, if not impossible, to determine the accuracy of the estimates. Until 1903 there was much discussion about the Representative Method. In this year the method was accepted by the international statistical community as a proper means for surveying a population.

Bowley (1906) was one of the first to contribute to a theory that could be used to quantify the uncertainty of estimates. He proposed to select samples with a random selection procedure. He could apply results from the theory of mathematical statistics to estimates based on random samples. He was able to prove that the sample mean had an asymptotically normal distribution.

The summary of Bowley's work in an appendix of an ISI report (Bowley, 1926), inspired Neyman (1934) to carry out further investigations. Neyman proved a number of fundamental theorems, which form the basis of subsequent development of sampling theory. He also proposed the confidence interval as a means of quantifying the accuracy of estimates of population characteristics.

The classical theory of sampling was more or less completed in 1952 with a paper by Horvitz and Thompson. They showed that equal selection probabilities are not a prerequisite for the construction of good estimates. As long as the selection probabilities are known and not equal to zero, it is always possible to construct proper estimators.

7.1.3   The survey process

Nowadays, the sample survey is a well established means of collecting information. This section describes the various steps you have to go through in order to carry out a survey. An overview of the process is given in Figure 7.1. The first step is, of course, the *survey design*, in which you specify the

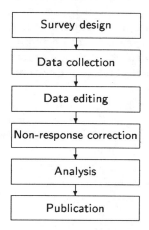

Figure 7.1: The survey process.

population to be investigated, the data to be collected, and the characteristics to be estimated. You also have to define a questionnaire, containing the questions to be asked of the respondents. Furthermore, in the case of a sample survey, you have to specify a sampling design, and you must see to it that the sample is selected properly.

The second step in the process is *data collection*. Traditionally, in many surveys the questionnaires are completed in face-to-face interviews: interviewers visit respondents, ask questions, and record the answers on (paper) forms. The quality of the collected data tends to be good (compared to other ways of interviewing). However, since it typically requires a large number of interviewers, who may all have to do much travelling, it can be expensive and time-consuming. Therefore, telephone interviewing is sometimes used as an alternative. The interviewers call the respondents from the data collecting agency, and thus no more travelling is necessary. However, telephone interviewing is not always feasible: only connected people can be contacted, and the questionnaire should not be too long or too complicated. A mail survey is cheaper still: no interviewers at all are needed. Questionnaires are mailed to potential respondents with the request to return the completed forms. Although reminders can be sent, the persuasive power of the interviewer is lacking, and therefore response in this type of survey response tends to be lower, and so does the quality of collected data.

If the data are collected by means of paper forms, completed questionnaires have to undergo extensive treatment. In order to produce high quality statistics, it is vital to remove any errors. This step is called *data editing*. Three types of errors can be distinguished: A *range error* occurs if a given answer is outside the valid set of answers, e.g. an age of 348 years. A *consistency error* indicates an inconsistency in the answers to a set of questions. An age of 8 years may be valid, a marital status 'married' is not uncommon, but if both answers are given by the same person, at least in the Netherlands, there is something definitely wrong. The third type of error is the *routing error*. This type of error occurs if the interviewer or the respondent fails to follow the specified skip instructions, i.e. the route through the questionnaire is incorrect: irrelevant questions are answered, or relevant questions are left unanswered.

Detected errors have to be corrected, but this can be very difficult if it has to be done afterwards, at the office. In many cases, particularly for household surveys, respondents cannot be contacted again, so other ways have to be found to do something about the problem. Sometimes it is possible to compute a reasonable approximation of a correct value using some kind of model (see Section 7.4.2 about imputation), but in other cases an incorrect value is replaced by the special code indicating the value is 'unknown'.

The rapid advent of the microcomputer in the last decades has made it possible to replace paper and pencil interviewing (PAPI) by computer-assisted interviewing. The paper questionnaire is replaced by a computer program containing the questions to be asked. The computer takes control of the interviewing process. It performs two important activities:

- o *Route control.* The computer program determines which question is to be asked next, and displays that question on the screen. Such a decision may depend on the answers to previous questions. Hence it relieves the interviewer of the task of taking care of the correct route through the questionnaire. As a result, it is not possible any more to make route errors.

- o *Error checking.* The computer program checks the answers to the questions which are entered. Range checks are carried out immediately after entry, and consistency checks after entry of all relevant answers. If an error is detected, the program gives a warning, and one or more of the answers concerned can be modified. The program will not proceed to the next question until all detected errors have been corrected.

Application of computer-assisted data collection has three major advantages. In the first place it simplifies the work of interviewer (no more route control), in the second place it improves the quality of the collected data, and in the third place data is entered in the computer during the interview resulting in a clean record, so no more subsequent data entry and data editing is necessary.

Computer-assisted interviewing started in the 1970s with Computer-assisted Telephone Interviewing (CATI). This is a form of telephone interviewing in which the computer selects the proper question to be answered. This question is displayed on the computer screen, and thus can be asked by the interviewer. The answer is typed in and the computer checks it for range errors and consistency errors. If an error is detected, the computer warns the interviewer that something is wrong, and corrections can be made.

More recently is the technique of Computer-assisted Personal Interviewing (CAPI). It is a form of face-to-face interviewing in which interviewers use a small laptop or notebook computer to ask the questions and to record the answers, instead of the traditional paper form.

Nowadays, there is also growing attention to computerize mail interviewing. This is called Computer-assisted Self Interviewing (CASI). A diskette with the interview program is sent to the respondents, which run it in their own computers, after which they return the diskette with the completed questionnaire. CASI can also be implemented in other ways, e.g. by modem and phone. A challenge for the near future is to carry out interviews using the Internet.

Whatever way of data collection is used, the result will be a 'clean' data file, i.e. a data file without errors. However, this file is not yet ready for analysis. The collected data may not be representative due to non-response, i.e. for some elements in the sample the required information is not obtained. If non-respondents behave differently with respect to the population characteristics to be investigated, the results will be biased.

In order to correct for non-response, often a *weighting adjustment* procedure is carried out. Every record is assigned some weight. These weights are computed in such a way that the weighted sample distribution of characteristics like sex, age, marital status and area is equal to the known distribution of these characteristics in the population.

In the case of item non-response, i.e. answers are missing on some, but not all, questions, an *imputation* procedure can be carried out. Using some kind of model, an estimate for a missing value is computed and substituted in the record.

Finally, a data file is obtained which is ready for analysis. The first step in the analysis phase will nearly always be tabulation of the basic characteristics. Next, a more extensive analysis will be carried out. Depending on the nature of the study, this will take the form of an exploratory analysis or an inductive analysis. The researcher carries out an exploratory analysis if he has no preset ideas, and wants to detect possibly existing patterns, structures and relationships in the collected data. If he wants to make inference on the population as a whole, he carries out an inductive analysis. This can take the form of estimation of population characteristics or testing of hypotheses that have been formulated about the population. The results of the analysis relate to the statistical models. In order to be able to draw conclusions about the subject-matter research area, these results will have to be translated and interpreted.

The results of the investigation will be published in a report, paper or book. On the one hand, the report must present the results of the study in a form that makes them readable for non-experts in the field of survey research. On the other hand, the report must contain a sufficient amount of information for experts to establish whether the study was carried out properly, and to assess the validity of the conclusions.

Usually results are published in a printed report, but there is an increased demand for electronic publications. This can take the form of an electronic analogue of the report on the Internet, or the dissemination of a data file. In the latter case, care must be taken that the file is properly documented. So, not only the data is made available, but also the meta data, i.e. data about the data. Furthermore, measures must be taken to see to it that respondents are sufficiently protected against unwanted disclosure of their (possibly sensitive) information.

7.2   Basic principles of sampling

7.2.1   The population

Sample surveys deal with investigating a finite population. Suppose the size of this population is denoted by N. Furthermore, suppose all elements are identifiable, i.e. they can all be uniquely labelled from 1 to N, and the label of each element is known. Then, the finite population U can be denoted by the set

$$U = \{1, 2, ..., N\} \qquad (7.1)$$

where element i indicates the element with label i (for $i = 1, 2, ..., N$).

Suppose Y is the target variable of the survey. The *target variable* represents the phenomenon to be investigated. For each element in the population, this variable has a value. All these values are indicated by

$$Y_1, Y_2, ..., Y_N. \qquad (7.2)$$

For example, if the target population consists of all people with a paid job, and the target variable is income, then $Y_1, Y_2, ..., Y_N$ are the incomes of all people with a job.

The objective of the sample survey is estimation of some characteristics of the target population. Only one basic characteristic will be considered here, and that is the population mean

$$\overline{Y} = \frac{1}{N} \sum_{i=1}^{N} Y_i. \qquad (7.3)$$

In the example, the population mean would be the mean income of all people with a job. Other basic characteristics are totals, percentages and fractions. Other characteristics, like correlations and covariances, can be derived from these basic characteristics.

7.2.2   Selecting a sample

To estimate the population mean, a random sample is selected. The elements in this sample are obtained by means of a random selection procedure. This procedure assigns to every element in the target population a fixed, positive and known probability of being selected. The most straightforward way to select a random sample is giving each element the same probability of being selected. Such a random sample is called a *simple random sample*.

Samples can be selected with replacement or without replacement. In *with replacement* selection procedures, a sample element is selected, and returned to the population after its characteristics have been recorded, before the next element is drawn. It is possible to select an element more than once. Since selecting an element more than once does not produce more information than selecting it once, selection *without replacement* is usually preferred.

A sample selected without replacement from the population, is denoted by a series of N indicators

$$t_1, t_2, ..., t_N. \tag{7.4}$$

To each element in the population, there corresponds an indicator. The indicator for element i is denoted by t_i (for $i = 1, 2, ..., N$). The indicator t_i assumes the value 1 if the corresponding element i is selected in the sample, and otherwise it assumes the value 0. Since the value of t_i is determined by the random selection mechanism, it is a *random variable*.

The sample size, i.e. the number of selected elements, is denoted by n. Since the t_i have a value 1 for all elements in the sample, and the value 0 for all other elements, the sample size can be written as the sum of the values of the indicators:

$$n = \sum_{i=1}^{N} t_i. \tag{7.5}$$

The *sample design* assigns to every possible sample a specific probability of selection. These probabilities can be used to compute the inclusion probabilities of the elements. The inclusion probability π_i of element i is defined as the probability that element i is selected in the sample. The inclusion probability π_i can be written as

$$\pi_i = P(t_i = 1) = E(t_i), \tag{7.6}$$

in which $E(t_i)$ is the expected value of the random variable t_i. It can be shown that the following simple relationship holds:

$$\sum_{i=1}^{N} \pi_i = n. \tag{7.7}$$

In order to be able to verify the accuracy of estimates, also the so-called second order inclusion probabilities are required. The second order inclusion probability π_{ij} of the elements i and j is the probability that both elements are selected in the sample. This probability can be written as

$$\pi_{ij} = P(t_i t_j = 1) = E(t_i t_j). \tag{7.8}$$

7.2.3   Computing an estimate

The values of the target variable can be observed for all sampled elements. These values must be used to estimate the population characteristic. The recipe to compute such an estimate is called an *estimator*, and the result of this computation is called the *estimate*. In order to be useful, an estimator must have a number of properties.

In the first place, the estimator must be *unbiased*. This means that average value of the estimates over all possible samples must be equal to the value of the (unknown) population characteristic to be estimated. On average, the estimator will result in the correct value. It will never under-estimate or over-estimate the population value in a systematic way. For an unbiased estimator z of a population characteristic Z, the expected value will be equal to the population value Z:

$$E(z) = Z \tag{7.9}$$

where $E(z)$ denotes the expected value of the estimator z.

In the second place, the estimator must be *precise*. It means that the variation in possible outcomes must be small. For an estimator z of a population characteristic Z, the variance must be small:

$$V(z) = E(z - E(z))^2 \tag{7.10}$$

where $V(z)$ denotes the variance of the estimator Z.

In the third place, estimators must be simple to compute. At a time in which powerful computers are readily available, this requirement has become less important. Still, the study of statistical properties is easier for simple estimators. This leads to the use of linear estimators. Estimates are computed as linear combinations of the observed values of the target variable.

Imposing the conditions of unbiasedness and linearity leads to the estimator introduced by Horvitz & Thompson (1952). This estimator for the population mean $\overline{Y}$ is defined as

$$\bar{y}_{HT} = \frac{1}{N} \sum_{i=1}^{N} \frac{t_i Y_i}{\pi_i}. \tag{7.11}$$

The indicators t_i see to it that only the available sample values of the target variable are used in the computation of the estimate. Note that each value Y_i is weighted with the inverse selection probability π_i. Thus, the estimator is corrected for the fact that elements with a large inclusion probability are over-represented in the sample.

It can be shown that the Horvitz-Thompson estimator is an unbiased estimator, and that its variance is equal to

$$V(\bar{y}_{HT}) = \frac{1}{2N^2} \sum_{i=1}^{N} \sum_{j=1}^{N} (\pi_i \pi_j - \pi_{ij}) \left(\frac{Y_i}{\pi_i} - \frac{Y_j}{\pi_j} \right)^2. \qquad (7.12)$$

This expression makes clear that by using a well chosen sampling design, the survey researcher can improve the precision of estimates. If the inclusion probabilities are taken more or less proportional to the values of the target variable, the quadratic term in the variance will be small, and thus the variance will be small. In practice, it is not possible to get exact proportionality. Having inclusion probabilities exactly proportional to the values of the target variable, i.e. $\frac{Y_i}{X_i}$ is constant for all values Y_i and X_i of the target variable Y and the auxiliary variable X, would imply that these values are known, and thus no survey would be necessary. In Section 7.2.6 it is shown how approximate proportionality can be used to improve the accuracy of estimates.

Note that no assumptions are made about the underlying distribution of the values of the target variable. The theory of sampling from finite populations provides a robust way of making inference.

7.2.4 The simple random sample

The most basic way to obtain a sample is drawing a simple random sample. It is a sample without replacement in which every population element has the same probability of selection. Imposing this condition in expression (7.7) results in each inclusion probability π_i being equal to $\frac{n}{N}$. If this result is substituted in the expression (7.11) for the Horvitz-Thompson estimator, the following simple result is obtained

$$\bar{y}_{HT} = \bar{y} = \frac{1}{n} \sum_{i=1}^{N} t_i Y_i. \qquad (7.13)$$

In the case of simple random sampling, the sample mean $\bar{y}$ is an unbiased estimator of the population mean $\overline{Y}$. This is an example of the *Analogy Principle* that often (but not always) applies in sampling theory: a population characteristic is estimated by computing the corresponding quantity for the sample.

The variance of this estimator is obtained by substituting

$$\pi_i = \frac{n}{N} \qquad (7.14)$$

for the first order inclusion probabilities and

$$\pi_{ij} = \frac{n(n-1)}{N(N-1)} \qquad (7.15)$$

for the second order inclusion probabilities in expression (7.12) for the variance of the Horvitz-Thompson estimator. The result is

$$V(\overline{y}) = \frac{1-f}{n} S^2 \qquad (7.16)$$

in which quantity f is called the *sampling fraction*. It is equal to $\frac{n}{N}$. The quantity S^2 is the *adjusted population variance* of the variable Y. It is defined by

$$S^2 = \frac{1}{N-1} \sum_{i=1}^{N} \left(Y_i - \overline{Y}\right)^2. \qquad (7.17)$$

The adjusted population variance is a measure of the homogeneity of the population with respect to the target variable: the larger the variation of the values of the target variable, the larger the variance. The variance is 0 if all values are equal.

By taking a closer look at expression (7.16), two important conclusions can be drawn:

1. The variance of the estimator decreases as the sample size increases. Thus, more precise estimates of population characteristics can be obtained by taking larger samples.

2. For samples from not too small populations, the variance can be approximated by S^2/n. This approximation does not depend on the size of the population. Hence, larger populations do not require larger samples to obtain the same degree of precision of the estimators.

Conclusion (2) may seem somewhat unexpected at first sight. This conclusion can be made more plausible by comparing it with a simple down-to-earth activity like tasting soup. One tastes soup by eating one spoonful. As long as the soup in the pan is well stirred, it does not matter how large the pan is; the same spoonful is sufficient to draw a conclusion.

7.2.5 The precision of estimates

A sample survey results in estimates of population characteristics. Once such estimates have been computed, the question arises how precise they are. How close are the estimates to the true, but unknown, value of the population characteristic? A first indicator of the precision is the variance of the estimate. An estimate with a small variance is more precise than one with a large variance. However, the interpretation of the value of the variance is not straightforward. For one thing, the variance has a different unit of measurement. If the target variable measures income in dollars, then the variance of the population mean is in squared dollars. A simple way to solve this problem is to take to the square root of the variance. The quantity obtained in this way, is called the *standard error* of the estimate. So, the standard error of the sample mean $\overline{y}$ is defined as

$$S(\overline{y}) = \sqrt{V(\overline{y})} \qquad (7.18)$$

Although the standard error has the same unit of measurement, it still is not simple to interpret its value. For what value of the standard error can we say the estimate is precise? The theory of statistics offers a way out. The solution is the use of the *confidence interval*. The confidence interval specifies a lower and an upper bound calculated on the basis of the available data. The bounds are calculated in such a way that the probability that the interval covers the (unknown) population characteristic is at least equal to a preset large probability $1 - \alpha$. The quantity $1 - \alpha$ is called the *confidence level*. Often, the value of α is set to 0.05 so that the confidence level is equal to 0.95. Such a confidence interval can be interpreted as follows: if you would repeat your study a large number of times, and you would compute the estimate and the confidence interval for each study, then in approximately 95 of the 100 cases the confidence interval would contain the value of the population characteristic. So you run a risk of 5% that conclusions based on confidence intervals are wrong.

You are free in your choice of the confidence level. If, on the one hand, you want to reduce the risk of making a wrong conclusion, you can take a smaller value of α, say $\alpha = 0.01$. But you have to pay a price for this reduced risk, because confidence intervals will be wider, and consequently you can make less precise statements about the values of the population characteristics. If, on the other hand, you want to have very precise estimates, you must increase the value of α, and this increases the risk of wrong conclusions. So, there is always a pay-off between precision and risk.

Calculation of confidence intervals is fairly straightforward. The sample mean and related statistics usually have an approximately normal distribution. Therefore, only the standard error is needed. For $\alpha = 0.05$, the confidence interval for the population mean $\overline{Y}$ of the target variable Y is equal to

$$(\overline{y} - 1.96S(\overline{y}), \overline{y} + 1.96S(\overline{y})), \qquad (7.19)$$

where $S(\overline{y})$ is the standard error of the sample mean $\overline{y}$. In practice, the confidence is approximated by substituting the sample estimate $s(\overline{y})$ for $S(\overline{y})$. For a different value of α, the value 1.96 is substituted by a different value.

If you publish the results of your survey research, it is not sufficient to restrict yourself to estimates. Confidence intervals must be mentioned too. In fact, an estimate without some indication of its precision is useless. This error is often made in the media when opinion polls are discussed. Just mentioning estimates creates a feeling of exactness that does not exist. It may even be better to publish no estimates at all, but to only give confidence intervals.

7.2.6   Advanced sampling strategies

The combination of a sampling design and an estimation procedure is called a *sampling strategy*. Thus far, only one sampling strategy was discussed, and this was simple random sampling in combination with the sample mean.

There are other sampling strategies possible. They have the advantage of producing more accurate estimates, but there is a price to be paid: they are less simple to implement, and they require extra information about the population. In this section, an overview is given of three such sampling strategies: stratified sampling, unequal probability sampling, and regression estimation.

In *stratified sampling*, the population is divided into a number of subpopulations. These subpopulations are called strata. The number of strata is denoted by L. The population sizes N_1, N_2, ..., N_L of the strata are supposed to be known. A sample is selected in each stratum. This requires a sampling frame to be available for each stratum. Usually, a simple random sample is selected in each stratum, but other sampling designs can also be used. Let $\bar{y}_h$ be the sample mean in stratum h, for $h = 1, 2, ..., L$. Then this sample mean is an unbiased estimate of the population mean in the stratum. The stratum estimates are combined into a population estimate with the following formula:

$$\bar{y}_S = \frac{1}{N} \sum_{h=1}^{L} N_h \bar{y}_h. \tag{7.20}$$

The subscript S indicates that the estimate is based on a stratified sample. Expression (7.20) represents an unbiased estimate of the population mean. It can be shown that its variance is small if the strata are homogeneous with respect to the target variable, i.e. variation within strata is less than variation between strata. A simple example illustrates the usefulness of stratification. For an income survey in a large town, it may be worthwhile to stratify by neighbourhood. If people with high incomes live in other neighbourhoods than people with low incomes, income distributions within neighbourhoods may have less variation than income distributions between neighbourhoods.

An additional advantage of stratification is that you have control over the sample sizes in the strata. This makes it possible to get reasonably accurate estimates within strata, giving more information about the population.

All sampling discussed up until now was sampling with equal selection probabilities. Horvitz & Thompson (1952) showed that it is also possible to make proper inference on a population based on *sampling with unequal probabilities*. If selection probabilities are used that are proportional to some auxiliary variable, and there is a sufficient amount of correlation between the target variable and this auxiliary variable, even much more precise estimates can be obtained.

It is not easy to find a practical procedure for a sample without replacement with unequal probabilities. The sequential nature of the selection procedure makes it hard to design a simple procedure with preset inclusion probabilities. Moreover, several of these procedures result in negative variance estimates. Therefore, sampling with replacement is preferred. This is much simpler to implement. The procedure requires all the values

$$X_1, X_2, ..., X_N$$

of the auxiliary variable X in the population to be known. In every draw, element i in the population is assigned a probability

$$p_i = \frac{X_i}{\sum_{k=1}^{N} X_k} \qquad (7.21)$$

of being selected. The simple sample mean cannot be used any more to calculate an estimate, because it does not correct for the unequal selection probabilities. The proper estimator is obtained by substituting inclusion probabilities $\pi_i = n p_i$ in expression (7.11) for the Horvitz-Thompson estimator. The resulting estimator is

$$\bar{y}_U = \frac{\overline{X}}{n} \sum_{i=1}^{N} t_i \frac{Y_i}{X_i}. \qquad (7.22)$$

The higher the correlation between the variables X and Y, the more accurate the estimate is.

A nice example of sampling with unequal probabilities is a survey on shop-lifting carried out by Statistics Netherlands. To estimate the magnitude of this problem, a sample of shops was selected. Since the floor area of shops was available as auxiliary variable, and there was a relationship between floor area and value of stolen goods, the sample was selected with probabilities proportional to the floor area. Due to this sampling scheme, large department stores had a high probability of being selected. They suffer most from shop-lifting, so a lot of information was obtained in this way, and precise estimates could be computed.

Estimates can be improved by using differing sampling designs. But there are also other ways. Sometimes it is possible to use different estimation procedures. One such procedure is *regression estimation*. This procedure can be applied if an auxiliary variable X is available that sufficiently correlates with the target variable. This auxiliary variable must be measured in the sample, and furthermore its population mean $\overline{X}$ must be known.

A simple random sample is selected, and using the sample data on both variables, the simple linear regression model

$$E(Y) = \alpha + \beta X \qquad (7.23)$$

is estimated. The sample based estimate of β is equal to

$$b = \frac{\sum_{i=1}^{N} t_i (X_i - \bar{x})(Y_i - \bar{y})}{\sum_{i=1}^{N} t_i (X_i - \bar{x})^2}, \qquad (7.24)$$

where $\bar{x}$ and $\bar{y}$ are the sample means of X and Y. The sample estimate for α is equal to

$$a = \bar{y} - b\bar{x}. \qquad (7.25)$$

Now, the regression estimate is defined by

$$\overline{y}_R = \overline{y} - b(\overline{x} - \overline{X}). \tag{7.26}$$

The regression estimate is approximately unbiased. It has a small bias due to the fact that expected value of the ratio of two random variables is not equal to the ratio of the expected values of the variables. Fortunately, this bias decreases in size as the sample size increases. In most practical situations the bias can be ignored. The variance of the estimate is equal to

$$V(\overline{y}_R) = V(\overline{y})(1 - R^2), \tag{7.27}$$

where R is correlation coefficient between the variables X and Y. If there is no correlation, the variance reduces to that of the simple sample mean. It is clear that as the correlation increases, the variance decreases. Hence, it pays to search for auxiliary variables that are correlated with the target variables of the surveys.

7.3   Practical problems

7.3.1   A taxonomy of errors

Usually, one of the main objectives of a sample survey is to compute estimates of population characteristics. Such estimates will never be exactly equal to the population characteristics. There will always be some error. This error can have many causes. Bethlehem & Kersten (1986) give a taxonomy of possible causes. It is reproduced in Figure 7.2. The taxonomy is a more extended version of one given by Kish (1967).

The ultimate result of all these errors is a discrepancy between the survey estimate and the population characteristic to be estimated. This discrepancy is called the *total error*. Two broad categories can be distinguished contributing to this total error: sampling errors and non-sampling errors.

Sampling errors are introduced by the sampling design. They are due to the fact that estimates are based on a sample and not on a complete enumeration of the population. Sampling errors vanish if the complete population is observed. Since only a sample is available, and not the complete data set, to compute population characteristics, you have to rely on an estimate. The sampling error can be split in a selection error and an estimation error.

A *selection error* occurs when wrong selection probabilities are used. For example, the true selection probabilities may differ from the anticipated selection probabilities when elements have multiple occurrences in the sampling frame. Selection errors are hard to avoid without thorough investigation of the sampling frame.

The *estimation error* denotes the effect caused by using a sample based on a random selection procedure. Every new selection of a sample will result in different elements, and thus in a different value of the estimator.

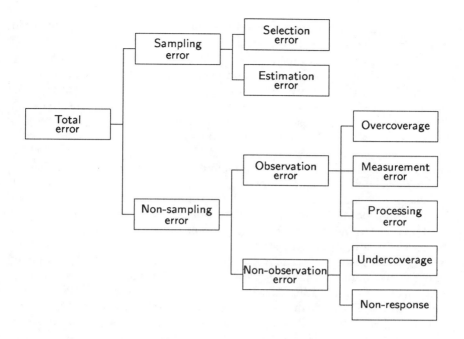

Figure 7.2: A taxonomy of errors.

The estimation error can be controlled through the sampling design. For example, by increasing the sample size, or by taking selection probabilities proportional to some well chosen auxiliary variable, you can reduce the error in the estimate.

Non-sampling errors may even occur if the whole population is investigated. They denote errors made during the process of recording the answers to the questions. Non-sampling errors can be divided in observation errors and non-observation errors.

Observation errors are one form of non-sampling errors. These denote errors made during the process of obtaining and recording the answers. *Overcoverage* means that elements are included in the survey not belonging to the target population. A *measurement error* occurs when the respondent does not understand the question, or does not want to give the true answer, or if the interviewer makes an error in recording the answer. Also, interview effects, question wording effects, and memory effects belong to this group of errors. A measurement error causes a difference between the true value and the value processed in the survey. A *processing error* denotes an error made during data processing, e.g. data entry.

Non-observation errors are errors made because the intended measurements could not be carried out. *Undercoverage* occurs when elements in the target population do not appear in the sampling frame. So, representatives of these elements can never be contacted. Another non-observation error is *non-response*. It is the phenomenon that people selected in the sample do not provide the required information.

The taxonomy above makes clear that a lot can go wrong during the process of collecting survey data, and usually it does. Some errors can be avoided by taking preventive measures at the design stage. However, some errors will remain. Therefore, it is important to check the collected data for errors, and where possible, to correct detected errors. This activity is called *data editing*. Data editing procedures are not able to handle every type of survey error. They are most suitable for detecting and correcting measurement errors, processing errors, and possibly overcoverage. Phenomena like selection errors, undercoverage, and non-response require a different approach. This approach often leads to the use of adjustment weights in estimation procedures, and not to correction of individual values in records.

Data editing may occur in many steps of the survey process. Edits can be part of the computer-assisted interviewing program. In this case, data editing takes place during data collection. If data is collected by means of paper forms, data editing is a separate activity that comes after data entry. Both ways of data editing focus on each form separately. This is called *micro-editing*. Data editing can also be carried out in the final steps of the survey process, by investigating tables and graphs that are produced using all available records. This is called *macro-editing*.

The aim of data editing is to detect errors, and if possible, to correct these errors. Error correction during interviewing is no problem. You can confront the respondent with the problem, so he or she can assist to solve it. Error correction is much more difficult if it has to be done after the field work has finished. Then the respondent is not available any more. So, it is generally not possible to determine the correct answer. The situation is even more difficult for consistency checks. Several variables are involved in such checks, and it is in most situations impossible to determine the variable(s) causing the error. Fellegi & Holt (1976) have developed a methodology for this situation. It is based on the principles that errors are relatively rare, and that the errors must be solved by making a minimal amount of change in the data.

The next sections are devoted to one of the most serious types of errors, and this is the phenomenon of non-response.

7.4   The non-response problem

Non-response is the phenomenon that elements in the selected sample do not provide the requested information, or that the provided information is unusable.

Due to non-response the sample size is smaller than expected. The main problem caused by non-response is that estimates of population characteristics may be biased. This situation occurs if, due to non-response, some groups in the population are over- or under-represented, and these groups

Year	Labour Force Survey	Consumer Sentiments Survey	Survey on Well being	Mobility Survey	Holiday Survey
1972		29			
1973	12	23			
1974		25	28		
1975	14	22			14
1976		28	23		13
1977	12	31	30		19
1978		36		33	22
1979	19	37	35	31	26
1980		39	39	32	26
1981	17	35		32	26
1982		40	36	34	29
1983	18	37	42	34	26
1984		35		36	31
1985	23	31		40	32
1986			41	40	34
1987	40			40	
1988	39			45	
1989	40			42	

Table 7.1: Non-response percentages in some Dutch surveys.

behave differently with respect to the characteristics to be investigated.

Indeed, estimators must be assumed to be biased unless very convincing evidence of the contrary is provided. Bethlehem & Kersten (1985) discuss a number of surveys of Statistics Netherlands. A follow-up study of the Victimization Survey showed that people who are afraid of being home alone at night, are less inclined to participate in the survey. In Housing Demand Surveys, refusers turned out to have lesser housing demands than respondents. For the Survey on the Mobility of the Population it is obvious that mobile people are relatively under-represented among the respondents. The magnitude of the non-response in many Dutch sample surveys is increasing to such an extent that without special adjustment techniques one has to reckon with a decrease of the quality of the results. Table 7.1 presents non-response figures of a number of surveys carried out by Statistics Netherlands.

It is difficult to compare response rates of different surveys, but for each of the surveys one can study its non-response trend over the years. The magnitude of the non-response is determined by a large number of factors, including the subject of the survey, the target population, the time period, the length of the questionnaire, the quality of the interviewers, the fieldwork in general, etc. It is clear from Table 7.1 that non-response is a considerable problem. It has an impact on the costs of a survey, since it takes more and more effort to obtain estimates with the same precision as originally specified in the sampling design.

Non-respondents can be classified in three groups. The first group are the *refusers*. These people refuse to co-operate. Sometimes it is possible to make an appointment for an interview at some later date. However, frequently the refusal can be considered permanent. Possible causes are lack of interest, fear of privacy intrusion, and interview fatigue.

The second group of non-respondents are the *not-contactable*. No contact is made due to the fact people are not at home, due to removal or due to other circumstances like watchdogs, dangerous neighbourhoods or houses which are difficult to reach. Generally speaking, people are increasingly hard to contact. Important factors are smaller family sizes, greater mobility, and a larger amount of spare time which is spent out-of-doors.

The third group of non-respondents consists of people who are physically or mentally *not able* to co-operate during the fieldwork period. Language problems can also cause this type of non-response.

To be able to build a well-founded theory of non-response adjustment, it is necessary to incorporate the phenomenon of non-response in the theory of survey sampling. The literature on non-response contains two different basic views on how non-response occurs. Here, these views are labelled the Random Response Model and the Fixed Response Model.

The *Random Response Model* assumes some kind of random mechanism determining whether or not a selected person will respond. Each element in the population is assigned an imaginary random number generator. This generator can only produce either the value 0 or 1. A value 1 means response, and a value 0 non-response. The probability with which the random number generator assumes the value 1, is different for each element in the population. For element i, this probability is denoted by δ_i (for $i = 1, 2, ..., N$). All response probabilities δ_1, δ_2, ..., δ_N are assumed to be unknown. Under the Random Response Model, there are two random processes controlling the availability of data: the sample selection mechanism defined by the researcher, and the response mechanism, which is not under his control.

The *Fixed Response Model* assumes the population to consist of two mutually exclusive and exhaustive subpopulations: the response stratum and the non-response stratum. Elements in the response stratum would participate in the survey with certainty, if selected in the sample. And elements in the non-response stratum would not participate with certainty, if selected. The Fixed Response Model can be regarded as a special case of the Random Response Model in which the response probabilities are either 0 or 1. Many authors consider the Fixed Response Model a too simple, and unrealistic model. Here, the Random Response Model is used.

To incorporate the phenomenon of non-response in the theory of sampling, the indicators r_1, r_2, ... r_N are introduced. The indicator r_i assumes the value 1 if element i is selected in the sample *and* responds (for $i = 1, 2, ..., N$). In all other situations, r_i assumes the value 0. Data becomes only available for element i if the indicator r_i has the value 1. The probability with which r_i assumes the value 1, is determined by the (known) selection probability and the (unknown) response probability δ_i. The number of available observations is denoted by m, where $m < n$. This quantity is equal to

$$m = \sum_{i=1}^{N} r_i. \tag{7.28}$$

Unlike n, m is not a fixed number. It is a random variable, and its value depends on the response behaviour. Ignoring non-response, and pretending that the available data represent the intended sample, may have serious consequences. Consider the mean

$$\bar{y}^* = \frac{1}{m} \sum_{i=1}^{N} r_i Y_i \tag{7.29}$$

of the available values of the target variable. Bethlehem (1988) shows that the expected value of this estimator is approximately equal to

$$Y^* = \frac{1}{N} \sum_{i=1}^{N} \frac{\delta_i Y_i}{\bar{\delta}} \tag{7.30}$$

where $\bar{\delta}$ is the population mean of the response probabilities. Generally, the quantity on the right-hand side of the expression is not equal to the population mean. So, the estimate is biased. It will systematically over- or under-estimate the population mean. The bias of estimator can be shown to be approximately equal to

$$B(\bar{y}^*) = E(\bar{y}^*) - \bar{Y} = \frac{C}{\bar{\delta}}, \tag{7.31}$$

where the quantity C is equal to

$$C = \frac{1}{N} \sum_{i=1}^{N} (\delta_i - \bar{\delta})(Y_i - \bar{Y}). \tag{7.32}$$

This is the population covariance between the target variable and the response probabilities. From expression (7.31) one can draw two conclusions:

o The estimator will be biased if there is a relationship between target variable and response behaviour. The stronger the relationship, the larger the bias.

o The size of the bias is also determined by the average value of the response probabilities: The lower this average, the higher the bias. Hence, if the non-response rate is high, consequences may be more serious.

In practice, it is very difficult to asses the possible negative effects of non-response. And even if such effects can be detected, it is no simple matter to correct for them. To be able to do something, it is very important to have auxiliary information. For example, if there is an auxiliary variable that has been measured in the sample, and for which the population distribution is known, then this variable can be used to check whether the available data show unbalancedness, i.e. they are not representative for the population.

It is important to realize already in the design stage of the survey that the survey will most likely be affected by non-response. As much as possible auxiliary information should be collected to cope with the consequences. One of the consequences is including extra questions in the questionnaire. Non-respondents should be asked for the reason of non-response, and this reason must be recorded in the data file.

There are several techniques available to correct for non-response bias (For example, see Bethlehem, 1988; Bethlehem & Keller, 1987; Bethlehem & Kersten, 1987, 1985; Kersten & Bethlehem, 1984). The next two subsections pay some attention to weighting and imputation.

7.4.1 Weighting

The situation in which all requested information on an element is missing is called *unit non-response*. To correct for a possible bias due to unit non-response, often a weighting method is carried out.

The basic principle of weighting is that every observed element is assigned a specific weight. Estimates for population characteristics are obtained by processing the weighted values instead of the values themselves. The easiest and most straightforward method used to compute weights is post-stratification. The population is divided into strata after selection of the sample. If each stratum is homogeneous with respect to the target variable of the survey, then the observed elements resemble the unobserved elements. Therefore, estimates of stratum characteristics will not be very biased, so they can be used to construct population estimates.

To carry out post-stratification, discrete auxiliary variables are needed, and preferable auxiliary variables having a strong relationship with the target variable. All observed elements within a stratum are assigned the same weight, and this weight is computed such that the weighted sample distribution of the auxiliary variables agrees with the population distribution of these variables. If the relationships are strong enough, also the weighted sample distribution of the target variable will agree with its population distribution.

Suppose, the auxiliary variables divide the population into L strata. Let N_h be the population size of stratum h, and let m_h be the number of observed elements in stratum h, for $h = 1, 2, ..., L$. The total number of observed elements is denoted by m, where $m < n$. In case of simple random sampling, post-stratification assigns each observed element i in stratum h the same weight

$$w_i = \frac{N_h}{N} \frac{m}{m_h} \qquad (7.33)$$

If the weighted sample mean is computed using these weights, the result is the following expression:

$$\bar{y}_{PS} = \frac{1}{N} \sum_{h=1}^{L} N_h \bar{y}_h,$$ (7.34)

where $\bar{y}_h$ is the unweighted sample mean in stratum h. This expression is exactly the same as the expression for the estimator in case of stratified sampling. However, the distributional properties of both formulae are different. This caused by the fact that for stratified sampling the sample sizes are fixed in advance, while for post-stratification estimation these sample sizes are random variables.

An example shows a simple application of weighting. A sample is selected from a population of 1000 persons, and 100 people respond. Two auxiliary variables are used for weighting: sex and age (in three categories). Table 7.2 shows the population distribution and sample distribution of these two variables.

Population	Male	Female	Sample	Male	Female
Young	226	209	Young	23	15
Middle	152	144	Middle	16	17
Old	133	136	Old	13	16

Table 7.2: Population and sample frequencies.

A closer look will show a difference between the population and sample distribution. For example, the percentage of old females in the population was 13.6%, whereas this percentage in the sample is equal to 16%. So, old females are over-represented in the sample.

Weights can be computed by dividing the population percentages by the corresponding sample percentages. The results are given in Table 7.3. For example, the weight for old females is 13.6/15 = 0.850. This weight is smaller than 1, indicating that the stratum is over-represented in the sample. Likewise, it can be noted that young females are under-represented in the sample, and therefore get a weight larger than 1.

Weights	Male	Female
Young	0.983	1.393
Middle	0.950	0.847
Old	1.023	0.850

Table 7.3: Adjustment weights.

This type of weighting only works as long as there are tables with population distributions available, and the cells in the corresponding sample tables are not empty. However, this is not always the case. New weighting techniques have been developed that can be applied where traditional post-stratification fails. For example, Bethlehem & Keller (1987) have proposed a technique called linear weighting, which is based on regression model which relate the target variables of the survey to the auxiliary variables used for weighting.

Since almost all surveys suffer from non-response, a weighting procedure is almost always required to correct a possible non-response bias. As a result, all subsequent analysis needs to take account of these weights. This may not be so simple, since many statistical analysis packages are not able to properly take account of weights.

7.4.2   Imputation

The situation in which only part of the requested information about an element is missing, is called item *non-response*. Item non-response requires a different approach. A great deal of additional information is available for the elements involved. All available responses to other questions can be used to predict the answer to the missing questions. This computation of a 'synthetic' answer to a question is called *imputation*. Predictions are usually based on models describing relationships between the variable with missing values and other variables for which the values are available. Of course, imputed values must satisfy the conditions set by range, consistency and route checks.

Imputation techniques can range from simple ad hoc procedures to sophisticated prediction techniques based on complex models. Kalton & Kasprzyk (1986) present a list of some commonly used imputation techniques:

o *Deductive imputation.* Sometimes, the missing answer to a question can be deduced with certainty from the available answers to other questions. When range, consistency and route checks restrict the answer to only one possible value, deductive imputation can be applied. This is the ideal form of imputation.

o *Imputation of the mean.* This technique assigns the mean of the available values of the variable to all missing responses.

o *Imputation of the group mean.* The sample is divided into groups using auxiliary variables. Within each group, the mean of the available values of the variable in the group is assigned to all missing responses.

o *Random imputation.* For each missing answer, a value is chosen at random from the set of available responses to the question.

o *Random imputation within groups.* The sample is divided into groups using auxiliary variables. Within each group, a missing response is assigned a randomly chosen value from the set of available responses to that variable within the group.

o *Hot-deck imputation.* This is a special implementation of random imputation within groups. For each group, a donor record is maintained. The records in the file are processed sequentially. If the field of the question to be imputed contains a real answer, the value is copied to the donor record. If the answer in the field is missing, the value from the donor record is copied to the field.

o *Regression imputation.* A regression model is constructed that explains the answers of the question to be imputed from other questions for which the answers are available. Then, the fitted regression model is used to predict the answer in missing cases. To conserve the distributional properties of the data, often a residual, drawn from some normal distribution, is added to the prediction.

The success of an imputation technique depends on properties of the mechanism generating item non-response. Suppose Y is the target variable of the survey, and it has some missing values. Let X be an auxiliary variable for which all survey values are available. Little & Rubin (1987) consider three types of patterns leading to missing data:

1. The probability of a missing value for Y is independent of the value of Y and independent of the value of X. This case is called *Missing Completely At Random* or MCAR. Then the observed values of Y form a random sub-sample from the sample. The mean of the observed values is an unbiased estimate of the population mean.

2. The probability of a missing value for Y is independent of the value depends on the value of Y, but is independent of the value of X. This case is called *Missing At Random* or MAR. Then the observed values of Y do not form a random sub-sample of the sample. However, they are a random sub-sample within the classes defined by the values of X. The auxiliary variable can be used to effectively correct for a bias due to missing values.

3. The probability of a missing value for Y depends both on the value of Y and the value of X. Then the observed values of Y do not form a random sub-sample of the sample. Also, they are not a random sub-sample within the classes defined by the values of X. Therefore, the auxiliary variable cannot be used to effectively correct for a bias due to missing values.

There are several considerations that play a role in selecting an imputation technique. One is the type of variable. All techniques listed above can be applied routinely on qualitative (continuous) variables. However, some of the techniques cannot be applied to qualitative (discrete or categorical) variables, because imputed values not necessarily have to belong to the domain of valid values. For example, imputation of the mean or regression imputation for the variable Sex with two possible answers (code 1 for male, and code 2 for female) may easily produce a value like 1.4. So, for qualitative variable it is better to only use random imputation (possibly within groups) or hot dock imputation, because these techniques always produce 'real' values.

Imputation techniques can be classified as random or deterministic, depending on whether imputed values are produced by means of a random mechanism. The deterministic techniques usually work in such a way that the mean of all values (observed and imputed) is equal to the mean of the observed values. For the random imputation methods, the expected value (of the imputed values of the producing mechanism) of the mean over all values is equal to the observed mean. So both methods have the same effect on the bias of estimates. However, adding imputed values introduces an extra source of uncertainty, and therefore reduces the precision of estimates. This may be a reason to prefer deterministic techniques for estimating the population mean.

Deterministic techniques have the disadvantage that they distort the properties of the distribution of the values of the variable. These techniques tend to predict values in the middle part of the distribution. Therefore, the distribution of Y in the imputed data set is much more peaked and much more concentrated than the original distribution. Standard errors computed from the imputed data set are generally too small. They create a too optimistic view of the precision of estimates. Random imputation methods do not have this nasty property. They are much better able to preserve the original distribution.

A final point to take into consideration is the effect of imputation on relationship between variables. Imputation of the overall mean and random imputation causes covariances and correlations to be biased. This occurs because imputed Y values are unrelated to the values of other variables in their records. By applying imputation within groups, the bias is decreased, but not avoided. Also, regression imputation introduces a bias in the covariance.

It is clear that the ideal imputation technique does not exist. A researcher always has to be careful in his analysis of a data set that has been subjected to imputation (unless the amount of imputation is small). Research for new imputation techniques is still in progress. An example is the multiple imputation technique proposed by Rubin (1979). This technique computes a set of, say m imputed values for each missing value. This results in m imputed data sets. Inference is based on the distribution of estimates obtained by computing the estimate for each of the m data sets.

Also, application of neural networks and of evolutionary algorithms looks promising. Experiments have shown that there are situations in which these techniques work. However, further research is necessary.

7.5   Analysis of survey data

7.5.1   About Dirty Data

Carrying out a cross-sectional study by means of a sample survey is a time consuming and costly activity. Therefore, the researcher will attempt to obtain as much as possible interesting results from the collected data. However, he must be careful. A lot can go wrong in the process of collecting and editing the data, and this has an impact on the results of his analysis.

Many data analysis techniques assume some kind of model stating that the data form an independent identically distributed random sample from some normal distribution. These assumptions are almost never satisfied in practical situations. More often, the *Dirty Data Theorem* applies. It states the data come from a sample that is obtained by a dependent sample with unknown and unequal selection probabilities from a bizarre and unspecified distribution, whereby some values are missing and many other values are subject to substantial measurement errors. It is clear that the researcher has to take into account that his data may be affected by measurement errors and non-response, that some values may not be observed but imputed, and that he has to use weights to compensate for a possible non-response bias.

This section gives an overview of some approaches to the analysis of survey data. It will not only describe possibilities, but also point at some caveats. The basic analysis approaches are exploratory and inductive analysis. And fairly new is an approach called data mining. All three approaches will be discussed in the following subsections.

7.5.2   Exploratory analysis

Exploratory analysis is an approach to investigating data without the ambition to make inference about the population the data came from. It is a collection of techniques that helps the researcher to discover unexpected patterns and structures in the data. One reason to do that could be a kind of check on the collected data. It may give indications as to whether the collection process and editing activities have worked properly. Another reason to carry out an exploratory analysis might be to come to the formulation of hypotheses on the population. Such hypotheses have to be tested independently. For this, see the next subsection on inductive analysis.

Exploratory analysis techniques let the data speak for themselves. The hope is to discover the unexpected. For such an analysis, graphical techniques work better than numerical techniques. Take the mean as an example. It is just one number indicating the central location of the values. But this is all the information it provides. Compare this with a proper graph of the distribution of values, which gives information about central location, variation, grouping of values, symmetry of the distribution, and the existence of possible outliers. Chambers, Kleiner, & Tukey (1983) give a dramatic example of the difference in numerical and graphical techniques. Figure 7.3 is reproduced from their work.

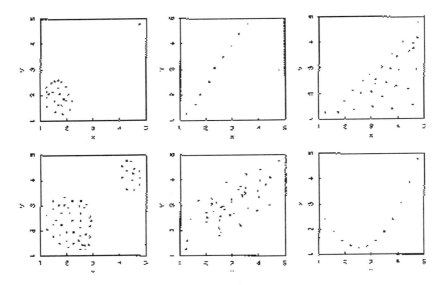

Figure 7.3: Limitations of the correlation coefficient.

The figure contains the six scatter plots. Each scatter plot displays the relationship between two variables X and Y. The nature of the relationship is different in each plot. However, the value of the correlation coefficient is the same in each plot: 0.7. In the upper left plot there is in fact no relationship, so the correlation coefficient should be 0. Unfortunately, the single outlier increases the value of the correlation coefficient to 0.7. In the upper middle plot the situation is the other way around. A perfect relationship is disturbed by an outlier. A final example is the lower right plot. There is a perfect relationship. However, since it is not linear, it is not properly reflected in the value of the correlation coefficient. The message from this example is clear: do not compute all kind of numerical quantities before having looked at some graphs!

Tukey (1977) has been one of the important men in the development of exploratory data analysis techniques. He is the inventor of many techniques that are now commonly used. Examples are the *stem and leaf display* and the *box and whisker plot*. He designed his techniques in an era in which the microcomputer had not yet been invented. So he worked on graph paper. With the emergence of the microcomputer it became possible to implement his graphical techniques in interactive data analysis programs. These programs offer a new approach to data analysis, in which the researcher is engaged in an interactive dialogue with the computer. The computer is able to respond very rapidly to requests for specific graphs. So, conclusions from one graph quickly can be explored further in other graphs.

An exploratory analysis is usually carried out in two steps. The first step concentrates on the distribution of single variables. Using techniques like one-way scatter plots, box-and-whisker plots and histograms, the distribution is displayed in a graphical way. In such graphs a number of aspects can be studied:

o *Outliers.* Outliers represent unusual values that are far from the location of the distribution. An outlier may indicate a wrong value that has to be corrected. It may also indicate an unusual element in the survey that has to be removed before carrying out the analysis. Of course, an outlier may also denote a correct value.

o *Groups.* If the data values fall apart in distinct groups, this may indicate that the values come from different distributions. It may be better to study these distributions separately.

o *Symmetry.* An asymmetric distribution is a clear indicator of non-normality of the distribution.

It is the hope of the researcher that the variables will have a more or less normal distribution. If this is the case, he can apply many of the analysis techniques that require normality. If distributions are skewed, he might consider carrying out a transformation on the variable, so that the transformed variable is more or less normally distributed. Often, a logarithmic or square root transformation helps. An example is income. Usually, the logarithm of the income is closer to normality than the income distribution itself.

The second step consists in investigating relationships between variables. At this point exploratory analysis has its limitations, one of the most important being that it is not able to investigate high-dimensional relationships. This is due to the two-dimensional nature of the computer screen. One way to extend the possibilities is offered by a collection of techniques that goes by the name of *dynamic graphics*. In essence, colour and movement are used to give more aspects of the data. For example, by rotating a two-dimensional scatter plot around a third axis, it becomes possible to study three-dimensional relationships. And colours can be used to mark a subset of points in a graph, and then study its behaviour in other graphs.

7.5.3   Inductive analysis

The power of cross-sectional studies lies in the fact that the application of proper sampling designs allows for generalization of the conclusions from the sample to the population. This is the area of inductive analysis. This type of analysis is based on some kind of model for the population. Such a model described the properties of the population. There are two approaches:

1. The model is completely specified. The data collected in the survey is used to check whether the model is correct or not. This type of analysis is called *hypothesis testing*.

2. The model is not completely specified. There is no statement about the values of a limited number of model parameters describing population characteristics. The survey data is used to estimate these parameters. This type of analysis is called *estimation.*

Estimation of population characteristics is nearly always carried out in cross-sectional studies. Typically, this is the most straightforward way to obtain new knowledge about a population. A proper estimation procedure requires the distribution of the estimator to be known. In the ideal situation (no non-response, no measurement errors) this is no problem. The distribution of the estimator is completely determined by the sampling design that was specified by the researcher. Particularly for not too small samples, the Central Limit Theorem applies to many of the sampling designs used. This means that estimators will have an approximately normal distribution. Computation of standard errors and confidence intervals is therefore straightforward. Usually, the situation is not ideal. Problems like non-response and measurement errors make life for the researcher hard. The presence of imputed values and the requirement to use weights may cause estimators to loose their nice properties. Modern information technology may offer some way out. *Bootstrap techniques* attempt to simulate the distribution of estimators by selecting a large number of subsamples from the collected data. These techniques are very computer-intensive but seem to work in many areas where classical model assumptions are not satisfied.

Cross-sectional studies concentrate less on hypothesis testing. One reason is that many of these studies have an exploratory nature. The researcher has no clear idea what to look for, so he is not able to formulate a hypothesis. Another reason is that hypothesis testing does not always work the way the researcher wants it to. Particularly in large surveys, statistical tests always produce a significant result. For example, to investigate the relationship between two variables, one could formulate the hypothesis that there is no relationship between the two variables, and then test this hypothesis. The test will almost always reject the hypothesis, even for the tiniest deviation from independence. This is not what the researcher is looking for. What he wants to know is whether there is a substantial relationship or not. Exploratory techniques might be sufficient to establish this kind of relationship.

As was said before, hypothesis testing requires a hypothesis. A naive researcher could take the approach to first use the survey data set to formulate the hypothesis, and then use the same data set to test this hypothesis. This is a fundamental error. The result of a statistical test is only of value, if the test is carried out on an independent data set. In fact, a new study is required to test the hypothesis. To avoid having to carry out a new study, a different approach can be taken. The survey data set is randomly divided into two parts. One part is used for an exploratory analysis, to form the hypotheses, and then the other part is used to test the hypotheses.

Hypothesis testing suffers from the same problems as estimation. Tests can only be carried out if certain model assumptions (like normality) are satisfied, and this is often not the case. So, it is important to check the model assumptions before performing any test. Also here, bootstrap methods may help.

7.5.4 Data mining

We now live in an era in which it becomes increasingly easy to collect, process and store data. Information technology has made data collection quicker and data storage cheaper. So, the question is not any more how to collect data, but what to do with all the collected data.

Raw survey data is usually not of direct benefit. Its true value lies in the ability to extract information from it that helps us to understand the process responsible for producing the data. This is, of course, the area of statistical analysis. Traditionally, statistical analysis is a manual process. The researcher would become intimately familiar with the data, carry out analyses, and publish reports. However, this approach is no longer feasible as the quantity of available data grows, and the number of dimensions increases. Which researcher is able to analyse 'millions' of cases, each with hundreds of variables. Furthermore, the amount of data is growing so fast the manual analysis simply cannot keep pace.

Data mining is an approach that can prevent the researcher from drowning in the data. It is a set of techniques sometimes defined as the non-trivial process of identifying valid, novel, potentially useful, and ultimately understandable patterns in the data. Data mining algorithms focus on classification and extracting models.

Data mining can be seen as a form of exploratory data analysis. Contrary to EDA, data mining is applied to data sets that are collected by others for other purposes, and on combinations of data sets from several sources. Furthermore, data mining attempts to automate the exploration process, whereas EDA remains a manual activity.

Blind application of data mining can be a dangerous activity leading to the discovery of meaningless patterns. For example, a data mining technique that carries out thousands of statistical tests on a meaningless data set, each test with a confidence level of $\alpha = 0.05$, will produce approximately 5% of significant results. Another danger lies hidden in the combination of data sets from different sources. Problems like different variable definitions, different measuring instruments and measurement points in time, may prevent proper inference from the combined data set.

Proper application of data mining requires to embed it in a more general methodology for discovering useful information in data. This general methodology is often referred to as *Knowledge Discovery in Databases* (KDD). The KDD process is interactive and iterative, requiring many decisions by the researcher. It is summarized in the following steps (see Figure 7.4):

1. Collecting all kinds of information on the domain of the application.

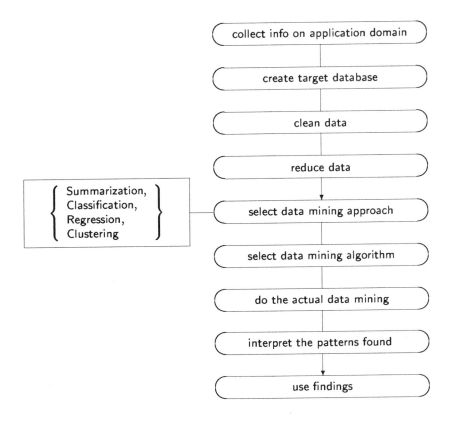

Figure 7.4: Data mining procedure.

2. Creating a target database. This may include combination of data sets, and/or making relevant selections from data sets.

3. Data cleaning. This includes search for and analyses of outliers, the treatment of missing values, accounting for non-response by means of weights, etc.

4. Data reduction. This includes the application dimensionality reduction techniques and transformation techniques (principal components analysis, factor analysis) that reduce the number of variables without affecting the amount of information.

5. Selection of the data mining approach. For example, the purpose can be summarization, classification, regression, or clustering.

6. Selection of data mining algorithms. This may include a selection of a family of models that may be appropriate.

7. Data mining. This is the actual search for interesting patterns.

8. Interpretation. This is the interpretation of the discovered patterns. This may result in going back to one of the previous steps. This step also includes deletion of irrelevant or redundant patterns, and translating useful patterns in terms understood by users.

9. Using the discovered knowledge. This could mean building new systems, or simply documenting the results in papers, and checking for consistency with other available knowledge in the subject-matter area.

Despite their rapid growth, KDD and data mining are still in their infancies. There are many challenges to overcome. The basic problems of statistical inference and knowledge discovery remain as difficult as they have always been. Automating the art of statistical analysis and the ability of the human brain to synthesize new knowledge from data still seems almost impossible to realize. However, the enormous amounts of data to be analysed, and the social and economic needs for more information, forces scientists to continue on this road. Therefore it is vital for researchers of cross-sectional data sets, to be kept informed about developments of data mining, its potentials and pitfalls. For an overview of the state of affairs (see, e.g. Fayyad, Piatetsky-Shapiro, & Smyth, 1996).

7.6   Further reading and Conclusions

This chapter presented an overview of ideas, concepts, possibilities and problems of cross-sectional surveys. It was by no means meant to be exhaustive. The vast literature on survey methodology provides more insight on all its aspects. Here are some suggestions for further reading.

More on the practical aspects of sampling strategies can be found in the standard textbooks on the subject (e.g. Cochran, 1977). A good reference for theoretical aspects is Särndal, Swensson, & Wretman (1992).

The field of data editing is developing at a fast rate. A basic paper was written by Fellegi & Holt (1976). Some new data editing strategies are described by Pol & Bethlehem (1997).

Computer-assisted interviewing is more and more becoming a standard procedure for data collection. The state of the art by the end of 1996 is described by Couper et al. (1998).

Non-response remains a serious problem. In many countries non-response rates are increasing, and this is a cause for concern. An overview of the non-response problem in the Netherlands, and some treatments, is given by Bethlehem & Kersten (1985).

One may wonder what the future of survey sampling will be in an era in which information technology is developing so fast. Indeed, there have been survey sampling experts predicting that sample surveys will have ceased to exist around the year 2020. The basis for this prediction is the assumption that by that time all information required for statistical purposes can be found in databases and registers. So, making statistics will have become a simple matter of putting together data that is retrieved from various electronic sources.

I think that in the year 2525, if man is still alive, there will still be sample surveys. But the way in which sample surveys are used, will have changed. Indeed, one can observe a trend of an increased use of database and register data. More and more data will become available through these sources. But even in the far future not all data can be found in databases. Information like opinions on important political issues, expectations of the development of the economic situation, assessment of personal health, feelings about housing conditions still will have to be collected through sample surveys.

However, the role of sample surveys in statistical information collection will change. More and more, data will be retrieved from registers and databases. But this will not be sufficient to fill the complete survey database. Sample surveys are still needed to fill the many remaining gaps.

Registers and databases are usually built for different purposes by different organizations using different conceptual frameworks. Also, the quality of the information will not be clear. Sample surveys provide very useful tools for quality control. Moreover, it will not be easy to construct a coherent and consistent survey database using information from various sources. Survey methodology techniques like editing, imputation and adjustment weighting will still be needed to put the pieces of this jigsaw puzzle together.

Chapter 8

Longitudinal Analysis

Peter C. M. Molenaar

Longitudinal analysis involves the analysis of change.
This preliminary definition of longitudinal analysis will be specified in several respects later on, but for the moment let it be understood in its common-sense meaning and let us consider the question why a study of change might be worthwhile to pursue. This question can be answered in several ways.

First, an analysis of change constitutes the royal road to understand the *causal mechanisms* underlying observed phenomena. For instance, all the basic causal laws of physics are differential equations explaining the change in particular physical phenomena (the Maxwell equations of electromagnetism, the Boltzman equation of statistical mechanics, the Schrödinger equation of quantum mechanics, etc.). In the next section, a simple example will be given of how the analysis of change in a biomedical setting can point the way to discovering the causal mechanisms underlying the observations.

A second answer is that an analysis of change leads to the possibility of *optimal control* of the processes under scrutiny. That is, the results of an analysis of change offer the possibility to carry out interventions, strategically chosen qua timing and dose that steer a particular process in the desired direction while minimizing the costs involved. A straightforward example is the determination of the times and doses of medication that maximize its positive effects while avoiding the occurrence of undesirable syndromes. Such optimal control based on the results of analyses of change is the standard approach in engineering but is much less known in the biological, medical and social sciences. In what follows we will discuss at some length applications of optimal control in psychotherapy and psychiatry.

Thirdly, and lastly, an analysis of change provides *more information in a statistical sense.* This not only pertains to the increased power of statistical tests of repeated measures designs, but also to the validity of inferences concerning the future course of processes under scrutiny. We will present a simple, but enlightening, illustration of this in the following section. Moreover, an analysis of change provides more information in a much more general sense, in that it allows for the detection and accommodation of unsuspected *heterogeneity* in subject samples. For instance, it may occur that the assumption that each subject in a population of interest obeys the same statistical model does not at all hold. This could for instance be the case in some populations of clinical or psychiatric interest. Yet standard statistical approaches may not be sufficient in order to detect and accommodate this structural heterogeneity, in contrast to specific analyses of change. In what follows this aspect of the analysis of change will be given due attention.

8.1   Preliminaries

Our first task is to further specify and discuss our preliminary definition of longitudinal analysis given in the previous section. Longitudinal analysis involves the analysis of change, but not all analysis of change is longitudinal. We will introduce that other main technique in the analysis of change, namely *time series analysis*, and provide more encompassing definitions that clearly show the communalities and differences between longitudinal analysis and time series analysis. In closing this section, we will present some simple examples of how (longitudinal or time series) analysis of change can uncover the causal mechanisms underlying the data in a valid way.

8.1.1   Two ways of analysing change

Change is not a simple, self-evident phenomenon, as witnessed by the perennial philosophical discussions devoted to it. Already in ancient Greek philosophy we find the diametrically opposed points of view of Parmenides, who denied the existence of change, and of Heraclitos who conceived of change as the basic ingredient of reality. But also in modern science, issues like Cambridge change in mathematical logic (Geach, 1972), the frame problem in artificial intelligence (Genesereth & Nilsson, 1987), and the irreversibility of time in theoretical physics (Zeh, 1992) attest to the complexity of the concept of change.

Within the confines of the present chapter, however, we will not be able to elaborate these complexities, but instead we will have to restrict attention to a limited point of view concerning change that leads to a suitable working definition for the discussion of the statistical analysis of change.

We define change as *time-dependent differences* in some aspect of a system. This simple definition implies that we do not consider spatial changes or spatio-temporal changes, only changes in time. As to the aspect of a system that changes in time, this can be its ongoing behaviour (or output) due to external or internal perturbations. In this case the structural aspects of the system stay invariant, like the function mapping input into output and the statistical characteristics of internal perturbations.

EXAMPLE 1

A possible illustration is the study of nerve conduction under stationary experimental conditions. Alternatively, some structural aspect of a system itself may be varying in time, like in the study of habituation of nerve activity.

In the latter case, new fundamental problems arise concerning the identity in time of changing systems, but these will have to be neglected here.

Our simple definition of change refers to a single system (e.g., a single subject). That is, it refers to within-system (e.g., within-subject) variation in time. The standard way to study such within-system variation in time is by means of time series analysis: the manifest time-dependent behaviour of some aspect of a single system is registered during a finite interval of time and subjected to appropriate statistical analysis. Hence, the results obtained in such a statistical analysis are generalizable to the previous and future behaviour of the given system at time points outside the finite observation interval. This can be summarized as follows: in a typical time series analysis the *system* is *fixed* whereas the *time points* are *random* (meaning that generalization takes place to a 'population' of time points).

It is noted that time series analysis of within-subject variation is not the standard way to analyse change in the social sciences. Instead of registering the time-dependent behaviour of a single system (usually a subject) during a finite, sufficiently long, interval of time, it is customary to register the behaviour of a sufficiently large sample of systems (subjects) at a few points in time. The between-systems variation at the given points in time then is subjected to a longitudinal analysis, the results of which are generalized to the population of systems from which the sample was drawn. This can be summarized as follows: in a typical longitudinal analysis the *time points* are *fixed*, whereas the *systems* are *random*.

Obviously, within-system variation of some behaviour and between-system variation of the same behaviour can be quite different. For instance, a particular behavioural aspect of each system may be constant in time, but this constant level may vary between different systems.

EXAMPLE 2

To give an example taken from Anderson (1992), the speed of conduction in a given peripheral nerve as well as the speed of basic information processing is constant in each human being across a large portion of the life-span, but these constant within-subject levels differ considerably between different subjects. Alternatively, a particular behavioural aspect of each system may be time-varying, but the way it varies in time may be the same across different systems. An example might be the entrainment of circadian rhythms of human beings living in the same environment: their daily variation of body temperature, for instance, is time-locked to (i.e., synchronized with) a common day–night cycle.

In view of these differences it is concluded that we will have to be careful to distinguish between two different types of analysis of change, namely one based on *within-system variation* (time series analysis) and another based on *between-systems variation* (longitudinal analysis). As will be explained at some length in what follows, this distinction mainly pertains to the possible lack of relationship between results obtained in a time series analysis of some behaviour and the results obtained in a longitudinal analysis of the same behaviour. That is, results obtained in an analysis of within-system variation may not be generalizable to a population of systems, and results obtained in an analysis of between-systems variation may not be generalizable to the future behaviour of a single system. This does not imply that the statistical models underlying time series analysis and longitudinal analysis have to be qualitatively different. In fact, we will see that longitudinal models as well as time series models can be regarded as special instances of the same canonical model of time-dependent change.

8.1.2 Simple examples of the merits of analyses of change

In the introductory section, three general answers were given to the question why a study of change might be worthwhile to pursue. We now give a couple of preliminary examples (in later sections, more elaborated examples will follow).

EXAMPLE 3

In their discussion of the advantages of longitudinal studies, Diggle, Liang, & Zeger (1994, pp. 17–18) present the following simple example. Consider first a cross-sectional study of the dependence of reading ability (Y) on age (x). Then one is restricted to the model:

$$Y_i = \beta_C x_i + \varepsilon_i$$

for subject $i = 1, \ldots, n$ where β_C represents the difference in average Y across two sub-populations which differ by one unit in x. With repeated observations obtained in a longitudinal study, this linear model can be extended to the form:

$$Y_{ij} = \beta_C x_{i1} + \beta_L (x_{ij} - x_{i1}) + \varepsilon_i$$

for subject $i = 1, \ldots, n$ and repeated measurements $j = 1, \ldots, m$, where β_C has the same interpretation as in the cross-sectional model and where β_L represents the expected change in Y over time per unit change in x for a given subject.

To estimate how an individual's reading ability changes with age from a cross-sectional study, one has to assume that $\beta_C = \beta_L$. In contrast, the latter strong assumption is unnecessary in a longitudinal study since both β_C and β_L can be estimated. Notice that there exists in general no *a priori* relationship between β_C and β_L (for instance, β_C and β_L can have opposite signs).

EXAMPLE 4

Granger-causality. Another example of the merits of an analysis of change is the possibility to identify causal relationships. This is best illustrated with the concept of Granger-causality in time series analysis, which is based on the standard notion of causality according to which (variation of) the cause precedes (variation of) its effect in time. Let $\mathbf{y}(t)' = [y_1(t), y_2(t)]$ be a bivariate time series, where the superscript ' denotes transposition (of the column vector $\mathbf{y}(t)$). For instance, $y_1(t)$ and $y_2(t), t = 1, 2, \ldots, T$ are repeated measurements of two distinct physiological response systems obtained with a single subject. Suppose that $\mathbf{y}(t)$ obeys the process model $\mathbf{y}(t) = \mathbf{B}\mathbf{y}(t-1) + \varepsilon(t)$, which in partitioned form is given by:

$$\left[\begin{array}{c} y_1(t) \\ y_2(t) \end{array} \right] = \left[\begin{array}{cc} \beta_{11} & \beta_{12} \\ \beta_{21} & \beta_{22} \end{array} \right] \left[\begin{array}{c} y_1(t-1) \\ y_2(t-1) \end{array} \right] + \left[\begin{array}{c} \varepsilon_1(t) \\ \varepsilon_2(t) \end{array} \right]$$

where $\beta_{ij}, i, j = 1, 2$, are autoregressive coefficients relating $\mathbf{y}(t)$ to $\mathbf{y}(t-1)$, and $\varepsilon(t)' = [\varepsilon_1(t), \varepsilon_2(t)]$ denotes residual unsystematic variation that cannot be predicted. With respect to this process model, if $y_1(t)$ Granger-causes $y_2(t)$ then $\beta_{12} = 0$. In contrast, if $y_2(t)$ Granger-causes $y_1(t)$ then $\beta_{21} = 0$.

Granger-causality is based on the notion that only the cause is a significant predictor of its effect. For a more general definition of Granger-causality and alternative ways to test it, the reader is referred to Lütkepohl (1991). In the realm of longitudinal analysis, a similar test of causality has been proposed in the context of crossed-lagged panel designs (cf. Baltes, Reese, & Nesselroade, 1977).

A fundamental discussion of empirical tests of causality is given in Nancy Cartwright's (1989) delightful treatise on philosophy of science. In Section 8.5 we will consider an alternative definition of causality.

8.2 A canonical model

Although one has to distinguish sharply between the structure of within-subject variation and the structure of between-subjects variation, this does not logically imply that the statistical models underlying longitudinal analysis and time series analysis are different. As a matter of fact, longitudinal models and time series models have so much in common that they both can be conceived of as special instances of a single canonical model. This canonical model, called the *state-space model*, will be introduced below. But we start with some general remarks.

As an extremely general canonical model, the state-space model covers all known linear and non-linear time series models, including for instance the Cox model (a standard model in Biometrics), the hidden Markov model (an increasingly popular model in speech recognition and artificial neural network theory) and time series versions of the loglinear model (Fahrmeir & Tutz, 1994).

The canonical state-space model allows for the definition of a unified estimation scheme that applies to all special instances, including time series and longitudinal variants. Only an outline of this estimation scheme will be given, in combination with ample references to the published literature on specific estimation techniques.

8.2.1   State-space model

Let $\eta(t)$ denote a q-variate stochastic process, $t \in \mathbb{N}$, where $\mathbb{N}$ denotes the integers. We will refer to $\eta(t)$ as the state at time t. In addition let the evolution of $\eta(t)$ be described by:

$$\eta(t+1) = \mathbf{f}_t[\eta(t)] + \zeta(t) \tag{8.1}$$

where $\mathbf{f}_t[.]$ is a non-linear vector-valued time-varying function obeying certain smoothness conditions (cf. Sage & Melsa, 1971) and where $\zeta(t)$ is a q-variate stochastic process called the *innovations process*. The state process is not observed directly, but instead the manifest p-variate process is $\mathbf{y}(t)$ given by:

$$\mathbf{y}(t) = \mathbf{h}_t[\eta(t)] + \varepsilon(t) \tag{8.2}$$

where the non-linear vector-valued function $\mathbf{h}_t[.]$ obeys the same smoothness conditions as $\mathbf{f}_t[.]$ and where $\varepsilon(t)$ denotes p-variate measurement noise.

The state-space model (8.1-8.2) is quite general, although an even more general definition could be given. But for our present purposes these equations suffice. Through additional specifications, many well-known types of process models are obtained as special instances of (8.1-8.2). These specifications mainly concern (a) the measurement scales of the state process $\eta(t)$ and manifest process $\mathbf{y}(t)$, which each can be metrical or categorical, (b) the forms of $\mathbf{f}_t[.]$ and $\mathbf{h}_t[.]$, which can be linear or non-linear, and (c) the distributional assumptions characterizing $\zeta(t)$ and $\varepsilon(t)$. Furthermore, the time index in (8.1-8.2) can be defined as real-valued ($t \in \mathbb{R}$) instead of integer-valued. We will not consider all possible specific types of process models thus obtained, but only present a few illustrations.

Linear state-space model.   Let $\eta(t)$ and $\mathbf{y}(t)$ be metrical processes, $\mathbf{f}_t[.]$ and $\mathbf{h}_t[.]$ be linear functions, and $\zeta(t)$ and $\varepsilon(t)$ be *Gaussian processes*[1]. Then the linear state-space model underlying normal (i.e., Gaussian) theory longitudinal factor analysis (Jöreskog, 1979) is obtained.

Denoting the linear functions $\mathbf{f}_t[.]$ and $\mathbf{h}_t[.]$ by, respectively, the (q,q)-dimensional matrix $\mathbf{F}_t$ and the (p,q)-dimensional matrix $\mathbf{H}_t$, yields the usual representation of the longitudinal factor model:

---

[1] A *Gaussian process* is defined as a stochastic time-dependent process for which the probability distributions at arbitrary finite subsets of time points are multivariate normal.

$$\begin{aligned}
\eta(t+1) &= \mathbf{F}_t\eta(t) + \zeta(t); \\
\mathbf{y}(t) &= \mathbf{H}_t\eta(t) + \varepsilon(t)
\end{aligned} \qquad (8.3)$$

where $\eta(t)$ is the longitudinal q-variate factor at measurement occasion t, $\mathbf{F}_t$ is the matrix of autoregression coefficients relating $\eta(t+1)$ to $\eta(t)$, and $\mathbf{H}_t$ is the matrix of factor loadings at t. For further details about the equivalence between the linear state-space model and the longitudinal factor model, the reader is referred to MacCallum & Ashby (1986) and Priestley & Subba Rao (1969).

The same representation (8.3) also underlies normal theory dynamic factor analysis of multivariate time series (Molenaar, 1994). In case the matrices $\mathbf{F}_t$ and $\mathbf{H}_t$ are invariant in time, $\mathbf{F}_t = \mathbf{F}$ and $\mathbf{H}_t = \mathbf{H}$, dynamic factor analysis can be carried out by means of the same structural equation modelling techniques which are commonly employed in longitudinal factor analysis (Molenaar, 1985; Molenaar & Nesselroade, 1998).

Generalized linear state-space model. Let the state evolution be defined as in (8.3), i.e., $\eta(t)$ is a metrical process, $\mathbf{f}_t[.]$ is a linear function given by the (q, q)-dimensional matrix $\mathbf{F}_t$ and $\zeta(t)$ is a Gaussian process.

In contrast, let $\mathbf{y}(t)$ be a categorical process and let $\mathbf{h}_t[.]$ be the natural response function (inverse of the canonical link function) associated with the particular exponential distribution family describing the categorical observations.

For instance, for the Bernoulli family the natural response function is

$$\mathbf{h}_t[\eta(t)] = \frac{\exp(\eta(t))}{1 + \exp(\eta(t))}$$

This specification yields the generalized linear state-space model for the analysis of categorical longitudinal and time series data. The excellent monograph of Fahrmeir & Tutz (1994) presents an in-depth discussion as well as applications of this particular variant of the state-space model.

Hidden Markov model. Let both $\eta(t)$ and $\mathbf{y}(t)$ be categorical processes and let $\mathbf{f}_t[.]$ and $\mathbf{h}_t[.]$ be given by, respectively, the (q, q)-dimensional matrix $\mathbf{F}_t$ and the (p, q)-dimensional matrix $\mathbf{H}_t$. This yields the hidden Markov model with discrete states and discrete observations. The hidden Markov model can be represented in exactly the same way as the linear state-space model (8.3), but now $\zeta(t)$ and $\varepsilon(t)$ have to be understood as martingale increments obeying a restricted covariance structure (cf. Elliott, Aggoun, & Moore, 1995, for a technical exposition). Hidden Markov models play an important role in such diverse fields as automatic speech recognition (e.g., Rabiner, 1989) and the learning behaviour of artificial neural networks (e.g., Crutchfield, 1994). When applied in the analysis of longitudinal categorical data, the same model is called the *latent Markov model* (Langeheine, 1994).

Doubly stochastic Poisson process. To give an example of a model in continuous time ($t \in \mathbb{R}$), let $\mathbf{y}(t)$ denote a categorical process, whereas $\eta(t)$ is a metrical process. More specifically, $\mathbf{y}(t)$ is defined as a univariate counting process in continuous time. For example the occurrence of each R-peak in ongoing cardiac activity defines a recurring event that gives rise to a counting process in continuous time. In addition, let $\eta(t)$ be composed of the time-varying intensity function $\lambda(t)$ in a Poisson process s and the $(q-1)$-variate metrical process $\xi(t)$:

$$\eta(t)' = [\lambda(t), \xi(t)]$$

In the context of our example in which $y(t)$ is a counting process of heart beats, the component $\xi(t)$ can be interpreted as describing the activity of the cardiac pacemaker determining $\lambda(t)$ (cf. Somsen, Molenaar, Van der Molen, & Jennings, 1991). Although the definition of $\mathbf{f}_t[.]$ is arbitrary, the function $\mathbf{h}_t[.]$ is simply the unity mapping.

In some regards, the doubly stochastic Poisson process (with $\mathbf{f}_t[.]$ linear) can be conceived of as a continuous-time version of the generalized linear state-space model. The definitive reference for time series applications of the doubly stochastic Poisson process is Snyder (1975). For applications to longitudinal data, the reader is referred to Andersen, Borgan, Gill, & Keiding (1993).

8.2.2   ML estimation in the state-space model

In this section a schematic presentation is given of a general technique for parameter estimation in the state-space model (8.1-8.2). Hence, in principle this technique is applicable to all specific variants discussed in Section 8.2.1.

To illustrate the schematic outline of the general technique, two simple applications will be given to time series analysis and longitudinal analysis, respectively.

Consider the state-space model (8.1-8.2) depending upon unknown, possibly time-varying and/or stochastic parameters $\theta_{t_j}, t \in \mathbb{N}, j = 1, 2, \ldots, J$, which are collected in the J-dimensional vector θ_t:

$$
\begin{aligned}
\eta(t+1) &= \mathbf{f}_t[\eta(t); \theta_t] + \zeta(t) \\
\mathbf{y}(t) &= \mathbf{h}_t[\eta(t); \theta_t] + \varepsilon(t) \\
\operatorname{cov}[\zeta(t), \zeta'(t+k)] &= \delta(k)\mathbf{C}_\zeta(\theta_t); \\
\operatorname{cov}[\varepsilon(t), \varepsilon'(t+k)] &= \delta(k)\mathbf{C}_\varepsilon(\theta_t)
\end{aligned}
\tag{8.4}
$$

where $\delta(k) = 1$ if $k = 0$ and $\delta(k) = 0$ if $k \neq 0$. Hence, $\zeta(t)$ and $\varepsilon(t)$ can each have non-zero covariance at each time t, but have zero covariances at different times t and $t+k$ (this is not a restrictive assumption because models in which this does not hold can always be rewritten in this way). An estimator for θ_t is obtained by minimizing the discrepancy function derived by means of an appropriate method of estimation (e.g., maximum likelihood, generalized least squares, etc.). Such a discrepancy function not only depends upon the manifest process $\mathbf{y}(t)$, but also on the latent state process $\eta(t)$ (or, equivalently, on $\varepsilon(t)$ and $\zeta(t)$). Hence, the *expectation-maximization (EM) algorithm* (cf. Orchard & Woodbury, 1971; Dempster, Laird, & Rubin, 1977) constitutes a natural approach to the minimization of this discrepancy function. The EM algorithm concerned consists of iteration of two steps (see Figure 8.1).

Choose an initial estimate of θ_t.

Until convergence, perform the following two steps:

E-step: given the estimate of θ_t obtained in the previous iteration, estimate the latent state process $\eta(t)$;

M-step: given the estimated latent state process $\eta(t)$ obtained in the E-step, maximize the discrepancy function with respect to θ_t and obtain a new estimate of θ_t.

Figure 8.1: The EM-algorithm.

8.2.2.1 Illustrative application to time series analysis

In this section we present a simple application of the general estimation technique to time series analysis. The illustration is taken from Molenaar (1994), to which the reader is referred for further details including algorithmic specification and additional illustrations. It concerns a linear time-varying instance of the state-space model (8.3) with metrical (Gaussian) 5-variate observations $\mathbf{y}(t)$ and ditto univariate state process $\eta(t)$ in discrete time $t \in \mathbb{N}$.

The parameter vector θ_t in (8.4) is allowed to vary in time, thus accommodating the eventual non-stationarity of $\mathbf{y}(t)$. In the application we have in mind it will generally be unknown which parameters are time-varying and how they vary in time. Given this lack of information, θ_t can be represented as

$$\theta_t = \theta_0 + \theta_1 t + \theta_2 t^2 + \ldots + \theta_d t^d \qquad (8.5)$$

This simple polynomial function can be replaced by any other function of t, for instance step functions, exponentials, and/or orthogonal (e.g. Chebyshev) polynomials. The important decision is whether θ_t is considered to be *non-random* as in (8.5), or *random*. Notice that in (8.5) the degree of the polynomial associated with each element of θ_t may be different.

EXAMPLE 5

As a simple application of the EM algorithm, consider the following instance of (8.3):

$$\eta(t+1) \quad = \quad (0.7 - 0.7\tau)\eta(t) + \zeta(t)$$

$$
\begin{aligned}
\mathbf{y}(t) &= \mathbf{h}\eta(t) + \varepsilon(t) & (8.6) \\
c_\zeta(0) &= 1, \\
\mathbf{h}' &= [0.9, 0.8, 0.7, 0.6, 0.5] \\
\mathbf{C}_\varepsilon(0) &= \mathrm{diag}[1, 1, 1, 1, 1]
\end{aligned}
$$

Here the state is a univariate non-stationary first-order autoregression and the autoregressive coefficient is given by $\mathbf{f}_t = 0.7 - 0.7\tau, \tau = \frac{t}{T}$, where T is the number of equidistant measurement occasions. Hence, the autoregressive coefficient is $f_1 = 0.7$ at $t = 1$ and decays linearly to $f_T = 0$ at $t = T$. $\mathbf{y}(t)$ is a manifest 5-variate series and diag[ ] denotes a diagonal matrix. Both $\zeta(t)$ and $\varepsilon(t)$ are white-noise processes.

This model is used to generate a single realization of $\mathbf{y}(t)$ for $T = 50$ time points. Next various candidate models are fitted to this particular realization by means of the EM algorithm (in which $c_\zeta(0)$ has been fixed at $c_\zeta(0) = 1$ because it is not identified). The best fitting model according to some suitable criterion is chosen, yielding the following estimates:

$$
\begin{aligned}
\widehat{\mathbf{f}}_t(\theta_\tau) &= 0.74 - 0.72\tau, \\
\widehat{\widetilde{\mathbf{h}}}'(\theta_t) &= [1.22, 0.82, 0.92, 0.63, 0.56], \\
\widehat{\mathbf{C}}_\varepsilon(\theta_t) &= \mathrm{diag}[0.74, 1.32, 1.02, 0.78, 1.08]
\end{aligned}
$$

Hence, it appears, even for these limited time series data ($T = 50$), that the EM algorithm correctly recovers the non-stationary coefficient of the state autoregression.

Illustrative application to longitudinal analysis. Next, we discuss an application of the general estimation technique to longitudinal analysis. In fact, the longitudinal data are simulated by means of the same linear time-varying state-space model as used in Section 8.2.2.1. To obtain a longitudinal data set, we first simulate N independent replications (cases) according to the same model (8.6), again with $T = 50$. This yields an ensemble of N manifest 5-variate time series $\mathbf{y}_i(t), i = 1, 2, \ldots, N; t = 1, 2, \ldots, 50$. Next, M time points $t_j, j = 1, 2, \ldots, M$ are chosen and the set $\{\mathbf{y}_i(t_j)|i = 1, 2, \ldots, N; j = 1, 2, \ldots, M\}$ comprises the longitudinal data.

More specifically, we take $N = 50$ replications and $M = 3$ fixed time points, at $t_j, j = 1, 2$ and 4. Accordingly, it follows (by substituting $\frac{t_j}{T}$ for τ in the first line of (8.6)) that the true autoregressive coefficient relating the state process at t_2 to t_1 equals $f_{2,1} = 0.672$, while in addition the true autoregressive coefficient relating the state process at t_4 to t_2 equals $f_{4,2} = 0.424$. The true values of the remaining parameters are the same as in (8.6).

Application of the EM algorithm yields the following estimates:

$$\widehat{f}_{2,1}(\theta_t) = 0.78,$$
$$\widehat{f}_{4,2}(\theta_t) = 0.41$$
$$\widehat{h}'(\theta_t) = [0.91, 0.79, 0.47, 0.74, 0.68]$$
$$\widehat{C}_\varepsilon(\theta_t) = \text{diag}[0.84, 0.93, 0.95, 0.98, 10.05]$$

It appears that the algorithm faithfully recovers the true parameter values. Notice that the current longitudinal data set comprises $N = 50$ 5-variate time series, one for each $n \in N$, each of length $M = 3$. In contrast, the simulated data set in the previous section (8.2.2.1) comprises $N = 1$ 5-variate time series of length $T = 50$. Hence, the current longitudinal data set is larger than the time series data set used in the previous section.

Notice also that the longitudinal analysis is based on the between-replications (between-cases) variation, whereas the time series analysis was based on the within-case variation. In fact, the longitudinal analysis corresponds to a longitudinal factor analysis that can be carried out by means of standardly available structural equation modelling software (e.g., Jöreskog & Sörbom, 1993). For similar comparisons between time series analysis and longitudinal analysis, the reader is referred to Molenaar (1994).

8.3   Optimal control

An analysis of change leads to the possibility of optimal control of the processes under scrutiny. That is, the results of an analysis of change may allow for the application of interventions, strategically chosen qua timing and dose, that steer a particular process in desired directions while minimizing the costs involved. Optimal control constitutes a basic tool in the engineering sciences (e.g., Goodwin & Sin, 1984), but its potential domain of application consists of all longitudinal and time series analyses where the measured process $\mathbf{y}(t)$ includes a subset of control variables that can be set at arbitrary values (for instance, the prescribed amount of medication intake). Modern control theory (e.g., Whittle, 1990) can handle the complexities that are characteristic of analyses of change in which no *a priori* information is available about the stochastic processes under investigation. In fact, optimal control can be applied while such an analysis of change is in progress (i.e., on-line).

In what follows we will consider the most basic version of optimal control in which it is assumed that $\mathbf{y}(t)$ is a linear Gaussian process. Moreover, the *cost function* (i.e., the criterion that the controller wants to minimize; see below) is chosen to be a quadratic function. This yields the Linear-Quadratic-Gaussian (LQG) control theory. For extensions to non-linear processes the reader is referred to Isidori (1989); extensions to more general types of cost function are described in Whittle (1990).

We already indicated that the linear state-space model (8.3) underlies both longitudinal factor analysis and linear time series analysis. It therefore will come as no great surprise that LQG control applies to longitudinal as well as linear time series models. Yet to the best of our knowledge the use of LQG control in a longitudinal setting appears to be almost non-existent (the only reference we know of is (Press, 1972, Chapter 14). Hence, we will restrict attention to application of LQG in time series analysis.

LQG control has several noteworthy characteristics. For instance, it yields a recursive closed-loop (feedback) controller that is easily implemented. That is, the optimal setting of the control variables at each time point is determined according to a model that is formally similar to the state-space model (8.1-8.2). The input to this model at each time t is the predicted deviance of the measured process with respect to its desired value at the next time point $t + 1$, the output consists of the optimal setting of the control variables at time t so that the cost function expressing this deviance is minimized. LQG control also has the interesting feature that its computation is not affected by the contingent fact whether or not the optimal values of the control variables are actually realized. This allows for a posteriori computation of optimal control in those cases where the actual experimental study of change already has been finished. It also can accommodate the situation where the true optimal settings of the control variables cannot be realized perfectly during an ongoing experimental study of change.

8.3.1   Outline of LQG control

Consider a time series analysis based on the linear state-space model (8.3). To ease the presentation we use a simplified version of (8.3) in which the state process is not latent, i.e., $\mathbf{y}(t) = \eta(t)$ (cf. Whittle (1990), for the general case). Moreover, the p-variate process $\mathbf{y}(t)$ is decomposed into the subset of r control variables $\mathbf{z}(t)$ and the $s = p - r$ dependent (controlled) variables $\mathbf{x}(t)$:

$$\mathbf{y}'(t) = [\mathbf{x}'(t), \mathbf{z}'(t)]$$

Then the following instance of the linear state-space model is obtained:

$$\mathbf{x}(t + 1) = \mu(t + 1) + \mathbf{F}_t \xi(t) + \mathbf{B}_t \mathbf{z}(t) + \zeta(t) \tag{8.7}$$

where $\mathbf{B}_t$ is (s, r)-dimensional and where $\mu(t+1)$ denotes an s-dimensional deterministic trend function.

Denote the desired value of $\mathbf{x}(t)$ by $\mathbf{x} * (t)$. Similarly, denote the desired value of $\mathbf{z}(t)$ by $\mathbf{z}^*(t)$. Both $\mathbf{x}^*(t)$ and $\mathbf{z}^*(t)$ are chosen by the controlling agent. The instantaneous cost function at each time t then is defined by

$$
\begin{aligned}
c(t) \;=\; & E\{[\mathbf{x}(t) - \mathbf{x}^*(t)]'\mathbf{M}_t[\mathbf{x}(t) - \mathbf{x}^*(t)] \\
& + [\mathbf{z}(t-1) - \mathbf{z}^*(t-1)]'\mathbf{N}_{t-1}[\mathbf{z}(t-1) - \mathbf{z}^*(t-1)]\}
\end{aligned}
\tag{8.8}
$$

where $\mathbf{M}_t$ and $\mathbf{N}_{t-1}$ are (s,s)-dimensional and (r,r)-dimensional matrices, respectively, chosen by the controlling agent. The instantaneous cost function $c(t)$ is a quadratic function of deviances $\mathbf{x}(t) - \mathbf{x}^*(t)$, weighted by $\mathbf{M}_t$, and deviances $\mathbf{z}(t-1) - \mathbf{z}^*(t-1)$, weighted by $\mathbf{N}_{t-1}$. The latter quadratic function of deviances $\mathbf{z}(t-1) - \mathbf{z}^*(t-1)$ penalizes the costs involved in exercising control. The total cost function is defined as the sum of $c(t)$ over time points $t = 1, 2, \ldots, T$, where T is called the *horizon* of the control problem.

It can be shown (cf. Whittle, 1990) that the total LQG cost function is minimized by an adaptive feedback function schematically given by

$$\bar{\mathbf{z}}(t) = \mathbf{A}_t \mathbf{x}(t) + \mathbf{g}_t \tag{8.9}$$

where $\mathbf{A}_t$ is a recursive function of $\mathbf{F}_t$ and $\mathbf{B}_t$ in (8.7) yielding the stochastic component of the optimal control. In addition, $\mathbf{g}_t$ is a recursive function of $\mu(t)$ and $\mathbf{x}^*(t)$, yielding the deterministic component of the optimal control (cf. Molenaar, 1987, for the defining equations).

8.3.2   Application to the psychotherapeutic process

To illustrate the abstract scheme of optimal LQG control given in the previous section, we will concisely consider its application in a psychotherapeutic process analysis as originally reported in Molenaar (1987).

EXAMPLE 6

The psychotherapy concerned consisted of 61 sessions, twice each week, with a 26-year-old client suffering from physical tension, anxiety, lack of self-confidence and social poise. The client variables were: x_1: emotional tone (EMOTION), x_2: self-esteem (SELF), x_3: social activities (SOCIAL), and x_4: physical fitness (PHYSICAL). They were scaled so that $+1$ indicates the presence of severe problems and -1 a complete lack of problems. The control variables were the intensity of the following therapeutic manipulations: z_1: counselling and modelling (COUNSEL), z_2: positive/negative reinforcement (REINFORCE), and z_3: interactive style (INTERACT). They were also scaled so that $+1$ indicates maximal intensity of a manipulation and -1 a complete lack of it. Figure 8.2 shows the time course of the client variables; Figure 8.3 depicts the time course of the therapist (control) variables.

Computation of LQG optimal control was carried out after completion of the psychotherapy. As noted before, this does not affect the obtained values of $\bar{\mathbf{z}}(t)$, although there were of course no benefits for the client concerned. The model (8.7) was fitted to the data in an on-line fashion (cf. Molenaar, 1987, for a listing of the estimation equations). The parameter estimates were then used in (8.9) to determine the optimal control at each time (session) $t = 1, 2, \ldots, 61$. The desired path for the client variables was chosen to be $\mathbf{x}^*(t)' = [-0.5, -0.5, -0.5, -0.5]$, indicating a low prevalence of problems. The desired path of the control variables was chosen in a similar way. Both weight matrices $\mathbf{M}_t$ and $\mathbf{N}_t$ were chosen to be the identity matrix of appropriate dimensions.

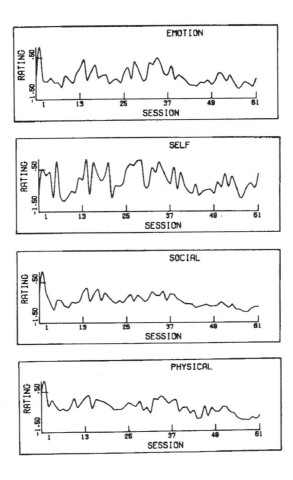

Figure 8.2: Time course of client variables.

Figure 8.4 depicts the time course of $\mathbf{g}_t$ in (8.9), i.e., the deterministic component of optimal LQG control. It is seen that COUNSEL is very instrumental in controlling the mean trend of the client variables during the initial part of the sequence of sessions, but its effectiveness is waning as the psychotherapy continues. In contrast, REINFORCE appears to have a distinctively negative effect on the trend of the client variables, especially during the initial and final parts of the sequence of sessions. This points at a counterproductive effect of REINFORCE during this psychotherapy, which was acknowledged a posteriori by the therapist. Finally, the effectiveness of INTERACT in controlling is increasing from counterproductive at the beginning of the sequence of sessions to instrumental at the end.

Apart from the deterministic component $\mathbf{g}_t$, (8.9) also provides the stochastic component $\mathbf{A}_t\mathbf{x}(t)$ of $\bar{\mathbf{z}}(t)$ which is important for short-term cor-

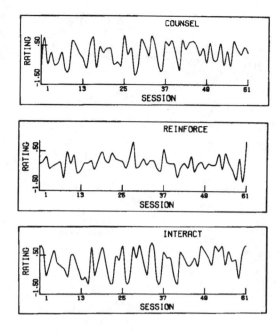

Figure 8.3: Time course of therapist variables.

rections. The elements of the time-varying matrix $\mathbf{A}_t$ can be plotted as function of time in the same manner as in Figure 8.4. Each of these plots shows the optimal stochastic feedback of one of the client variables on one of the control variables. The reader is referred to Molenaar (1987) for a complete presentation of these plots.

8.4 Ergodicity

In this section we will discuss the relationship between state-space analyses of time series describing intra-individual (co-)variation (e.g., Molenaar, 1985) and longitudinal factor analyses of inter-individual (co-)variation (Jöreskog, 1979). The main question to be answered is:

> *'Under which conditions an application of the linear state-space model (8.3) to longitudinal data will yield results that are lawfully related to (e.g., are qualitatively the same as) the results of an application of (8.3) to analogous time series data.'*

More specifically, consider a given test-battery composed of p tests which is used in both a longitudinal study and a time series study.

In the longitudinal study the test-battery is administered at T measurement occasions (where T usually is small) to a sample of N subjects (N

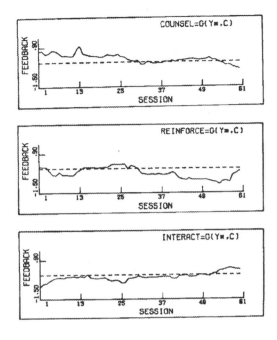

Figure 8.4: Time course of $\mathbf{g}_t$ in Equation 8.9.

usually is large), randomly drawn from some homogeneous population $\mathcal{P}$. In the time series study the same test-battery is administered at T measurement occasions (T usually is large) to a single subject ($N = 1$), randomly drawn from the same population $\mathcal{P}$. Suppose that an instance of the linear state-space model (8.3) with q-dimensional latent state process yields a satisfactory fit to the longitudinal data. Phrased in more customary jargon, suppose it is found that a longitudinal q-factor model yields a satisfactory fit to the data obtained in the longitudinal design. Then: *under which conditions can we expect that this instance of (8.3) with q-variate latent state process $\eta(t)$ (i.e., a dynamic q-factor model) also will yield a satisfactory fit to the data obtained in the time series design?*

An answer to this question has major theoretical and practical implications. We will discuss theoretical implications below, but first will consider some practical implications. Suppose that there exist conditions under which there is no lawful relationship between a longitudinal factor analysis and dynamic factor analysis. Then it would follow that the results obtained in a longitudinal factor analysis are not predictive of the sequential behaviour of each single subject belonging to the longitudinal sample. Now longitudinal factor analysis is a much more fashionable technique than dynamic factor analysis (or stated more generally, statistical analysis of interindividual variation is much more common in the social sciences than time series analysis). Hence, there is a fair chance that, for instance, psychological tests will have been constructed and validated in a standard longitudinal factor analysis. It may thus have been concluded, for instance, that a particular test obeys a 1-factor model at each measurement occasion, that the factor loadings stay invariant between measurement occasions and that the intercorrelations of the factor between measurement occasions are high. If this test then is used in a clinical or counselling setting to predict the scores of a *single* subject belonging to the population from which the longitudinal sample was drawn, it may yield entirely irrelevant results!

That is, it may happen that the factorial structure of the test scores of this subject across time lacks all the features of the longitudinal factor model. For instance, the scores of this particular subject may actually obey a (dynamic) factor model with a different number of factors at consecutive measurement occasions, the factor loadings for this subject may change substantially across time, and/or the stability of factor scores may be low. Evidently, this state of affairs (a large discrepancy between the factor models for inter- and intra-individual (co-)variation) will negatively affect the appropriateness of decisions based on the longitudinal factor structure of the test in individual counselling or clinical intervention.

As to the more theoretical consequences of a possible lack of lawful relationships between analyses of inter- and intra-individual variation, it is noted that there are some which would seem to affect the foundations of Psychometrics. This is perhaps best illustrated in Lord & Novick's (1968) authoritative monograph on classical test theory, at the point where they introduce the concept of *true score*. First, the concept of true score is defined for a single subject, namely as the mean of the distribution of observed scores which would be obtained by taking a large number (infinitely many in theory) of repeated measurements of this subject. Of course this distribution is a measure of intra-individual variation:

> '... we conceive initially of a sequence of independent observations, ..., and consider some effects, such as the subject's ability, to be constant, and others, such as the transient state of the person, to be random. We then consider the distribution that might be obtained over a sequence of such statistically independent measurements if each were governed by the propensity distribution $F_{ga}(x_{ga})$ of the random variable X_{ga}. The function $F_{ga}(x_{ga})$ is a cumulative distribution function defined over repeated statistically independent measurements on the same person.'

And further on:

> 'A mathematically convenient way of defining a true score is as the expected observed score with respect to the propensity distribution of a given person a on a given measurement g.'

(Lord & Novick, 1968, p. 30)

Then a shift in perspective is made, because it is deemed impossible to actually obtain the requisite stationary series of scores to determine the distribution for a single subject. Instead of considering a large number of repeated measurements with a single subject, classical test theory then is derived for the situation where a large number of subjects is measured at a single measurement occasion:

> 'We have to this point dealt with hypothetical replications (described by the propensity distribution) on one person. Primarily, test theory treats individual differences or, equivalently, the distribution of measurements over people.'
> (Lord & Novick, 1968, p. 32)

Hence, in the foundation of classical test theory, a shift is made from the characterization of intra-individual variation to a characterization of inter-individual variation. It is evident that the plausibility of this shift is at stake in those cases where there exists no lawful relationship between the two distributions concerned. Now what can be said about the conditions under which there is, and the conditions under which there is not, a lawful relationship between longitudinal and time series analysis? This question is at a formal level addressed in the mathematical statistical discipline called *ergodic theory* (e.g., Petersen, 1983). An ensemble of stochastic systems is called *ergodic* if a statistical analysis of the time series describing the sequential behaviour of a single system yields asymptotically (i.e., when the length of the analysed series approaches infinity) the same results as a statistical analysis of the ensemble of systems at a single time. Hence, ergodic theory provides a principled answer to the question under which conditions longitudinal and time series analysis yield the same results. Although the classical ergodic theorems are quite abstract and delicate, their content can for our purposes be roughly summarized as follows.

In order to be ergodic, an ensemble of stochastic systems has to be such that the time series describing the sequential behaviour of each system is *stationary*. For the present purposes, stationarity can be defined as follows: *the parameter matrices in (8.3) should not depend upon time t.* More specifically, $F_t = F$ and $H_t = H$ in (8.3). It is noted that the relation between ergodicity and stationarity is much more intricate than this simple equivalence, but we will not enter into such elaborations since they are complicated and out of scope in the present chapter.

Bearing in mind this qualification, the preliminary conclusion from ergodic theory is that there is a lawful relationship between longitudinal and time series analysis if the manifest process under study is stationary. In contrast, the existence of this lawful relationship is questionable if the process is non-stationary.

Molenaar (1997) presents results of a Monte Carlo simulation study which show that the following situation may be easily obtained: the structure of intra-individual covariation is different for each subject in a population, but a standard factor analysis of the inter-individual covariation for these same subjects yields a satisfactorily fitting 1-factor solution! The latter 1-factor solution, while faithfully describing the structure of inter-individual covariation, does not conform to any dynamic factor model describing the structures of intra-individual covariation in the population concerned. Nesselroade & Molenaar (1999) describe a statistical test of ergodicity for application to an ensemble of short time series obtained with multiple subjects.

8.4.1 Simulation study

We now will describe the results of an illustrative simulation study to present a concrete instance of the differences between the structure of intra-individual and inter-individual covariation we have been discussing thus far. In broad outline the present study follows the design used in the analogous study reported in Molenaar (1997). There is one important distinction, however. Presently we will compare a longitudinal factor analysis with dynamic factor analysis, whereas in Molenaar (1997) this comparison was restricted to a cross-sectional factor analysis and dynamic factor analysis.

Consider the situation in which we have a sample of N distinct subjects (cases), where each subject $i = 1, \ldots, N$ has been repeatedly administered the same p-variate test at $t = 1, \ldots, T$ measurement occasions. This yields an ensemble of N p-variate time series $\mathbf{y}_i(t), t = 1, \ldots, T; i = 1, \ldots, N$. Suppose that the structure of intra-individual covariation of $\mathbf{y}_i(t)$ is *different* for *each* distinct subject i. More specifically, suppose that the dynamic factor model (8.3) describing the intra-individual covariance structure for each subject i differs from all other $N - 1$ subjects in the sample. Clearly, such an ensemble would be non-ergodic. In fact, such an ensemble would be heterogeneous in a more strong sense than mere non-ergodicity. The question which we would like to answer now is, what will be the results of carrying out a longitudinal factor analysis on this ensemble.

To answer this question we generate an ensemble of artificial data in the following way. For $N_1 = 100, p = 4$ variate time series are generated ($T = 250$) according to a dynamic 1-factor model:

$$
\begin{aligned}
\eta_i(t+1) &= \mathbf{F}_i \eta_i(t) + \zeta_i(t) \\
\mathbf{y}_i(t) &= \mathbf{H}_i \eta(t) + \varepsilon_i(t); \\
&\quad (i = 1, \ldots, 100; t = 1, \ldots, 250)
\end{aligned}
\tag{8.10}
$$

Notice that the autoregressive coefficient $\mathbf{F}_i$, the loadings $\mathbf{H}_i$, as well as the covariances $\text{cov}[\zeta_i(t), \zeta_i(t)'] = \mathbf{C}_{\zeta_i}(0)$ and $\text{cov}[\varepsilon_i(t), \varepsilon_i(t)'] = \mathbf{C}_{\varepsilon_i}(0)$ are all different for each subject i.

In a similar vein, we generate for another $N_2 = 100$ cases $p = 4$ variate time series according to a dynamic 2-factor model obeying the same general form as (8.10), but where $\eta_i(t)$ and $\zeta_i(t)$ now are 2-variate processes. Again, all coefficient matrices are different for each subject i. Finally, for another $N_3 = 100$ cases $p = 4$ variate time series are generated in the same way as before according to a dynamic 3-factor model obeying (8.10) with $\eta_i(t)$ and $\zeta_i(t)$ 3-variate processes and with all coefficient matrices different for each distinct subject i. We thus obtain a completely heterogeneous ensemble of $N = N_1 + N_2 + N_3 = 300$ 4-variate time series.

Within the time interval $t = 1, \ldots, 250$ we arbitrarily choose two consecutive time points t_1 and $t_2 = t_1 + 1$. At these two time points the 4-variate vectors $\mathbf{y}_i(t_1)$ and $\mathbf{y}_i(t_2), i = 1, \ldots, 300$, comprise our longitudinal data set. Next, the longitudinal data set thus obtained is subjected to a straightforward longitudinal factor analysis, yielding the estimated structure of inter-individual covariation of $\mathbf{y}_i(t)$.

```
2.40
1.22   3.19
0.94   1.77   3.52
0.95   1.74   1.84   3.21
0.53   0.53   0.40   0.27   2.52
0.48   0.80   0.86   0.66   1.15   3.79
0.39   0.81   0.77   0.57   1.02   2.13   3.82
0.47   0.84   0.66   0.71   0.93   2.09   2.56   3.63
```

Table 8.1: Observed longitudinal covariance matrix $N = 300$ 4-variate test scores at two measurement occasions.

	η_1	η_2
$y_1(t_1)$	1.00	–
$y_2(t_1)$	1.74 (0.22)	–
$y_3(t_1)$	1.68 (0.22)	–
$y_4(t_1)$	1.64 (0.21)	–
$y_1(t_2)$	–	1.00
$y_2(t_2)$	–	2.05 (0.31)
$y_3(t_2)$	–	2.42 (0.36)
$y_4(t_2)$	–	2.36 (0.35)

Table 8.2: H-matrix. Estimated factor loadings in longitudinal factor analysis (Standard errors are within parentheses).

The observed $(8,8)$-dimensional longitudinal covariance matrix is given in Table 8.1. This covariance matrix does not appear to have any special features and could have been obtained with a typical empirical data set. It turns out that a longitudinal factor model yields a satisfactory description of the inter-individual longitudinal covariance structure of the $N = 300$ subjects: $\chi^2 = 27.34, df = 19, p \approx 0.10$. Moreover, the standardized residuals are small (only one is just significant). The matrix of estimated factor loadings is presented in Table 8.2 and does not seem to require special comment. The same can be said with respect to the estimated specific variances: they

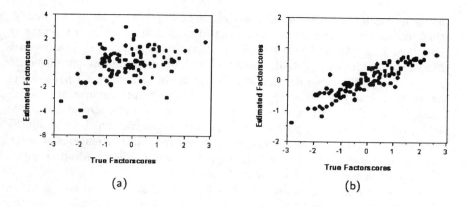

Figure 8.5: True and estimated factor scores at (a) t_1 and (b) t_2.

are all significantly different from zero. Also the variances of the longitudinal factor $\eta(t)$ at time points t_1 and t_2 are significantly different from zero, as is the intercorrelation between $\eta(t_1)$ and $\eta(t_2)$.

It appears that the fit of the linear state-space model (8.2) to the intersubjective covariance structure of $\mathbf{y}_i(t)$ is satisfactory. Stated otherwise, the longitudinal factor analysis of our strongly heterogeneous (non-ergodic) ensemble yields a satisfactorily fitting model. This clearly shows that the results of an analysis of the inter-subjective structure of covariance may have no relationship to the intra-individual covariance structure characterizing each of the subjects comprising the longitudinal sample. To elucidate some of the implications of this remarkable result for applied psychology, we will estimate the factor scores of each subject according to the longitudinal factor model and compare these estimated longitudinal factor scores with the true dynamic factor scores used in simulating the data.

To compare the estimated factor scores in the fitted longitudinal factor model with the true factor scores in the dynamic factor model used to generate the data ensemble, we have to take notice that this ensemble comprises three distinct subensembles. In the first subensemble ($N_1 = 100$) the structure of intra-individual covariation of each subject obeys a dynamic 1-factor model (in which the parameters differ between subjects). Hence, the number of true factor scores to be considered for each subject in this subensemble is two; one at t_1 and one at t_2. In the second subensemble ($N_2 = 100$) each subject obeys a dynamic 2-factor model (in which the parameters differ between subjects). Hence, the number of true factor scores to be considered in this subensemble is four; two at t_1 and two at t_2. The number of true factor scores in the third subensemble ($N_3 = 100$) is six; three at t_1 and three at t_2.

Starting with the subensemble in which subjects obey idiosyncratic dynamic 1-factor models, it is found that the correlation between the true and estimated factor scores at t_1 is 0.407, while the analogous correlation at t_2 is 0.896. The observed correlation of 0.407 at t_1 is much smaller than commonly found in simulation studies of estimated factor scores in standard longitudinal factor analysis of homogeneous data (e.g., Boomsma, Molenaar, & Orlebeke, 1990). In the latter kind of simulation studies each subject obeys the same longitudinal factor model (in which all parameters are invariant across subjects), in conformance with the assumptions underlying standard longitudinal factor analysis. For a sample size of $N_1 = 100$ and given the pattern of parameter values in the longitudinal 1-factor model currently obtained, one then can expect to find that the correlations between estimated and true factor scores are higher than 0.9. Figure 8.5 shows plots of the true and estimated factor scores at t_1 and t_2.

In the second subensemble each subject is characterized by two true (dynamic) factor scores at t_1 and two at t_2. The correlations of the estimated longitudinal factor scores at t_1 and t_2 with the true scores on the first dynamic factor are, respectively, 0.372 and 0.593. The correlations of the estimated longitudinal factor scores at t_1 and t_2 with the true scores on the second dynamic factor are, respectively, -0.366 and 0.676. Especially at t_1, but also at t_2, these correlations are disturbingly low. In the third subensemble each subject is characterized by three true (dynamic) factor scores at t_1 and three at t_2.

The correlation of the estimated longitudinal factor scores at t_1 with the true scores on the first dynamic factor is 0.343 (see Figure 8.6(a)), while the analogous correlation at t_2 is 0.573 (see Figure 8.6(b)). The correlation of the estimated longitudinal factor scores at t_1 with the true scores on the second dynamic factor is -0.306 (see Figure 8.6(c)), while the analogous correlation at t_2 is 0.556 (see Figure 8.6(d)). Finally, the correlation of the estimated longitudinal factor scores at t_1 with the true scores on the third dynamic factor is -0.326 (see Figure 8.6(e)), while the analogous correlation at t_2 is 0.452 (see Figure 8.6(f)). Again, all these correlations are very low, implying that the longitudinal factor model of inter-individual covariance structure bears no clear relationship to the intra-individual covariance structure characterizing individual time-dependent trajectories. In particular, the longitudinal factor model will yield very unreliable predictions concerning the future course of individual subjects.

8.5   General discussion and conclusion

In the initial sections of this chapter an attempt was made to specify the merits of analyses of change. One of these merits concerns the possibility to identify causal relationships, for instance by means of a test for Granger-causality. Tests for Granger-causality are based on the standard notion that a cause precedes its effects in time. This standard notion of causality would seem plausible in the study of most physical processes, but may be questionable if applied to the actions of rational human beings. Consider for instance a subject who has certain expectations about a future state

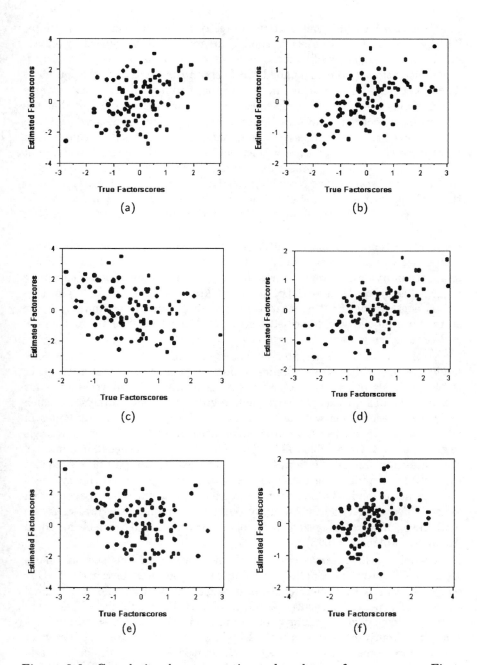

Figure 8.6: Correlation between estimated and true factor scores. First factor: (a) at t_1, Correlation: 0.343; (b) at t_2, Correlation: 0.573. Second factor: (c) at t_1, Correlation: -0.306; (d) at t_2, Correlation: 0.556. Third factor: (e) at t_1, Correlation: -0.326; (f) at t_2, Correlation: 0.452.

of affairs and bases his/her current course of action on these expectations. The behaviour of this subject at some time point t will be caused by a state of affairs that is expected to materialize at a later time point $t' > t$. Objective registrations (from a so-called *third-person perspective*) of this subject's time-dependent behaviour as function of the manifest environmental states of affair may not obey Granger-causality, yet our assumption was that the behaviour concerned is causally determined. Apparently, one needs a different notion of causality than the one underlying Granger-causality in order to capture the effects of expectations on human actions. Such a different notion of causal relationships based on expectations has been developed in the context of state-space modelling (cf. Holly & Hallett, 1989). It is found that taking into account the distinct effects on human actions caused by expectancies often leads to improved prediction and control of econometric processes.

Another major emphasis in this chapter was on showing the many communalities which exist between a wide range of parametric models of intra- and inter-individual change. It was shown that the state-space model can be regarded as a canonical model of almost all known time series and longitudinal models. Moreover, a general technique for parameter estimation in the state-space model was described which pertains to all special longitudinal and time series variants of this model.

At the close of this chapter it should be stressed that the state-space model concerned is also a canonical model for more traditional approaches to the analysis of change. That is, standard MAN(C)OVA techniques for the analysis of repeated measurement, regression (trend) analyses of such repeated measures, as well as non-standard design analysis techniques in which the within-subject covariance structure is modeled in alternative ways (e.g., Vonesh & Chinchilli, 1997), can all be regarded as special instances of the state-space model. In fact, for many of these techniques it is sufficient to rewrite the underlying model as an instance of the normal theory longitudinal factor model (which is an instance of the linear state-space model, as explained earlier) and then apply publicly available structural equation modelling software (Jöreskog & Sörbom, 1993). Details can be found in Rovine & Molenaar (1998).

It would seem a fair assessment of this chapter on longitudinal analysis to characterize its contents as being somewhat non-conventional. One reason for this is that there exists a growing literature on the longitudinal analysis of repeated measures which is of very high quality. To mention only a few recent monographs of outstanding quality (which should be consulted for many more references): Diggle et al. (1994); Hand & Crowder (1996); and Vonesh & Chinchilli (1997). It would be very difficult to add something substantial to this literature in a chapter like this. Another reason is that the topics which have been put to the fore in this chapter do not figure predominantly in the literature on longitudinal analysis. Yet, we hope to have made clear that each of these topics (the communalities between time series and longitudinal models, the possibility to exercise optimal control, the qualitative differences between the structure of intra- and inter-individual covariation) may have important consequences for analyses of change. If this is indeed the case, then we consider our mission in this chapter fulfilled.

Chapter 9

Measurement Models

Gideon J. Mellenbergh[1]

In the empirical sciences data are used for investigating substantive hypotheses and theories, and for making practical decisions. Many researchers are mainly interested in the substantive aspects. These theories contain constructs, and in empirical research constructs must be operationalized and data must be analysed. Although the interest is in substantive hypotheses and theories, other theories are always needed for operationalizing constructs and analysing data. These types of theories are called auxiliary theories (Hox & Mellenbergh, 1990).

This chapter discusses psychometric theories, that is, auxiliary theories at the level of the operationalization of theoretical constructs. It is remarked that substantive and auxiliary theories must be interlocked: misspecifications at the level of the auxiliary theories may have profound effects on the validity of conclusions about substantive theories.

The emphasis is on measurement of human properties, such as blood pressure, verbal intelligence, or mathematical skills. For the measurement of most of these properties the cooperation of persons is needed. It means that the persons can react to the measurement situation, for example, persons may be nervous if their blood pressure or verbal intelligence is assessed. In contrast, non-reactive measurements do not need persons' cooperation. An example is the measurement of liquor consumption in a city without package stores by counting the number of empty bottles in the city's trash (Webb, Campbell, Schwartz, & Sechrest, 1966, Study of Sawyer, p. 41). The measurement models apply to both types of measurements.

Psychometric theories are further subdivided into theories about the measurement of theoretical constructs themselves and theories about the application of measured constructs for making practical decisions (psychometric decision models). An example of psychometric decision-making is

---

[1] The author thanks Herman J. Adèr, Wulfert P. van den Brink, David J. Hand, Peter F. de Jong and Willem E. Saris for their valuable comments.

job selection based on applicants' test scores. This chapter is, however, on measurement models; for an overview of psychometric decision models the reader is referred to Van der Linden (1991).

Two main types of measurement models are distinguished, that is, *test score models* and *item response models*. Most measurement instruments yield one or more scores per person, for example, a patient's blood pressure, a subject's verbal intelligence, or a student's mathematics examination result. These scores can be *continuous* or *discrete*, for example, blood pressure is a continuous variable, whereas the number of correctly answered problems of a mathematics examination is a discrete variable. Score models for both continuous and discrete scores are discussed.

Many of the measurement instruments of the behavioural and social sciences consist of a set of n elements, which will be called items; and the person is requested to respond to each of the items. For example, intelligence and achievement tests consist of a series of problems which must be solved by the subject or examinee, and questionnaires and interviews consist of a series of questions which must be answered by the respondent. These types of instruments yield responses per item, and the subject's or examinee's responses are described by item response models.

9.1   Score models

In this section score models are discussed. A distinction is made between continuous and discrete score models.

9.1.1   Continuous score models

The score is a continuous variable. Examples of really continuous variables are weight, blood pressure, and the time a student needs to solve a number of mental arithmetic problems. Many of the behavioural and social science instruments consist of a series of items. A long existing tradition is to score the separate items, to take the unweighted sum of the item scores, and to treat this score as a continuous variable. An example is an achievement test consisting of 30 items: A correctly answered item is scored 1 and an incorrectly answered item is scored 0, and the examinee's score is the sum of the item scores, that is, the number of correctly answered items. Another example is an attitude questionnaire consisting of ten so-called Likert items. A Likert item consists of a statement and a number of ordered options, where the subject responds by choosing one of the options, for example, an item of Likert's (1932) 'Surveys of Opinions' is given in Figure 9.1. The items are scored by assigning the rank number of the option to the respondent's choice, e.g., if the student chooses the first option the score is 1, if the student chooses the second option the score is 2, etc. The test score is the unweighted sum of the item scores. This procedure of scoring a test or questionnaire can be criticized on different grounds: The unweighted sum of the item scores is not a continuous but a discrete variable. Usually, however,

*We must strive for loyalty to our country before we can afford
to consider world brotherhood.*

Strongly Approve	Approve	Undecided	Disapprove	Strongly Disapprove
(1)	(2)	(3)	(4)	(5)

Figure 9.1: Item from Likert's (1932) Surveys of Opinions.

it is assumed that the number of items is sufficiently large and the discrete
score (sum of item scores) can be approximated by a continuous variable.
A more fundamental criticism is that the item scores are rank numbers and
that a sum of rank numbers does not have the properties of a continuous
variable. The classical model is applied to continuous variables, such as
time to solve a number of arithmetic problems, and to sum scores, which
are considered to be continuous, such as the unweighted sum of item scores.

Some concepts of the classical score model were firstly mentioned by
Edgeworth (1888), but the model originates from an article of Spearman
published in 1904 (Gulliksen, 1950, p. 1). The model is called classical test
theory. A comprehensive overview of the theory was given by Gulliksen and
the statistical foundation was given by Lord & Novick (1968).

9.1.1.1 Classical model for one person

Lord & Novick (1968, Chapter 2) derived the classical model for one person
by a thought-experiment: A measurement instrument is administered to a
given person p, and the person's observed score is recorded. The measurement procedure is repeated an infinite number of times, and it is assumed
that the person (a) does not change from occasion to occasion and (b)
does not remember previous measurement occasions. Under this thought-
experiment the person's observed score is a random variable X_p with values
x_p in a (hypothetical) population of independent replications (repeated measurements). The person's *true score* τ_p is defined as the expected value of
the person's observed score:

$$E_r(X_p) = \tau_p \tag{9.1}$$

where E_r means expectation with respect to replications. The person's true
score, τ_p, is the person's parameter. From this definition follows the classical
model for the person's observed score:

$$X_p = \tau_p + \varepsilon_p \tag{9.2}$$

where ε_p is a random measurement error variable. The model has some
important consequences. First,

$$E_r(X_p) = E_r(\tau_p) + E_r(\varepsilon_p) = \tau_p + E_r(\varepsilon_p) = \tau_p$$

and, therefore, the expected error is zero:

$$E_r(\varepsilon_p) = 0. \tag{9.3}$$

Second, it follows that the within-person observed score variance is equal to the error variance:

$$Var_r(X_p) = Var_r(\tau_p + \varepsilon_p) = Var_r(\varepsilon_p) = \sigma_p^2 \tag{9.4}$$

where Var_r means that the variance is computed over replications.

A weak and a strong form of the classical model are distinguished. In the weak form it is only assumed that the person's observed score has a distribution with finite mean and variance in the population of (hypothetical) replications. If the instrument is administered only once to the person, the actual administration is considered to be a single random draw from the population of replications. The least squares criterion for estimating the person's true score is $(x_p - \tau_p)^2$. The minimum of this function is obtained for

$$\hat{\tau}_p = x_p \tag{9.5}$$

that is, the least squares estimator of the person's true score is his or her observed score.

In the strong form of the model it is assumed that the within-person distribution of the observed score is normal. The likelihood of the score is equal to its density, and the log likelihood is:

$$\ln L = c - \frac{(x_p - \tau_p)^2}{2\sigma_p^2} \tag{9.6}$$

where c is a constant that does not depend on τ_p. Assuming that σ_p^2 is known, the maximum of this function is obtained for

$$\hat{\tau}_p = x_p \tag{9.7}$$

that is, the maximum likelihood estimator is the same as the least squares estimator.

9.1.1.2   Classical model for a population of persons

The model is extended to a population of persons. It is assumed that the classical model Formulas (9.1) and (9.2) apply to each of the persons of the population. The observed score model of a randomly selected person is:

$$X = T + \varepsilon \tag{9.8}$$

where T is the random true score variable and ε the random error in a population of persons. The classical model Formula (9.8) is a linear regression model because

$$E_r(X|T = \tau_p) = \tau_p$$

and, therefore, a path analytic representation of the model can be given. Figure 9.2(a) shows the path analytic representation. The latent true score T is indicated by a circle, the regression of X on T is represented by an arrow from X to T, and the error is indicated by ε and an arrow from ε to X.

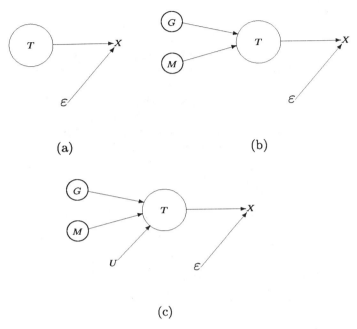

Figure 9.2: Path analytic representation of (a) the classical score model, (b) Jöreskog's score model, and (c) Saris' score model.

9.1.1.3 Method effects

A limitation of the classical model is the assumption that the observed score is determined by one latent variable T. It might be that the observed score is also influenced by other person variables. For example, a student's mathematics achievement can be measured in different ways, e.g., an achievement test or a teacher's rating. Both test and rating assess the student's achievement, but each of the two methods might also measure specific aspects. For example, next to a general aspect the test might measure the student's ability to express him(her)self on paper, whereas the teacher's rating might measure the student's ability to express him(her)self verbally. This problem was handled by decomposing the true score in a general and a method part.

The concept of this modification of classical test theory was introduced by Campbell & Fiske (1959). Jöreskog (1974) presented the following decomposition of the true score:

$$T = G + M \qquad (9.9)$$

where G is a general random person variable and M a method-specific random person variable. Usually, it is also assumed that G and M are uncorrelated in the population of persons. The model is a regression model with two predictors, i.e., G and M; the path analytic representation is given in Figure 9.2(b).

It is, however, possible that the true score T is not completely determined by the G and M variables, and that a part of the true score remains unexplained. Saris (1990) proposed the following modification of the classical model:

$$T = G + M + U \qquad (9.10)$$

where U is an unexplained residual of the true score. Usually, it is also assumed that G, M, and U are uncorrelated in the population. The path analytic representation of this model is given in Figure 9.2(c).

In general, it is impossible to estimate parameters of these modified models using data from one single instrument administration. The parameters can, however, be estimated using special designs for instrument administration; for further information the reader is referred to Jöreskog (1974) and Saris & Andrews (1991), respectively.

9.1.2   Discrete score models

The situation is considered of an instrument consisting of n items. Each of the items is dichotomously scored: 1 for a correctly answered or endorsed item and 0 for an incorrectly answered or non-endorsed item. The instrument score is the unweighted sum of the n item scores, i.e., the score is the number of correctly answered or endorsed items. Therefore, the person's score can take the discrete values $0, 1, 2, \ldots, n$. The binomial error model (Lord & Novick, 1968, Chapter 23) applies to this situation of discrete test scores.

The model is also defined in two steps: First, a model for a single person is specified and, second, the model is extended to a population of persons. It is assumed that a large domain of items is available. For a given person p a random sample of n items is selected from the domain, these items are administered to the person, and the person's score is computed. In a thought-experiment this procedure is repeated an infinite number of times: Each of the times a new random sample of n items is selected from the domain and this sample is administered to the person. The pth person's true score is defined as the expected value of the person's observed score X_p over repeated random samples of n items from the domain:

$$E_r(X_p) = \tau_p \qquad (9.11)$$

The mean true score computed over the items, i.e., $\frac{T_p}{n}$, can be interpreted as the person's probability of giving a correct answer (endorsing) a randomly selected item from the domain.

It is assumed that at an instrument administration the person's item responses are independently distributed and that his or her observed test score has a binomial distribution with parameters $\frac{T_p}{n}$ and n:

$$P(X_p = x_p) = \binom{n}{x_p}(\frac{T_p}{n})^{x_p}(1 - \frac{T_p}{n})^{n-x_p}, x_p = 0, 1, \ldots, n. \qquad (9.12)$$

The expected value of this distribution is τ_p and its variance is a function of the expected value:

$$Var_r(X_p) = \frac{\tau_p(n - \tau_p)}{n}. \qquad (9.13)$$

The likelihood of one single administration of the n-item instrument is equal to its density, and the log likelihood is:

$$\ln L = x_p \ln(\frac{T_p}{n}) + (n - x_p)\ln(\frac{n - T_p}{n}). \qquad (9.14)$$

The maximum likelihood estimator of the true score is obtained by taking the derivative of the log likelihood to τ_p, setting the result equal to 0, and solving for τ_p:

$$\hat{\tau}_p = x_p \qquad (9.15)$$

that is, the observed score is the maximum likelihood estimator of the true score.

The binomial error model Formula (9.12) is formulated for one single person p. The model can be extended to a population of persons. For each of the persons a new sample of n items is randomly selected from the domain of items, and it is assumed that the binomial error model applies to each of the persons. Moreover, it is assumed that the true score T has a Beta distribution in the population of persons. The combination of the individual binomial error model and a population Beta distribution yields the so-called *Beta-binomial* model for discrete test scores.

9.2   Item response models

Most of the existing tests, questionnaires, and interviews consist of items. Therefore, it is possible to use the persons' item responses for model building. The first models of this type were published in the forties by Lawley (Lord & Novick, 1968, p. 368) and Guttman (1950). Their early work resulted in the models of Rasch (1960), Birnbaum (1968), Samejima (1969) and Mokken (1970), which are the basis of modern *item response theory*.

Three types of item answer scales will be distinguished: (a) continuous, (b) dichotomous, and (c) ordinal-polytomous; and different models are needed for each of these types of answer scales. Continuous scales require the person to give an answer on a continuous scale, e.g., the person's time to solve a mental arithmetic problem. Dichotomous answer scales yield two different item responses, e.g., `correct-incorrect`, `yes-no`, and `agree-don't agree`. Ordinal-polytomous answer scales yield responses in more than two ordered categories, e.g., `correct-half correct-incorrect` and `strongly agree-agree-neutral-disagree-strongly disagree`.

Most of the existing item response models have a number of common elements (Mellenbergh, 1994a). First, a distribution of a person's responses to a given item over repeated administrations is assumed. The assumed distribution depends on the item answer scale, for example, a normal distribution for a continuous scale, a Bernoulli distribution for a dichotomous scale, and a multinomial distribution for a polytomous scale. Second, it is assumed that the person's observed item responses are explained by at least one latent variable. The models differ in the nature and number of assumed latent variables. The latent variable can be a discrete or a continuous variable. Latent discrete variable models are called *latent class models* and continuous latent variable models *latent trait models*. Latent trait models using only one trait are called *unidimensional* latent trait models and models using more than one trait are called *multidimensional* latent trait models. Third, it is assumed that given the values of the latent variable(s) the person's responses to the n instrument items are independently distributed. This conditional independence assumption is called *local independence*. Finally, all item response models assume a *regression function* of the observed item response on the latent variables. Item response models differ between each other in the regression function which is assumed.

Some well-known examples of item response models are discussed. The emphasis is on models having only one continuous latent variable, i.e., unidimensional latent trait models. Models for continuous, dichotomous, and ordinal-polytomous answer scales are discussed. For dichotomous responses, also an example of a latent class model is given. The discussion is concentrated on the regression functions which are used in these models. Parameter estimation and model testing are not discussed.

9.2.1   Continuous response

The person's item response is on a continuous scale, for example, a student's time to answer a mental arithmetic item. In a thought-experiment item i is repeatedly administered to person p. It is assumed that the pth person's response to the ith item, X_{ip}, is normally distributed with mean μ_{ip} and homogeneous variance σ_i^2 over (hypothetical) replications. The mean μ_{ip} depends on both the item and the person, but it is assumed that the variance σ_i^2 only depends on the item. It is further assumed that the person's item response, X_{ip}, is explained by one latent trait, i.e., the model is a unidimensional latent trait model for continuous item responses (Mellenbergh, 1994b). Moreover, it is assumed that the person's responses to n items of the same instrument are independently distributed over (hypothetical) replications, which is the assumption of local independence.

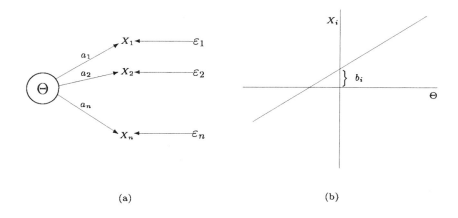

(a)   (b)

Figure 9.3: (a) Path analytic representation, where $\varepsilon_1, \ldots \varepsilon_n$ indicate random errors, and (b) regression function of the one-factor model for continuous item responses.

The model for a given person p is extended to a population of persons. It is assumed that the model holds for each of the persons of a population. Moreover, it is assumed that the regression of the observed item score on the latent trait is linear:

$$E_r(X_{ip}|\Theta = \theta_p) = \mu_{ip} = b_i + a_i\theta_p \qquad (9.16)$$

where θ_p is the value of a randomly selected person p on the random latent trait Θ, b_i is the intercept and a_i the slope of the ith regression function. The b_i - parameter indicates the item 'difficulty', for example, the larger b_i the more time the student needs to solve the mental arithmetic item. The a_i is the item discrimination parameter, e.g., the larger a_i the better the item discriminates between low and high latent mental arithmetic ability students. The model is Spearman's one-factor model applied to continuous item responses. The path analytic representation is given in Figure 9.3(a) and the linear regression function in Figure 9.3(b). The parameters of the model can be estimated using factor analytic methods.

9.2.2   Dichotomous response

The person's answer is on a dichotomous scale, for example, yes–no, agree–don't agree, or an answer which is scored correct–incorrect. It is assumed that the person's responses are Bernoulli distributed in a (hypothetical) population of independent replications. The answers are scored 1 for a correct (yes) answer and 0 for an incorrect (no) answer and, therefore, the pth person expected response to the ith item is the person's probability of giving a correct (yes) answer to the ith item; this probability is indicated by Π_{ip}. Moreover, it is assumed that the observed item response is determined

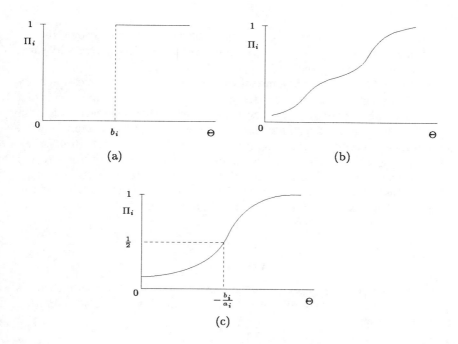

Figure 9.4: Regression functions for (a) the Guttman model, (b) the Mokken model, and (c) the Birnbaum model for dichotomous item responses.

by one latent trait and that the person's responses to n items are locally independent.

A number of unidimensional latent trait models for dichotomous responses were proposed in the history of psychometrics. All of these models make the assumptions of Bernoulli distributed and locally independent responses, but the models differ among each other in the regression function that is used.

One of the first models of this type was described by Guttman (1950). He used a step regression function:

$$\Pi_{ip} = E_r(X_{ip}|\Theta = \theta_p) = \left\{ \begin{array}{l} 1 \text{ if } \theta_p > b_i \\ 0 \text{ if } \theta_p \le b_i \end{array} \right. . \qquad (9.17)$$

The graph of the function is shown in Figure 9.4(a).

The Guttman model is a very restrictive model because it is of a *deterministic* nature: a person with latent trait value above the item's difficulty answers the item correctly (or endorses the item) for sure and a person with latent trait value equal to or below the item's difficulty answers the item incorrectly (or does not endorse the item) for sure.

Under the Guttman model the person (θ) and item (b) parameter values cannot be estimated. However, it is possible to estimate the rank order of the person latent trait values and of the item difficulties.

The restrictive Guttman model was relaxed by using monotonic regression functions instead of a step function. Both *non-parametric* and *parametric* functions were used.

Mokken (1970) presented a model with a non-parametric regression function. He assumed that the regression is a monotonically non-decreasing function of the latent trait. Moreover, he assumed that the regression functions of the n items of an instrument do not intersect. An example of a monotonically non-decreasing regression function is given in Figure 9.4(b). Under the Mokken model it is not possible to estimate the person (θ) and item (b) parameter values, but their rank orders can be estimated.

The Rasch (1960) and Birnbaum (1968) models are parametric generalizations of Guttman's deterministic model. Birnbaum used a two-parameter logistic regression function:

$$\Pi_{ip} = \frac{\exp(b_i + a_i\theta_p)}{1 + \exp(b_i + a_i\theta_p)} \tag{9.18}$$

where exp denotes the exponential function. The graphic of the function is given in Figure 9.4(c). Usually, the Birnbaum model is presented in another parametrization:

$$\Pi_{ip} = \frac{\exp\{a_i(\theta_p - b_i^*)\}}{1 + \exp\{a_i(\theta_p - b_i^*)\}}$$

where $b_i^* = \frac{-b_i}{a_i}$, but this parametrization will not be used in the sequel. The Rasch model is obtained by setting the item discrimination parameters of the n items equal to each other, that is, by setting $a_i = a(i = 1, 2, \ldots, n)$:

$$\Pi_{ip} = \frac{\exp(b_i + a\theta_p)}{1 + \exp(b_i + a\theta_p)}. \tag{9.19}$$

The parameters of the Birnbaum and Rasch models can be estimated; for further information on estimation see, for example, Hambleton & Swaminathan (1985).

An example of a latent class model for dichotomous item responses is mastery testing in educational measurement. An n-item test is administered to a group of examinees to assess their performance in an educational skill, such as, the multiplication of two-digit numbers. It is assumed that the examinees either master or do not master the skill. A master may make a mistake and give an incorrect answer to a particular item, and a non-master may have luck and give a correct answer to a particular item. It is assumed that the latent skill variable consists of only two classes, i.e., masters and non-masters, and that an examinee's responses are Bernoulli distributed in a (hypothetical) population of independent administrations of the same item to the same examinee.

The latent class mastery testing model is of a similar structure as the latent trait model Formula (9.18). The continuous latent trait is replaced by a dichotomous latent class variable which has values $\Theta = 1$ for masters and $\Theta = 0$ for non-masters. Analogously to model Formula (9.18), an examinee's probability of giving a correct answer to the ith item is written as

$$\Pi_{i|\theta} = \frac{\exp(b_i + a_i\theta)}{1 + \exp(b_i + a_i\theta)} \qquad (9.20)$$

From Formula (9.20) it follows that a master's probability of giving a correct response to the ith item is:

$$\Pi_{i|1} = \frac{\exp(b_i + a_i 1)}{1 + \exp(b_i + a_i 1)} = \frac{\exp(b_i^*)}{1 + \exp(b_i^*)}. \qquad (9.21)$$

where $b_i^* = b_i + a_i$, and a non-master's probability of giving a correct response to the ith item is

$$\Pi_{i|0} = \frac{\exp(b_i + a_i 0)}{1 + \exp(b_i + a_i 0)} = \frac{\exp(b_i)}{1 + \exp(b_i)} \qquad (9.22)$$

Model Formulas (9.21) and (9.22) are equivalent to the two-state mastery model of Macready & Dayton (1980). A master's probability of giving an incorrect answer to the item is $1 - \Pi_{i|1}$ and is called *the omission error probability*. A non-master's probability of giving a correct answer is $\Pi_{i|0}$ and is called the *intrusion error probability*.

Formulas (9.21) and (9.22) do not constrain the conditional probabilities $\Pi_{i|1}$ and $\Pi_{i|0}$. Constrained versions of the model are obtained by restricting the parameters. An example is the restriction $a_i = -2b_i$ which implies that the omission and intrusion error probabilities are equal to each other, i.e., $1 - \Pi_{i|1} = \Pi_{i|0}$.

9.2.3   Ordinal-polytomous response

The answer scale consists of more than two ordered categories, such as a five-point Likert scale. It is assumed that a person's responses to the item are multinomially distributed over (hypothetical) replications and that the person's responses to n items are locally independent.

An ordinal K-category variable can conceptually be split into a series of $K-1$ order preserving dichotomous variables. But, the splitting can be done in three different ways: adjacent-categories, continuation, and cumulative splitting (Agresti, 1990, Section 9.3). Applying these three types of splittings to ordinal-polytomous answer scales yields models of similar structure, but with different interpretation of their parameters (Mellenbergh, 1995).

Here, only cumulative splitting of an ordinal K-category answer scale into $K-1$ dichotomous variables is discussed. For example, the cumulative splitting of a four-category answer scale yields three order preserving dichotomous variables; see Figure 9.5.

At each of the splittings the higher categories are coded 1 and the lower categories are coded 0. The pth person's probability of scoring 1 at the kth splitting of the ith item is indicated by $\Pi_{ikp} (k = 1, 2, \ldots, K - 1)$. The

| Cat. 1 |
| Cat. 2 |
| Cat. 3 |
| Cat. 4 |

| Cat. 1: Code 0 |
| Cat. 2, 3 & 4: Code 1 |

| Cat. 1 & 2: Code 0 |
| Cat. 3 & 4: Code 1 |

| Cat. 1, 2 & 3: Code 0 |
| Cat. 4: Code 1 |

Figure 9.5: Cumulative splitting and dummy coding of a four-category ordinal item response scale.

cumulative splitting of the K-category variable implies that the cumulative probabilities are ordered:

$$\Pi_{i1p} \geq \Pi_{i2p} \geq \ldots \geq \Pi_{i(K-1)p}$$

Unidimensional latent trait models for ordinal-polytomous items come into being by applying unidimensional latent trait models for dichotomous items to the $(K-1)$ splittings of the ordinal K-category scale. The ordering of the cumulative probabilities implies that the $(K-1)$ within-item regression functions cannot intersect each other.

The extension of the Guttman model to ordinal-polytomous items specifies $(K-1)$ step regression functions (Guttman, 1950). The three regression functions of a four-category answer scale are shown in Figure 9.6(a). The requirement that the regression functions cannot intersect is automatically fulfilled because step functions are non-intersecting.

The extension of the Mokken model to ordinal-polytomous items was given by Molenaar (1982). The $(K-1)$ regression functions must be monotonically increasing functions of the latent trait and they must be non-intersecting. An example of a four-category answer scale is given in Figure 9.6(b).

The extension of the Birnbaum model of Formula (9.18) to ordinal-polytomous items was given by Samejima (1969). The requirement that the regression functions are non-intersecting implies that the within-item discrimination parameters must be equal. Therefore, the homogeneous case of Samejima's model is:

$$\Pi_{ikp} = \frac{\exp(b_{ik} + a_i\theta_p)}{1 + \exp(b_{ik} + a_i\theta_p)}, k = 1, 2, \ldots, K-1 \tag{9.23}$$

where b_{ik} is an item- and splitting-specific location parameter and a_i the discrimination parameter, which is specific for the item but does not depend on the splitting. An example of a four-category item is given in Figure 9.6(c).

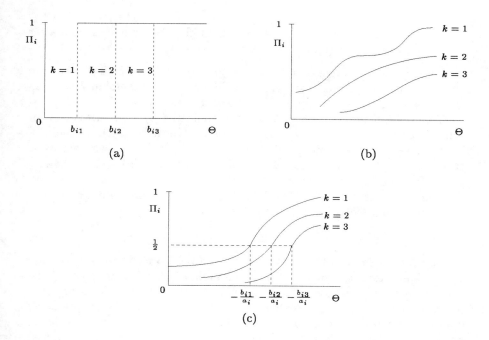

Figure 9.6: Regression functions corresponding to cumulative splitting of a four-category ordinal item response scale for (a) the Guttman model, (b) the Molenaar model, and (c) the Samejima model.

9.2.4 Item response measurement model violation

Classical test theory assumes that the observed test score is explained by one latent true score variable, and unidimensional item response models assume that a person's item responses are explained by one latent trait. It was remarked that the observed score can also be influenced by other variables, which were denoted as method effects in Section 9.1.1.3. In the same way, it is possible that, next to the latent trait, also other variables effect a person's item responses. If the measurement procedure does not intend to measure these other variables, they are called violators of the unidimensional item response measurement model (Oort, 1996, Chapter 1).

Violators can be variables of different types. Two distinctions are made. First, a violator can be a continuous or a discrete variable and, second, a violator can be an observed or a latent variable. Combining these two distinctions yields four types of violators:

1. continuous and observed, for example, age;

2. continuous and latent, for example, the latent trait to produce a certain picture of oneself (response set);

3. discrete and observed, for example, group membership (`male-female`, `minority-majority group`);

4. discrete and latent, for example a latent class of students who master the examination topic and a latent class of non-masters.

The best known example of a violator is group membership. The violation of an unidimensional item response model by group membership was called *item bias* and, more recently, *differential item functioning*.

The violator model with one violator, indicated by V, is discussed for continuous and dichotomous item responses. The discussion of the violator model for dichotomous responses is restricted to the two-parameter Birnbaum model, which is usually applied to differential item functioning research of dichotomous items.

The measurement model Formula (9.16) for continuous item responses is extended to a violator model as follows:

$$E_r(X_{ip}|\Theta = \theta_p, V = v_p) = b_i + a_i\theta_p + c_iv_p + d_i\theta_pv_p \qquad (9.24)$$

where v_p is the value of the randomly selected person p on the violator, and c_i and d_i are item parameters. If $c_i \neq 0$ and $d_i \neq 0$ the measurement model is called *non-uniformly* violated and if $c_i \neq 0$ and $d_i = 0$ the measurement model is called *uniformly* violated. A discrete violator is specified by using dummy variables. For example, a dichotomous group membership variable, such as `male-female`, is specified by setting $V = 0$ for members of the first group and $V = 1$ for members of the second group. Using this dichotomous violator model, Formula (9.24) becomes:

$$E_r(X_{ip}|\Theta = \theta_p, V = 0) = b_i + a_i\theta_p \qquad (9.25)$$

for members of the first group, and

$$E_r(X_{ip}|\Theta = \theta_p, V = 1) = b_i + a_i\theta_p + c_i + d_i\theta_p = b_i^* + a_i^*\theta_p \qquad (9.26)$$

for members of the second group, where $b_i^* = b_i + c_i$ and $a_i^* = a_i + d_i$. If $c_i \neq 0$ and $d_i \neq 0$, Formulas (9.25) and (9.26) specify two parallel regression lines with different intercepts and slopes (non-uniform violation); and, if $c_i \neq 0$ and $d_i = 0$ (9.25) and (9.26) specify two parallel regression lines with different intercepts (uniform violation) studied by Oort (1996).

For dichotomous item responses the two-parameter Birnbaum model Formula (9.18) is extended to a violator model as follows:

$$E_r(X_{ip}|\Theta = \theta_p, V = v_p) = \frac{\exp(b_i + a_i\theta_p + c_iv_p + d_i\theta_pv_p)}{1 + \exp(b_i + a_i\theta_p + c_iv_p + d_i\theta_pv_p)} \qquad (9.27)$$

For a dichotomous group membership violator model, Formula (9.27) becomes:

$$E_r(X_{ip}|\Theta = \theta_p, V = 0) = \frac{\exp(b_i + a_i\theta_p)}{1 + \exp(b_i + a_i\theta_p)} \qquad (9.28)$$

for members of the first group, and

$$E_r(X_{ip}|\Theta = \theta_p, V = 1) = \frac{\exp(b_i^* + a_i^*\theta_p)}{1 + \exp(b_i^* + a_i^*\theta_p)} \qquad (9.29)$$

for members of the second group. Model Formulas (9.28) and (9.29) specify two logistic regression functions. If $c_i \neq 0$ and $d_i \neq 0$, Formulas (9.28) and (9.29) represent the model for non-uniform item bias or differential item functioning; and, if $c_i \neq 0$ and $d_i = 0$ Formulas (9.28) and (9.29) represent the model for uniform item bias or differential item functioning; see, for example, Mellenbergh (1989) and Millsap & Everson (1993).

Formulas (9.24) and (9.27) show that d_i is an item parameter for the product of the latent trait and the violator. The product term of these models can be interpreted as a special type of interaction of the latent trait and the violator. If the measurement model is uniformly violated, the parameter $d_i = 0$ which means that the latent trait and violator do not interact. If the measurement model is non-uniformly violated, the parameter $d_i \neq 0$ which means that the latent trait and violator interact with each other via their product.

9.3   Measurement precision

An important question is the *precision* of measurements. Two aspects of precision are distinguished: *information* and *reliability*. Mostly, information is associated with item response models and reliability with test score models, but both concepts apply to both types of models (Mellenbergh, 1996). These two concepts are discussed for the two most common situations, that is the classical test score model and the parametric Birnbaum model for item responses.

9.3.1   Information

The concept of information applies to the precision of the measurement of a given person. Information is high if the within-person variance, computed over (hypothetical) repeated measurements, is small and information is low if this variance is large. High information (small within-person variance) means that confidence intervals of the person's estimated true score or latent trait value are narrow, while low information (large within-person variance) means that these intervals are broad.

In statistics, the concept of information on a parameter β is defined as (Lindgren, 1976, section 4.5.4):

$$I(\beta) = -E\left(\frac{\partial^2 \ln L}{\partial \beta^2}\right) \tag{9.30}$$

where $\ln L$ denotes the natural logarithm of the likelihood, and the expectation is taken over the observations. The concept of information is used in the context of maximum likelihood estimation. If $\hat{\beta}$ is the maximum likelihood estimator of β then asymptotically, according to Lindgren (1976, section 5.2.2.), $\hat{\beta}$ has a normal distribution with variance:

$$Var(\hat{\beta}|\beta) = \frac{1}{I(\beta)}. \tag{9.31}$$

The maximum likelihood estimator of the true score of the classical score model Formula (9.1) is the person's observed test score Formula (9.7). Using Formulas (9.6) and (9.30), it follows that the information is:

$$I(\tau_p) = \frac{1}{\sigma_p^2}. \tag{9.32}$$

A problem of classical test theory is that it is not possible to estimate σ_p^2 from one single instrument administration, but an approximate estimate can be obtained using estimates of population parameters (Lord & Novick, 1968, Chapter 2).

Under Birnbaum's model Formula (9.18) for dichotomous item responses, the maximum likelihood estimator of the person's latent trait value θ_p can be derived (Lord & Novick, 1968, Chapter 20). Using Formula (9.30), person p's test information is:

$$I(\theta_p) = \sum_{i=1}^{n} I_i(\theta_p) = \sum_{i=1}^{n} a_i^2 \Pi_{ip}(1 - \Pi_{ip}) \tag{9.33}$$

where $I_i = a_i^2 \Pi_{ip}(1 - \Pi_{ip})$ is the *item information* function. Formula (9.33) shows that the test information is the sum of the separate item informations. Moreover, the information is a function of the latent trait because Π_{ip} is a function of the latent trait (see Formula (9.18)).

9.3.2   Reliability

Information is a population-independent concept of measurement precision. It is determined by the within-person variance of (hypothetical) repeated measurements. In contrast, reliability is a population-dependent concept of precision. It is the squared correlation between the true score or latent trait and its estimate in a population of persons (Mellenbergh, 1996). Therefore, reliability can be interpreted as the proportion true score or latent trait variance that can linearly be predicted from its estimate.

In classical test theory model Formula (9.8), the reliability is defined as the squared correlation between the true score variable T and its estimate, the observed score variable X, in a population of persons. Lord & Novick (1968, Chapter 3) proved that the reliability is:

$$Rel(X) = Cor_p^2(T, X) = \frac{Var_p(T)}{Var_p(X)} = \frac{Var_p(T)}{E_p(Var_r(X_p)) + Var_p(T)} \tag{9.34}$$

where Rel denotes reliability and Cor_p and Var_p population correlation and variance, respectively. $E_p(Var_r(X_p))$ is the population mean of the within-person test score variance over repeated test administrations. The reliability cannot directly be computed because the true score variable T is latent and its variance cannot be obtained from empirical test data. This problem is solved by defining parallel instruments. Two scores, X and X', are said to be *parallel* if they measure the same true score for each of the persons and if their errors are uncorrelated with equal variances (Lord & Novick, 1968, Chapter 2). Using the definition of parallel tests, it was proved that (Lord & Novick, 1968, Chapter 3),

$$Cor_p(X, X') = \frac{Var_p(T)}{Var_p(X)} \qquad (9.35)$$

which shows that the parallel instrument correlation is equal to the reliability Formula (9.34). Several practical methods for estimating the reliability are described in the literature; for an overview of the conventional methods, see Lord & Novick (1968, Chapter 9). One method is to construct parallel instruments, to administer them to a random sample of persons, and to compute the parallel instrument correlation.

The reliability of the latent trait estimates of the parametric item response models for dichotomous items is usually not considered. The reliability can, however, analogously, be defined as the squared correlation between the latent trait and its estimate in a population of persons. Suppose that $\hat{\Theta}$ is an unbiased estimator of the latent trait Θ. The reliability of the estimates is (Mellenbergh, 1996):

$$Rel(\hat{\Theta}) = Cor_p^2(\Theta, \hat{\Theta}) = \frac{Var_p(\Theta)}{E_p(Var_r(\hat{\Theta}|\Theta = \theta_p)) + Var_p(\Theta)} \qquad (9.36)$$

where $E_p(Var_r(\hat{\Theta}|\Theta = \theta_p))$ is the population mean of the within-person variances of the estimated latent trait value over (hypothetical) repeated test administrations. The reliability of Formula (9.36) can be estimated using factor-analytic methods.

9.4   Sensitivity and specificity

In Epidemiology, the concepts of information and reliability are usually not used. Instead of these concepts, *sensitivity* and *specificity* are used for the assessment of the quality of medical diagnostic instruments.

A person can be in two true, but unknown, states: a disease is present or absent. A diagnostic test based on, for example, a blood sample or an X-ray, is applied to the person. A positive outcome of the test indicates the presence of the disease, while a negative outcome indicates the absence of the disease. Usually, the test is not perfect and errors are made: some healthy persons are diagnosed as patients, and some patients are diagnosed as healthy. The sensitivity of a test is defined as the probability of a positive outcome of the test conditional that the person suffers from the disease (Miettinen, 1985, p. 340). The specificity of a test is defined as the probability that the outcome of the test is negative conditional that the person does not have the disease (Miettinen, 1985, p. 341).

The situation of the medical test to diagnose whether the disease is present or absent is formally equivalent to the situation of the achievement test item to indicate whether an examinee is a master or non-master. However, the terminology differs between the fields of epidemiological and educational measurement. The sensitivity of the diagnostic test is equivalent to the probability that a master gives a correct answer to the achievement test, i.e., $\Pi_{i|1}$. The specificity of the diagnostic test is equivalent to the probability that a non-master gives an incorrect answer to the item, i.e., $1 - \Pi_{i|0}$.

Sensitivity and specificity are defined conditional on the health status of the person. The sensitivity is defined for persons having the disease and the specificity for persons not having the disease. Sensitivity and specificity are concepts, which do not depend on the distribution of the disease in the population of persons. In this sense sensitivity and specificity are population-independent concepts, which play a similar part in epidemiological measurement as the information concept in educational and psychological measurement.

9.5 Discussion

Measurement models were discussed for test scores and item responses. In both types of models, the concepts of information and reliability are defined. Information is a within-person concept of measurement precision, whereas reliability is a between-persons concept of measurement precision. Both concepts are useful, but they apply to different situations. The emphasis was on educational and psychological measurement, but it was remarked that the epidemiological concepts of sensitivity and specificity have a similar status as the information concept.

Information is used for assessing the precision of a given person's measurement. Information does not depend on other persons and is, therefore, a population-independent concept of precision. It is used for constructing confidence intervals for the person's true score or latent trait value.

Reliability is the squared correlation of true score or latent trait and its estimate in a population of persons, and, therefore, it is a population-dependent concept of precision. As demonstrated by Formulas (9.34) and (9.36), reliability depends on both the true score or latent trait variance and the mean within-person variance of the estimate over repeated test administrations. For a constant value of the mean within-person variance, the reliability depends on the true score or latent trait variance: The reliability is higher in a heterogeneous population (large true score or latent trait variance) than in a homogeneous population (small true score or latent trait variance). Reliability is relevant for determining a person's true score or latent trait with respect to other persons of the population: low reliability implies that a person's relative position in a group of persons cannot be determined.

The concepts of information and reliability apply to both test score and item response models and they do not distinguish these two types of models. The main distinction between the two types of models is that in item response models person and item parameters are separated, whereas that is not the case in test score models. For example, the classical test model Formula (9.1) for continuous scores specifies the person's true score at a given test. Suppose that a second test measures the same ability, but that this test is harder. The person has another, lower true score on this second test. In contrast, the item response model Formula (9.16) for continuous responses has a person parameter (θ_p) and separate item parameters $(a_i$ and $b_i)$. Two tests may differ in their item parameters, but their person parameters remain the same. Therefore, the parameters of item response models have invariance properties, which test score models do not have. A consequence is that item response models have advantages over test score models in practical applications such as test construction, adaptive testing, and equating; see, for example, Hambleton & Swaminathan (1985).

9.6   Further reading

In this section some references to publications on measurement models are given. The most advanced and complete book on test score models is Lord & Novick (1968). Introductory books on this topic were published by Allen & Yen (1979), and Crocker & Algina (1986). The classical test score model was extended to generalizability theory, which was not discussed in this chapter; for further information the reader is referred to the book of Cronbach, Gleser, Nanda, & Rajaratnam (1972) and the more elementary texts of Brennan (1983) and Shavelson, Webb, & Rowley (1989).

The binomial error model for discrete test scores is described in Chapter 23 of Lord & Novick. An overview of binomial error models is given in an article of Van den Brink (1982).

An introductory book on latent trait models for item responses is Hambleton, Swaminathan, & Rogers (1991), while Hambleton (1989), Hambleton & Swaminathan (1985), and Lord (1980) are more advanced texts on this topic. The book of Heinen (1996) gives an overview of latent class models for item responses. Van der Linden & Hambleton (1997) edited a volume, wherein a large number of the existing item response models are described. Thissen & Steinberg (1986) presented a taxonomy of item response models, and Mellenbergh (1994a) put most of the existing item response models in the framework of generalized linear item response theory.

Finally, a general discussion of measurement theories and their relations is given by Hand (1996).

Chapter 10

Graphical Modelling

Joe Whittaker and Pete Sewart

Almost without exception empirical studies in the social sciences collect and interpret multiple observations: whether the sampling units are persons, points in time, or households, observations on the same unit are generally dependent and often highly correlated. Furthermore these associations can be of central interest to the investigation. For instance in a study of poverty and access to education, an accurate description of their interrelationship over the sample might be the principal outcome of the analysis. Such dependences are rarely deterministic and so naturally require statistical descriptions allowing for variation over the units in the sample. One dimensional summaries of the data are presented as *histograms* and two dimensional as *scatter diagrams*. Sufficiently complex descriptions ideally require multi-dimensional displays of the empirical data base.

A particularly simple case arises when two variables are *statistically independent*: imagine a scatter diagram when the principal directions of the cloud are parallel to the axes. In this case the joint display of the variables is unnecessary, and each variable may be separately summarized in their respective one dimensional margins.

Graphical models build multivariate probability distributions that capitalize on the *conditional* independence inherent in the empirical structure of the observations. Graphical models simplify the analysis of multivariate data: associations between the variables comprising the data are summarized by a *graph* consisting of nodes and edges. *Variables* are represented by *nodes*, and the *absence of edges* between any two nodes signify a *conditional independence* between the two corresponding variables.

The idea of representing log-linear models by independence graphs was originally introduced by Darroch, Lauritzen, & Speed (1980). Whittaker (1990) explains in detail the properties of graphical models and includes numerous case studies. Edwards (1995) provides another recent practical introduction while Lauritzen (1996) gives an extensive account of the theory.

While other techniques designed to analyse multivariate data, such as principal component analysis, for example Krzanowski (1988) or, Flury (1997), reduce dimension by replacing the original variables by (linear) combinations of variables, with graphical models, the variables remain distinct and it is the relationships between the variables on their original scale that are examined.

The purpose of this chapter is, through illustration, to indicate the use of conditional independence in analysing data, and to show how conditional independence relates to graphical models. From a multitude of graphical models we concentrate on just a few in this chapter. Our archetypical graph has one type of vertex and one type of edge, and is applied to represent the conditional independence in models for continuous and for categorical variables. Here we focus on undirected graphs, and only briefly mention directed graphs (often called *Bayesian belief nets*).

To illustrate the methods, the analysis concentrates on modelling two examples: (a) one is a subset of variables taken from a credit card application form and (b) the other is a subset of exchange rates from the foreign currency markets. There is much that can be gained from examining even a relatively small subset of variables. The undirected graphical model of these variables allows an improved understanding of the inter-relationships between the application characteristics. This is useful for analysts keen to learn about the social, demographic and economic behaviour of the population of interest. An insight into the differences between distinct populations is obtained if they are modelled separately and their graphs compared.

The chapter begins with the notions of independence and of conditional independence, and introduces the representation of conditional independence as a missing edge in a graph. This is followed in Section 10.2 by a discussion of marginalizing and conditioning, which correspond to the familiar operations for simplifying data inspection by summing out variables (for instance, to build two-way cross-classifications) or by selecting only those units with a given value of a particular variable (to examine a slice of a larger table). An example of *Simpson's paradox*, which emphasizes the importance of modelling the joint distribution, is given. Conditioning, which may be used to model more general selection processes for entry to a survey, and occurs, for instance, in applications for financial credit, is explained in terms of directed graphs and conditional independence.

In Section 10.3 potential models for describing cross-sectional survey data are discussed in the context of a specific example of variables taken from a credit card application form. These are somewhat generally specified, and in the next section, Section 10.4, log-linear models for categorical data and their relation to graphical models are described. Firstly, the all-way log-linear model is used, along with an explanation of the edge exclusion deviance test statistic which is used to select acceptable models. However, it turns out that the log-linear all-way interaction model is usually impractical for modelling a large number of variables because of sparsity, or lack of observations, in many cells of the associated contingency table.

This problem is solved by constraining interactions higher than two to vanish, which still retains the conditional independence structure, but gives models with a sensible number of parameters. In Section 10.5, this modelling approach is illustrated on a stratified sample of applicants to the credit card division of a major bank. To illustrate the methods, three graphical models are produced for the subset of application variables: the first constructed using all individuals in the sample, the second constructed on the sub-population of 'young' applicants, and the third on the separate subpopulation of 'old' applicants. Inferences are drawn from the first graph and the other two graphs are briefly compared.

The model for continuous data, corresponding to the graphical log-linear model for categorical data, is the graphical Gaussian model presented in Section 10.6. An indication of the parallel mathematics is outlined, which provides a formal procedure for testing the adequacy of an independence graph against data. The chapter ends with an illustrative example of multiple exchange rate variation in Section 10.7. Correlation, the usual method of measuring association, does not reveal the joint structure of association, which only becomes apparent by evaluating the *partial (or conditional) correlations*. This structure is simply described by the conditional independence graph and the model is found to fit the data well.

The final section summarizes some of the benefits of using independence graphs and graphical models, suggests further reading, and discusses some available software for fitting such models.

10.1   Conditional independence

Graphical models are concerned with summarizing association and dependence between the variables in a multivariate data set. They work by determining which conditional independence statements are true and then representing this information graphically. We first have to define independence and conditional independence.

Definition 10.1 (Independence) *Events A and B are independent, written $A \perp\!\!\!\perp B$, if and only if $P(A \cap B) = P(A)P(B)$, where $P(\cdot)$ is the probability.*

An equivalent formulation is $P(A|B) = P(A)$, which states that the outcome of event B has no influence on the outcome of event A.

In applications it is necessary to work in terms of the probability density or mass functions and use random variables or vectors rather than events. The random vectors X and Y are independent,

$$X \perp\!\!\!\perp Y,$$

if and only if the joint density function factorizes:

$$p_{XY}(x,y) = p_X(x)p_Y(y) \text{ for all values of } x \text{ and } y$$

(i)   (ii)

Figure 10.1: Graphs representing dependence and independence: (i) X and Y dependent, (ii) X and Y independent.

It is straightforward to represent two random variables as graphs as Figure 10.1 illustrates.

Directed independence graphs are used to represent the dependence of Y on X as opposed to the association between X and Y. Interest lies in the distribution p_X and the conditional distribution $p_{Y|X}$, rather than their joint distribution p_{XY}. This is illustrated in Figure 10.2.

Figure 10.2: An example of a directed graph: Y is dependent on X.

The definition of independent events, can be rewritten by replacing the unconditional probabilities with conditional probabilities to give the definition of conditional independence.

Definition 10.2 *Events A and B are independent, conditional on C, $A \perp\!\!\!\perp B|C$, if and only if*

$$P(A \cap B|C) = P(A|C)P(B|C)$$

Expressed in terms of probability density functions, the random vectors X and Z are independent, conditional on the random vector Y, if and only if

$$p_{XZ|Y}(x,z|y) = p_{X|Y}(x|y)p_{Z|Y}(z|y)$$

for all values of x, y, z. An alternative formulation is

$$p_{XYZ}(x,y,z) = p_{XY}(x,y)p_{YZ}(y,z)/p_Y(y) \tag{10.1}$$

With three random variables, the conditional independence is signified by the absence of a connecting edge, as illustrated in Figure 10.3.

More generally, in an arbitrary undirected graph, two subsets of variables are independent conditional upon any *separating* subset of variables. In the context of prediction, say, where one variable is unknown but the others have been observed to guess or predict the outcome of the unknown variable, it is only necessary to use those variables that are directly joined to it with an edge. Variables that are separated from the outcome variable in the graph,

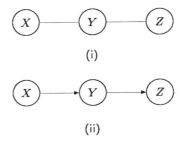

(i)

(ii)

Figure 10.3: Representing the conditional independence $X \perp\!\!\!\perp Z | Y$ in an undirected (i) and directed (ii) graph.

in other words those that are not connected by an edge, are conditionally independent given the separating variables and hence provide no additional information for prediction.

The separation properties of directed graphs, though potentially rewarding, are somewhat harder to formulate simply. In consequence we omit them from this chapter but refer the reader to Whittaker (1990) or Lauritzen (1996).

10.2   Marginalizing and Conditioning

Simpson's paradox

It is important to understand the difference between marginal and conditional independence. Examples 1 and 2 illustrate Simpson's paradox (Simpson, 1951). It refers to seemingly contradictory interpretations of independence and association present simultaneously in the marginal and conditional distributions.

EXAMPLE 1
Marginal dependence does not imply conditional dependence. Consider a simple, though contrived example related to sexual discrimination. A sample of 1200 bank loan applicants are classified according to gender [male/female], loan status [rejected/accepted], and bank applied to [A/B/C]. Examining the marginal table between gender and loan status suggests that sexual discrimination is taking place:

	rejected	accepted	% accepted
male	250	350	58
female	350	250	42

If the three bank categories refer to different branches of the same national bank, and a decision is made centrally on whether to grant loans, then this is the whole picture, and the conclusion of sexual discrimination is a valid one. The variables gender and loan status are marginally correlated, and the graph of their distribution is shown in Figure 10.4.

Figure 10.4: The marginal dependence between gender and loan status.

However, it may well be the case that the banks are competitors or deal with different types of loans and hence have different loan granting policies. It is sensible then to break down the figures by bank, since the decision to grant loans is made locally:

bank A	rejected	accepted	% accepted
male	75	25	25
female	225	75	25
bank B	rejected	accepted	% accepted
male	100	100	50
female	100	100	50
bank C	rejected	accepted	% accepted
male	75	225	75
female	25	75	75

The truth is now that, within each bank, gender and loan status are independent. The suggestion of sexual discrimination is shown to be false, and instead it is apparent that males tend to apply to the banks with high acceptance rates and females to the banks with low acceptance rates. The reason the banks have different sex ratios applying for loans might perhaps be explained by the banks marketing strategy, for instance if directed towards a particular gender. Another possibility is that the banks specialize in loans designed for specific items which are traditionally gender orientated. The acceptance rates for the three banks are likely to be pre-determined by the bank's history, or the type of loan specialization.

It is evident that gender no longer provides any information about the outcome of the loan decision once it is known which bank the application was made to. The full graph, illustrating the conditional independence, is shown in Figure 10.5 (i). Collapsing the full table over bank applied to gives the initial marginal table and induces the observed dependence between gender and loan status.

This example carries a typical feature of latent variable analysis. Suppose the value of Bank is unknown and so presumed latent. The observed dependency in the marginal distribution of the observed variables (Gender and Loan status in Figure 10.4) is explained by the latent variable (Bank in Figure 10.5(ii)). In such an analysis it is usual to model the marginal distribution of the latent variable, and the conditional distribution of the observed variables given the latent variable, and for this, the second graph Figure 10.5(ii) is appropriate.

But for both graphs of the Figure 10.5 the dependency is explicitly induced by marginalization over Bank.

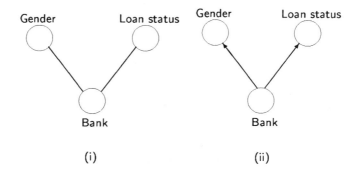

Figure   10.5:   Two   independence   graphs   representing: Gender⊥⊥Loan status|Bank: (i) undirected, (ii) directed.

Figure 10.6: Wealth is independent of default status.

EXAMPLE 2

Marginal independence does not imply conditional independence. This fictional example illustrates how certain characteristics might influence the probability of defaulting on credit card repayments. A sample of 4500 credit card holders are classified according to wealth [poor/rich], default status [no/yes], and credit card usage [light/heavy].

First, consider the effect of wealth on defaulting. Equal percentages of defaulters in both categories indicate that wealth provides no information about defaulting:

	defaulted		
wealth	no	yes	% default
poor	2250	60	3.75
rich	2250	60	3.75

The subgraph in Figure 10.6, displays the marginal independence of the variables.

By breaking this table down by light and heavy credit card users the previous conclusion that wealth and defaulting are independent is reversed, and they are dependent, conditional on credit card usage:

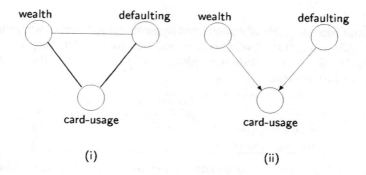

Figure 10.7: Wealth and defaulting are dependent in the joint distribution.

usage	wealth	defaulted no	defaulted yes	% default
light users	poor	2000	10	0.5
	rich	250	10	3.8
heavy users	poor	250	50	16.7
	rich	2000	50	2.4

If it is known whether an individual is a light or a heavy user, then their wealth becomes an important factor in predicting whether they are likely to default or not. The first graph of the three variables, shown in Figure 10.7(i), has no edges missing, and represents the joint distribution.

The second graph Figure 10.7(ii) combines the information from Figure 10.6 that wealth and defaulting are marginally independent, with the fact that usage is dependent on both.

In a causal graph a plausible scenario might be that wealth 'causes' usage and that wealth and usage 'cause' default status, which would lead to a different set of directed edges.

Selection bias and conditioning

The statistical analysis of data has to contend with the problem of selection. This may occur for several reasons, including attrition and experimental design. It is often the case that all the relevant issues are not fully considered and a misleading sample is obtained, or complex mechanisms lead to biased samples.

Example 10.2 above might lead to a selection bias: if, for example, the survey only comprises light users, then one would conclude that wealth and default status are dependent; though in fact it is a dependence only in the sub-population of light users.

EXAMPLE 3

Selection bias and work training. Consider an investigation into the success of training schemes for the unemployed. An obvious cross-classification is to build the two-way table of current employment status [unemployed/employed], against the indication of whether they received training [no/yes], for a sample of people who were recently unemployed. The table here, although artificial, might well be realistic.

	current employment status		
	unemployed	employed	%
no training received	100	100	50
training received	50	50	50

It appears that training has no effect on increasing job prospects, and in fact, employment is independent of training. The graphical model would show no edges joining these two variables.

However, it is predominantly the case that employment training is offered to the long-term unemployed in the belief that the recently unemployed find it possible to obtain a job without the need for training. The sub-population that is of greater interest to this investigation is the sample of people who are long-term unemployed and hence were in a position to be offered retraining. The two-way table of this conditional sample displays the more reassuring result that training doubles the chances of obtaining a job.

	current employment status		
	unemployed	employed	%
no training received	75	25	25
training received	40	40	50

The graphical model of this population would now show an edge between these two variables.

In the majority of social science investigations data for analysis requires individual consent and non-response has serious implications to the validity of the sample, especially when it is correlated with the question of interest. Continuing the previous example, suppose that a selection of people who were long-term unemployed are sent a postal questionnaire. Response levels to this survey are likely to be influenced by the individual's experience. For example, those who are now employed are more likely to respond, as are people who received training, so that the responding sub-sample of the above table might produce the next table which would lead to an erroneous independence statement.

	current employment status		
	unemployed	employed	%
no training received	8	15	66
training received	12	24	66

The prospects of employment are heavily exaggerated, and once again the effect of training is disguised by the sub-population analysed - this time the population of respondents. The graph in Figure 10.8 illustrates.

These three examples emphasize the importance of examining the whole picture wherever possible. It is the joint distribution of all relevant variables that is of interest if an understanding of how all the variables interact

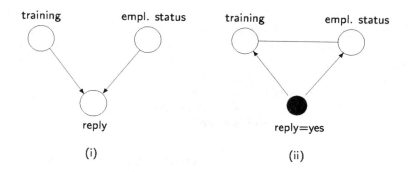

Figure 10.8: In (i) training and status are independent in the marginal distribution before conditioning on response to the postal questionnaire. In (ii) the solid circle indicates that the variable is given (conditioning) and training and status are dependent in this selected sample.

is desired. When only the marginal distribution of a subset is examined, either by choice, or because other variables are unobserved or unobservable, then interesting associations may be missed and spurious relationships may be misleadingly presented. Similarly the method of drawing samples may inadvertently imply conditioning on an unobserved variable, and again may lead to spurious relationships.

10.3 Graphical models in survey analysis

There are a number of graphical models that, depending on the contents of the dataset, can be used to describe different features of interest. It is simplest to proceed within the context of an example.

EXAMPLE 4

Credit scoring is the process whereby the applicant for credit is 'scored' in order to estimate his or her risk and so determines whether the application for a credit card should be accepted or declined. To calculate the overall score, predetermined scores are allocated to the individual characteristics which describe the applicant. These characteristics, associated with credit risk, are generally taken from the application form and credit reference agencies. Any applicant whose overall score falls below a cut-off value is declined credit. Credit scoring is a relatively straightforward field in which to describe the use of graphical models.

The 'scorecards' are built using previous customers for whom credit performance is known. This credit performance is usually categorized as 'Good', corresponding to satisfactory customers, and 'Bad', corresponding to customers the credit company regretted accepting, usually customers with a history of delinquency. The scores are calculated to provide the greatest discrimination between the Good and Bad customers. Note that the sample used to construct the scorecard can only be taken from the previously accepted sub-population about whom credit performance is known.

We consider some of various features of the credit scoring process that can be described by graphical models. Let (X_a, X_b, X_c) denote three *subsets* of variables taken from the application form and used to build the scorecard, with X_d denoting the subset of variables not used in card's construction. This subsetting notation means that if $b = \{4, 6, 8, 11\}$, then $X_b = (X_4, X_6, X_8, X_{11})$. Let Y be the eventual credit performance indicator and S the score or credit performance prediction.

A graphical model for the explanatory variables

A model of the joint distribution of the variables from the application form, $X = (X_a, X_b, X_c, X_d)$, using undirected edges is straightforward, see Figure 10.9. No assumptions about causal influences are made and a graph with just undirected edges is appropriate. The X variables are known for all applicants so inferences can be made about the through-the-door population.

We need to check various statements of conditional independence in order to construct the whole graph for all variables. However testing for independence from such data requires more substantive assumptions. By assuming a statistical model, for example, a bivariate normal distribution, one may relate the independence statement to the hypothesis that within the model, a specific parameter (or group of parameters) are zero (*e.g.* $\rho = 0$).

We shall begin by assuming that all variables on the application form are categorical and follow a (graphical) log-linear model, as discussed in the following sections. Had the variables all been continuous and jointly Gaussian, as is the case with the multiple exchange rate data discussed in Section 10.7, we would use the graphical Gaussian model discussed in Section 10.6.

More complex graphical models are possible

Inclusion of the credit performance indicator, Y, is clearly of interest to credit scorers. The conditional distribution of the indicator given the application form variables is of principal interest and a logistic regression model is generally used to model this conditional distribution (see, for instance, Agresti, 1990). Note that such an analysis only allows analysis of the accepted population since the performance indicator, Y, is not observable on the group declined a credit card; this selection may bias the conclusions drawn from the model as discussed above.

The distribution of the application variables together with the credit performance indicator may be jointly modelled, as in Figure 10.10, with a graph containing both directed edges and undirected edges. Such a model permits the assessment of which variables directly influence credit behaviour; and also, for example, to check whether the variables X_d that were not utilized in the score card construction do not, in fact, have any predictive ability for performance, Y.

Further including the score in this model, see Figure 10.11, the main focus of interest is in checking whether credit performance is conditionally independent of the application variables given the score, or whether the X variables contain additional information which could have improved the predictions. The score is a deterministic function of the observed application variables.

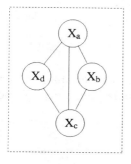

Figure 10.9: A possible graph of the application variables.

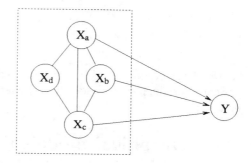

Figure 10.10: Graph of the application variables and credit performance indicator.

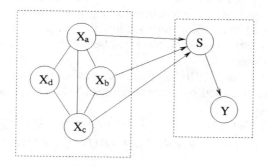

Figure 10.11: Graph of the application variables, credit performance indicator and the score.

An alternative way of modelling the relationship between X and Y is in a latent variable analysis. It may be reasonable to assume that people possess an unobserved underlying characteristic that determines their credit behaviour. This variable, Z, is such that credit performance, Y, is conditionally independent of the X variables, given Z, as Figure 10.12 illustrates.

In this model, the score would estimate the expected value of Z given the application form variables, X. If the arrows from Z to X were reversed this would be the graph of a reduced rank regression model.

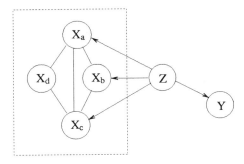

Figure 10.12: Latent variable situation. The application variables are independent of credit performance given the latent variable Z, underlying credit behaviour.

10.4 Graphical models for categorical variables

A systematic way of eliciting conditional independences from an observed categorical data set is to fit a log-linear model to the joint distribution of the variables in the study. Fitting models with certain log-linear parameters set to zero produces likelihood ratio tests of conditional independence with good statistical properties. An account of log-linear model analysis is given by Agresti (1990) and, using independence graphs, in Whittaker (1990). By their very construction such tests can be interpreted as part of a model selection procedure.

To briefly summarize, the log-linear all-way interaction expansion for a three-way table, classified by three variables (X_1, X_2, X_3), is

$$\log p_{123}(x_1, x_2, x_3) = u_\phi + u_1(x_1) + u_2(x_2) + u_3(x_3) + u_{12}(x_1, x_2) + $$
$$u_{13}(x_1, x_3) + u_{23}(x_2, x_3) + u_{123}(x_1, x_2, x_3) \ (10.2)$$

where, for example, the u-term $u_{12}(x_1, x_2)$ is the two-way interaction term between X_1 and X_2. In the special case of binary variables taking the values 0 and 1 the interaction terms may be simplified; for instance $u_{12}(x_1, x_2)$ can be replaced by:

$$u_{12}x_1x_2,$$

where u_{12} is a scalar, and the term only adds to (10.2) when both $x_1 = 1$ and $x_2 = 1$. This separates the parameter from the variables and makes the parameter explicit. More generally to avoid over parameterization constraints on the interaction terms, u, need to be imposed.

A table in which the conditional independence, $X_2 \perp\!\!\!\perp X_3 | X_1$, is satisfied has all interaction terms containing x_2 and x_3 set to zero, i.e. $u_{23} = 0$ and $u_{123} = 0$. The density function corresponding to this conditional independence is then

$$\log p_{123}(x_1, x_2, x_3) = u_\phi + u_1(x_1) + u_2(x_2) + u_3(x_3) + u_{12}(x_1, x_2) + u_{13}(x_1, x_3)$$
$$(10.3)$$

which satisfies the factorization at (10.1). Thus this model of conditional independence, with the same graph as in Figure 10.3 (i), is a sub-model of the saturated log-linear model above. The parameterization is easily extended from three to k dimensions.

Undirected independence graphs may be defined by the correspondence between a missing edge and the pairwise independence of two variables conditioned on the remaining variables, the rest. Within the log-linear model this corresponds to setting to zero all two-way and higher-way interactions containing that pair of variables.

The way to test for conditional independence is to fit the model at (10.3) by maximum likelihood and then compare the fitted values with the observed values using the deviance. The deviance of a particular model is twice the maximized log-likelihood ratio test statistic and measures the divergence between the observed values and the fitted values. It has a particularly simple form

$$\text{dev} = 2 \sum_{\text{cells}} \text{obs} \times \log \left(\frac{\text{obs}}{\text{fitted}} \right) \qquad (10.4)$$

and is closely approximated by Pearson's X^2 statistic. The fitted values are calculated from the specified log-linear model. Under the null hypothesis that the model specification is correct, the deviance has an asymptotic chi-squared distribution. The degrees of freedom are equal to the number of parameters set to zero in the saturated model's log-linear expansion to give the specified conditional independence model.

Edge exclusion deviances

A missing edge in the graph corresponds to a conditional independence between that pair of variables in the probability model. Edge exclusion deviances are those deviances corresponding to testing a pairwise conditional independence. To calculate any one edge exclusion deviance, that particular edge is dropped from the model M, say, and a new model, M' is defined. The deviance calculated by fitting the model M' is then compared with the deviance from the fitted model M. The difference between these two deviances defines the edge exclusion deviance, and is effectively a measure of how important that edge is in determining a good fit to the observed data. Small edge exclusion deviances correspond to near conditional independences while large deviances correspond to conditional dependences. The deviances may be calculated for each of the edges present in the graph of the model.

There is no neat formula for the edge exclusion deviance at (10.4), unlike (10.7) in the continuous case discussed later, but this deviance is easy to

compute numerically and may be taken as a measure of 'edge strength'
reflecting how confidently the null hypothesis of conditional independence
can be rejected.

Sparsity in the contingency table

It is common to have a large amount of information on the individuals in
the database. If attempts are made to model these variables simultaneously,
sparsity may soon become a problem.

For example, in a study at Lancaster with a sample size of some seven
thousand individuals and variables that typically contained between two and
five categories, the all-way saturated log-linear model was fitted to subsets
of around six variables. We found that (i) all of the edges were significant,
even at the 1% level; and (ii) that the edge exclusion deviances *increased*
disproportionately when additional variables were introduced to the model,
even after accounting for the extra degrees of freedom due to higher dimensions. Although this second latter point is theoretically possible, as
Simpson's paradox illustrates, it is expected that the extra information on
an additional variable should *reduce* the strength of the dependence between
the two variables on that specific edge.

It is sparsity that is causing the problems. Sparse tables have cells
with low frequencies due either to relatively small sample sizes, or to a
high number of categories classifying the variables, or to a large number of
variables. The failure to satisfy the large sample assumptions causes the
deviance to drift from the asymptotic chi-squared distribution and hence
induce misleading model selection.

EXAMPLE 5
**How sparsity may cause the deviance to increase upon further condi-
tioning.** Consider the edge exclusion deviance between variables X_1 and X_2.
As the dimension of the table is increased, each partial table is divided over the
levels of the additional conditioning variable. Each partial table contributes to
the edge exclusion deviance. Consider one such sparse observed partial table
between the two variables:

	$x_2 = 0$	$x_2 = 1$
$x_1 = 0$	1	1
$x_1 = 1$	1	2

This partial table's contribution to the edge exclusion deviance is 0.138 calculated from (10.4). Further conditioning on a variable X_3, independent of X_1
and X_2 with $p(x_3 = 1) = 0.5$, should not effect the edge exclusion deviance
between X_1 and X_2. However the expected table includes non-integer cell
counts, which is not possible:

	$x_3 = 0$		$x_3 = 1$	
	$x_2 = 0$	$x_2 = 1$	$x_2 = 0$	$x_2 = 1$
$x_1 = 0$	0.5	0.5	0.5	0.5
$x_1 = 1$	0.5	1	0.5	1

The sparsity of the table therefore forces the observations into one or the other of the levels of X_3, and dependences are induced. Two such possible tables are:

	$x_3 = 0$		$x_3 = 1$	
x_2 :	0	1	0	1
$x_1 = 0$	1	0	0	1
$x_1 = 1$	0	0	1	2

and

	$x_3 = 0$		$x_3 = 1$	
x_2 :	0	1	0	1
$x_1 = 0$	0	1	1	0
$x_1 = 1$	0	1	1	1

The contribution to the edge exclusion deviance is 1.73 and 1.05 respectively from these two tables, and by considering all possible tables, the expected edge exclusion deviance is 1.485, a large increase from the expected value of 0.138.

The cell frequencies of this example may seem artificially small, but they are typical of real survey data when interest is focused on the simultaneous analysis of several variables. While a larger sample size would avoid this problem, with a fixed sample size, high dimensions induce sparse sub-tables which inevitably increase the edge exclusion deviances. We propose the examination of the full two-way log-linear model as a remedy.

Two-way interaction models

A method for dealing with sparse data is to restrict models to the class of two-way interaction models. All-way interaction models have the complete table as a sufficient statistic, but the two-way interaction class only requires the set of all two-way marginal tables. These marginal tables are not sparse whatever the dimension of the data set. The number of parameters to estimate is correspondingly and drastically reduced. The conditional distributions derived from a two-way interaction model are necessarily additive in the log-odds ratio scale, which has to be assumed as a working hypothesis, though may be later modified.

The two-way interaction models are constructed by constraining all terms higher than two-way interaction terms in the log-linear expansion to be zero. So in 3-dimensions the model (10.2) is replaced by:

$$\log p_{123}(x_1, x_2, x_3) = u_\phi + u_1(x_1) + u_2(x_2) + u_3(x_3) + \\ u_3(x_3) + u_{12}(x_1, x_2) + u_{13}(x_1, x_3) + u_{23}(x_2, x_3)$$

and more generally in k dimensions

$$\log p(x_1, ..., x_k) = u_\phi + \sum_i u_i(x_i) + \sum_{i<j} u_{ij}(x_i, x_j). \qquad (10.5)$$

It is easily shown (see Whittaker, 1990), that the conditional independence:

$$X_1 \perp\!\!\!\perp X_2 | (X_3, X_4, \ldots, X_k)$$

is equivalent to $u_{12} = 0$ and so the independence graph is determined by the non-zero pairwise interaction terms, u_{ij}. Due to the reduced number of parameters in the model the tests for conditional independences in the full two-way interaction model are determined by relatively small degrees of freedom yielding far more powerful tests, and better asymptotic approximations. The price to pay is that if higher order interactions are non-zero, this may not necessarily be recognized and the model may fit parts of the table poorly.

In practice, unlike the saturated all-way interaction models, the two-way interaction model gives sensible results.

Model selection

When the contingency table is of dimension higher than three, there are a large number of possible models, each with its own graph, that might represent the data. It is useful to have a procedure to help select an acceptable model and one simple, but rather naive, model selection procedure is to fit the saturated model, determine which u-terms are negligible and then use this to decide the structure of the independence graph.

A substantial improvement is to drop the edges according to the size of the edge exclusion deviance which is computed for each of the edges in the graph. A further improvement is to use a backward elimination procedure where the edges are dropped sequentially according to the size of the edge exclusion deviances which are recomputed at each step. The process continues until a final model is determined. The edge strengths in the final model in which all edges are retained are used to highlight the relatively important interactions in the fitted graphs.

Forward selection procedures add edges to the graph. Edge inclusion deviances can be calculated in a similar manner by comparing the deviances in the models with and without the edge of interest. The edge is added to the graph if a large drop in deviance is apparent in the model which includes this edge. Stepwise model selection procedures move from model to model using the information provided by the array of edge inclusion and exclusion deviances.

10.5 A graphical model for credit card applications

EXAMPLE 6

The application form data. The data analysed in this section is a stratified sample of current account holders of a major bank who applied for a credit card to the bank's credit card division between June and November 1992. The total sample size is 7702 which includes 'Goods', 'Bads', 'indeterminates' and 'rejects'. Note that the data is a sample of the through-the-door population and hence the credit performance variable is not known for some of the applicants, namely the rejects, and we do not consider it in this application.

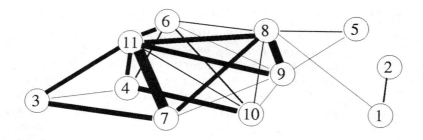

Figure 10.13: Independence graph of the scorecard application form variables.

The variables analysed in this paper, taken from the application form are given in Table 10.1.

1. bank account type,
2. own cheque guarantee card,
3. children,
4. employment status,
5. own phone,
6. income band,
7. marital status,
8. residential status,
9. time at address,
10. time at employment and
11. age.

Table 10.1: Variables of the credit card applicants data set.

The subset of variables selected here are not only potential scorecard covariates but are chosen to describe the social and demographic characteristics of the population. The data has been coarsely classified into the credit card company's usual groupings in order to reduce the number of categories, and most variables contain between two and five levels.

The fitted graphical model and graph

Using software developed at the University of Lancaster we model this subset of variables by fitting the full two-way interaction model eliminating insignificant edges. This led to the graph in Figure 10.13.

There are a number of observations worth noting.

o The banking variables, bank account type (1), and own cheque guarantee card (2), are conditionally independent from the rest of the variables given residential status. People who possess their own property are more likely to have both deposit and current accounts; tenants are more likely to have deposit accounts; and people who live with their parents are less likely to have both types of account. People with deposit accounts are less likely to have cheque guarantee cards. The other variables provide no additional information about the banking variables.

o Owning a phone (5) depends only on residential status (8) and time at address (9). People who rent property are less likely to have their own phone, as are people who have only recently moved into a new property.

o Once information is known about an individual's employment status (4), marital status (7), and age (11), the other variables have no additional power in predicting whether the person has children (3).

o Marital status (7) and age (11) are very strongly dependent. It is obvious that very young people have a lower probability of being married, let alone separated, divorced or widowed.

o Residential status (8), time at address (9), and age (11) are strongly dependent. We can explain this association by considering that young people who live with their parents have generally lived at the same address for a number of years. Apart from this sub-population, we would expect to see that, in the main, time at address increases linearly with age.

o Marital status (7) is conditionally independent of employment status (4), given income (6), residential status (8) and age (11).

A comparison of distinct age groups.

We compare graphical models built for distinct sub-populations based on young and older age groups.

It is evident from Figure 10.13 that age (11) has an important role in the model. It is also likely that the two-way interaction model is not sufficient to explain some of the associations, and that some of the more complex relationships could be modelled by considering age groups separately. For example, the relationship between time at address and residential status is dependent on age: young people have not had the opportunity to live in rented or owned accommodation as long as older people. By modelling age groups separately, three-way interactions with age are included.

Furthermore a separate score card is often used for applicants under a certain age. The graphs of the two distinct age groups can reveal the differences between the structure of the two populations and hence suggest the importance of using separate scorecards. To carry out this comparison the data has been split into two, approximately equal sized groups of 'young' and 'old' applicants.

The graphs of the 'young' and 'old' applicants are shown in Figure 10.14 and Figure 10.15 respectively.

Note that edges present in the graph in Figure 10.13 almost always exist in at least one of the sub-population graphs. While the graphs are substantially similar, there are a number of evident differences, confirming that the inter-relationships between these variables change with age. A discriminant function, built without including higher interactions with age, would not succeed in modelling these differences.

We comment on some of the differences between the two graphs here, although this list is by no means comprehensive:

o Bank account type (1) and residential status (8) are independent of the other variables in the young sub-population. This perhaps reflects a difference between generations. The older sub-population are perhaps more reluctant to change their ways and are less often targeted by the banks marketing departments, and hence older tenants are less likely to have deposit accounts.

o The conditional dependence between children (3) and employment status (4) is only apparent in the older population, where the self-employed, and non-workers are more likely to have children. There are obviously less young people with children, so it is difficult to judge whether a relationship exists.

o Owning a phone (5) and residential status (8) are independent in the young sub-population. Young people are just as likely to have a phone wherever they live.

o The relationship between income band (6) and residential status (8), time at address (9), and time at employment (10), is stronger in the young population. For young people, a high income increases the opportunity for moving out of the parental home.

o Marital status (7) and time at address (9) are conditionally independent in the old population. People tend to change residence or ownership when they get married. In the young population, married people have only been married for a short time, and so marital status is associated with a short time at address.

o In the young population, time at employment (10) is associated with residential status (8), and is conditionally independent of time at address (9). The converse is true in the old population. We hypothesize that living with parents is associated with not having worked very long. Older people are more likely to live with their parents for different reasons other than waiting to find a new job.

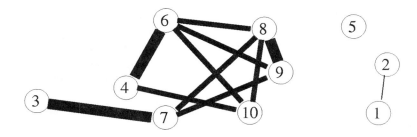

Figure 10.14: Independence graph of the young sub-population.

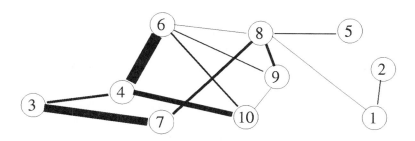

Figure 10.15: Independence graph of the older sub-population.

The graphs of the application variables allow a structured and systematic discussion of the many possible inter-relationships between the variables on the forms. Of course, this is no replacement for the examination of the details of particular relationships within sub-tables of interest, but does provide an overall context.

Finally we note that modelling in high dimensions inevitably leads to sparsity and misleading model selections from fitting the all-way log-linear interaction model. The asymptotic approximation to the chi-squared distribution becomes invalid and it is not possible to obtain reasonable parameter estimates. The all two-way interaction model overcomes the problems of sparsity whilst still retaining the conditional independence structure. It has strong links with logistic regression, the interactions are easily interpretable, and it provides sensible estimates of the edge exclusion deviances. On the downside, it may neglect higher order interactions.

10.6 Graphical Gaussian models for continuous variables

The simplest assumption for random variables measured on a continuous scale is that they have a *normal* or *Gaussian joint distribution*. The key benefit of such an assumption, in terms of constructing graphical models, is that uncorrelated normal random variables are independent and partially uncorrelated normal random variables are conditionally independent. Furthermore partial correlation coefficients are zero whenever the corresponding element in the inverse variance matrix is zero. Detailed exploitation of these relationships is discussed in Whittaker (1990).

Suppose $X = (X_1, X_2, \ldots, X_q)'$ is a q-dimensional random vector with a multivariate normal distribution, mean $E(X) = \mu$ and variance var $(X) = V$. The inverse variance is $D = V^{-1}$. The ij-th element of D is d_{ij}. The density of X, written in terms of the inverse variance, is

$$f(x) \quad = \quad (2\pi)^{-k/2} D^{1/2} \exp\left\{-\frac{1}{2}(x-\mu)'D(x-\mu)\right\},$$

which may be rearranged as

$$f(x) = \exp\left\{\alpha + \sum_{i=1}^{q} \beta_i x_i - 1/2 \sum_{i=1}^{q}\sum_{j=1}^{q} d_{ij} x_i x_j\right\}, \qquad (10.6)$$

where the α and β are suitably determined constants. Note how similar it is to the full two-way log-linear interaction model at (10.5). When $d_{ij} = 0$, the quadratic terms in the density separate into two parts, one not depending on x_i and the other not depending on x_j. This is enough, see (10.1), to establish the conditional independence $X_i \perp\!\!\!\perp X_j | X_{\text{rest}}$.

It is apparent from this that setting elements of the inverse variance matrix, the parameters, to zero is equivalent to modelling conditional independences and hence defining the corresponding graphical model. Models specified in this way are known as *graphical Gaussian models*. For example, in a three-dimensional setting, setting the element d_{13} to zero corresponds to requiring that $X_1 \perp\!\!\!\perp X_3 | X_2$, and the edge connecting the nodes 2 and 3 in the corresponding graph would be missing, giving the graph in Figure 10.3 (i).

The parameters are determined empirically by maximizing the appropriate likelihood function. For certain models the maximum can be found directly, although for other models an iterative method such as the iterative proportional fitting procedure, is necessary to solve the likelihood equations indirectly (Whittaker, 1990).

As in the categorical case, alternative models are compared by using the deviance, the maximized log-likelihood ratio test statistic. When just one edge is excluded from the complete graph the formula is particularly simple,

$$\mathrm{dev}_{ij} = -N \log(1 - r^2_{ij|rest}) \qquad (10.7)$$

where the sample size is N, and $r_{ij|rest}$ is the partial correlation of the pair given the rest. To use this as a statistical test, its value is compared to the chi-squared distribution with 1 degree of freedom. For the deviance in the more general situation of comparing models differing by dropping several edges, see Agresti (1990) and, using independence graphs, Whittaker (1990) or Edwards (1995).

10.7 A graphical model for foreign exchange rates

The plots in Figure 10.16 are the logged daily changes of five exchange rates recorded by the Swiss Bank Corporation, from Jan 96 to Apr 97. There are 334 working days in these series. The five rates are the Swiss Franc, the German Mark, the French Franc, the Great British Pound and the Japanese Yen all measured against the American Dollar.

There are good economic reasons to believe these increments are independent in time because, if not, then it is possible to use previous values of the series to predict the future course of the rates; and so, in a free market, it would be possible to make money without cost.

Inspection of the five increment series suggests that they are stationary, namely that the average behaviour of a series in any one time window is much the same for any other window. Histograms of these increments are shown in the diagonal of Figure 10.17 and are not inconsistent with Normal (or Gaussian) distributions for their marginal distributions.

The pairs plot of one increment against each of the others, reveals that these variables are all correlated. Most pairs of increments show a positive linear association, but with varying strengths. For instance, there is an

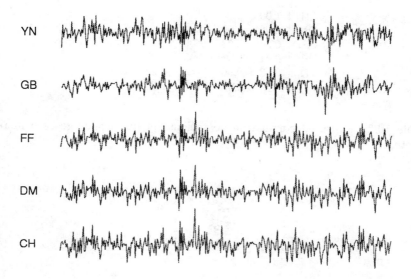

Figure 10.16: Exchange rates increments: logged daily changes in five exchange rates, 333 points from Jan 96 to Apr 97.

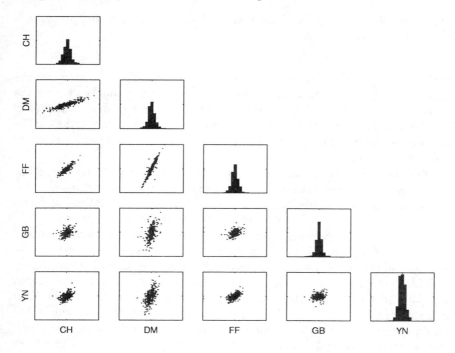

Figure 10.17: Pairs plot of five exchange rate increments, with histograms on the diagonal.

	CH	DM	FF	GB	YN
CH	1.00				
DM	0.90	1.00			
FF	0.86	0.93	1.00		
GB	0.41	0.46	0.43	1.00	
YN	0.53	0.56	0.54	0.22	1.00

Table 10.2: Marginal correlation coefficients of five exchange rate increments.

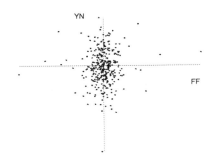

Figure 10.18: Scatter plot of the French Franc against the Yen having adjusted for the Mark.

extremely pronounced linear relationship between the French Franc and the Mark. The Swiss Franc is also highly correlated with the Mark. At the other extreme the correlation between the Yen and the British pound is relatively small. The relationships are linear and so their strengths can be adequately summarized by the matrix of correlation coefficients given in Table 10.2.

The conclusion that everything is correlated with everything else is not one we particularly wish to draw: it neither yields any financial insight, nor is it a parsimonious statistical model. However these correlations measure the marginal association between each pair of variables.

A more fruitful approach is to examine some of the conditional associations between the pair, while conditioning on the values of another variable. The *partial* (or conditional) correlation, is easily calculated for continuous variables. Consider the relationship between the Yen and French Franc in the pairs plot of Figure 10.17, clearly showing a positive correlation with value corr$(FF, YN) = 0.5387$ as given in Table 10.2. Now calculate the residuals in the ordinary least squares regression of the Franc on the Mark; and separately calculate the residuals of the Yen on the Mark. The scatter plot of these residuals is displayed in Figure 10.18.

These residuals are virtually uncorrelated. The partial correlation coefficient is defined as the ordinary correlation between these two residuals.

	CH	DM	FF	GB	YN
CH	1.00				
DM	0.53	1.00			
FF	0.13	0.68	1.00		
GB	-0.03	0.17	0.02	1.00	
YN	0.05	0.15	0.04	-0.05	1.00

Table 10.3: Partial correlation coefficients of five exchange rate increments, each partialled on the rest.

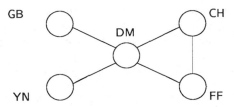

Figure 10.19: Independence graph of the five exchange rate increments.

Numerically we find that the partial correlation of the Franc and the Yen given the Mark is corr $(FF, YN|DM) = 0.0455$. It is almost zero, suggesting that the marginal association between the Franc and the Yen is due to a common correlation with the Mark. With just these three variables, taking the near zero partial correlation to be statistically indistinguishable from zero, the independence graph is

There is no edge between the Franc and the Yen. We write $FF \perp\!\!\!\perp YN|DM$ as, by normality, the Franc and the Yen are independent conditional on the Mark.

This technique generalizes to five variables by computing the partial correlations of each pair given the 'rest'. The ordinary regression on one exogenous variable is now a multiple regression on the variables determined by the 'rest'. Thus we can compute corr $(FF, YN|CH, DM, GB) = 0.0398$ by regressions of the Franc and the Yen on the Swiss Franc, Mark and Pound. Similarly, the partial correlations of all the $\binom{5}{2} = 10$ pairs are reported in Table 10.3.

These partial correlations reveal a structure concealed in the marginal correlations. There are five partial correlations less than 0.05, say, in absolute value. This suggests the independence graph (more precisely, the conditional independence graph displayed in Figure 10.19).

Fitting the graphical Gaussian model defined by this graph to the data leads to an acceptable model with an overall deviance of 2.53 on 5 degrees of freedom (corresponding to the five missing edges).

DM	108.7913			
FF	5.7672	202.7131		
GB	-0.2251	9.4959	0.1147	
YN	0.6886	7.7903	0.5287	-0.7850
	CH	DM	FF	GB

Table 10.4: Edge exclusion deviances.

The graph reveals important features of the joint distribution of the five exchange rate increments. The Markov property of the graph states that one variable, or group of variables, is independent of another group, conditionally upon the values of the variables that *separate* these two groups. Note that a set of variables separates if its removal from the graph leaves the two groups unconnected.

In this instance, among many other relationships, we can see that

$$FF \perp\!\!\!\perp YN | DM, \quad FF \perp\!\!\!\perp YN | (CH, DM, GB)$$

and,

$$(CH, FF) \perp\!\!\!\perp YN | DM \quad GB \perp\!\!\!\perp YN | DM.$$

Several further substantive conclusions can be drawn from this independence graph:

- o the more complex 5-dimensional object is decomposed into three simpler objects, one of 3 and two of 2 dimensions;

- o the Mark is highlighted as the one crucial exchange rate in analysing the exchange rate inter-relationships;

- o the graph asserts that the Mark is sufficient to predict the Pound, the Mark and the Swiss Franc are needed to predict the French Franc, and that all four rates are needed to predict the Mark.

Figure 10.20 is a version of the independence graph that displays edge strengths. While there are several ways to measure strength we choose one that equally well applies to categorical and mixed data: the edge exclusion deviance (See Table 10.4). Here our model is a graphical Gaussian model, and the array of edge exclusion deviances, is from (10.7) with sample size $N = 333$.

A comparison of the graphs in Figures 10.19 and 10.20 show that the Mark is very closely related to the Swiss and French Francs, while the relationship between the two Francs conditioned on the Mark is much weaker, but still not to be neglected.

The graphical model determined is specified by stating that the joint distribution of the exchange rate increments has a 5-dimensional Gaussian distribution, with mean vector estimated by the sample mean [-0.71 -0.55 -0.51 0.14 -0.59] and variance matrix estimated by:

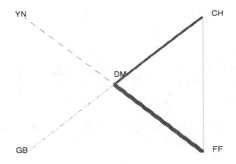

Figure 10.20: Independence graph of five exchange rates with edge strengths indicated.

CH	36.55				
DM	28.25	26.75			
FF	25.92	23.96	24.74		
GB	11.45	10.85	9.72	20.58	
YN	15.44	14.62	13.09	5.93	25.14
	CH	DM	FF	GB	YN

This model fits extremely well, its deviance of 2.53 is well within the 5% point of the chi-squared distribution on 5 degrees of freedom. The fitted marginal and fitted partial correlations are displayed in Tables 10.5 and 10.6. Note how close these fitted correlations are to the empirical correlations in Tables 10.2 and 10.3. There are exact zeros in the five partial correlations corresponding to the 5 missing edges in the graph of Figure 10.19. We have determined a well fitting model that characterizes the contemporaneous variation in the exchange rates by the graphs of Figures 10.19 and 10.20.

10.8   Concluding remarks

Graphical models is a novel but now rapidly expanding area of statistics which has many connections to long established branches of statistical modelling, including, for instance, path and regression analysis, log-linear, latent variable and structural equation models, time series and stochastic

CH	1.00				
DM	0.90	1.00			
FF	0.86	0.93	1.00		
GB	0.42	0.46	0.43	1.00	
YN	0.51	0.56	0.53	0.26	1.00
	CH	DM	FF	GB	YN

Table 10.5: Fitted marginal for the multiple exchange rate data.

CH	-1.00				
DM	0.53	-1.00			
FF	0.13	0.68	-1.00		
GB	0.00	0.15	-0.00	-1.00	
YN	0.00	0.20	0.00	-0.00	-1.00
	CH	DM	FF	GB	YN

Table 10.6: Fitted partial correlations for the multiple exchange rate data.

processes. There are numerous fields of application of graphical models, especially in the human social, economic, medical and biological sciences; some applications are directly practical, as exemplified by the credit scoring example, while others are more theoretical leading to insights in, for example, Simpson's paradox.

There are as many graphical models as there are systems of random variables with a specified probability distribution. Because of the ubiquitous nature of conditional independence, independence graphs abound throughout statistics and statistical modelling. The graph to represent the regression of a variable Y on X has just two nodes and the directed edge from X to Y. It of course conceals as much as it reveals, and for instance, the graph is the same whether the regression be ordinary or logistic regression, and whatever the link function.

There are some classes of models for which the graph is rather informative, in particular, we would point to: *Bayesian (belief) networks* which use directed models; models with latent variables, be they continuous, discrete, ordinal or just categorical, such as models with random effects, structural equation models, state space models, and more general Bayesian hierarchical models; and models for missing data mechanisms. In these models the graph may be relatively sparse, and relatively structured, and thereby more informative than a graph with all edges present. The ideas of graphical models have been used to build probabilistic expert systems, solve pedigree trees, enhance image analysis, and are now being extended to encompass neural networks.

Relation to other chapters in this volume

It is clear that graphs and graphical models are related to causality and causal inference. This is the underlying topic of the accompanying Chapter 12 by Pearl on 'Graphs, causality and structural equation models' and Chapter 11 by Saris on 'Structural equation modelling'.

The independence graphs described in this chapter are graphs of conditional independence relationships in probability distributions, and are not representations of causality. This is not to say that they cannot be representations of causal links, but that no such claim is made; and nor is one necessary: many interesting problems of scientific analysis are exploratory, descriptive and comparative, and do not require associations to be explicitly causal. Furthermore scientific tests for causal structures require controlled experimentation, while assessment of joint probabilities only require observational studies.

An illustration of the difference between *independence graphs* of probability distributions and *causal graphs* of causal relationships is furnished by retrospective studies of smoking and cancer. It is known that smoking is a cause of lung cancer, so that in a causal graph a parent of lung cancer is smoking. However, in a comparison of equal numbers of lung cancer patients with controls the statistical response variate is smoking and the causal dependence on the risk factor would be depicted by an arrow from cancer to smoking in the independence graph. **The general point is that information in the form of probabilities can flow in two directions while causation can only flow in one.**

10.8.1 Further reading

We have already mentioned the seminal article of Darroch et al. (1980) and the books of Whittaker (1990), Edwards (1995), and Lauritzen (1996). The book by Edwards is the most practical, and also describes the program MIM for fitting these models, Lauritzen is theoretically orientated, while Whittaker attempts to strike a balance.

The text by Cox & Wermuth (1996) has several real-life scale examples taken from the social sciences, especially education and psychology, and the monograph by Dean (1993) includes chapters containing examples taken from the health sciences.

Bayesian belief networks, which are directed graphs defined by sequences of conditional probabilities are used in probabilistic expert systems. See, for example Pearl (1988) or, more recently, Jensen (1996). For applications of Bayesian belief networks to artificial neural networks, see Bishop (1995) or Ripley (1996). Closely related to directed graphs are the influence diagrams of decision theory, which may be viewed as graphical models that contain nodes relating to individual decisions, see Marshall & Oliver (1995) for a thorough account.

Perhaps especial mention should be made of the use of independence graphs in defining Bayesian statistical models, see Spiegelhalter (1998).

The credit industry is a major part of the economy's financial services. With the relentless developments in electronics and computing many financial applications are now automated with judgements essentially made on the basis of the statistical analysis of large data bases. In this Chapter we have given examples set in the context of credit card usage, and we have shown how a graphical model may be useful in the analysis of real data. A start to the credit scoring literature is Lewis (1992) or the volume edited by Thomas, Crook, & Edelman (1992). References to the more general applications of statistics in finance are given in the recent volume edited by Hand & Jacka (1997). Graphical models have been applied to data from the credit industry by Hand, McConway, & Stanghellini (1996) and Whittaker & Sewart (1998).

10.8.2 Software

Computing gets easier and easier but the demand for higher and higher specifications makes writing one's own software a daunting task. While the machinery to fit all the graphical models discussed here is, in principle, available its usage is far from automatic. General purpose statistical software is widely available (Matlab, SPSS, SAS, S+) and can sometimes be cajoled into fitting graphical models. However, their main defect is that they do not support decent graphics for the display of independence graphs.

For modelling a joint distribution, and when the data sets are not too large the PC-program MIM of Edwards (1995) is most useful. It is based on a broad family of statistical models for discrete and continuous variables, including hierarchical log-linear models, graphical Gaussian models, graphical association models, standard MANOVA models and various other models used in multivariate analysis. MIM includes facilities for defining and reading data, defining and manipulating models, displayng their independence graphs, fitting models to data by maximum likelihood, tests for comparison of models (including exact tests), several methods of model selection, estimation for incomplete data or latent variables using the EM-algorithm.

CoCo is a statistics package for analysis of associations between discrete variables, obtained by loading CoCo into Xlisp-Stat. With this graphical user interface a model selection on graphical models can be performed by mouse interaction with the independence graph. An idea of its capabilities can be gleaned from the key words: *statistical analysis of discrete data, contingency table, decomposable, graphical and hierarchical models, log-linear model, interactions, independence graph, conditional independence, closed form expression for maximum likelihood estimates, IPS algorithm, large sparse tables, zero partial association, exact conditional test, incomplete tables, quasi-independence.* The package has model editing commands, and implementations of model selection strategy: coherence, incremental search procedures: backward and forward, restricted incremental search, global search.

Internet addresses for the graphical modeller

A file of hyperlinks to web pages of interest to the graphical modeller is maintained at the address:

    http://www.maths.lancs.ac.uk/~whittake

This list includes addresses, from which technical reports, advice and free software may sometimes be obtained.

10.9   Summary

Graphical models and their associated conditional independence statements
have a role to play in many areas of science, especially the human sciences,
and, to illustrate, we have taken two substantive examples from financial
science. We have shown that examination of the independence relationships
has revealed structure that is otherwise unseen in more standard analyses of
these data. We have argued that to avoid interpreting spurious relationships
and to understand the more complex associations, it is necessary to examine the joint probability distribution of the variables of interest. Through
didactic and practical examples set in the financial context we have shown
that graphical models provide the means to:

- display the multivariate interactions between variables expressed in
  the original coordinate system;

- simplify and describe the association between variables, that may lead
  to models for the causal system generating the data;

- directly compare sub-populations;

- illustrate possible effects on variable inter-dependency, such as bias,
  due to marginalization, selection and stratification.

Acknowledgements

This work was carried out with assistance from the credit card division of
a major UK bank; the cooperation of the Swiss Bank Corporation and of
Yadolah Dodge of the University of Neuchatel; support from the ALCD
(Analysis of Large and Complex Data) initiative of the ESRC, award
H519255029.

Chapter 11

Structural Equation Modelling

Willem E. Saris

In some fields of research it is not possible to apply experimental designs to control for confounding variables and to manipulate the causal variable. Some authors, like Cook & Campbell (1979), take the position that in such fields causal inferences are nearly impossible. This is, however, not the point of view of those working in the field of Structural equation models. We will show in this chapter, why we share this opinion.

Structural equation modelling started in Biology with a paper by Wright (1934) and was introduced into the Social Sciences by Simon (1954) and Blalock (1964) who advocated the use of partial correlation coefficients. Later on, many others used a slightly different approach which has been labelled 'path analysis' (e.g., Duncan, 1966, 1975) and the close relation to linear regression analysis was better understood. The methodology became better developed after a meeting in 1971 of psychologists, working on factor analysis; economists, working with simultaneous equations; sociologists, working on causal models with latent variables; and statisticians interested in the statistical aspects of these very models (Goldberger & Duncan, 1973). At this meeting a structural equation model was introduced and discussed which allows representation of the above models as special cases. At the same meeting, Jöreskog presented the first version of his now famous LISREL program (Jöreskog, 1973). These developments have led to the present situation in which structural equation modelling is widely and intensively used to derive causal inferences using data originating from non-experimental research.

In this chapter we will introduce the basic principles and assumptions of *Structural Equation Modelling* (or *SEM*, by abbreviation). The emphasis will not be on the statistical details but rather on the logic of the approach and its assumptions. For the statistical details we refer to the textbooks. Saris & Stronkhorst (1984) gives a simple introduction, while Bollen (1989) provides a more advanced and thorough coverage of the topic.

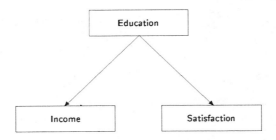

Figure 11.1: Diagram of causal influences.

11.1   Formulation of Structural equation models

Often researchers start with only a vague notion that one variable might have an effect on another variable. For example, in the life satisfaction research it is very common to suppose that Income is causally related to Satisfaction. Veenhoven (1996) has given ample evidence of this relationship on an aggregate level, using countries as units. On the other hand, the empirical evidence of this relationship on an individual level is rather weak. In a cross-cultural study in thirteen different countries, the correlation between these two variables was larger than 0.2 in only one country (Saris, Veenhoven, Scherpenzeel, & Bunting, 1996).

A major problem with causal inferences in non-experimental research is the eventuality of confounding variables. For example, in the case mentioned above the possibility that the weak relationship between Income and Satisfaction is a *spurious* one, can not be excluded. The explanation is that people with a higher eduction usually get a higher income and that the level of education also effects satisfaction. This simple idea is presented in Figure 11.1 where an arrow represents a direct causal effect. This figure is based on the two assumed direct causal effects:

  o *Higher Education will cause higher Income.*

  o *Higher Education will cause more Satisfaction.*

As a consequence of these two statements we may conclude that:

Higher Income is associated with higher Satisfaction.

This last statement follows from the previous two without any assumption about the direct effect of Income on Satisfaction. This *could* be a typical example of a spurious relationship between the variables Income and Satisfaction due to the effects of a *third* variable, Education.

Note that a 'spurious relationship' is *not* a non-existent relationship! Such a relationship is real enough but it is not a *causal* relationship. It

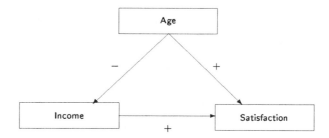

Figure 11.2: A diagram indicating possible causal effects between three variables.

would have been better to speak of a spurious effect but the term spurious relationship or spurious correlation is so widely used that this habit is not easily changed.

It is also possible that the association between two variables of interest is moderate or even absent due to a spurious relationship with a third variable. For example we could image the following three relationships:

o *Older people have lower incomes.*

o *The older people become, the higher their Satisfaction.*

o *Income has a positive effect on Satisfaction.*

This model is presented in Figure 11.2.
From the first two relationships, it follows that:

The lower the Income the more satisfied people are.

This spurious relationship is negative, while we expect a positive effect of Income on Satisfaction. The consequence of this combination of relationships can be that the correlation between these two variables is approximately zero if the spurious relationship and the causal effect cancel each other out. This example indicates that an important assignment of non-experimental research is to distinguish between spurious and causal relationships. Having formulated the problem in this way, an obvious solution may be the following:

Prescription 1 *In non-experimental research, all those variables that may cause a spurious relationship between the variables of interest have to be collected and included in the data set.*

If we take care of this, we can assess whether the relationship between the variables of interest is at all spurious. If not, we can conclude that the relationship is a causal one. This argument is based on the following principle:

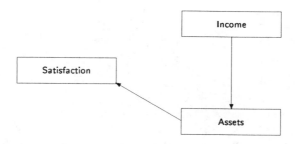

Figure 11.3: Example of an indirect effect.

Principle 1 *If the covariance between the variables of interest can be entirely explained by variables that cause spurious relationships between them, we conclude that the variables of interest have no causal relationship.*

Consequently, if the covariance between the variables of interest can not be explained by the variables which cause spurious relationships between the variables of interest, one can conclude for the time being that the variables of interest have a causal relationship.

Although this principle is undoubtedly correct, in everyday research we can never be sure that Prescription 1 is satisfied and that all variables producing spurious relationships have been collected. Besides that, statistical evaluation can only be performed correctly if the variables are measured without error. We will come back to this later.

The requirement to include all variables that can cause spurious relationships entails that a very serious effort has to be made to elicit all those variables. This leads to the following approach:

Before the actual design is formulated, one has to list all variables that could possibly cause spurious relationships between the variables of interest. In order to do so, diagrams of the kind shown in Figure 11.1 and 11.2 can be used.

Such diagrams are called *path diagrams*. The arrows in these diagrams indicate direct effects of one variable on another. Indirect effects and spurious relationships do not have to be presented in the diagrams because they are automatically derived from the direct effects. Figure 11.3 may serve as an example of this way of reasoning: In this case, the two direct effects are:

o *Income has an effect on Assets.*

o *Assets has an effect on Satisfaction.*

From these two causal relationships it follows that:

Income influences Satisfaction.

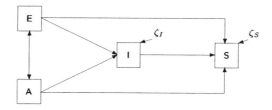

Figure 11.4: A path diagram of the causal model for a study on income satisfaction.
E: Education, A: Age, I: Income, S: Satisfaction.

However, Figure 11.3 shows no direct arrow from Income to Satisfaction: the causal relationship is indirect and this is represented by two direct effects. Note that the relationship between Income and Satisfaction is not spurious: there *is* an effect although it is an indirect one. An intervening (or mediating) variable like 'Assets' does not have to be included in the study because it does not cause a spurious relationship, being an intervening variable. However, sometimes such variables are useful to understand why a causal effect occurs.

Other types of variables that do not have to be included in the study are variables that effect only the cause or the effect but not both. Such variables can not cause a spurious relationship and can be omitted. For example, satisfaction with one's marriage will probably have an effect on satisfaction but not on the income of a person. Therefore, this variable can not produce a spurious relationship between the variables of interest and can thus be ignored. Such variables in combination are represented by variables called *disturbance terms*. We represent them by the symbol ζ_i for the ith variable. Such variables are only attached to the effect variables.

Figure 11.4 illustrates the use of a path diagram for the satisfaction example. In this model two variables are included which are expected to produce spurious relationships between the variables Income and Satisfaction. The first is Education and the second is Age. For the sake of the argument we assume that these two variables are the only variables causing spurious relationships between Income and Satisfaction.

In path diagrams two directional arrows are used to indicate a correlation between two variables that is unaffected by other variables in the model. These correlations are an essential part of the model. To see this, imagine that some other variable is introduced in the model that is a causal variable for both Education and Age (for instance: Age of the parent). This new variable could indirectly cause a spurious relationship between Income and Satisfaction. If we do not want to allow for this possibility in our model, we implicitly assume that Education and Age are first in the causal chain. Such variables are called *exogeneous*. These exogeneous variables are not further explained by other variables in the model but can be correlated.

	Causal variables			
	Income	Satisfaction	Education	Age
Effect variables				
Income			×	×
Satisfaction	×		×	×

Table 11.1: Effect matrix of path diagram of Figure 11.2.

This brings us to a second set of conditions a path diagrams should fulfill:

Prescription 2 *Each diagram should include:*

○ *The cause and effect variables of interest.*

○ *All variables that may cause spurious relations between cause and effect variables.*

○ *The direct effects between the variables indicating causal relationships.*

○ *Correlations between exogeneous variables.*

○ *Disturbance terms representing all variables that need not be explicitly represented.*

In this way a more elaborate theory is formulated to study the causal relationship of interest. To make sure that no effects have been forgotten, a different representation is suggested by some authors called *the effect matrix* (Saris & Stronkhorst, 1984).

The rows of this matrix contain the effect variables, while the columns contain the causal variables. The cells of the matrix contain indications of the presence or absence of an effect relationship between row and column entries.

Table 11.1 gives the effect matrix that corresponds to the model of Figure 11.4.

The representation of a theory in an effect matrix has the advantage that the assumptions with respect to the zero effects are clearly shown. From Table 11.1, it is immediately apparent that we have omitted the effect of Satisfaction on Income. Since in this case that seems plausible, no changes to the model are necessary.

Another advantage of the effect matrix is that it can represent any theory independent of the number of variables, while path diagrams may become confusing if the number of variables increases. In this specific case, the number of variables is not too large and both representations work well. But the difference in emphasis may be clear: from a path diagram we can immediately deduce which effects are expected to exist, while from an effect matrix it is at once apparent which effects supposedly do *not* exist. In this way, the two representations are complementary.

So far we have described only two approaches to represent a causal model. Before such a model can be statistically analysed, it has to be translated into a system of linear equations called *structural equations*. The term 'structural' only means that we try to represent causal relationships and not merely the covariance between the variables of the model or even functional relationships.

This translation step can be done routinely either starting from the path diagram or from the effect matrix. For instance, in the above model two linear equations would result having the following form:

$$I = g_{11}E + g_{12}A + \zeta_I \qquad (11.1)$$
$$S = b_{21}I + g_{21}E + g_{22}A + \zeta_S. \qquad (11.2)$$

This type of model is frequently used to estimate the effect of Income and other variables on Satisfaction. In many cases the effect of Income on Satisfaction turns out very weak. Possibly the reason is that the last step is made too easily.

The above direct translation into a set of linear equations may not be optimal, due to two major conditions that have to be taken into account and that have not yet been mentioned:

Prescription 3

1. *For any value of the causal variable, the effects on the effect variables should be the same.*

2. *The effect should be the same for any value of another causal variable in the model.*

If both requirements are satisfied, the set of linear equations can be specified immediately. If one of the conditions does not hold, the linear equations are not correct and a transformation into linear equations has to be worked out. That this situation is not unusual can be illustrated by means of the Income-Satisfaction study.

There is a lot of evidence suggesting that the Income-Satisfaction model assuming linear effects and additivity is too simple. First of all, there is ample evidence that the satisfaction level depends not only on the income of a person but rather on the deviation of Income from the income *aspirations*. Most recently, this point was made by Saris (1996).

Secondly, it may be assumed that the effect of an income increase is not the same for all initial values of Income. Instead, Hamblin (1974) found that the effect of the same income increase is smaller if the initial income is higher. So it seems that the relationship between Income and Satisfaction is non-linear and even non-additive. If this non-linearity is inherent to the relation between Income and Satisfaction, this may be one of the reasons the relationship normally found between these two variables while using a linear model is much weaker than one would expect.

Let us for a moment assume that satisfaction gets larger if the ratio of real income and income aspiration level becomes larger than one and that Satisfaction is smaller if this ratio is smaller than one. In order to represent the phenomenon that the effect becomes smaller for larger values of the ratio we can use a power function. Our model would then take the following form:

$$S = a_2 (\frac{I}{As})^g \tag{11.3}$$

where As is the person's income aspiration level.

For Income we assume the following relationship:

$$I = a_1 E^{g_{11}} A^{g_{12}} \tag{11.4}$$

(The coefficients g_{11} and g_{12} have been introduced to allow for unequal effects for different values of the causal variables.)

This equation suggests that Income varies as a multiplicative power function of Education and Age. This kind of a relationship was found to hold in a number of contexts (Hamblin, 1974). In our case it means that the increase in income due to Age is largely depending on the education level a person has. For some countries at least, an income policy exists that makes this model realistic.

Furthermore, we expect a person's income aspiration level to be determined by Age and Education:

$$As = aE^{g_{11}} A^{g_{12}}. \tag{11.5}$$

We specified the coefficients in this equation to be the same as in equation 11.4 to suggest that people would react on deviations from what they normally expect to happen. Substitution of this equation in (11.3) gives

$$S = a_2 (\frac{I}{aE^{g_{11}} A^{g_{12}}})^g. \tag{11.6}$$

All these equations are clearly non-linear and non-additive. However, when we take the natural logarithm at both sides of the equations, we get:

$$\ln(I) = \ln(a_1) + g_{11} \ln(E) + g_{12} \ln(A) + \zeta_1 \tag{11.7}$$

$$\ln(S) = \ln(a_2) + g \ln(I) - g \times g_{11} \ln(E)$$
$$-g \times g_{12} \ln(A) + \zeta_2 \tag{11.8}$$

or, writing $y_1 = \ln(I); y_2 = \ln(S); x_1 = \ln(E); x_2 = \ln(A)$ and $\alpha_1 = \ln(a_1), \gamma_{11} = g_{11}, \gamma_{12} = g_{12}, \alpha_2 = \ln(a_2), \gamma_{21} = g \times g_{11}, \gamma_{22} = g \times g_{12}$ and $\beta_{21} = g$:

$$y_1 = \alpha_1 + \gamma_{11} x_1 + \gamma_{12} x_2 + \zeta_1 \tag{11.9}$$

$$y_2 = \alpha_2 + \beta_{21} y_1 + \gamma_{21} x_1 + \gamma_{22} x_2 + \zeta_2. \tag{11.10}$$

Model (11.7–11.8) is derived from model (11.3–11.6).

An alternative model could hypothesize that the relationship between Income and Satisfaction be spurious. In that case, the income equation (11.4) remains the same but the equation for Satisfaction (11.6) has to be formulated in terms of exogeneous variables assuming that higher education provides better, more pleasant work and that older people have lower aspirations in any field and therefore are happier with their life. Following Hamblin again, we express the relationship as a multiplicative power function in which the effects get smaller if the values of the causal variables get larger. In line with this idea the relationship would become:

$$I = a_1 E^{g_{11}} A^{g_{12}} \tag{11.11}$$

$$S = a_2 E^{g_{21}} A^{g_{22}}. \tag{11.12}$$

From equations (11.11) and (11.12) the same linear model specified in (11.9) and (11.10) can be derived by a logarithmic transformation except that in this case the coefficient $\beta_{21} = 0$, while $\gamma_{21} = g_{21}$ and $\gamma_{22} = g_{22}$. The result of the log transformation has led to sets of linear and additive structural equations which can be handled as before. Only a limited set of examples of non-linear models has been studied until now (Kenny & Judd, 1984; Jaccard, Turrisi, & Wan, 1990; Yang Jonsson, 1997).

Our example shows that after the specification of the model in a path model or an effect matrix, the next step is the formulation of a system of linear structural equations. In this case, this is not a straightforward activity. A more detailed discussion of the issue can be found in Saris & Stronkhorst (1984) and (Christ, 1966).

A last point that has to be mentioned is that if we proceed in this way, no variables are omitted which can cause spurious relationships between the variables of interest and between the variables of interest and the disturbance terms. Therefore, after a serious effort has been made to formulate a realistic model, we can add to the theory the assumptions that:

Assumptions:

- o *The disturbance terms are independent of each other.*

- o *The disturbance terms are independent of the causal variables in the equations.*

These two assumptions are essential in the whole process as we will see in the next section. They play an important role in drawing conclusions for a causal theory. If not all variables have been measured, the omitted variables will be present in the disturbance terms which will be correlated in that case. Technically this approach is possible but it makes the causal modelling less clear since one can not decide with certainty if the correlation between the causal and the effect variable are completely spurious or not.

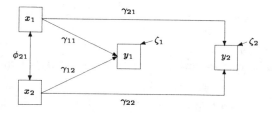

Figure 11.5: A path diagram of the causal model for a study on income satisfaction.

11.2 Estimation and Testing

The estimation and testing of structural equation model is based on a second fundamental principle of Linear Structural equation modelling:

Principle 2 *The correlation between two variables is the sum of the direct effects, the indirect effects, eventual spurious relationships and the joint effects.*

In this formulation, the term *joint effect* indicates a contribution to the correlation which can not be assigned to a specific variable but can come from two different exogenous variables which are correlated. In order to apply this basic principle we must be able to indicate the direct effects, the indirect effects, eventual spurious relationships and the joint effects.

In case the variables are standardized, the following principle can be proven:

Principle 3 *Each indirect effect, spurious relationship and joint effect can be expressed as a product of the standardized[1] parameters which connect the two variables of interest.*

For the proof of this statement and a more detailed discussion we refer to Saris & Stronkhorst (1984). Our example will clarify the second basic principle. In order to do so, we first draw another path diagram, this time including the (effect) parameters of the standardized variables as they have been given in model (11.9-11.10) and assuming $\beta_{21} = 0$ (see Figure 11.5).

Using this path diagram the correlations (ρ_{ij}) between the variables can be expressed in the (effect) parameters of the model using the second basic principle. This gives the following set of equations:

---

[1] By standardizing, variables get a mean of zero and a variance of one, while the form of the relationships does not change except for the fact that the intercepts in the equations become zero and thus can be omitted while the effects are expressed in standard deviations instead of the original units of measurement.

$$\rho_{x_2 x_1} = \phi_{21} \tag{11.13}$$
(a correlation between the exogeneous variables)

$$\rho_{y_1 x_1} = \gamma_{11} + \phi_{21}\gamma_{12} \tag{11.14}$$
(a direct effect + a joint effect)

$$\rho_{y_1 x_2} = \gamma_{12} + \phi_{21}\gamma_{11} \tag{11.15}$$
(a direct effect + a joint effect)

$$\rho_{y_2 x_1} = \gamma_{21} + \phi_{21}\gamma_{22} \tag{11.16}$$
(a direct effect + a joint effect)

$$\rho_{y_2 x_2} = \gamma_{22} + \phi_{21}\gamma_{21} \tag{11.17}$$
(a direct effect + a joint effect)

$$\rho_{y_2 y_1} = \gamma_{11}\gamma_{21} + \gamma_{12}\gamma_{22} + \gamma_{11}\phi_{21}\gamma_{22} + \gamma_{12}\phi_{21}\gamma_{21} \tag{11.18}$$
(the sum of four spurious relationships)

These derived relationships are very important for the estimation of the effects and to test the fit of the model.

We start with *estimation*. The correlations between these variables can in principle be estimated from the data.

Given the stated relationships between these correlations and the parameters of the model one can estimate these parameters from these correlations. This is done by calculating those parameter values which minimize the sum of the squared (or weighted) residuals between the observed correlations (r_{ij}) and the reproduced correlations (ρ_{ij}) or, by minimizing:

$$f_{uls} = \sum_{i>j}(r_{ij} - \rho_{ij})^2, \text{ or } f_{wls} = \sum_{i>j} w_{ij}(r_{ij} - \rho_{ij})^2$$

f_{uls} is the function which is minimized to obtain an unweighted least squares solution and f_{wls} is the function which is minimized to obtain a weighted least squares solution where the weights w_{ij} can be chosen in different ways, leading to different estimation procedures (Jöreskog & Sörbom, 1989; Bollen, 1989). We will not go into any detail here, but in all cases the parameters have the property that they in some way or another minimize the residuals defined above.

These estimation procedures only provide *unique solutions* when the number of parameters is at most equal to the number of distinct elements in the correlation matrix. This is a necessary condition for what has been called the *identifiability* of the model. Sufficient conditions are rather complex and will not be discussed here (see Fox, 1984; Bollen, 1989). In our example there are six correlations and only five coefficients to be estimated. This means that the necessary condition is satisfied.

It can also be verified that the sufficient condition is satisfied because it is clear that from equation (11.13), ϕ_{21} can be obtained. After that, using

	ln(A)	ln(E)	ln(I)	ln(S)
Correlations				
ln(A)	1.00			
ln(E)	-0.445	1.00		
ln(I)	-0.343	0.382	1.00	
ln(S)	-0.024	0.068	0.273	1.00
Effects				
ln (I)	-0.22	0.29	-	-
	(0.02)	(0.02)		
ln(S)	0.01	0.07	-	-
	(0.02)	(0.02)		

Table 11.2: The estimated correlations and effects between these variables in Russia ($n = 2000$).

equation (11.14) and (11.15) the parameters γ_{11} and γ_{12} can be obtained, and from equations (11.16) and (11.17) the parameters γ_{21} and γ_{22} can be derived. Note that in this case there is even one equation, namely (11.18) which is not needed for identification of the model. There is what is called, *one degree of freedom* in the model.

The remaining equation (11.18) could be used as a test of the model because if all parameters have been estimated the last equation can be used to test the model. If the model is correct and $\beta_{21} = 0$ then equation (11.18) should hold. In this test we use the second basic principle.

Table 11.2 provides the correlations between these variables from a representative sample of 2000 households in Russia during 1996. From these correlations the effect parameters have been estimated. The table also gives the estimated values of the parameters with, in parentheses, the standard errors. Given these parameters, the test gives the following. The predicted value of $r_{y_2 y_1}$ according to this model should be:

$$
\begin{aligned}
r_{y_2 y_1} &= 0.29 \times 0.07 + -0.22 \times 0.01 + \\
&\quad 0.29 \times -0.45 \times 0.01 + -0.22 \times -0.45 \times 0.07 \\
&= 0.023
\end{aligned}
$$

But from the data we know that $r_{y_2 y_1}$ is 0.273. This means that the residual for this equation would be

$$
r_{y_2 y_1} - \rho_{y_2 y_1} = 0.273 - 0.023 = 0.250
$$

which is rather large. This means that the variables which are supposed to cause the spurious relationship between the variables of interest can not explain the obtained correlation. Therefore, given this model, we have to conclude that the correlation is not only spurious but that the largest part of the correlation is due to a direct effect of Income on the Satisfaction. Of

	ln(A)	ln(E)	ln(I)	ln(S)
ln(I)	-0.22	0.29	-	-
	(0.02)	(0.02)		
ln(S)	0.07	-0.02	0.30	-
	(0.02)	(0.02)	(0.02)	

Table 11.3: The estimated values of the parameters using model (11.7-11.8) with $\beta_{21} = 0$.

course, more rigorous statistical tests are available for the type of hypotheses we discuss here. The reader is referred to textbooks like Saris & Stronkhorst (1984), Jöreskog & Sörbom (1989) or Bollen (1989) for an in-depth discussion.

Given the result that there seems to be a real effect of Income on Satisfaction, this effect can be estimated by using model (11.7-11.8) instead of the restricted model for this data. The disadvantage of the former model is that the number of parameters is exactly the same as the number of correlations. Therefore there are no degrees of freedom. Such a model, if identified, can not be tested because it will always fit the data perfectly. However, it can be used for the estimation of the effects. Table 11.3 gives the results.

This table shows that the effect of Income is much larger than the other two effects. It is also interesting to see that the effect is even slightly larger than the original correlation. This is due to the fact that the spurious effect produced by the variables Age and Education is mainly negative and that the effect of Income on Satisfaction is positive.

On the other hand, it should be noted that the variable Income only explains $(0.30)^2$ or 9% of the variance in Satisfaction which is only a small amount. One would expect this to be a larger figure[2]. There is one other possible reason for this weak relationship which is the *Measurement error* in the Satisfaction measurement. We will explore this possibility in the next section.

11.3   Correction for Measurement error

Any data contains errors. Some of these errors will be random due to mistakes that respondents, interviewers, coders or typists make. Other errors are related to the research method used and thus can be systematic. We will concentrate here on random errors and refer for systematic errors to other

---

[2]In this case, transformation of the variables has improved the explained variance only slightly since in the linear version of the model the explained variance was 7%. The non-linear form was introduced here to illustrate that the linear version of the model is not always the only alternative and that sometimes the non-linear version of the model gives superior results.

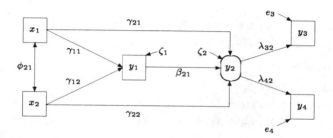

Figure 11.6: The path diagram with a measurement model for the satisfaction variable.

texts (see e.g. Schuman & Presser, 1981; Belson, 1981; Andrews, 1984; Költringer, 1993; Scherpenzeel & Saris, 1993; Saris & Münnich, 1995).

It is well-known that random error can disturb the relationships between variables and make them weaker than they really are. Therefore, one has to correct for measurement error to get better estimates. This was one of the reasons why procedures like Structural equation modelling and the LISREL program have been developed (for a discussion, see Goldberger, 1973).

In order to do so, the substantive model can be extended with a measurement model. To clarify this point, we will do this for the Income-Satisfaction model assuming that only Satisfaction is measured with error. It could in fact be assumed for each of the other variables in the model.

In the Russian study, Satisfaction is assessed twice: once at the beginning of the interview and once at the end. In this way, two measurements were obtained. It is likely that the respondents could not remember what they had said at the first occasion given that there were more than 20 minutes between the two questions (Saris & Van Meurs, 1990). The previous model can be extended to include the measurement equations (see Figure 11.6).

In the model y_2 is placed in an oval because it is now assumed that Satisfaction is not directly observed but that there are two separate observations of Satisfaction y_3 and y_4 each with its own associated error term e_3 and e_4. The quality of the measurement is expressed in the strength of the relationship between y_2, y_3 and y_4 expressed in the regression coefficients λ_{32} and λ_{42}.

Using the same decomposition rule for the correlations, one can derive the following system of equations from this model:

$$\rho_{x_2x_1} = \phi_{21} \tag{11.19}$$

$$\rho_{y_1x_1} = \gamma_{11} + \phi_{21}\gamma_{12} \tag{11.20}$$

$$\rho_{y_1x_2} = \gamma_{12} + \phi_{21}\gamma_{11} \tag{11.21}$$

$$\rho_{y_2x_1} = \gamma_{21} + \phi_{21}\gamma_{22} + \beta_{21}\gamma_{11} + \beta_{21}\gamma_{12}\phi_{21} \tag{11.22}$$

$$\rho_{y_2 x_2} = \gamma_{22} + \phi_{21}\gamma_{21} + \beta_{21}\gamma_{12} + \beta_{21}\gamma_{11}\phi_{21} \tag{11.23}$$

$$\rho_{y_2 y_1} = \beta_{21} + \gamma_{11}\gamma_{21} + \gamma_{12}\gamma_{22} + \gamma_{11}\phi_{21}\gamma_{22} + \gamma_{12}\phi_{21}\gamma_{21} \tag{11.24}$$

$$\rho_{y_3 y_2} = \lambda_{32} \tag{11.25}$$

$$\rho_{y_4 y_2} = \lambda_{42} \tag{11.26}$$

$$\rho_{y_3 x_1} = \lambda_{32}\gamma_{21} + \lambda_{32}\phi_{21}\gamma_{22} + \lambda_{32}\beta_{21}\gamma_{11} + \lambda_{32}\beta_{21}\gamma_{12}\phi_{21} \tag{11.27}$$

$$\rho_{y_3 x_2} = \lambda_{32}\gamma_{12} + \lambda_{32}\phi_{21}\gamma_{21} + \lambda_{32}\beta_{21}\gamma_{12} + \lambda_{32}\beta_{21}\gamma_{11}\phi_{21} \tag{11.28}$$

$$\rho_{y_4 x_1} = \lambda_{42}\gamma_{21} + \lambda_{42}\phi_{21}\gamma_{22} + \lambda_{42}\beta_{21}\gamma_{11} + \lambda_{42}\beta_{21}\gamma_{12}\phi_{21} \tag{11.29}$$

$$\rho_{y_4 x_2} = \lambda_{42}\gamma_{12} + \lambda_{42}\phi_{21}\gamma_{21} + \lambda_{42}\beta_{21}\gamma_{12} + \lambda_{42}\beta_{21}\gamma_{11}\phi_{21} \tag{11.30}$$

$$\rho_{y_3 y_1} = \lambda_{32}\beta_{21} \tag{11.31}$$

$$\rho_{y_4 y_1} = \lambda_{42}\beta_{21} \tag{11.32}$$

$$\rho_{y_4 y_3} = \lambda_{42}\lambda_{32}. \tag{11.33}$$

It may be clear that errors are very easily made while writing down these equations. Fortunately, one does not have to do this any more. The user of programs like LISREL, EQS or AMOS have only to specify the graphical or algebraic representation of the model. All the other steps are done automatically by the program.

The equations $(11.19) - (11.24)$ are the same as before except that effects of y_1 on y_2 have been added to the equations because now we assume that $\beta_{21} > 0$. In this case, the model contains six variables and the correlation matrix consists of fifteen distinct elements. Therefore, we also get fifteen derived equations for the relationships between the correlations and the parameters of the model. However, in this case y_2 is an unobserved variable. So all correlations between y_2 and other variables are not available from the data[3].

This means that equations $(11.22) - (11.26)$ can not be used for estimation of the parameters. So only ten equations remain for correlations that can be estimated from the data. From these ten equations, one ϕ coefficient, four γ's, one β coefficient and two λ's coefficients have to be estimated. Thus, from ten equations eight parameters have to be estimated. Without further proof we state that this model is also identified and unique estimates of the parameters of this model can be obtained. Thus, we can also estimate β_{21} in this model, even though it represents an effect of an observed variable on a variable that is not directly observed. The advantage of this approach is that this estimate of the effect of Income on Satisfaction is corrected for measurement error.

Table 11.4 presents the results of an analysis performed with the LISREL procedure. The ML estimator has been used for estimation. The model has two degrees of freedom and the likelihood ratio χ^2 goodness-of-fit statistic is

---

[3]In this analysis the correlations of Table 11.2 have been used extended with one more measure of satisfaction with the following correlations with the other variables: $-0.041, 0.076, 0.323$ while this measure correlated 0.75 with the first measure of satisfaction. The ML estimator has been used for estimation.

	ln(A)	ln(E)	ln(I)	ln(S)
$y_1 = \ln(I)$	-0.22	0.29	-	-
$y_2 = \ln(S)$	0.08	-0.03	0.38	-
$y_3 = \ln(S_1)$	-	-	-	0.80
$y_4 = \ln(S_2)$	-	-	-	0.94

Table 11.4: The parameter estimates for model (11.19 – 11.33).

0.9. The critical value for the χ^2 test with two degress of freedom would be 5.6. So the model fits very well. Constraining β_{21} to zero, gives a χ^2 with three degrees of freedom of 228, which indicates that β_{21} is really needed to get an acceptable fit of the model.

This result shows that the correction for measurement error increases the effect of Income on Satisfaction as expected. Without correction the effect was 0.30 and after correction for measurement error the coefficient is 0.38. However, this increase is not impressive because the measurement error is relatively small for the Satisfaction variable. This confirms previous research (Saris et al., 1996).

11.4   Data requirements

So far it was assumed that the variables in the models are continuous and have at least interval measurement level. However, the satisfaction variables in these examples are not continuous but discrete and can only be considered ordinal since the distances between the categories are unknown. Both variables are measured on a five point scale which is very common in social sciences survey research. This means that in this respect the observed variables do not satisfy the measurement requirements of the SEM approach. There are several ways to tackle this problem.

Some researchers take a strict point of view and hold that one should not analyse data of an ordinal measurement level with statistical procedures developed for interval level variables. This principled stand has led to a parallel literature on structural equation models based on categorical data. One of the most promising approaches in this area is *Latent class analysis*. It would lead too far to discuss this large field here but very good textbooks are available, for example Hagenaars (1990, 1993) and the more advanced introduction in Clogg (1995, pp. 311–361).

There are also researchers who say that the fundamentalists forget that most of the variables of interest like opinions, attitudes, feelings etc. are basically continuous. Only due to the crude measurement of these variables these continuous variables are forced on an ordinal measurement scale. They recognize that therefore the correlations between the variables are not consistent estimates of the true correlations. To correct for the influence of the crude measurements they suggest to use alternative estimation procedures.

Assuming that the underlying continuous variables are multivariate normally distributed, their intercorrelations can be estimated (Muthen, 1984; Jöreskog, 1973). In this way the whole approach discussed above can be applied after obtaining appropriate estimates of the correlations between the variables in the model, i.e. after correction for crude measurement.

Finally, there are two groups of researchers who suggest that it does not matter much that measurement requirements are not satisfied. One group argues that the correlations between the variables of interest will not be very different if the number of categories of the variables is five or more (Borgatta & Bohrnstedt, 1981). Implicitly they suggest that equal intervals between categories may be assumed. They trust the approach explained above can be reliably applied as long as the number of categories in the scales does not go below five.

Then there is another group that argues that, indeed, the crude measurement has a considerable effect on the estimated correlations, especially if the number of categories is small. But if one uses models with multiple indicators like we did for Satisfaction, then the relationship between the theoretical variables behind these multiply observed variables will be approximately consistent because the crude measurement error will be corrected for in the measurement relations. This argument has been supported by a large number of simulation studies (Homer & O'Brien, 1988; Coenders, Satorra, & Saris, 1997).

All these approaches to this measurement problem have their own value. The latent class approach has led to a whole new range of Structural equation and measurement models. This is in itself attractive from the point of view of everyday research. We think, however, that there is some truth in the objection that most variables of interest in the social sciences are continuous and that these models move too far away from the phenomenon we want to model.

The correction procedures for the estimation of the correlations are also attractive but the price one has to pay for this solution is the assumption of bivariate or even multivariate normality of the underlying variables. In many cases this will not be justified.

The more practice oriented solutions have at least the advantage of simplicity. Their drawback, however, is that it can not be proven that they are valid in all situations. Therefore, one has to be careful with these approaches, too.

Probably the best way is to try several approaches simultaneously. If they lead to the same result, one can be sure of their correctness; if they differ, one has to study the reasons for the differences and matters may become complicated. In that case one has to choose to report those solutions that are most plausible and defendable.

11.5   Summary

In this chapter we have shown that the Structural equation modelling approach has been developed to perform tests of causal hypotheses in non-experimental research. In order to do such tests the major problem is to properly control for confounding variables. Of most concern should be those variables that cause spurious relationships between the cause and effect variables. This spurious relationship can be either positive or negative. Variables that produce spurious correlations with signs opposite to what might be expected are most difficult to handle and interpret.

A basic principle in non-experimental research is that one has to partial out all spurious correlation from the observed correlation between the variables of interest. If no significant correlation is left, the hypothesis that there is any causal effect has to be rejected. If some correlation is left, then one may assume that there is a causal relationship between the variables of interest.

In the procedure described in this chapter, the following steps are taken:

1. A scrupulous literature search is performed for variables that may eventually produce spurious correlations between the variables of interest;

2. These variables and the variables of interest are assessed during the implementation of the research and, in the end, produce a data set that can be analysed;

3. A model is specified indicating, between other relationships, the causal relationships between the variables of interest;

4. Eventually, a transformation of the variables is applied in order to obtain a model with linear relationships;

5. The identifiability of the model is checked;

6. The model is fitted to the data and the parameters are estimated;

7. If sufficient degrees of freedom remain, a test can be done on the causal relationship between the variables of interest.

Figure 11.7 summarizes the procedure (see also Saris & Stronkhorst, 1984, p. 7). This procedure has obvious limitations. The most important one is that all variables producing spurious relationships have to be included in the model. How can one ever be sure that one has succeeded in doing so and that all these confounding variables are present in the study design?

Although the researcher can do his utmost to include all variables that are relevant, he can always be criticized at this point.

In a sound scientific dialogue it is the task of the critic to show that with some other confounding variables the correlation can indeed be shown to be spurious. There is an analogy here with experimental research where it is

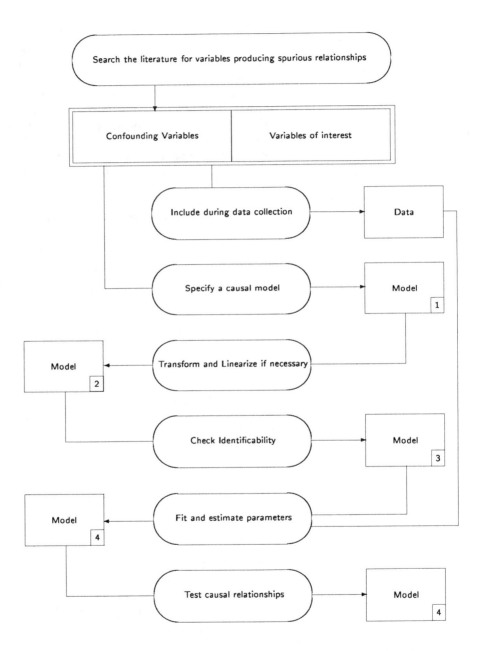

Figure 11.7: Steps taken during the procedure described in this chapter.

always possible that new research will show that it was not the manipulated variable which had the effect that was claimed but another variable related to the manipulation. In this way, experimental and non-experimental sciences progress.

Another limitation of the Structural equation modelling approach is that it only works in the simple form described here if all variables are measured without error. However, this is never the case. Thus it may occur that the estimated effects are too small compared to the error present in them and therefore the estimates of the spurious relationships as well.

One may argue that in that case also the relationships between the cause and effect variables are too low due to measurement error and therefore neglecting the measurement error does not matter. However, it is not necessarily so that all variables have approximately equally large error contributions (see Andrews, 1984; Alwin & Krosnick, 1991; Scherpenzeel & Saris, 1993). Therefore, it is advisable to correct for measurement error before causal relationships are tested. LISREL and other SEM programs are especially efficient to this respect. However, in order to estimate measurement error one needs repeated observations as we did show in the example. Recent research provides also possibilities for the estimation of measurement error on the basis of separate methodological research (see e.g. Andrews, 1984; Költringer, 1993; Scherpenzeel & Saris, 1993). For a full description of the problems of measurement error in structural equations models we again refer to Bollen (1989).

Chapter 12

Graphs, Causality, and Structural Equation Models

Judea Pearl

Structural equation modeling (SEM) has dominated causal analysis in the social and behavioral sciences since the 1960s. Currently, many SEM practitioners are having difficulty articulating the causal content of SEM and are seeking foundational answers. Recent developments in the areas of graphical models and the logic of causality show potential for alleviating such difficulties and thus for revitalizing structural equations as the primary language of causal modeling. This chapter summarizes several of these developments, including the prediction of vanishing partial correlations, model testing, model equivalence, parametric and nonparametric identifiability, control of confounding, and covariate selection. These developments clarify the causal and statistical components of structural equation models and the role of SEM in the empirical sciences.

12.1   Introduction

12.1.1   Causality in search of a language

The word *cause* is not in the vocabulary of standard probability theory. It is an embarrassing yet inescapable fact that probability theory, the official mathematical language of many empirical sciences, does not permit us to express sentences such as 'Mud does not cause rain'; all we can say is that the two events are mutually correlated, or dependent – meaning that if we find one, we can expect to encounter the other. Scientists seeking causal explanations for complex phenomena or rationales for policy decisions must therefore supplement the language of probability with a vocabulary for causality, one in which the symbolic representation for the causal relationship 'Mud does not cause rain' is distinct from the symbolic representation for 'Mud is independent of rain'.

Oddly, such distinctions have not yet been incorporated into standard scientific analysis[1].

Two languages for causality have been proposed: *path analysis* or *structural equation modeling (SEM)* (Wright, 1921; Haavelmo, 1943) and Neyman-Rubin's *potential-response model* (Rubin, 1974, 1990).

The former has been adopted by economists and social scientists (Goldberger, 1972; Duncan, 1975) while a small group of statisticians champion the latter (Rubin, 1974; Robins, 1986; Holland, 1988). These two languages are mathematically equivalent[2], yet neither has become standard in causal modeling – the structural equation framework because it has been greatly misused and inadequately formalized (Freedman, 1987), and the potential-response framework because it has been only partially formalized and, more significant, because it rests on an esoteric and seemingly metaphysical vocabulary of counterfactual variables that bears no apparent relation to ordinary understanding of cause-effect processes.

Currently, potential-response models are understood by few and used by even fewer, while structural equation models are used by many but their causal interpretation is generally questioned or avoided. The main purpose of this chapter is to formulate the causal interpretation and outline the proper use of structural equation models, and thus to reinstate confidence in SEM as the primary (and perhaps the only) formal language for causal analysis in the social and behavioral sciences. But first, a brief analysis of the current crisis in SEM research in light of its historical development.

12.1.2   Causality and structural models

As already has been briefly indicated in the previous chapter (Chapter 11) on structural equation modeling, SEM was developed by geneticists (Wright, 1921) and economists (Haavelmo, 1943; Koopmans, 1953) so that qualitative cause-effect information could be combined with statistical data to provide quantitative assessment of cause-effect relationships among variables of interest. Thus, to the often asked question, '*Under what conditions can we give causal interpretation to structural coefficients?*' Wright and Haavelmo would have answered, '*Always!*'. According to the founding fathers of SEM, the conditions that make the equation $y = \beta x + \epsilon$ *structural* are precisely those that make the causal connection between X and Y have no other value but β and nothing about the statistical relationship between x and ϵ can ever change this interpretation of β. Amazingly, this basic understanding of SEM has all but disappeared from the literature, leaving modern econometricians and social scientists in a quandary over β.

---

[1] A summary of unsuccessful attempts by philosophers to reduce causality to probabilities is given in Pearl (1996, pp. 396–405) and Pearl (1999).

[2] The equivalence of the potential-response and structural equation frameworks, anticipated by Holland (1986), Pratt & Schlaifer (1988), Pearl (1995), and Robins (1995) is proven formally in Galles & Pearl (1998).

Most SEM researchers today are of the opinion that extra ingredients are necessary for structural equations to qualify as carriers of causal claims. Among social scientists, James, Mulaik, & Brett (1982, p. 45) for example, state that a condition called *self-containment* is necessary for consecrating the equation $y = \beta x + \epsilon$ with causal meaning, where self-containment stands for $cov(x, \epsilon) = 0$. According to James, Mulaik and Brett, whenever self-containment does not hold *'neither the equation nor the functional relation represents a causal relation'*. Bollen (1989, p. 44) reiterates the necessity of self-containment (under the rubric *isolation* or *pseudo-isolation*), contrary to the understanding that structural equations attain their causal interpretation prior to, and independently of, any statistical relationships among their constituents. Since the early 1980s, it has become exceedingly rare to find an open endorsement of the original SEM logic, namely, that ϵ is defined in terms of β, not the other way around, and that the orthogonality condition $cov(x, \epsilon) = 0$ is neither necessary nor sufficient for the causal interpretation of β (see Section 12.4.1). In fact this condition is not necessary even for the identification of β, once β is interpreted (see the identification of α in Figures 12.8 and 12.10, below).

Econometricians have just as much difficulty with the causal reading of structural parameters. Leamer (1985, p. 258) observes, *'It is my surprising conclusion that economists know very well what they mean when they use the words 'exogenous', 'structural', and 'causal', yet no textbook author has written adequate definitions.'* There has been little change since Leamer made these observations. Hendry (1995, p. 62), for instance, amplifies the necessity of the orthogonality condition, and states:

> *'... the status of β may be unclear until the conditions needed to estimate the postulated model are specified. For example, in the model:*
>
> $$y_t = z_t \beta + u_t \text{ where } u_t \sim \mathcal{N}(0, \sigma_u^2),$$
>
> *until the relationship between z_t and u_t is specified the meaning of β is uncertain since $E[z_t u_t]$ could be either zero or non-zero on the information provided.'*

LeRoy (1995, p. 211) goes even further:

> *'It is a commonplace of elementary instruction in economics that endogenous variables are not generally causally ordered, implying that the question 'What is the effect of y_1 on y_2?' where y_1 and y_2 are endogenous variables is generally meaningless.'*

According to LeRoy, causal relationships cannot be attributed to any variable whose causes have separate influence on the effect variable, a position that denies causal reading to most of the structural parameters that economists and social scientists labor to estimate.

Cartwright (1995, p. 49), a renowned philosopher of science, addresses these difficulties by initiating a renewed attack on the tormenting question,

'*Why can we assume that we can read off causes, including causal order, from the parameters in equations whose exogenous variables are uncorrelated?*' Cartwright, like SEM's founders, recognizes that causes cannot be derived from statistical or functional relationships alone and that causal assumptions are prerequisite for validating any causal conclusion. Unlike Wright and Haavelmo, however, she launches an all-out search for the assumptions that would endow the parameter β in the regression equation $y = \beta x + \epsilon$ with a legitimate causal meaning and endeavors to prove that the assumptions she proposes are indeed sufficient. What is revealing in Cartwright's analysis is that she does not consider the answer Haavelmo would have provided, namely, that the assumptions needed for drawing causal conclusions from parameters are already encoded in the *syntax* of the equations and can be read off the associated graph as easily as a shopping list[3].

Briefly, if G is the graph associated with a causal model that renders a certain parameter identifiable, then two assumptions are sufficient for authenticating the causal reading of that parameter, namely, (1) every missing arrow, say between X and Y, represents the assumption that X has no effect on Y once we intervene and hold certain other variables fixed, and (2) every missing bi-directed arc $X \leftarrow - - \rightarrow Y$ represents the assumption that all omitted factors that affect Y are uncorrelated with those that affect X. Each of these assumptions is *testable* in experimental settings, where interventions are feasible (Section 12.4.1.3). They need not be searched for elsewhere, nor do they require specialized proofs of sufficiency. Haavelmo's answer applies to models of any size and shape, including models with correlated exogenous variables.

Cartwright's analysis partakes of an alarming tendency among economists and social scientists to view a structural equation as an algebraic object that carries functional and statistical assumptions but is void of causal content. This statement from one leading social scientist is typical: '*It would be very healthy if more researchers abandoned thinking of and using terms such as cause and effect*' (Muthen, 1987, p. 180). Perhaps the boldest expression of this tendency was recently voiced by Holland (1995, p. 54):

'*I am speaking, of course, about the equation: $y = a + bx + \epsilon$. What does it mean? The only meaning I have ever determined for such an equation is that it is a shorthand way of describing the conditional distribution of y given x[4].*'

The founders of SEM had an entirely different conception of structures and models. Wright (1923, p. 240) declared that '*prior knowledge of the*

---

[3] These assumptions will be explicated and operationalized in Section 12.4.

[4] Holland's interpretation is at variance with the structural reading of the equation (Haavelmo, 1943), which is '*In an ideal experiment where we control X to x and any other set Z of variables (not containing X or Y) to z, Y is independent of z and is given by $a + bx + \epsilon$*' (*see Section 12.4.1.1s*)).

causal relations is assumed as prerequisite' in the theory of path coefficients, and Haavelmo (1943) explicitly interpreted each structural equation as a statement about a hypothetical controlled experiment. Marschak (1950) and Koopmans (1953) stated clearly that the purpose of postulating a structure behind the probability distribution is to cope with the hypothetical changes that can be brought about by policy. One wonders, therefore, what has happened to SEM over the past 50 years, and why the basic (and still valid) teachings of Wright, Haavelmo, Marschak, and Koopmans have been forgotten.

Some economists attribute the decline in the understanding of structural equations to Lucas' critique (Lucas Jr., 1976), according to which economic agents anticipating policy change would tend to act contrary to SEM's predictions which often ignore such anticipations. However, since Lucas' critique merely shifts the burden of structural modeling from the behavioral level to a deeper level, involving agents' motivations and expectations, it does not exonerate economists from defining and representing the causal content of structural equations at some level of discourse.

I believe that the causal content of SEM has gradually escaped the consciousness of SEM practitioners mainly for the following reasons:

1. SEM practitioners have sought to gain respectability for SEM by keeping causal assumptions implicit, since statisticians, the arbiters of respectability, abhor assumptions that are not directly testable.

2. The algebraic language that has dominated SEM lacks the notational facility needed to make causal assumptions, as distinct from statistical assumptions, explicit. By failing to equip causal relations with precise mathematical notation, the founding fathers in fact committed the causal foundations of SEM to oblivion. Their disciples today are seeking foundational answers elsewhere.

Let me elaborate on the latter point. The founders of SEM understood quite well that in structural models the equality sign conveys the asymmetrical relation 'is determined by', and hence behaves more like an assignment symbol (:=) in programming languages than like an algebraic equality. However, perhaps for reasons of mathematical purity (*i.e.*, to avoid the appearance of syntax sensitivity), they refrained from introducing a symbol to represent the asymmetry. According to Epstein (1987), in the 1940s Wright gave a seminar on path coefficients to the Cowles Commission (the breeding ground for SEM), but neither side saw particular merit in the other's methods.

Why? After all, a diagram is nothing but a set of non-parametric structural equations in which, to avoid confusion, the equality signs are replaced with arrows.

My explanation is that the early econometricians were extremely careful mathematicians who thought they could keep the mathematics in purely equational-statistical form and just reason about structure in their heads.

Indeed, they managed to do so surprisingly well, because they were truly remarkable individuals who *could* do it in their heads. The consequences surfaced in the early 1980s, when their disciples began to mistake the equality sign for an algebraic equality. The upshot was that suddenly the 'so-called disturbance terms' did not make any sense at all (Richard, 1980, p. 3). We are living with the sad end to this tale. By failing to express their insights in mathematical notation, the founders of SEM brought about the current difficulties surrounding the interpretation of structural equations, as summarized by Holland's 'What does it mean?'

12.1.3 Graphs as a mathematical language: an example

Certain recent developments in graphical methods promise to bring causality back into the mainstream of scientific modeling and analysis. These developments involve an improved understanding of the relationships between graphs and probabilities, on the one hand, and graphs and causality, on the other. But the crucial change has been the emergence of graphs as a mathematical language. This mathematical language is not simply a heuristic mnemonic device for displaying algebraic relationships, as in the writings of Blalock, Jr. (1962) and Duncan (1975). Rather, graphs provide a fundamental notational system for concepts and relationships that are not easily expressed in the standard mathematical languages of algebraic equations, and probability calculus. Moreover, graphs provide a powerful symbolic machinery for deriving the consequences of causal assumptions when such assumptions are combined with statistical data.

A concrete example that illustrates the power of the graphical language will set the stage for the discussions in Sections 12.2 and 12.3. One of the most frustrating problems in causal analysis has been *covariate selection* – for instance, determining whether a variate Z can be added to a regression equation without biasing the result. More generally, whenever we try to evaluate the effect of one factor (X) on another (Y), we wonder whether we should adjust for possible variations in some other variable, Z, sometimes called a *covariate, concomitant*, or *confounder*. Adjustment amounts to partitioning the population into groups that are homogeneous relative to Z, assessing the effect of X on Y in each homogeneous group, and, finally, averaging the results.

The elusive nature of such an adjustment was recognized as early as 1899, when Pearson and Yule discovered what is now called *Simpson's paradox*, namely, that any statistical relationship between two variables may be reversed or negated by including additional factors in the analysis. For example, we may find that students who smoke obtain higher grades than those who do not smoke; but after we adjust for age, smokers obtain lower grades than non-smokers in every age group; but after we further adjust for family income, smokers obtain higher grades than non-smokers in every income-age group; and so on.

The classic case demonstrating Simpson's reversal is the study of Berkeley's alleged sex bias in graduate admission (Bickel, Hammel, & O'Connell, 1975), where data showed a higher rate of admission for male applicants overall but, when broken down by departments, yielded a slight bias toward female applicants.

Despite a century of analysis, Simpson's reversal phenomenon continues to 'trap the unwary' (Dawid, 1979, p. 5), and the main question – whether an adjustment for a given covariate Z is appropriate in any given study – continues to be decided informally, case-by-case, with the decision resting on folklore and intuition rather than on hard mathematics. The standard statistical literature is remarkably silent on this issue. Aside from noting that one should not adjust for a covariate that is affected by the putative cause (X)[5], it provides no guidelines as to what covariates might be admissible for adjustment and what assumptions would be needed for making such a determination formally. The reason for this silence is clear: the solution to the covariate selection problem rests on causal assumptions, as we shall see in Section 12.3, and such assumptions cannot be expressed formally in the standard language of statistics.

In the potential-response framework, a criterion called *ignorability* has been advanced to address the covariate selection problem (Rosenbaum & Rubin, 1983). It states that Z is an admissible covariate relative to the effect of X on Y if, for every x, the value that Y would obtain had X been x is conditionally independent of X, given Z. This criterion paraphrases the problem in the language of counterfactuals without providing a working test for covariate selection. Because counterfactuals are not observable, and judgments about the conditional independence of counterfactuals are not readily made using our ordinary understanding of causal processes, ignorability has remained a theoretical construct with only a minor impact on practice. Epidemiologists, for example, well apprised of ignorability analysis via the admirable papers of Robins (1986) and Greenland & Robins (1986), are still debating the meaning of 'confounding' (Grayson, 1987) and often adjust for the wrong sets of covariates (Weinberg, 1993). Social scientists, likewise, despite the potential-response analyses of Holland & Rubin (1983) and Sobel (1995), are still struggling with various manifestations of the Lord paradox (a version of Simpson's paradox) in psychometric research (Wainer, 1991) and are still not distinguishing *collapsibility* from *non-confounding* (Steyer, Gabler, & Rucai, 1996).

In contrast, formulating the covariate selection problem in the language of graphs immediately yields a general solution that is both natural and formal. The investigator expresses causal knowledge (*i.e.*, assumptions) in the familiar qualitative terminology of path diagrams, and, once the diagram

---

[5]This advice, which rests on the causal relationship 'not affected by' is, to the best of my knowledge, the *only* causal notion that has found a place in statistics textbooks. The advice is necessary, but it is not sufficient. The other common guideline, that X should not precede Z (Shafer, 1996, p. 326), is neither necessary nor sufficient, as will become clear in Section 12.3.

is complete, a simple procedure decides whether a proposed adjustment (or regression) is appropriate relative to the quantity under evaluation.

This procedure, called the *back-door criterion* in Section 12.3 (Theorems 6 and 7) proceeds roughly as follows:

> To determine whether a set of variables Z should be adjusted for when we wish to evaluate the total effect of X on Y, we delete all arrows emanating from node X and then test whether, in the resulting graph, all paths between X and Y are *blocked* by nodes corresponding to Z. If the direct effect is to be evaluated, then only the arrow from X to Y should be deleted before applying the test (Theorem 6).

The notion *blocked* is defined formally in Section 12.2.1.2 (Definition 12.1).

This example is not an isolated instance of graphical methods affording clarity and understanding. In fact, the conceptual basis for SEM achieves a new level of precision through graphs. What makes a set of equations 'structural', what assumptions the authors of such equations should examine, what the testable implications of those assumptions are, and what policy claims a given set of structural equations advertize are some of the questions that receive simple and mathematically precise answers via graphical methods. These and related issues in SEM will be discussed in the following sections. A systematic account fo the new approach to causality is given in Pearl (1999).

12.1.4   Chapter outline

The testable implications of structural models are explicated in Section 12.2. For recursive models (herein termed *Markovian*), we find that the statistical content of a structural model can be fully characterized by a set of vanishing partial correlations that are entailed by the model. These vanishing partial correlations can be read off the graph using a simple criterion, called *d-separation*, which applies to both linear and non-linear models (Section 12.2.1). The application of this criterion to model testing is discussed in Section 12.2.2. The *d*-separation criterion leads to graphical tests of model equivalence, which, again, apply to both linear and non-linear models (Section 12.2.3).

Section 12.3 deals with the issue of determining the identifiability of structural parameters prior to gathering any data. In Section 12.3.1, simple graphical tests of identifiability are developed for linear Markovian and semi-Markovian models (*i.e.*, acyclic diagrams with correlated errors). Extensions to non-parametric models are developed in Sections 12.3.2 and 12.3.3, and their ramifications for practical problems of covariate selection are clarified in Section 12.3.4.

Section 12.4 discusses the logical foundations of SEM and resolves a number of difficulties that were kept dormant in the past. These include operational definitions for structural equations, structural parameters, error terms, total and direct effects.

12.2   Graphs and model testing

In 1919, Wright developed his 'method of path coefficients', which allows researchers to compute the magnitudes of cause-effect relationships from correlation measurements, as long as the path diagram represents correctly the causal processes underlying the data. Wright's method consists of writing a set of equations, one for each pair of variables (X_i, X_j), and equating the correlation coefficient ρ_{ij} with a sum of products of path coefficients and residual correlations along the various paths connecting X_i and X_j. Whenever the resulting equations give a unique solution to some path coefficient p_{mn} that is independent of the (unobserved) residual correlations, that coefficient is said to be *identifiable*. If every set of correlation coefficients ρ_{ij} is compatible with some choice of path coefficients, the model is said to be *untestable* or *unfalsifiable* (also called *saturated, just identified*, and so on), because it is capable of perfectly fitting any data whatsoever.

Whereas Wright's method is partly graphical and partly algebraic, the theory of directed graphs permits us to analyse questions of testability and identifiability in purely graphical terms, prior to data collection, and it also enables us to extend these analyses from linear to non-linear or non-parametric models. This section deals with issues of testability in linear and non-parametric models.

12.2.1   The testable implications of structural models

When we hypothesize a model of the data-generating process, that model often imposes restrictions on the statistics of the data collected. In observational studies, these restrictions provide the only view under which the hypothesized model can be tested or falsified. In many cases, such restrictions can be expressed in the form of vanishing partial correlations and, more significant, the restrictions are implied by the structure of the path diagram alone, independent of the numerical values of the parameters. Blalock, Jr. (1962), having recognized the importance of vanishing partial correlations that are implied by path diagrams, worked out an exhaustive list of those correlations in all path diagrams involving four variables. He also expressed doubt that the list would ever be extended to path diagrams with five (or more) variables. Nonetheless, a method is now available for identifying vanishing partial correlations in path diagrams of any size or form. The method is based on a test called *d*-separation (Pearl, 1988), to be discussed next.

12.2.1.1   Preliminary notation

The graphs we discuss in this chapter represent a set of structural equations of the form

$$x_i = f_i(pa_i, \epsilon_i) \qquad i = 1, \dots, n \qquad (12.1)$$

where pa_i (connoting *parents*) stand for the set of variables judged to be immediate causes of X_i, and ϵ_i represent errors due to omitted factors. Equation (12.1) is a non-linear, non-parametric generalization of the standard linear equations

$$x_i = \sum_{k \neq i} \alpha_{ik} x_k + \epsilon_i \qquad i = 1, \dots, n \qquad (12.2)$$

in which pa_i correspond to those variables on the right-hand side of Equation (12.2) that have non-zero coefficients. A set of equations in the form of Equation (12.1) used to represent the data-generating process will be called a *causal model*[6]. The graph G obtained by drawing an arrow from every member of pa_i to X_i will be called a *causal diagram*. In addition to full arrows, a causal diagram should contain a bi-directed (*i.e.*, double-arrowed) arc between any pair of variables whose corresponding errors are dependent (as in Figure 12.3). A diagram may include directed cycles (*e.g.*, $X \longrightarrow Y$, $Y \longrightarrow X$), representing mutual causation or feedback processes, but not self loops (*e.g.*, $X \longrightarrow X$). An *edge* is either an arrow or a bi-directed arc, and two variables connected by an edge are called *adjacent*.

We make free use of the terminology of kinship (*e.g.*, *parents, children, descendants, ancestors*) to denote the relationships in a graph. These kinship relations are defined along the full arrows in the diagram, including arrows that form directed cycles but ignoring bi-directed arcs. In Figure 12.5(c), for example, Y has two parents (X and Z), three ancestors (X, Z, and W), and no children, while X has no parents (hence, no ancestors) and one child (Y).

Causal diagrams play the same role in non-linear structural equation models as path diagrams play in linear structural equation models. Causal diagrams differ from path diagrams in that their pa_i are defined as non-trivial arguments of the function f_i, rather than variables obtaining non-zero coefficients, and their bi-directed arcs reflect dependency, rather than correlation. It is important to emphasize that causal diagrams (as well as traditional path diagrams) should be distinguished from the wide variety of graphical models in the statistical literature whose construction rests solely on properties of the joint distribution (Cox & Wermuth, 1996; Lauritzen, 1996; Andersson, Madigan, Perlman, & Richardson, 1998). The missing links in those statistical models represent conditional independencies, while the missing links in causal diagrams represent absence of causal connections

---

[6]Causal models, structural equations, and error terms will be defined in terms of response to interventions in Section 12.4. Formal treatments of these notions are given in Galles & Pearl (1997) and Galles & Pearl (1998).

(see Section 12.4) which may or may not imply conditional independencies in the distribution.

A causal model will be called *Markovian* if its graph contains no directed cycles and if its ϵ_i''s are mutually independent (*i.e.*, no bi-directed arcs). A model is *semi-Markovian* if its graph is acyclic and if it contains dependent errors.

Markovian models, (the parallel term in the SEM literature is *recursive models*[7] (Bollen, 1989)), possess useful features, shared by both linear and non-linear systems, that make their statistical implications transparent. One fundamental property of Markovian models is *parent screening*: given the state of its parents pa_i, each variable X_i is conditionally independent of all its non-descendants in the graph. This follows immediately from the independence of the errors ϵ_i and supports the intuition that once the direct causes of X_i are known, the probability of X_i is completely determined; no other event preceding X_i could modify this probability. As a result, the statistical parameters of Markovian models can be estimated by ordinary regression analysis.

An immediate consequence of this Markovian property is that the joint distribution of variables generated by Equation (12.1) can be decomposed (using the chain rule of probability calculus) into the product

$$P(x_1,\ldots,x_n) = \prod_i P(x_i \mid pa_i) \qquad (12.3)$$

where pa_i are the values of the parents of X_i in the causal graph G. For example, the model illustrated in Figure 12.1 induces the decomposition

$$P(x_1, x_2, x_3, x_4, x_5) = P(x_1)\, P(x_2|x_1)\, P(x_3|x_1)\, P(x_4|x_2, x_3)\, P(x_5|x_4).$$
$$(12.4)$$

This decomposition holds for any distribution of the error terms, regardless of the functional form of f_i; it depends only on the structural features of the generating model in Equation (12.1) as captured by the graph G. The product decomposition, in turn, entails certain conditional independence relationships that hold regardless of the functional form of f_i and regardless of the error distribution. Such independencies are said to be *entailed* by the graph and can be read from the graph using a criterion called *d-separation* (the d denotes *directional*).

12.2.1.2   The *d*-separation criterion

Consider three disjoint sets of variables, X, Y, and Z, which are represented as nodes in a directed acyclic graph (DAG) G. To test whether X is independent of Y given Z in any Markovian model represented by G, we need to test whether the nodes corresponding to variables Z 'block' all paths from nodes in X to nodes in Y. By *path* we mean a sequence of consecutive edges

---

[7]The term *recursive* is ambiguous; some authors exclude correlated errors, but others do not.

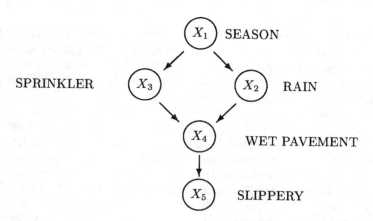

Figure 12.1: Causal graph illustrating causal relationships among five variables.

(of any directionality) in the graph, and '*blocking*' is to be interpreted as stopping the flow of information (or the correlation) between the variables that are connected by such paths.

Definition 12.1 (d-separation) *A path p is said to be d-separated (or blocked) by a set of nodes Z iff*

1. *p contains a chain $i \longrightarrow m \longrightarrow j$ or a fork $i \longleftarrow m \longrightarrow j$ such that the middle node m is in Z, or*

2. *p contains an inverted fork (or collider) $i \longrightarrow m \longleftarrow j$ such that the middle node m is not in Z and such that no descendant of m is in Z.*

   A set Z is said to d-separate X from Y iff Z blocks every path from a node in X to a node in Y.

The intuition behind d-separation is simple. In causal chains:

$$i \longrightarrow m \longrightarrow k$$

and causal forks:

$$i \longleftarrow m \longrightarrow j$$

the two extreme variables are marginally dependent but become independent of each other (*i.e.*, blocked) once we condition on the middle variable. Figuratively, conditioning on m appears to 'block' the flow of information along the path, since learning about i has no effect on the probability of j, given m. Inverted forks $i \longrightarrow m \longleftarrow j$, representing two causes having a common effect, act the opposite way; if the two extreme variables are (marginally) independent, they will become dependent (*i.e.*, unblocked) once we condition on the middle variable (*i.e.*, the common effect) or any of its descendants. This can be confirmed in the context of Figure 12.1. Once we know the season, X_3 and X_2 are independent (assuming that sprinklers are set in advance, according to the season) but finding that the pavement is wet or slippery renders X_2 and X_3 dependent, because refuting one of these explanations increases the probability of the other.

In Figure 12.1, $X = \{X_2\}$ and $Y = \{X_3\}$ are d-separated by $Z = \{X_1\}$, because both paths connecting X_2 and X_3 are blocked by Z. The path $X_2 \longleftarrow X_1 \longrightarrow X_3$ is blocked because it is a fork in which the middle node, X_1, is in Z, while the path $X_2 \longrightarrow X_4 \longleftarrow X_3$ is blocked because it is an inverted fork in which the middle node, X_4, and all its descendants are outside Z. However, X and Y are not d-separated by the set $Z' = \{X_1, X_5\}$: the path $X_2 \longrightarrow X_4 \longleftarrow X_3$ (an inverted fork) is not blocked by Z', since X_5, a descendant of the middle node X_4, is in Z'. Metaphorically, learning the value of the consequence X_5 renders its causes X_2 and X_3 dependent, as if a pathway were opened along the arrows converging at X_4.

Readers might find it a bit odd that conditioning on a node not lying on a blocked path may unblock the path. However, this corresponds to a general rule about causal relationships: observations on a common consequence of uncorrelated causes tend to render those causes correlated. This rule is known as *Berkson's paradox* in the statistical literature (Berkson, 1946) and as the *explaining away effect* in artificial intelligence (Kim & Pearl, 1983). For example, if the admission criteria to a certain graduate school call for either high grades as an undergraduate or special musical talents, then these two attributes will be found to be negatively correlated in the student population of that school, even if these attributes are uncorrelated in the population at large. Indeed, students with low grades are likely to be exceptionally gifted in music, which explains their admission to graduate school.

Algebraically, the partial correlations associated with $i \longrightarrow m \longleftarrow j$ are governed by the equation

$$\rho_{ij \cdot m} = (\rho_{ij} - \rho_{im}\rho_{jm})/(1 - \rho_{im}^2)^{\frac{1}{2}}(1 - \rho_{jm}^2)^{\frac{1}{2}}$$

which renders $\rho_{ij \cdot m} \neq 0$ when $\rho_{ij} = 0$. The same applies to the partial correlation $\rho_{ij \cdot m'}$ where m' is any descendant of m.

Theorem 1 (Verma & Pearl, 1988; Geiger, Verma, & Pearl, 1990)
If sets X and Y are d-separated by Z in a DAG G then X is independent of Y conditional on Z in every Markovian model structured according to G. Conversely, if X and Y are not d-separated by Z in a DAG G, then X and Y are dependent conditional on Z in almost all Markovian models structured according to G.

Because conditional independence implies zero partial correlation, Theorem 1 translates into a graphical test for identifying those partial correlations that must vanish in the model.

Corollary 1 *In any Markovian model structured according to a DAG G, the partial correlation $\rho_{XY \cdot Z}$ vanishes whenever the nodes corresponding to the variables in Z d-separate node X from node Y in G, regardless of the model's parameters. Moreover, no other partial correlation would vanish for all the model's parameters.*

Unrestricted semi-Markovian models can always be emulated by Markovian models that include latent variables, with the latter accounting for all dependencies among error terms. Consequently, the d-separation criterion remains valid in such models if we interpret bi-directed arcs as emanating from latent common parents. This is not always possible in linear semi-Markovian models if each latent variable is restricted to influence at most two observed variables (Spirtes, Richardson, Meek, Scheines, & Glymour, 1996). However, it has been shown that the d-separation criterion remains valid in such restricted systems (Spirtes et al., 1996) and, moreover, that the validity is preserved when the network contains cycles (Koster, 1996; Spirtes, Richardson, Meek, Scheines, & Glymour, 1997). These results are summarized in the next theorem.

Theorem 2 *For any linear model structured according to diagram D, which may include cycles and bi-directed arcs, the partial correlation $\rho_{XY \cdot Z}$ vanishes if the nodes corresponding to the set of variables Z d-separate node X from node Y in D, where each bi-directed arc $i \leftarrow - - \rightarrow j$ is interpreted as a latent common parent $i \longleftarrow L \longrightarrow j$.*

For linear structural equation models (see Equation (12.2)), Theorem 2 implies that those (and only those) partial correlations identified by the d-separation test are guaranteed to vanish independent of the model parameters α_{ik} and independent of the error variances. This suggests a simple and direct method for testing models: rather than going through the standard exercise of finding a maximum likelihood estimate for the model's parameters and scoring those estimates for fit to the data, we can directly test for each zero partial correlation implied by the free model. The advantages of using such tests were noted by Shipley (1997), who also devised implementations of these tests.

The question arises however whether it is feasible to test for the vast number of vanishing partial correlations entailed by a given model. Fortunately, these partial correlations are not independent of each other, but can be derived from a relatively small number of partial correlations that constitutes a *basis* for the entire set (Pearl & Verma, 1987).

Definition 12.2 (Basis) *Let S be a set of partial correlations. A basis B for S is a set of zero partial correlations that (1) implies (using the laws of probability) the vanishing of every element of S, and (2) no proper subset of B sustains such implication.*

An obvious choice of a basis for the zero partial correlations entailed by a DAG D is the set of equalities $B = \{\rho_{ij \cdot pa_i} = 0 | i > j\}$, where i ranges over all nodes in D, and j ranges over all predecessors of i in any order that agrees with the arrows of D. This set of equalities reflects in fact the 'parent screening' property of Markovian models, which is the source of all the probabilistic information encoded in a DAG. Testing for these equalities is sufficient therefore for testing all the statistical claims of a linear Markovian model. Moreover, when the parent sets pa_i are large, it may be possible to select a more economical basis, as shown in the next theorem[8].

Theorem 3 (Graphical basis) *Let (i, j) be a pair of non-adjacent nodes in a DAG D, and Z_{ij} any set of nodes that are closer to i than j is to i, and such that Z_{ij} d-separates i from j. The set of zero partial correlations $B = \{\rho_{ij \cdot Z_{ij}} = 0 | i > j\}$, consisting of one element per non-adjacent pair, constitutes a basis for the set of all vanishing partial correlations entailed by D.*

Theorem 3 states that the set of zero partial correlations corresponding to any separation of the non-adjacent nodes in the diagram encapsulates the entire statistical information conveyed by a linear Markovian model. A formal proof of Theorem 3 is given in (Pearl & Meshkat, 1998).

Examining Figure 12.2, we see that each of following two sets forms a basis for the model in the figure:

$$
\begin{aligned}
B_1 &= \{\rho_{32 \cdot 1} = 0, \rho_{41 \cdot 3} = 0, \rho_{42 \cdot 3} = 0, \rho_{51 \cdot 43} = 0, \rho_{52 \cdot 43} = 0\} \\
B_2 &= \{\rho_{32 \cdot 1} = 0, \rho_{41 \cdot 3} = 0, \rho_{42 \cdot 1} = 0, \rho_{51 \cdot 3} = 0, \rho_{52 \cdot 1} = 0\}
\end{aligned}
\tag{12.5}
$$

The basis B_1 employs the parent set pa_i for separating i from j, $i > j$. Basis B_2, on the other hand, employs smaller separating sets, thus leading to tests involving fewer regressors. Note that each member of a basis corresponds

---

[8]The possibility that linear models may possess more economical bases came to my attention in a conversation with Rod McDonald.

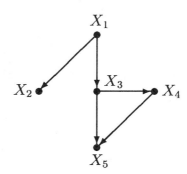

Figure 12.2: Model testable with two regressors for each missing link (Equation (12.5)).

to a missing arrow in the DAG; therefore, the number of tests required to validate a DAG is equal to the number of missing arrows it contains. The sparser the graph, the more it constrains the covariance matrix and more tests are required to verify those constraints.

12.2.2   Testing the Testable

In linear structural equation models, the hypothesized causal relationships between variables can be expressed in the form of a directed graph annotated with coefficients, some fixed *a priori* (usually to zero) and some free to vary. The conventional method for testing such a model against the data involves two stages. First, the free parameters are estimated by iteratively maximizing a fitness measure such as the maximum likelihood function. Second, the covariance matrix implied by the estimated parameters is compared to the sample covariances and a statistical test is applied to decide whether the latter could originate from the former (Bollen, 1989; Chou & Bentler, 1995).

There are two major weaknesses to this approach:

1. If some parameters are not identifiable, the first phase may fail to reach stable estimates for the parameters and the investigator must simply abandon the test.

2. If the model fails to pass the data-fitness test, the investigator receives very little guidance about which modeling assumptions are wrong.

For example, Figure 12.3 shows a path model in which the parameter α is not identifiable if $cov(\epsilon_1, \epsilon_2)$ is assumed unknown, which means that the maximum likelihood method may fail to find a suitable estimate for α, thus precluding the second phase of the test. Still, this model is no less

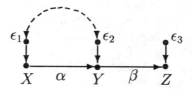

Figure 12.3: A testable model containing unidentified parameter (α).

testable than the one in which $cov(\epsilon_1, \epsilon_2) = 0$, α is identifiable, and the test can proceed. These models impose the same restrictions on the covariance matrix, namely, that the partial correlation $\rho_{XZ \cdot Y}$ should vanish (*i.e.*, $\rho_{XZ} = \rho_{XY}\rho_{YZ}$), yet the model with free $cov(\epsilon_1, \epsilon_2)$, by virtue of α being non-identifiable, cannot be tested for this restriction.

Figure 12.4 illustrates the weakness associated with model diagnosis. Suppose the true data-generating model has a direct causal connection between X and W, as shown in Figure 12.4(a), while the hypothesized model

(Figure 12.4(b)) has no such connection. Statistically, the two models differ in the term $\rho_{XW \cdot Z}$, which should vanish according to Figure 12.4(b) and is left free according to Figure 12.4(a). Once the nature of the discrepancy is

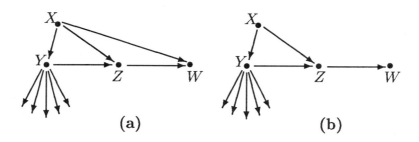

Figure 12.4: Models differing in one local test, $\rho_{XW \cdot Z} = 0$.

clear, the investigator must decide whether substantive knowledge justifies alteration of the model, namely, adding either a link or a curved arc between X and W. However, because the effect of the discrepancy will be spread over several covariance terms, global fitness tests will not be able to isolate the discrepancy easily. Even multiple fitness tests on various local modifications of the model (such tests are provided by LISREL) may not help much, because the results may be skewed by other discrepancies in different parts of the model, such as the subgraph rooted at Y. Thus, testing for global fitness is often of only minor use in model debugging.

Local fitness testing is an attractive alternative to global fitness testing. This involves listing the restrictions implied by the model and testing them one by one. Local testing may help isolate the discrepancy and can be performed more reliably than testing the overall model as one unit. A restriction such as $\rho_{XW \cdot Z} = 0$, for example, can be tested locally without measuring Y or any of its descendants, thus keeping errors associated with those measurements from interfering with the test for $\rho_{XW \cdot Z} = 0$, which is the real source of the lack of fit. More generally, typical SEM models are often close to being 'saturated', claiming but a few restrictions, in the form of a few edges missing from a large, otherwise unrestrictive diagram. Local and direct tests for those restrictions are more reliable than global tests, as they involve fewer degrees of freedom and are not contaminated with irrelevant measurement errors. The missing edges approach described in Section 12.2.1 provides a systematic way of detecting and enumerating the local tests needed for testing a given model.

12.2.3   Model equivalence

An important criterion for determining whether two given causal models are observationally equivalent follows from the d-separation test.

Definition 12.3 (Observational equivalence) *Two structural equation models are said to be* observationally equivalent *if every probability distribution that is generated by one of the models can also be generated by the other.*

Theorem 4 (Verma & Pearl, 1990) *Two Markovian models are observationally equivalent iff they entail the same sets of conditional independencies. Moreover, two such models are observationally equivalent iff their corresponding graphs have the same sets of edges and the same sets of v-structures (two converging arrows whose tails are not connected by an arrow).*

In standard SEM, models are assumed linear and data are characterized by covariance matrices. Thus, two such models are observationally indistinguishable if they are *covariance equivalent*, that is, if every covariance matrix generated by one model (through some choice of parameters) can also be generated by the other. It can be easily verified that Theorem 4 extends to covariance equivalence.

Theorem 5 *Two Markovian linear-normal models are covariance equivalent iff they entail the same sets of zero partial correlations. Moreover, two such models are covariance equivalent iff their corresponding graphs have the same sets of edges and the same sets of v-structures.*

In Theorems 4 and 5, the first part defines the testable implications of any Markovian structural equation model. These theorems state that, in non-manipulative studies, Markovian structural equation models cannot be tested for any feature other than those zero partial correlations that the d-separation test reveals. They provide as well a simple test for equivalence which requires, instead of the checking of all d-separation conditions, merely a comparison of corresponding edges and their directionalities.

For example, reversing the direction of the arrow between X_1 and X_2 in Figure 12.1 does not introduce any new v-structure. Therefore, this reversal yields an observationally equivalent network, and the directionality of the link $X_1 \longrightarrow X_2$ cannot be determined from probabilistic information. The arrows $X_2 \longrightarrow X_4$ and $X_4 \longrightarrow X_5$ are of a different nature, however; their directionality cannot be reversed without creating a new v-structure. Thus, we see that some arrows retain their directionality in all models equivalent to a given model and, hence, that this directionality is testable whenever the equivalence class (of models) is testable. Algorithms for automatically identifying such arrows in the graph have been devised by Chickering (1995), Meek (1995), and Andersson et al. (1998). We further see that some kinds of statistical data (such as those generated by the model in Figure 12.1), unaccompanied by temporal information, can reveal the directionality of some arrows and, hence, the directionality of the causal relationships among the corresponding variables. This feature is used in various discovery algorithms that elicit causal relationships from complex patterns of statistical associations (*e.g.* Pearl & Verma (1991); Spirtes, Glymour, & Scheines (1993)), but discussion of such algorithms lies beyond the scope of this chapter.

In semi-Markovian models (DAGs with correlated errors), the d-separation criterion is still valid for testing independencies (see Theorem 2) but independence equivalence no longer implies observational equivalence[9]. Two models that entail the same set of zero partial correlations among the observed variables may yet impose different inequality constraints on the covariance matrix. Nevertheless, Theorems 2 and 4 still provide necessary conditions for testing equivalence.

12.2.3.1   Generating equivalent models

By permitting arrows to be reversed as long as no v-structures are destroyed or created, we can use Theorems 4 and 5 to generate equivalent alternatives to any Markovian model. Meek (1995) and Chickering (1995) have shown that $X \longrightarrow Y$ can be replaced by $X \longleftarrow Y$ iff all parents of X are also parents of Y, and, moreover, that for any two equivalent models, there is always some sequence of such edge reversals that takes one model into the other. This simple rule for edge reversal coincides with those proposed by Stelzl (1986) and Lee & Hershberger (1990).

In semi-Markovian models, the rules for generating equivalent models are more complicated. Nevertheless, Theorems 4 and 5 yield convenient graphical principles for testing the correctness of edge-replacement rules. The basic principle is that if we regard each bi-directed arc $X \; \text{-}\;\text{-}\;\text{-} \; Y$ as representing a latent common cause $X \longleftarrow L \longrightarrow Y$, then the 'if' part of Theorem 4 remains valid, that is, any edge-replacement transformation that does not destroy or create a v-structure is allowed. Thus, for example, an edge $X \longrightarrow Y$ can be replaced by a bi-directed arc $X \; \text{-}\;\text{-}\;\text{-} \; Y$ whenever X and Y have no other parents, latent or observed. Likewise, an edge $X \longrightarrow Y$ can be replaced by a bi-directed arc $X \; \text{-}\;\text{-}\;\text{-} \; Y$ whenever (1) X and Y have no latent parents and (2) every parent of X or Y is a parent of both. Such replacements do not introduce new v-structures. Since v-structures may now involve latent variables, however, we can tolerate the creation or destruction of some v-structures as long as this does not effect partial correlations among the observed variables. Figure 12.5(a) demonstrates that the creation of certain v-structures can be tolerated. If we reverse the arrow $X \longrightarrow Y$ we create two converging arrows $Z \longrightarrow X \longleftarrow Y$ whose tails are connected, not directly, but through a latent common cause. This is tolerated, because, although the new convergence at X blocks the path (Z, X, Y), the connection between Z and Y (through the arc $Z \; \text{-}\;\text{-}\;\text{-} \; Y$) remains unblocked and, in fact, cannot be blocked by any set of observed variables.

---

[9]Verma & Pearl (1990) present an example using a non-parametric model, and Richardson has devised an example using linear models with correlated errors (Spirtes & Richardson, 1996).

We can carry this principle further by generalizing the concept of v-structure. Whereas in Markovian models, a v-structure is defined as two converging arrows whose tails are not connected by a link, we now define v-structure as any two converging arrowheads whose tails are *separable*. By separable, we mean that there exists a conditioning set S capable of d-separating the two tails. Clearly, the two tails will not be separable if they are connected by an arrow or by a bi-directed arc. But a pair of nodes in a semi-Markovian model can be inseparable even when not connected by an edge (Verma & Pearl, 1990). With this generalization in mind, we can state necessary conditions for edge replacement:

Rule 1: An arrow $X \longrightarrow Y$ is interchangeable with $X \leftarrow - - \rightarrow Y$ only if every neighbor or parent of X is inseparable from Y. (By *neighbor* we mean a node connected (to X) through a bi-directed arc.)

Rule 2: An arrow $X \longrightarrow Y$ can be reversed into $X \longleftarrow Y$ only if, before reversal, (i) every neighbor or parent of Y (excluding X) is inseparable from X and (ii) every neighbor or parent of X is inseparable from Y.

For example, consider the model $Z \leftarrow - - \rightarrow X \longrightarrow Y$. The arrow $X \longrightarrow Y$ cannot be replaced with a bi-directed arc $X \leftarrow - - \rightarrow Y$ because Z (a neighbor of X) is separable from Y by the set $S = \{X\}$. Indeed, the new v-structure created at X would render X and Y marginally independent, contrary to the original model. As another example, consider the graph in Figure 12.5(a). Here, it is legitimate to replace $X \longrightarrow Y$ with $X \leftarrow - - \rightarrow Y$

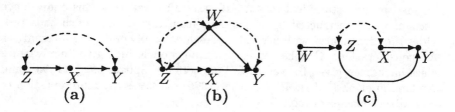

(a)   **(b)**   **(c)**

Figure 12.5: Models permitting ((a) and (b)) and forbidding (c) the reversal of $X \to Y$.

or with a reversed arrow $X \longleftarrow Y$ because X has no neighbors and Z, the only parent of X, is inseparable from Y. The same considerations apply to Figure 12.5(b); variables Z and Y, though non-adjacent, are inseparable, because the paths going from Z to Y through W cannot be blocked.

A more complicated example, one that demonstrates that the rules above are not sufficient to ensure the legitimacy of a transformation, is shown in Figure 12.5(c). Here, it appears that replacing $X \longrightarrow Y$ with $X \leftarrow - - \rightarrow Y$ would be legitimate because the (latent) v-structure at X is shunted by the arrow $Z \longrightarrow Y$. However, the original model shows the path from W to Y to be d-connected given Z, while the post-replacement model shows the same path d-separated given Z. Consequently, the partial correlation $\rho_{WY \cdot Z}$ vanishes in the post-replacement model but not in the pre-replacement model. A similar disparity also occurs relative to the partial correlation $\rho_{WY \cdot ZX}$. The original model shows that the path from W to Y is blocked, given $\{Z, X\}$, while the post-replacement model shows that path d-connected, given $\{Z, X\}$. Consequently, the partial correlation $\rho_{WY \cdot ZX}$ vanishes in the pre-replacement model but is unconstrained in the post-replacement model[10]. Evidently, it is not enough to impose rules on the parents and neighbors of X; remote ancestors (*e.g.*, W) should be considered too.

These rules are just a few of the implications of the d-separation criterion when applied to semi-Markovian models. A necessary and sufficient criterion for testing the d-separation equivalence of two semi-Markovian models has been devised by Spirtes & Verma (1992). Spirtes & Richardson (1996) have extended that criterion to include models with feedback cycles. We should keep in mind, though, that, because two semi-Markovian models can be zero-partial-correlation equivalent and yet not covariance equivalent, criteria based on d-separation can provide merely the necessary conditions for model equivalence.

12.2.3.2   The significance of equivalent models

Theorem 4 is methodologically significant because it clarifies what it means to claim that structural models are 'testable' (Bollen, 1989, p. 78)[11]'. It asserts that we never test *a* model but, rather a whole class of observationally equivalent models from which the hypothesized model cannot be distinguished by any statistical means. It asserts as well that this equivalence class can be constructed by inspection, from the graph, which thus provides the investigator with a vivid representation of competing alternatives for consideration. Graphs representing all models in a given equivalence class have been given by Verma & Pearl (1990), Spirtes et al. (1993), and Andersson et al. (1998). Richardson (1996) discusses the representation of equivalence classes of models with cycles.

While it is true that (over-identified) structural equation models have testable implications, those implications are but a small part of what the model represents, namely, a set of claims, assumptions, and implications. Failure to distinguish among causal assumptions, statistical implications, and policy claims has been one of the main reasons for the suspicion and confusion surrounding quantitative methods in the social sciences (Freedman, 1987; Goldberger, 1992; Wermuth, 1992). However, because they make the distinctions among these components vivid and crisp, graphical

---

[10] This example was brought to my attention by Jin Tian, and a similar one, by two anonymous reviewers.

[11] In response to an allegation that 'path analysis does not derive the causal theory from the data, or test any major part of it against the data' (Freedman, 1987, p. 112), Bollen (1989, p. 78) state, 'we can test and reject structural models.... Thus the assertion that these models cannot be falsified has little basis.'

methods promise to make SEM more acceptable to researchers from a wide variety of disciplines.

By and large, the SEM literature has ignored the explicit analysis of equivalent models. Breckler (1990), for example, found that out of 72 articles in the areas of social and personality psychology only one acknowledged the existence of an equivalent model. The general attitude has been that the combination of data fitness and model over-identification is sufficient to confirm the hypothesized model. Recently, however, the existence of multiple equivalent models seems to have jangled the nerves of some SEM researchers. MacCallum, Wegener, Uchino, & Fabrigar (1993) conclude that 'the phenomenon of equivalent models represents a serious problem for empirical researchers using CSM' and 'a threat to the validity of interpretation of CSM results'. Breckler (1990) reckons that 'if one model is supported, so too are all of its equivalent models' and, consequently, ventures that 'the term *causal modeling* is a misnomer'.

Such extremes are not justifiable. The existence of equivalent models is logically inevitable if we accept the fact that causal relations cannot be inferred from statistical data alone; as Wright (1921) stated, 'prior knowledge of the causal relations is assumed as prerequisite' in SEM. But this does not make SEM useless as a tool for causal modeling. The move from the qualitative causal premises represented by the structure of a path diagram to the quantitative causal conclusions advertized by the coefficients in the diagram is neither useless nor trivial. Consider, for example, the model depicted in Figure 12.6, which Bagozzi & Burnkrant (1979) use to illustrate problems associated with equivalent models. Although this model is saturated (*i.e.*, just identified) and although it has (at least) 27 semi-Markovian equivalent models, finding that the influence of AFFECT on BEHAVIOR is almost three times stronger (on a standardized scale) than the influence of COGNITION on BEHAVIOR is still very illuminating — it tells us about the relative effectiveness of different behavior-modification policies if some are known to influence AFFECT and others COGNITION. The significance of this quantitative analysis on policy analysis may be more dramatic when a path coefficient turns negative while the corresponding correlation coefficient measures positive. Learning that such a reversal is logically implied by the qualitative causal premises embedded in the diagram may have profound impact on policy decisions.

In summary, social scientists need not abandon SEM altogether; they need only abandon the notion that SEM is a method of *testing* causal models. SEM is a method of testing a tiny fraction of the premises that make up a causal model and, in cases where that fraction is found to be compatible with the data, the method elucidates the necessary quantitative consequences of both the premises and the data. It follows, then, that users of SEM should concentrate on examining the implicit theoretical premises that enter into a model. As we will see in Section 12.4, graphical methods make these premises vivid and precise.

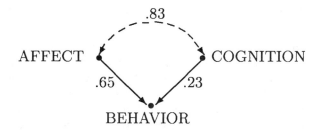

Figure 12.6: Untestable model displaying quantitative causal information derived.

12.3   Graphs and identifiability

12.3.1   Parameter identification in linear models

Consider a directed edge $X \longrightarrow Y$ embedded in a path diagram G, and let α stand for the path coefficient associated with that edge. It is well known that the regression coefficient $r_{YX} = \rho_{XY}\sigma_Y/\sigma_X$ can be decomposed into the sum

$$r_{YX} = \alpha + I_{YX}$$

where I_{YX} is not a function of α, since it is computed (*e.g.*, using Wright's rules) from other paths connecting X and Y excluding the edge $X \longrightarrow Y$. (Such paths traverse both uni-directed and bi-directed arcs.) Thus, if we remove the edge $X \longrightarrow Y$ from the path diagram and find that the resulting subgraph entails zero correlation between X and Y, then we know that $I_{YX} = 0$ and $\alpha = r_{YX}$; hence, α is identified. Such entailment can be established graphically by testing whether X is d-separated from Y (by the empty set $Z = \{\emptyset\}$) in the subgraph. Figure 12.7 illustrates this simple test for identification: all paths between X and Y in the subgraph G_α are blocked by converging arrows, and α can immediately be equated with r_{YX}.

We can extend this basic idea to cases where I_{YX} is not zero but can be made zero by adjusting for a set of variables $Z = \{Z_1, Z_2, \ldots, Z_k\}$ that lie on various d-connected paths between X and Y. Consider the partial regression coefficient $r_{YX\cdot Z} = \rho_{YX\cdot Z}\sigma_{Y\cdot Z}/\sigma_{X\cdot Z}$, which represents the residual correlation between Y and X after Z is 'partialled out'. If Z contains no descendant of Y, then again we can write[12]

$$r_{YX\cdot Z} = \alpha + I_{YX\cdot Z}$$

where $I_{YX\cdot Z}$ represents the partial correlation between X and Y resulting from setting α to zero, that is, the partial correlation in a model whose

---

[12]This can be seen when the relation between Y and its parents, $Y = \alpha x + \sum_i \beta_i w_i + \epsilon$ is substituted into the expression for $r_{YX\cdot Z}$, which yields α plus an expression $I_{YX\cdot Z}$ involving partial correlations among the variables $\{X, W_1, \ldots, W_k, Z, \epsilon\}$. Since Y is assumed not to be an ancestor of any of these variables, their joint density is unaffected by the equation for Y; hence, $I_{YX\cdot Z}$ is independent of α.

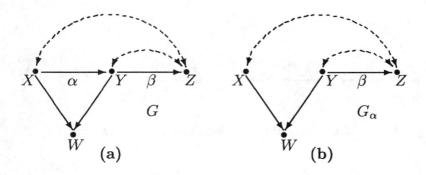

Figure 12.7: Testing whether structural parameter α can be equated with regression coefficient r_{YX}.

graph, G_α, lacks the edge $X \longrightarrow Y$ but is otherwise identical to G. If Z d-separates X from Y in G_α, then $I_{YX \cdot Z}$ would indeed be zero in such a model, and we can conclude that in our original model, α is identified and is equal to $\alpha = r_{YX \cdot Z}$. Moreover, since $r_{YX \cdot Z}$ is given by the coefficient of x in the regression of Y on X and Z, α can be estimated using the regression

$$y = \alpha x + \beta_1 z_1 + \ldots + \beta_k z_k + \epsilon$$

This result provides a simple graphical answer to the questions, alluded to in Section 12.1.3, of what constitutes an adequate set of regressors and when a regression coefficient provides a consistent estimate of a path coefficient. The answers are summarized in the following theorem[13].

Theorem 6 (Single-link criterion) *Let G be any path diagram in which α is the path coefficient associated with link $X \longrightarrow Y$, and let G_α denote the diagram that results when $X \longrightarrow Y$ is deleted from G. The coefficient α is identifiable, if there exists a set of variables Z such that Z contains no descendant of Y, and Z d-separates X from Y in G_α. If Z satisfies these two conditions, then α is equal to the regression coefficient $r_{YX \cdot Z}$. Conversely, if Z does not satisfy these conditions, then $r_{YX \cdot Z}$ is not a consistent estimand of α, except in rare instances of measure zero.*

The use of Theorem 6 can be illustrated as follows. Consider the graphs G and G_α in Figure 12.8. The only path connecting X and Y in G_α is the one traversing Z, and since that path is d-separated (blocked) by Z, α is identifiable and is given by $\alpha = r_{YX \cdot Z}$. The coefficient β is identifiable, of course, since Z is d-separated from X in G_β (by the empty set $\{\emptyset\}$) and thus $\beta = r_{XZ}$.

We now extend the use of d-separation to facilitate the identification of total, rather than direct, effects. Consider the graph G in Figure 12.9. If we form the graph G_α (by removing the link $X \longrightarrow Y$), we observe

---

[13]This result is also presented in Spirtes et al. (1997).

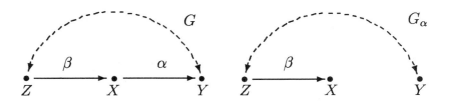

Figure 12.8: Illustrating the identification of α (Theorem 6).

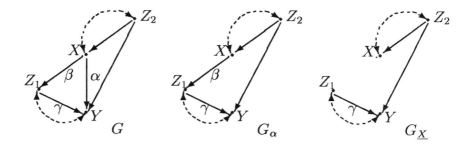

Figure 12.9: Graphical identification of the total effect of X on Y, $\alpha + \beta\gamma = r_{YX \cdot Z_2}$.

that there is no set Z of nodes that d-separates all paths from X to Y. If Z contains Z_1, then the path $X \longrightarrow Z_1 \leftarrow - - \rightarrow Y$ will be unblocked through the converging arrows at Z_1. If Z does not contain Z_1, the path $X \longrightarrow Z_1 \longrightarrow Y$ is unblocked. Thus we conclude that α cannot be identified using our previous method. However, suppose we are interested in the total effect of X on Y, given by $\alpha + \beta\gamma$. For this sum to be identified by r_{YX}, there should be no contribution to r_{YX} from paths other than those leading from X to Y. However, we see that two such paths, called *confounding* or *back-door* paths, exist in the graph, namely, $X \longleftarrow Z_2 \longrightarrow Y$ and $X \leftarrow - - \rightarrow Z_2 \longrightarrow Y$. Fortunately, these paths are blocked by Z_2, and we conclude that adjusting for Z_2 would render $\alpha + \beta\gamma$ identifiable and given by

$$\alpha + \beta\gamma = r_{YX \cdot Z_2}$$

This line of reasoning leads to a general test for the identifiability of total effects, called the *back-door* criterion (Pearl, 1993a, 1995):

Theorem 7 (Back-door criterion) *For any two variables X and Y in a causal diagram G, the total effect of X on Y is identifiable if there exists a set of measurements Z such that:*

1. no member of Z is a descendant of X, and

2. *Z d-separates X from Y in the subgraph $G_{\underline{X}}$ formed by deleting from G all arrows emanating from X.*

Moreover, if the two conditions are satisfied, then the total effect of X on Y is given by $r_{YX \cdot Z}$.

The two conditions of Theorem 7, as we will see in the next subsection, are also valid in non-linear non-Gaussian models, as well as in models with discrete variables. It is for this reason that the back-door criterion can serve as a general test for covariate selection, as described in Section 12.1.3. The reason for deleting the arrows in step 2 is to ensure that only confounding (*i.e.*, back-door) paths participate in the *d*-separation test. The test ensures that, after adjustment for Z, X and Y are not associated through confounding paths, which means that the partial correlation $r_{YX \cdot Z}$ is equal to the total effect. In fact, we can view Theorems 6 and 7 as special cases of a more general scheme: to identify any *partial effect*, as defined by a select bundle of causal paths from X to Y, we ought to find a set Z of measured variables that block all non-selected paths between X and Y. The partial effect will then equal the regression coefficient $r_{YX \cdot Z}$.

Figure 12.9 demonstrates that some total effects can be determined directly from the graphs, without having to identify their individual components. Standard SEM methods (Bollen, 1989; Chou & Bentler, 1995), which focus on the identification and estimation of individual parameters, may miss the identification and estimation of effects such as the one in Figure 12.9, which can be estimated reliably even though some of the constituents remain unidentified.

Some total effects cannot be determined directly, as a unit, but require the determination of each component separately. In Figure 12.8, for example, the effect of Z on $Y (= \alpha\beta)$ does not meet the back-door criterion, yet this effect can be determined from its constituents α and β, which meet the back-door criterion individually and evaluate to

$$\beta = r_{XZ} \qquad \alpha = r_{YX \cdot Z}$$

There is still a third kind of causal parameter which cannot be determined directly or through its constituents, but requires the evaluation of a broader causal effect of which it is a part. The structure shown in Figure 12.10 represents an example of this case. The parameter α cannot be identified directly, yet it can be determined from $\alpha\beta$ and β, which represent the effect of Z on Y and that of Z on X, respectively. These two effects can be identified directly, since there are no back-door paths from Z to either Y or X, giving $\alpha\beta = r_{YZ}$ and $\beta = r_{XZ}$. Thus,

$$\alpha = r_{YZ}/r_{XZ}$$

which is familiar to us as the *instrumental-variable formula* (Bowden & Turkington, 1984).

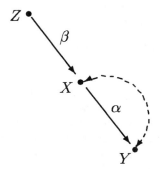

Figure 12.10: Graphical identification of α using instrumental variable Z.

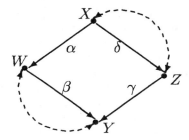

Figure 12.11: Graphical identification of α, β and γ.

The example shown in Figure 12.11 combines all three methods considered thus far. The total effect of X on Y is given by $\alpha\beta + \gamma\delta$, which is not identifiable because it does not meet the back-door criterion and is not part of another identifiable structure. However, suppose we wish to estimate β. By conditioning on Z, we block all paths going through Z and obtain $\alpha\beta = r_{YX \cdot Z}$, which is the effect of X on Y mediated by W. Because there are no back-door paths from X to W, α itself evaluates directly to $\alpha = r_{WX}$. We therefore obtain

$$\beta = r_{YX \cdot Z} / r_{WX}$$

In contrast, γ can be evaluated directly by conditioning on X (thus blocking the back-door path from Z to Y through X), which gives

$$\gamma = r_{YZ \cdot X}$$

The methods we have been using suggest a systematic procedure for recognizing identifiable coefficients in a graph (see Figure 12.12).

The process described in Figure 12.12 is not complete, because our insistence on labeling coefficients one at a time may cause us to miss certain opportunities. This is shown in Figure 12.13. Starting with the pairs

1. Start by searching for identifiable causal effects among pairs of variables in the graph, using the back-door criterion and Theorem 6. These can be either direct effects, total effects, or partial effects, that is, effects mediated by specific sets of variables.

2. For any such identified effect, collect the path coefficients involved and put them in a bucket.

3. Begin labeling the coefficients in the buckets according to the following procedure:
   If a bucket is a singleton, label its coefficient I (denoting *identifiable*).
   If a bucket is not a singleton but contains only a single unlabeled element, label that element I.

4. Repeat this process until no new labeling is possible.

5. List all labeled coefficients; these are identifiable.

Figure 12.12: Procedure for recognizing identifiable coefficients in a graph.

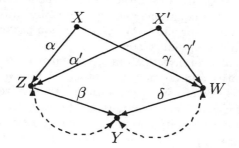

Figure 12.13: Identifying β and δ using two instrumental variables.

$(X, Z), (X, W), (X', Z)$, and (X', W), we discover that α, γ, α', and γ' are identifiable. Going to (X, Y), we find that $\alpha\beta + \delta\gamma$ is identifiable, and, likewise, from (X', Y), that $\alpha'\beta + \gamma'\delta$ is identifiable. This does not enable us to label β or δ yet, but we can solve two equations for the unknowns β and δ, as long as the determinant $\begin{vmatrix} \alpha & \gamma \\ \alpha' & \gamma' \end{vmatrix}$ is non-zero. Since we are not interested in identifiability at a point, but rather in identifiability 'almost everywhere' (Koopmans, Rubin, & Leipnik, 1950; Simon, 1953), we need not compute this determinant. We merely inspect the symbolic form of the determinant's rows to make sure that the equations are non-redundant; each imposes a new constraint on the unlabeled coefficients for at least one value of the labeled coefficients.

With a facility to detect redundancies, we can increase the power of our procedure by adding the following rule:

3b. If there are k non-redundant buckets that contain at most k unlabeled coefficients, label these coefficients, and continue.

Another way to increase the power of our procedure is to list not just identifiable effects, but also expressions involving correlations due to bi-directed arcs, in accordance with Wright's rules. Finally, one can endeavor to list effects of several variables jointly. A modified back-door criterion for evaluating joint effects has been reported by Pearl & Robins (1995). However, such enrichments tend to make the procedure more complex and might compromise our main objective of providing investigators with a way of immediately recognizing the identified coefficients in a given model and immediately understanding those features in the model that influence the identifiability of the target quantity. We now address the problem of identification in non-parametric models, where the machinery of linear algebra can be of little help and where graph theoretical techniques have led to significant progress.

12.3.2   Identification in non-parametric models

non-parametric models are structural equation models in which both the functional forms of the equations and the probability distributions of the disturbances remain unspecified. We consider non-parametric models for both practical and conceptual reasons.

On the practical side, investigators often find it hard to defend the assumptions of linearity and normality, or other functional-distributional assumptions, especially when categorical variables are involved. Non-parametric results are valid for non-linear functions and for any distribution of errors. Moreover, having such results allows us to gauge how sensitive standard techniques are to assumptions of linearity and normality. On the conceptual side, non-parametric models, which are stripped of algebraic connotations, illuminate the distinctions between structural and algebraic equations. The search for alternatives to path coefficients (which are non-existent in non-parametric models) and to the standard definitions of direct and total causal effects (which are normally defined in terms of path coefficients) forces explication of what path coefficients really mean and of where their empirical content comes from.

12.3.2.1   Parametric vs. non-parametric models: an example

Consider the set of structural equations:

$$x = f_1(u, \epsilon_1) \tag{12.6}$$

$$z = f_2(x, \epsilon_2) \tag{12.7}$$

$$y = f_3(z, u, \epsilon_3) \tag{12.8}$$

where X, Z, and Y are observed variables, f_1, f_2, and f_3 are unknown arbitrary functions, and $U, \epsilon_1, \epsilon_2$, and ϵ_3 are unobservables that we can regard either as latent variables or as disturbances. For the sake of this discussion, we will assume that $U, \epsilon_1, \epsilon_2$, and ϵ_3 are mutually independent and arbitrarily distributed. Graphically, these influences can be represented by the path diagram of Figure 12.14.

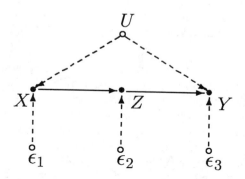

Figure 12.14: Path diagram corresponding to Equations (12.6)–(12.8), where $\{X, Z, Y\}$ are observed and $\{U, \epsilon_1, \epsilon_2, \epsilon_3\}$ are unobserved.

The problem is as follows: we have drawn a long stream of independent samples of the process defined by Equations (12.6)–(12.8) and have recorded the values of the observed variables X, Z, and Y, and we now wish to estimate the unspecified quantities of the model to the greatest extent possible.

To clarify the scope of the problem, let us consider its linear version, which is given by

$$x \;=\; u + \epsilon_1 \tag{12.9}$$

$$z \;=\; \alpha x + \epsilon_2 \tag{12.10}$$

$$y \;=\; \beta z + \gamma u + \epsilon_3 \tag{12.11}$$

where $U, \epsilon_1, \epsilon_2$, and ϵ_3 are uncorrelated, zero-mean disturbances[14]. It is not hard to show that parameters α, β, and γ can be determined uniquely from the correlations among the observed quantities X, Z, and Y. This identification was demonstrated already in the example of Figure 12.8, where the back-door criterion yielded

$$\beta = r_{YZ \cdot X} \qquad \alpha = r_{ZX} \tag{12.12}$$

and hence

$$\gamma = r_{YX} - \alpha\beta \tag{12.13}$$

Thus, returning to the non-parametric version of the model, it is tempting to generalize that for the model to be identifiable, the functions $\{f_1, f_2, f_3\}$

---

[14] An equivalent version of this model is obtained by eliminating U from the equations and allowing ϵ_1 and ϵ_3 to be correlated.

must be determined uniquely from the data. However, the prospect of this happening is unlikely, because the mapping between functions and distributions is known to be many to one. In other words, given any non-parametric model M, if there exists one set of functions $\{f_1, f_2, f_3\}$ compatible with a given distribution $P(x, y, z)$, then there are infinitely many such functions. Thus, it seems that nothing useful can be inferred from loosely specified models such as the one given by Equations (12.6)–(12.8).

Identification is not an end in itself, however, even in linear models. Rather it serves to answer practical questions of prediction and control. At issue is not whether the data permit us to identify the form of the equations but rather whether the data permit us to provide unambiguous answers to questions of the kind traditionally answered by parametric models.

When the model given by Equations (12.6)–(12.8) is used strictly for prediction (*i.e.*, to determine the probabilities of some variables given a set of observations on other variables), the structural content of the parameters becomes irrelevant; the predictions can be estimated directly from either the covariance matrices or the sample estimates of those covariances. If dimensionality reduction is needed (*e.g.*, to improve estimation accuracy), the covariance matrix can be encoded in a variety of simultaneous equation models, all of the same dimensionality. For example, the correlations among X, Y, and Z in the linear model M of Equations (12.9)–(12.11) might well be represented by the model M' (Figure 12.15):

$$x = \epsilon_1 \tag{12.14}$$

$$z = \alpha' x + \epsilon_2 \tag{12.15}$$

$$y = \beta' z + \delta x + \epsilon_3 \tag{12.16}$$

which is as compact as Equations (12.9)–(12.11) and is covariance equivalent to M with respect to the observed variables X, Y, and Z. Upon setting $\alpha' = \alpha, \beta' = \beta$, and $\delta = \gamma$, model M' will yield the same probabilistic predictions as those of the model of Equations (12.9)–(12.11). Still, when viewed as data-generating mechanisms, the two models are not equivalent; each tells a different story about the processes generating X, Y, and Z, and, naturally, their predictions about the changes that would result from subjecting these processes to external interventions differ.

12.3.3 Causal Effects: the interventional interpretation of structural equation models

The differences between models M and M' illustrate precisely where the structural reading of simultaneous equation models comes into play. Model M', defined by Equations (12.14)–(12.16), regards X as a direct participant in the process that determines the value of Y, while model M, defined by Equations (12.9)–(12.11), views X as an indirect factor whose effect on Y is mediated by Z. This difference is not manifested in the data but in the way the data would change in response to outside interventions. For example,

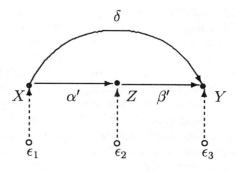

Figure 12.15: Diagram representing model M' of Equations (12.14)–(12.16).

suppose we wish to predict the expectation of Y after we intervene and fix the value of X to some constant x, denoted $E(Y|do(X = x))$[15]. After $X = x$ is substituted into Equations (12.15) and (12.16), model M' yields:

$$E[Y|do(X = x)] = E[\beta'\alpha'x + \beta'\epsilon_2 + \delta x + \epsilon_3] \qquad (12.17)$$
$$= (\beta'\alpha' + \delta)x \qquad (12.18)$$

while model M yields:

$$E[Y|do(X = x)] = E[\beta\alpha x + \beta\epsilon_2 + \gamma u + \epsilon_3] \qquad (12.19)$$
$$= \beta\alpha x \qquad (12.20)$$

Upon setting $\alpha' = \alpha$, $\beta' = \beta$, and $\delta = \gamma$ (as required for covariance equivalence, see Equations (12.12) and (12.13)), we see clearly that the two models assign different magnitudes to the (total) causal effect of X on Y; model M predicts that a unit change in x will change $E(Y)$ by the amount $\beta\alpha$, while model M' puts this amount at $\beta\alpha + \gamma$.

At this point, it is tempting to ask whether we should substitute $x - \epsilon_1$ for u in Equation (12.11) prior to taking expectations in Equation (12.19). If we permit the substitution of Equation (12.10) into Equation (12.11), as we did in deriving Equation (12.19), why not permit the substitution of Equation (12.9) into Equation (12.11) as well? After all, so the argument goes, there is no harm in upholding a mathematical equality, $u = x - \epsilon_1$, that the modeler deems valid.

This argument is fallacious, however. Structural equations are not meant to be treated as immutable mathematical equalities. Rather, they are introduced into the model to describe a state of equilibrium, and they are *violated* when that equilibrium is perturbed by outside interventions. In fact, the

---

[15] Pearl (1993b) and Pearl (1995) used the notation $set(X = x)$. Currently, however, the $do(X = x)$ notation (taken from Goldszmidt & Pearl (1992)) seems to be winning broader popular support.

power of structural equation models is that they not only encode the initial equilibrium state but also the information necessary for determining which equations must be violated to account for a new state of equilibrium. For example, if the intervention merely consists of holding X constant at x, then the equation $x = u + \epsilon_1$, which represents the pre-intervention process determining X, should be overruled and replaced with the equation $X = x$. The solution to the new set of equations then represents the new equilibrium. Thus, the essential characteristic of structural equations that sets them apart from ordinary mathematical equations is that they stand not for one but for many sets of equations, each corresponding to a subset of equations taken from the original model. Every such subset represents some hypothetical physical reality that would prevail under a given intervention.

If we take the stand that the value of structural equations lies not in summarizing distribution functions but in encoding causal information for predicting the effects of policies (Haavelmo, 1943; Koopmans, 1953; Marschak, 1950), when dealing with non-parametric models it is natural to view such predictions as the proper generalization of structural coefficients. For example, the proper generalization of the coefficient β in the linear model M would be the answer to the control query, '*What would be the change in the expected value of Y if we were to intervene and change the value of Z from z to z + 1*', which is different, of course, from the observational query, '*What would be the difference in the expected value of Y if we were to* find *Z at level z + 1 instead of level z*.' Observational queries can be answered directly from the joint distribution $P(x, y, z)$, while control queries require causal information as well. Structural equations encode this causal information in their syntax, by treating the variable on the left hand side of the equality sign as the effect and those on the right as causes. To distinguish between the two types of queries, we will use the symbol $do(\cdot)$ to indicate externally controlled quantities. For example, we write:

$$E(Y|do(x)) \triangleq E[Y|do(X = x)] \qquad (12.21)$$

for the controlled expectation and

$$E(Y|x) \triangleq E(Y|X = x) \qquad (12.22)$$

for the standard conditional or observational expectation. That

$$E(Y|do(x)) \neq E(Y|x)$$

can easily be seen in the model of Equations (12.9)–(12.11), where

$$E(Y|do(x)) = \alpha\beta x, \quad \text{but} \quad E(Y|x) = r_{YX}x = (\alpha\beta + \gamma)x$$

Indeed, the passive observation $X = x$ should not violate any of the equations, and this is the justification for substituting both Equations (12.9) and (12.10) into Equation (12.11) before taking the expectation.

In linear models, the answers to questions of direct control are encoded in the so-called path coefficients or structural coefficients, and these can be used to derive the total effect of any variable on another. For example, the value of $E(Y|do(x))$ in the model defined by Equations (12.9)–(12.11) is $\alpha\beta x$, namely, x times the product of the path coefficients along the path $X \longrightarrow Z \longrightarrow Y$. In the non-parametric case, computation of $E(Y|do(x))$ would be more complicated, even when we know the functions f_1, f_2, and f_3. Nevertheless, this computation is well defined and requires the solution (for the expectation of Y) of a modified set of equations in which f_1 is 'wiped out' and X is replaced by the constant x:

$$z = f_2(x, \epsilon_2) \tag{12.23}$$
$$y = f_3(z, u, \epsilon_3) \tag{12.24}$$

Thus, computation of $E(Y|do(x))$ requires evaluation of

$$E(Y|do(x)) = E\{f_3[f_2(x, \epsilon_2), u, \epsilon_3]\}$$

where the expectation is taken over U, ϵ_2, and ϵ_3. Graphical methods for performing this computation are discussed in Section 12.3.4.

What, then, is an appropriate definition of identifiability for non-parametric models? One reasonable definition is that *answers to interventional queries are* unique. Accordingly, we call a model *identifiable* if there exists a consistent estimate for every query of the type '*Find $P(r|do(s)) \triangleq P[R = r|do(S = s)]$*', where R and S are subsets of observables and r and s are any realizations of these variables. The set of probabilities $P(r|do(s))$ is called the *causal effect* of S on R, as it describes how the distribution of R varies when S is changed by external control[16].

Naturally, we need to allow for instances in which some queries are identifiable while the system as a whole is not. Hence, we say that $P(r|do(s))$ is identifiable in model M if every choice of the model's parameters (*i.e.*, functional forms and distributions) compatible with the observed distribution P yields the same value for $P(r|do(s))$.

Remarkably, many aspects of non-parametric identification, including tests for deciding whether a given interventional query is identifiable, as well as formulas for estimating such queries, can be determined graphically, almost by inspection, from the diagrams that accompany the equations.

12.3.4   Identification of Causal Effects

Definition 12.4 (Causal effect) *Given a causal model M (cf. Equation (12.1)) and two disjoint sets of variables, X and Y, the* causal effect *of the set X on the set Y, denoted $P_M(y|do(x))$, is the probability of $Y = y$*

---

[16]Technically, the adjective 'causal' is redundant. It serves to emphasize, however, that the changes in S are enforced by external control and do not represent stochastic variations in the observed value of S.

*induced by deleting from the model all equations corresponding to variables
in X and substituting $X = x$ in the remaining equations*[17].

Clearly, the graph corresponding to the reduced set of equations is an edge
subgraph of G from which all arrows to X have been pruned (Spirtes et al.,
1993).

Readers accustomed to thinking of causal effects in terms of random-
ized experiments may interpret $P(y|do(x))$ as the conditional probability
$P_{exp}(Y = y|X = x)$ corresponding to a controlled experiment in which X
is randomized. An equivalent interpretation can be formulated using the
potential-response notation (Rubin, 1974) to read

$$P(y|do(x)) = P(Y_x = y)$$

where Y_x is the value that Y would obtain under the hypothetical control (or
treatment) $do(X = x)$. Rubin's definition of causal effect, $E(Y_{x'}) - E(Y_{x''})$,
where x' and x'' are two levels of a treatment variable X, corresponds to
the difference $E(y|do(x')) - E(Y|do(x''))$, and can always be obtained from
the generic distribution $P(y|do(x))$. Definition 12.4 forms the bridge be-
tween structural equation models and the potential-response framework. It
provides a precise model-theoretic definition for the counterfactual variable
Y_x, which in the potential-response framework is taken as a hypothetical
mental construct. The SEM equivalent of Y_x is: *the solution for Y, after
deleting from the model all equations corresponding to variables in the set
X, and substituting $X = x$ in the remaining equations.*

Definition 12.5 (Causal effect identifiability) *The causal effect of X
on Y is said to be identifiable in a class C of models if the quantity $P(y|do(x))$
can be computed uniquely from the probabilities of the observed variables V,
that is, if for every pair of models M_1 and M_2 in C for which $P_{M_1}(v) =
P_{M_2}(v)$, we have $P_{M_1}(y|do(x)) = P_{M_2}(y|do(x))$.*

Our analysis of identifiability will focus on a class C of models that have
the following characteristics in common:

1. they share the same causal graph G, and

2. they induce positive distributions on the observed variables, that is,
   $P_M(v) > 0$.

Analysis of causal effects becomes particularly simple when dealing with
Markovian models. In such models, all causal effect queries are identifiable,
that is, they can be computed directly from the conditional probabilities

---

[17]Explicit translation of interventions to 'wiping out' equations from the model was
first proposed by Strotz & Wold (1960) and has since been used by Fisher (1970) and
Sobel (1990). Graphical ramifications of this translation were explicated first by Spirtes
et al. (1993) and later by Pearl (1993b). A related mathematical model using event trees
has been introduced by Robins (1986, pp. 1422–1425).

$P(x_i|pa_i)$, even when the functional forms of the functions f_i and the distributions of the disturbances are not specified (Pearl, 1993c; Spirtes et al., 1993). This is seen immediately from the following observations.

On the one hand, the distribution induced by any Markovian model M is given by the product in Equation (12.3),

$$P_M(x_1,\ldots,x_n) = \prod_i P(x_i|pa_i) \tag{12.25}$$

where pa_i are (values of) the parents of X_i in the diagram representing M.

On the other hand, the submodel $M_{x'_j}$, representing the action $do(X_j = x'_j)$, is also Markovian; hence, it also induces a product-like distribution

$$P_{M_{x'_j}}(x_1,\ldots,x_n) = \begin{cases} \prod_{i\neq j} P(x_i|pa_i) = \frac{P(x_1,\ldots,x_n)}{P(x_j|pa_j)} & \text{if } x_j = x'_j \\ 0 & \text{if } x_j \neq x'_j \end{cases} \tag{12.26}$$

where the partial product reflects the removal of the equation $x_j = f_j(pa_j, \epsilon_j)$ from the model. Thus, we see that both the pre-action and the post-action distributions depend only on observed conditional probabilities, but they are independent of the particular functional forms of $\{f_i\}$ and of the error distributions that generated those probabilities.

It is possible to show that certain, although not all, causal effects are identifiable in semi-Markovian non-parametric models (Pearl, 1995). An important result in this direction has been the extension of the back-door criterion (Theorem 7) to non-parametric models:

Theorem 8 (Non-parametric back-door criterion.) *For any disjoint sets of variables X and Y in a causal diagram G, if the two conditions of Theorem 7 are satisfied, then the causal effect of X on Y is identified and is given by*

$$P(y|do(x)) = \sum_z P(y|x,z)P(z) \tag{12.27}$$

This theorem provides a formal definition for the concepts of *exogeneity* and *confounding* in econometrics (Engle, Hendry, & Richard, 1983) and epidemiology (Greenland, Pearl, & Robins, 1999), respectively. A variable X is said to be *exogenous (unconfounded)* relative to Y if $P(y|do(x)) = P(y|x)$, that is, if the conditions of the back-door criterion hold when Z is the empty set. Alternatively, X is said to be conditionally exogenous (unconfounded) relative to Y, given measurements on set Z, if Equation (12.27) holds, that is, if the conditions of the back-door criterion hold for Z. Section 12.3.1 proposes an explanation why the definitions of these two basic concepts have encountered difficulties in econometrics and epidemiology (see also Pearl (1998) and Pearl (1999, Chapter 6)).

Pearl (1995) introduces a symbolic calculus for the $do(\cdot)$ operator, which facilitates the identification of additional causal effects in non-parametric models. Using this calculus, Galles & Pearl (1995) have devised graphical criterion for identifying causal effects in any semi-Markovian model. Finally, if the objective of a study is to evaluate the direct, rather than the total, causal effect of X on Y, as was the case with the Berkeley graduate admissions study (see subsection 12.1.3), then some other graphical criteria that determine identifiability are available (Pearl & Robins, 1995). Applications to policy analysis and to the management of non-compliance are presented in Balke & Pearl (1995, 1997).

In light of these results, the reader might want to know whether the model defined by Equations (12.6)–(12.8) is identifiable. The answer is yes; this model permits the identification of all interventional queries. For example, from inspection of the graph in Figure 12.14, we can conclude immediately that

1. $P(x|do(y), do(z)) = P(x)$,
   consistent with the intuition that consequences can have no effect on their causes;

2. $P(z|do(x)) = P(z|x)$,
   because ϵ_1 is independent of X, and hence Z is not confounded by X (alternatively, and hence all back-door paths between Z and X are blocked);

3. $P(y|do(z)) = \sum_x P(y|z, x)P(x)$,
   because the back-door criterion qualifies X as an appropriate covariate for adjustment; and

4. $P(y|do(x)) = \sum_z P(z|x) \sum_{x'} P(y|x', z)P(x')$,
   which results from chaining $P(z|do(x))$ with $P(y|do(z))$, as is shown formally in Pearl (1995).

12.4 Some conceptual underpinnings

12.4.1 What do structural parameters really mean?

Every student of SEM has stumbled on the following paradox at some point in his or her career. If we interpret the coefficient β in the equation

$$y = \beta x + \epsilon$$

as the change in $E(Y)$ per unit change of X, then after rewriting the equation as

$$x = (y - \epsilon)/\beta$$

we ought to interpret $1/\beta$ as the change in $E(X)$ per unit change of Y. But this conflicts both with intuition and with the prediction of the model: the change in $E(X)$ per unit change of Y ought to be zero if Y does not appear as an independent variable in the equation for X.

Teachers of SEM generally evade this dilemma via one of two escape routes. One route involves denying that β has any causal reading and settling for a purely statistical interpretation in which β measures the reduction in the variance of Y explained by X (*e.g.*, Muthen (1987)). The other route permits causal reading of only those coefficients that meet the so-called isolation restriction (Bollen, 1989; James et al., 1982), namely, the explanatory variable must be uncorrelated with the error in the equation. Since ϵ cannot be uncorrelated with both X and Y, so the argument goes, β and $1/\beta$ cannot both have causal meaning, and the paradox dissolves.

The first route is self-consistent, but it compromises the founders' intent that SEM function as an aid to policy-making and clashes with the intuition of most SEM users. The second is vulnerable to attack logically. It is well known that every pair of bi-variate normal variables, X and Y, can be expressed in two equivalent ways:

$$y = \beta x + \epsilon_1$$

and

$$x = \alpha y + \epsilon_2$$

where $cov(X, \epsilon_1) = cov(Y, \epsilon_2) = 0$, and $\alpha = r_{XY} = \beta \sigma_X^2 / \sigma_Y^2$. Thus, if the condition $cov(X, \epsilon_1) = 0$ endows β with causal meaning, then $cov(Y, \epsilon_2) = 0$ ought to endow α with causal meaning as well. But this, too, conflicts with both intuition and the intentions behind SEM; the change in $E(X)$ per unit change of Y is zero, not r_{XY}, if there is no arrow from Y to X.

What then *is* the meaning of a structural coefficient? Or a structural equation? Or an error term? The interventional interpretation of causal effects, when coupled with the $do(x)$ notation introduced in Section 12.3.3, provides simple answers to these questions. The answers explicate the operational meaning of structural equations and thus should, I hope, end an era of controversy and confusion regarding these entities.

12.4.1.1   Structural equations: Operational definition

Definition 12.6 (Structural equations) *An equation $y = \beta x + \epsilon$ is said to be* structural *if it is to be interpreted as follows: In an ideal experiment where we control X to x and any other set Z of variables (not containing X or Y) to z, the value y of Y would be independent of z and is given by $\beta x + \epsilon$.*

This definition is operational because all quantities are observable, albeit under conditions of controlled manipulation. That manipulations cannot be performed in most observational studies does not negate the operationality of the definition, in much the same way that our inability to observe bacteria with the naked eye does not negate their observability under a microscope. The challenge of SEM is to extract the maximum information on what we wish to observe, from the little we can observe.

Note that the operational reading given above makes no claim about how X (or any other variable) will behave when we control Y. This asymmetry makes the equality signs in structural equations different from algebraic equality signs; the former act symmetrically in relating observations on X or on Y (*e.g.*, observing $Y = 0$ implies $\beta x = -\epsilon$), but they act asymmetrically when it comes to interventions (*e.g.*, setting Y to zero tells us nothing about the relation between x and ϵ). The arrows in path diagrams make this dual role explicit, and this may account for the insight and inferential power gained through the use of diagrams.

The strongest empirical claim of the equation $y = \beta x + \epsilon$ is made by excluding other variables from the right-hand side of the equation, thus proclaiming X the *only* immediate cause of Y. This translates into a testable claim of *invariance*: the statistics of Y under condition $do(x)$ should remain invariant to the manipulation of any other variable in the model (Pearl, 1996; Galles & Pearl, 1998)[18]. This can be written symbolically as

$$P(y|do(x), do(z)) = P(y|do(x)) \qquad (12.28)$$

for all Z disjoint of $\{X \cup Y\}$.

Note that this invariance holds relative to manipulations, not observations, of Z. The statistics of Y under condition $do(x)$, given the measurement $Z = z$, written $P(y|do(x), z)$, would certainly depend on z if the measurement was taken on a consequence (*i.e.*, descendant) of Y. Note also that the ordinary conditional probability $P(y|x)$ does not enjoy such a strong property of invariance, since $P(y|x)$ is generally sensitive to manipulations of variables other than X in the model, unless X and ϵ are independent. Equation (12.28), in contrast, remains valid regardless of the statistical relationship between ϵ and X.

Generalized to a set of several structural equations, Equation (12.28) explicates the assumptions underlying a given causal diagram. If G is the graph associated with a set of structural equations, then the assumptions are embodied in G as follows: (1) every missing arrow, say between X and Y, represents the assumption that X has no causal effect on Y once we intervene and hold the parents of Y fixed; and (2) every missing bi-directed link between X and Y represents the assumption that the omitted factors that influence Y are uncorrelated with those that influence X. Sections 12.4.1.3 and 12.4.1.4 discuss the operational meaning of the latter assumption.

---

[18]This statistical claim is in fact only part of the message conveyed by the equation; the other part consists of a counterfactual claim (Lewis, 1973; Rubin, 1990; Galles & Pearl, 1998): if we were to control X to x', instead of x, then Y would attain the value $\beta x' + \epsilon$. In other words, plotting the value of Y under various hypothetical controls of X, and under the same external conditions (ϵ), should result in a straight line with slope β. Such claims can only be tested under the assumption that ϵ, representing external conditions or properties of experimental units remains unaltered as we switch from x to x' (Pearl, 1996, p. 404).

12.4.1.2 The structural parameters: Operational definition

The definition of a structural equation as a statement about the behavior of Y under a hypothetical intervention yields a simple definition for the structural parameters. The meaning of β in the equation $y = \beta x + \epsilon$ is simply

$$\beta = \frac{\partial}{\partial x} E[Y|do(x)] \tag{12.29}$$

namely, the rate of change (relative to x) of the expectation of Y in an experiment where X is held at x by external control. This interpretation holds regardless of whether ϵ and X are correlated in non-experimental studies (*e.g.*, via another equation $x = \alpha y + \delta$).

12.4.1.3 The mystical error term: Operational definition

The interpretations given in Sections 12.4.1.1 and 12.4.1.2 provide an operational definition for that mystical error term

$$\epsilon = y - E[Y|do(x)] \tag{12.30}$$

which, despite being unobserved in non-manipulative studies is far from being metaphysical or definitional as suggested by some researchers (*e.g.*, Richard, 1980; Holland, 1988; Hendry, 1995). Unlike errors in regression equations, ϵ measures the deviation of Y from its controlled expectation $E[Y|do(x)]$ and not from its conditional expectation $E[Y|x]$. The statistics of ϵ can therefore be measured from observations on Y once X is controlled. Alternatively, since β remains the same, regardless of whether X is manipulated or observed, the statistics of $\epsilon = y - \beta x$ can be measured in observational studies, if we know β.

Likewise, the assumption of uncorrelated errors can be estimated empirically. For any two variables in the model, X and Y, we have

$$E[\epsilon_Y \epsilon_X] = E\{[Y - E[Y|do(pa_Y)]][X - E[X|do(pa_X)]]\} \tag{12.31}$$

Once we determine the structural coefficients, the controlled expectations $E[Y|do(pa_Y)]$ and $E[X|do(pa_X)]$ become known linear functions of the observed variables pa_Y and pa_X, hence the expectation on the right-hand side of Equation (12.31) can be estimated in observational studies. Alternatively, if the coefficients are not determined, the expression can be assessed directly in interventional studies, by holding pa_X and pa_Y fixed (assuming X and Y are not in parent–child relationship) and estimating the covariance of X and Y from data obtained under such conditions.

Finally, we are often interested not in assessing the numerical value of $E[\epsilon_Y \epsilon_X]$ but rather in determining whether ϵ_Y and ϵ_X can be assumed uncorrelated. For this determination, it suffices to test whether the equality

$$E[Y|x, do(s_{XY})] = E[Y|do(x), do(s_{XY})] \tag{12.32}$$

holds true, where s_{XY} stands for (any setting of) all variables in the model excluding X and Y. This test can be applied to any two variables in the model, except when Y is a parent of X, in which case the symmetrical equation is applicable, with X and Y interchanged.

12.4.1.4   The mystical error term: Conceptual interpretation

The authors of SEM textbooks usually interpret error terms as representing the influence of omitted factors. Many SEM researchers are reluctant to accept this interpretation, however, partly because unspecified omitted factors open the door to metaphysical speculations, and partly because arguments based on such factors were improperly used as a generic, substance-free license to omit bi-directed arcs from path diagrams (McDonald, 1997). Such concerns are answered by the operational interpretation of error terms, Equation (12.30), since it prescribes how errors are measured, not how they originate.

It is important to note, though, that the operational definition is no substitute for the omitted-factors conception when it comes to deciding whether pairs of error terms can be assumed to be uncorrelated. Since such decisions are needed at a stage when the model's parameters are still 'free', they cannot be made on the basis of numerical assessments of correlations but must rest instead on qualitative structural knowledge about how mechanisms are tied together and how variables affect each other. Such judgemental decisions are hardly aided by the operational criterion of Equation (12.31), because that criterion instructs the investigator to assess whether two deviations, taken on two different variables under two different experimental conditions, would be correlated or uncorrelated. Such assessments are cognitively infeasible.

In contrast, the omitted-factors conception instructs the investigator to judge whether there could be factors that simultaneously influence several observed variables. Such judgments are cognitively manageable, because they are qualitative and rest on purely structural knowledge – the only knowledge available during this phase of modeling.

Another source of error correlation is *selection bias*. If two uncorrelated unobserved factors have a common effect that is omitted from the analysis but influences the selection of samples for the study, then the corresponding error terms will be correlated in the sampled population, that is, the expectation in Equation (12.31) will not vanish when taken over the sampled population (see discussion of Berkson's paradox following Definition 12.1).

We should emphasize, however, that the arcs *missing* from the diagram, not those *in* the diagram, demand the most attention and careful substantive justification. Adding an extra bi-directed arc can only compromise the identifiability of parameters, but deleting an existing bi-directed arc may produce erroneous conclusions together with a false sense of model testability. Thus, bi-directed arcs should be assumed to exist, by default, between any two nodes in the diagram. They should be deleted only by well-motivated justifications, such as the unlikely existence of a common cause for the two variables and the unlikely existence of selection bias. Although we can never be cognizant of all the factors that may affect our variables, substantive knowledge sometimes permits us to state that if a common factor exists, its influence is not likely to be significant.

Thus, as often happens in the sciences, the way we measure physical entities does not offer the best way of thinking about them. The omitted-factor conception of errors, because it rests on structural knowledge, is a more useful guide than the operational definition when building, evaluating, and thinking about causal models.

12.4.2   Interventional interpretation of effect decomposition

In this section, we show that the interventional interpretation of structural equations provides simple, unambiguous definitions of effect decomposition for both parametric and non-parametric models.

We start with the general notion of a causal effect $P(y|do(x))$ from Definition 12.4, which applies to arbitrary sets of variables, X and Y. This interpretation of causal effect can be specialized to define total and direct causal effects, as follows.

Definition 12.7 (Total effect) *The total effect of X on Y is given by $P(y|do(x))$, namely, the distribution of Y while X is held constant at x and all other variables are permitted to run their natural course.*

Definition 12.8 (Direct effect) *The direct effect of X on Y is given by $P(y|do(x), do(s_{XY}))$ where S_{XY} is the set of all observed variables except X and Y in the system.*

In linear analysis, Definition 12.7 and 12.8 yield, after differentiation w.r.t. x, the path coefficients that are normally associated with direct and indirect effects, yet they differ from conventional definitions in several important aspects. First, direct effects are defined in terms of hypothetical experiments in which intermediate variables are held constant by *physical intervention*, not by statistical adjustment (which is often disguised under the misleading phrase 'control for'). Figure 12.11 depicts a simple example where adjustmenting for the intermediate variables (Z and W) would not give the correct value ($= 0$) for the direct effect of X on Y, while $\frac{\partial}{\partial_x} E(Y|do(x, z, w))$ does yield the correct value: $\frac{\partial}{\partial_x}(\beta w + \gamma z) = 0$. Second, there is no need to limit control to only intermediate variables; *all* variables in the system may be held constant (excluding X and Y). Thus, the measurement of direct effects is ascribed to an ideal laboratory; the scientist controls for all possible conditions S_{XY}, and measurements may commence without knowing the structure of the diagram. Finally, our definitions differ from convention by interpreting total and direct effects independently of each other, as outcomes of two different experiments. Textbook definitions (*e.g.*, Bollen (1989, p. 376)) usually equate the total effect with a power series of path coefficient matrices. This algebraic definition coincides with the operational definition (Definition 12.7) in recursive (semi-Markovian) systems, but yields erroneous expressions in models with feedback. For instance, given the pair of equations $\{y = \beta x + \epsilon, \; x = \alpha y + \delta\}$, the total effect of X on Y is simply β, not $\beta(1 - \alpha\beta)^{-1}$ as stated in Bollen (1989, p. 379). The latter has no operational significance worthy of the phrase 'effect of X[19]'.

Note that when the structure of the causal diagram is known, there is no need to actually hold *all* other variables constant; holding constant the direct parents of Y (excluding X) would have the same effect on Y as holding all variables except X and Y constant. Thus, we obtain the following equivalent definition of a direct effect.

Corollary 2 *The direct effect of X on Y is given by $P(y|do(x),\, do(pa_{Y\setminus X}))$, where $pa_{Y\setminus X}$ stands for any realization of the variables appearing in the equation for Y, excluding X.*

Readers versed in linear analysis may find it a bit strange that the direct effect of X on Y involves variables other than X and Y. However, given that we are dealing with non-linear interactions, the effect of X on Y should indeed depend on the levels at which we hold the other parents of Y. If we wish to average over these values and take the expectation of Y, we obtain the expression

$$\Delta_{x,x'}(Y) \;=\; \sum_{pa_{Y\setminus X}} [E(Y|do(x'), do(pa_{Y\setminus X})) - E(Y|do(x), do(pa_{Y\setminus X}))] \times$$
$$P(pa_{Y\setminus X}|do(x))$$

where $\Delta_{x,x'}(Y)$ stands for the average change in $E(Y)$ induced by changing X from x to x' while keeping the other parents of Y constant at whatever value they obtain under $do(x)$. This expression explicates what we actually wish to measure in race or sex discrimination cases, where we are instructed to assess the effect of one factor (X) while keeping 'all other factors constant'. If X is an exogenous variable, as 'gender' is in Berkeley's sex discrimination case (see subsection 12.1.3), then $do(x)$ can be replaced with x. However, we are not at liberty to replace $do(pa_{Y\setminus X})$ with $pa_{Y\setminus X}$ unless we can safely assume that the factors represented by $pa_{Y\setminus X}$ (*e.g.*, student's qualifications and the choice of department) are not confounded with Y (as defined in Theorem 8). In general, we see that the average direct effect $\Delta_{x,x'}(Y)$ is identifiable whenever both $E[Y|do(x), do(pa_{Y\setminus X})]$ and $P(pa_{Y\setminus X}|do(x))$ are identifiable. Note that if X does not appear in the equation for Y, then $P(y|do(x), do(pa_{Y\setminus X}))$ defines a constant distribution on Y, independent of x, which matches our understanding of 'having no

---

[19]This error was noted by Sobel (1990) but, perhaps because constancy of path coefficients was presented as new and extraneous assumptions, Sobel's correction has not brought about a shift in practice or philosophy.

direct effect'. Note as well that, in linear models, $\Delta_{x,x'}(Y)$ reduces to $x' - x$ times the path coefficient between X and Y.

In standard linear analysis, an indirect effect may be defined as the difference between the total and the direct effects (Bollen, 1989). In non-linear analysis, differences lose their significance, and one must isolate the contribution of mediating paths in some other way. Expressions of the form $P(y|do(x), do(z))$ cannot be used to isolate such contributions, however, because there is no physical means of selectively disabling a direct causal link from X to Y by holding some variables constant. This suggests that the notion of indirect effect has no intrinsic operational meaning apart from providing a comparison between the direct and the total effects.

In other words, a policy-maker who asks for that part of the total effect transmitted by a particular intermediate variable or by a group Z of such variables is really asking for a comparison of the effects of two policies, one where Z is held constant, the other where it is not. The expressions corresponding to these policies are $P(y|do(x), do(z))$ and $P(y|do(x))$, and this pair of distributions should be taken as the most general representation of indirect effects. Similar conclusions have been expressed by Robins (1986) and Robins & Greenland (1992).

12.5   Conclusion

Today the enterprise known as structural equation modeling (SEM) is increasingly under fire. The founding fathers have retired, their teachings are forgotten, and today's practitioners, teachers, and researchers find the methodology they inherited difficult to either defend or supplant. Modern SEM textbooks are preoccupied with parameter estimation and rarely explicate the role that those parameters play in causal explanations or in policy analysis; examples dealing with the effects of interventions are conspicuously absent, for instance. Research in SEM now focuses almost exclusively on model fitting, while foundational issues pertaining to the meaning of SEM's models are subjects of confusion and controversy. The contemporary crisis in SEM originates, I am thoroughly convinced, in the lack of a mathematical language that can handle the causal information embedded in structural equations. Recently, graphical models have provided such a language. They have thus helped us answer many of the unsettled foundational questions that drive the current crisis, including:

1. *Under what conditions can we give causal interpretation to structural coefficients?*

2. *What are the causal assumptions underlying a given structural equation model?*

3. *What are the statistical implications of any given structural equation model?*

4. *What is the operational meaning of a given structural coefficient?*

5. *What are the policy-making claims of any given structural equation model?*

6. *When is an equation non-structural?*

In this chapter, I have summarized the conceptual developments that now resolve such foundational questions. In addition, by way of illustrating the soundness of the proposed approach, I have presented several tools to be used in answering questions of practical importance. Questions of this type include:

1. *When are two structural equation models observationally indistinguishable?*

2. *When do regression coefficients represent path coefficients?*

3. *When would the addition of a regressor introduce bias?*

4. *How can we tell, prior to taking any data, which path coefficients can be identified?*

5. *When can we dispose of the linearity-normality assumption and still extract causal information from the data?*

I am hopeful that researchers will recognize the benefits of these concepts and tools and use them to revitalize causal analysis in the social and behavioral sciences.

Acknowledgments

This chapter owes its inspiration to the generations of statisticians who have asked, with humor and disbelief, how SEM's methodology could make sense to any rational being, and to the social scientists who, perhaps unwittingly, have saved the SEM tradition from drowning in statistical interpretations.

I am grateful to two (anonymous) referees for their exceptionally detailed comments on the original version of this chapter and for correcting several oversights and omissions. The comments of Herman Adèr, Jacques Hagenaars, and Rod McDonald have helped me gain a greater understanding of SEM practice and vocabulary. Jin Tiang was instrumental in revising Sections 12.2.3.1 and 12.3.1.

This investigation has also benefited from discussions with John Aldrich, Peter Bentler, Nancy Cartwright, David Chickering, David Freedman, Arthur Goldberger, Sander Greenland, Scott Hershberger, Jim Heckman, Paul Holland, Guido Imbens, Jan Koster, Ed Leamer, Christopher Meek, Thomas Richardson, Jamie Robins, William Shipley, Peter Spirtes, and Rolf Steyer.

This research was partially supported by grants from AFOSR, NSF, Northrop, and Rockwell.

Chapter 13

Meta-Analysis

John Cornell and Cynthia Mulrow

Glass (1976) first coined the term meta-analysis to describe a systematic quantitative alternative to narrative literature reviews that enhances the scientific rigor of the review process.

Today the term is often associated with statistical methods used to combine study estimates of a treatment's effect on some response measure, to evaluate the degree of consistency in these estimates across studies, and to explain variation in the response to treatment across studies (Cooper & Hedges, 1994; Hedges & Olkin, 1985). DerSimonian & Laird (1986), for example, define meta-analysis as the *'statistical analysis of a collection of analysis results from individual studies for the purpose of integrating the findings'* (p. 117). As such, the term meta-analysis refers to a set of methodological and statistical tools that aid in the production of an integrative literature review (Mulrow, Cook, & Davidoff, 1997).

Meta-analysis, according to Glass's definition, however, is more than a compendium of statistical methods. It is itself a research methodology whose statistical aspects are appropriately understood and applied only within the context of critical scientific appraisal of the research evidence. As such, meta-analysis is another realization of the scientific method within clinical medicine; which, like any research study, requires careful planning and execution to guarantee the clinical appropriateness and relevance of its results (Jones, 1995). Meta-analysis is not only the statistical methods used to combine and summarize study results. It is the application of scientific strategies to the systematic assembly, critical appraisal, and synthesis of all relevant studies on a topic that limits bias and reduces random errors in the review process (Cook, Sackett, & Spitzer, 1995).

A carefully executed meta-analysis also assesses how limitations in the available evidence impact the strength and generalizibility of the research evidence. Failure to consider meta-analysis within the context of the scientific process leads to biased, inappropriate and misleading estimates of medical interventions (Jadad & McQuay, 1996).

The review process requires that the reviewer integrate multiple, and often heterogeneous, pieces of evidence into a comprehensive summary through categorization and ordering of data (Cooper, 1984; Mulrow, Langhorne, & Grimshaw, 1997). The primary goal of a review is to detect consistent patterns of results across studies that advance our theoretical and practical knowledge (Bangert-Drowns, 1995). A comprehensive critical review identifies the boundaries of our knowledge, provides insight into the sources of inconsistencies found in the research evidence, and gives a perspective on the generalizibility and applicability of the research evidence (Cook & Sackett, 1995). Traditional narrative reviews, however, approach this task in an unsystematic and, at times, unscientific way (Light & Pillemer, 1984; Chalmers, 1991; Cook, Mulrow, & Haynes, 1997).

Reviewers need to realize that any review, whether strictly narrative or one that involves a quantitative summary, is a retrospective observational study that is subject to subjective bias and random error. Quantitative summaries alone do not guarantee that the conclusions drawn from an integrative review are valid or that the 'meta-analysis' provides a synthesis of the 'best evidence' available to evaluate an area of knowledge (Oxman, 1993; Slavin, 1995). In fact, the best evidence available in either the published or unpublished literature may be no evidence at all. No amount of quantification or statistical manipulation can turn weak evidence into strong evidence. Quantification can, however, give the illusion of scientific rigor and objectivity to a body of evidence that is seriously flawed (Gould, 1981; Letzel, 1995). The tendency among some researchers and statisticians to over-emphasize statistical methodology and under-emphasize the scientific and clinical issues involved in a research synthesis lend support to the criticism of meta-analysis as the 'statistical alchemy of the 21st century' (Feinstein, 1995).

13.1 Brief history and the role of meta-analysis in medicine

The concept of combining information from separate studies to make a judgement about a treatment effect originated with the work of Tippett (1931), Fisher (1932) and Pearson (1933) on the combination of p-values (see Hedges & Olkin, 1985; Wolf, 1986; Olkin, 1990). The earliest example of data pooling in medicine may be Pearson's (1904) study of enteric fever inoculations (Jones, 1995). Interest in meta-analysis in medicine lay dormant, however, until the 1980s. Only about 100 articles that either discussed or applied meta-analyses were published in medicine in the decade from 1976 to 1986. MEDLINE© added meta-analysis as a subject heading in 1989 and as a publication type in 1993. A crude MEDLINE search based on publication type found 269 published meta-analyses indexed in 1990, growing to 462 in 1996. This growth represents a 72% increase in the rate of publication between 1990 and 1996.

The Cochrane Collaboration[1], established as part of the new Research and Development Program within the National Health Service of the United Kingdom in 1992, provided a key stimulus to the use of meta-analysis in medical and health services research (Chalmers, 1991). Named in honor of the late Archie Cochrane, the Cochrane Collaboration is an international effort that 'aims to help people make well-informed decisions about healthcare by preparing, maintaining and promoting the accessibility of systematic reviews of the effects of healthcare interventions' (Collaboration, 1998). The work of the Collaboration is supported by 15 centers worldwide — Africa (1), Europe (7), Australasia (1), North America (5), and South America (1) — and over 40 collaborative review groups. To date the Cochrane Collaboration has identified and cataloged 179, 546 randomized trials in its trial registry. The members of the collaborative review groups have produced 377 systematic reviews and have 360 reviews in process. All the Collaboration's efforts are updated quarterly and distributed on an annual subscription basis on disk, CD-ROM, and via the Internet. The motivation for this international effort is Archie Cochrane's guiding principle that optimal healthcare decisions are based on the best available evidence about the effectiveness of healthcare interventions.

Meta-analysis provides graphical and numerical tools to display, summarize, and explain variation in the quantitative evidence. As such, meta-analysis plays an important role in the production of systematic reviews in medicine. Systematic reviews are concise summaries of the research evidence based on scientifically rigorous explicit methods for identifying, critically appraising, and integrating the relevant studies (Mulrow, 1995). The principal goal of a systematic review is to efficiently integrate research findings in order to provide a rational basis for decision making in clinical practice and to guide the development healthcare policy. Systematic reviews attempt to establish whether treatment effects are consistent across populations, settings, and difference in how treatments are implemented. In contrast to traditional narrative reviews, systematic reviews employ explicit systematic methods designed to limit bias and reduce random errors. Placed in this larger context, meta-analysis is simply *'a systematic review that employs statistical methods to combine and summarize the results of several studies'* (Cook et al., 1995, p. 167).

---

[1]You are invited to visit one of the Cochrane Collaboration Websites to obtain more detailed information on the principles and organization of the Cochrane Collaboration: `http://som.flinders.edu.au/fusa/cochrane`, `http://hiru.mcmaster.ca/cochrane/defalut.html`, or `http://www.imbi.uni-freiberg.de/cochrane`.
For more details on the Cochrane Library go to `http://www.cochrane.co.uk`

13.2   Combining estimators of treatment effectiveness

13.2.1   Measures of treatment effectiveness

A measure of *treatment effectiveness*, or *effect size*, is the fundamental building block in a meta-analysis. This measure assesses a study result in terms of the actual magnitude of the observed relationship, change, or group difference, rather than the *p*-value of a particular statistical test. An effect size measure, therefore, provides a more precise and meaningful answer to the clinical question that motivated the original study and our systematic review. It is relatively easy to construct confidence intervals for effect size measures that allow us to estimate the overall clinical significance of a study result, as well as estimate the level of precision or reliability of the observed treatment effect.

Effect size measures assess the magnitude of a treatment effect for either continuous or categorical outcomes. Continuous outcomes produce parametric effect size measures based on either a correlation coefficient or a mean difference. Rosenthal (1991, 1994) refers to these measures as members of the *r family* and *d family*, respectively. Measures based on a correlation coefficient are standardized effect size measures of the relationship between two variables. Measures based on a mean difference are either left in their original *raw score* form or they are transformed to a *standardized* form by dividing the mean difference by an estimate of its variation. Categorical outcomes produce effect size estimates based either on an *absolute measure* of treatment effectiveness or a *relative measure* of treatment effectiveness that adjusts the estimate relative to the event rate in the control group. Our choice of effect size measure depends on substantive meaning, as well as on its scale of measurement and its statistical properties. In general, while standardized or relative effect size measures have better statistical properties, effect size measures based on actual mean difference or absolute measures have stronger intuitive appeal to clinicians (Chatellier, Zapletal, Lamaitre, Menard, & Degoulet, 1996; Cook & Sackett, 1995; Rajkumar, Sampathkumar, & Gustafson, 1996).

13.2.2   Continuous effect size measures

The *r* family is based on the Pearson product moment correlation and its related indices: *e.g.*, the Phi coefficient for dichotomous measures, the point-biserial correlation coefficient for mixed dichotomous and continuous measures, or the Spearman rank order correlation coefficient for ordered categorical measures. Since the directionality of an association is often as important to us as its magnitude, we seldom use the square of these indices in meta-analysis (Rosenthal, 1994). Fisher's *z*-transformation is applied to *r* family measures prior to combining their information into an overall measure of a treatment's effectiveness or a relationship between two variables.

The primary outcomes of interest with most healthcare interventions are based on differences between means or proportions. Even in the area of diagnostic testing, the focus is on the operating characteristics of medical tests — their sensitivity, specificity, and response-operator characteristics — rather than correlation based validity coefficients. Thus, effect measures within the r family, though common in the social and behavioral sciences, are seldom used in meta-analytic studies on healthcare interventions. Consequently, we confine our discussion of effect size measures for continuous outcomes to members of the d family. The interested reader is referred to one of the major texts on meta-analysis for a review of r family measures (Hedges & Olkin, 1985; Rosenthal, 1991; Cooper & Hedges, 1994).

Type	Effect Size Measure(d_i)
Raw Score Mean Difference	$\overline{x_1} - \overline{x_2}$
Standardized Mean Difference	
Glass' Δ	$\frac{\overline{x_1} - \overline{x_2}}{s_2}$
Hedge's g	$\frac{\overline{x_1} - \overline{x_2}}{s_{pooled}}$

Table 13.1: Summary of d family effect size measures.

Effect size measures for continuous outcomes within the d family are reported either as a mean difference or a standardized mean difference between two groups, typically a treatment and control group. Let d_i represent the d family effect size measure for the ith study. Table 13.1 presents a summary of these effect size measures. The *raw score* effect size is the simple difference between the two means. Glass's Δ and Hedge's g are the most popular approaches to computing a standardized mean difference. Glass's Δ uses the control or reference group standard deviation, to standardize the mean difference, while Hedge's g uses the pooled standard deviation. It has a small sample bias that is minimized by:

$$g_i^* \equiv \left(1 - \frac{3}{4(n_1 + n2)}\right) g_i$$

The bias and variance for Hedge's g are smaller than those for Glass's Δ, so that, g provides a uniformly better estimator than Δ. The variance for g_i is

$$s_{g_i}^2 = \frac{n_1 + n_2}{n_1 n_2} + \frac{g_i^2}{2(n_1 + n_2)}.$$

The decision whether to use the raw mean difference or the standardized mean difference is fairly simple. When all studies measure a continuous outcome in the same units, the best choice is the mean difference. Interpretation of the mean difference is straightforward and clinically meaningful.

The standardized mean difference is useful for those situations where studies may use different instruments with different units of measurement to assess a continuous outcome.

EXAMPLE 1

Suppose you want to combine data on measures of depression from a series of randomized controlled trials comparing selective serotonin reuptake inhibitors (SSRI) with either a tricyclic antidepressant or a placebo. A majority of depression trials use the Hamilton Rating Scale for Depression (HRS-D). Different trials, however, use different versions of the HRS-D. Some use the 17-item version while others use a 24-, 25-, 28-, or 29-item version of the HSR-D. The only way to pool effect sizes across these trials, assuming that the different versions are relatively equivalent measures of depression, is to use the standardized mean difference.

Many measures of clinical interest are continuous. These measures range from clinical and laboratory values such as blood pressure (mmHg) or triglyceride levels (mmol/L) to psychometric measures of quality of life or functional status such as the SF-36. Suppose our (research) question is, *'Do pharmacologic therapies produce a long-term decrease in diastolic blood pressure in older persons with mild to moderate hypertension?'*

Group	N	M	SD
Active Drug Treatment	300	-13 mmHg	10.47 mmHg
Placebo Control	287	-6 mmHg	11.22 mmHg

Table 13.2: Change in diastolic blood pressure measured one year after initiation of anti-hypertensive drug therapy.

EXAMPLE 2

Table 13.2 presents study results from the European Working Party Study on Hypertension in the Elderly (Amery et al., 1986). Since all blood pressure measurements are recorded in the same units, mmHg, the raw mean difference is the best choice for our effect size measure.

The mean difference effect size (d_i) measure at 1-year post-treatment for the EWPHE trial is easily computed as

$$d_i = \overline{x_i} - \overline{x_i} = -13 \text{ mmHg} - (-6 \text{ mmHg}) = -7 \text{ mmHg}$$

and its variance is

$$
\begin{aligned}
s_{\overline{x_i}-\overline{x_i}} &= \left(\frac{(n_1 - 1)s_1^2 + (n_2 - 1)s_2^2}{n_1 + n_2 - 2} \right) \left(\frac{n_1 + n_2}{n_1 n_2} \right) \\
&= \left(\frac{(300 - 1)(10.47)^2 + (287 - 1)(11.26)^2}{(300 + 287 - 2)} \right) \left(\frac{300 + 287}{300.287} \right) \\
&= 0.8045
\end{aligned}
$$

Thus, we know that the pharmacotherapy group, on average, had a decrease in DBP mmHg lower than the decrease observed in the placebo control group. We now have two additional questions to answer: (a) *Is this result statistically significant.* and (b) *Is this result clinically important?* We construct a 95% confidence interval (95% $C.I.$) to answer both questions.

A *Confidence Interval* provides clinicians with the information needed to judge the clinical importance of a study result, as well as whether or not the result is statistically significant. A confidence interval for a mean difference that included zero indicates that the test of significance fails to reject the null hypothesis at the $p < 0.05$ level. In addition, the limits of the confidence interval must include only values deemed clinically important. Suppose that clinicians judge a 5 mmHg long-term decrease in DBP to be clinically important in older adults with mild to moderate hypertension. The 95% $C.I.$ for a clinically important result should exclude values indicating a less than 5 mmHg decrease in DBP.

For large samples, $N_i = n_{\Delta t} + n_{\Delta c} > 60$, the two-tailed 95th percentile z-score from the standard normal distribution can be used to calculate the 95% $C.I.$ for the mean difference. Small samples require use of the two-tailed 95th percentile value from the t distribution. Since the EWPHE trial involved a large sample, the 95% $C.I.$ for difference in mean change DBP is

$$d_i \pm z_{.975} \sqrt{s^2_{\overline{x_1} - \overline{x_2}}} = -7 \text{ mmHg} \pm 1.96\sqrt{0.8045} = (-8.76 \text{ mmHg}, -5.24 \text{ mmHg})$$

The interval clearly does not contain zero; and, therefore, indicates that antihypertensive drug therapy produced a statistically significant larger decrease in DBP among elderly hypertensive patients relative to the placebo. We also note that its upper limit is -5.24 mmHg. This value suggests that the result is clinically important, as well. The pooled standard deviation for our DBP example is:

$$s_{pooled} = \sqrt{\frac{(n_1 - 1)s_1^2 + (n_2 - 1)s_2^2}{n_1 + n_2 - 2}}$$
$$= 10.8634$$

Hedge's g for the EWPHE trial is:

$$g_i = \frac{\overline{x_1} - \overline{x_2}}{s_{pooled}} = -0.6444$$

The variance for g_i is 0.0072.

The 95% $C.I.$ for the standardized mean difference in DBP is:

$$-0.6444 \pm 1.96\sqrt{0.0072} = (-0.8107, -0.4781)$$

This confidence interval indicates that the pharmacotherapy group shows a significant long-term decrease in DBP relative to the placebo control group. The upper limit of the 95% $C.I.$ is close to half a standard deviation below a zero treatment effect. We might assume that a decrease of this magnitude in DBP is substantial, but clinicians often find it difficult to judge clinical importance from standardized values. Standardized mean difference values can be converted back to approximate raw mean differences by the following transformation

$$\overline{x_1} - \overline{x_2} = \overline{x_{\text{ref}}} - d_i(s_{pooled})$$

where x_{ref} is the mean value for the reference distribution. Here we are interested in the value for the upper limit of the 95% C.I. relative to a reference distribution with a zero treatment effect. For our example, this transformation yields a raw mean difference for the upper limit of the 95% C.I. of approximately $-0.4781(10.8634) \approx -5.19$ mmHg, which is very close to the upper 95% C.I. value for the raw mean difference.

The point of this exercise is two-fold. First, it demonstrates our need to consider both clinical meaning and statistical properties in our selection of effect size measures; and, second, it illustrates the usefulness of maintaining, whenever possible, the original units of measurement in our selection of effect size measures.

With respect to psychometric Quality of Life or Functional Status measures we often have little choice but to use a standardized mean difference to measure a treatment's effectiveness. The rich variety of psychometric instruments available to researchers has as a consequence that different studies invariably use different instruments to measure the same treatment outcome. Fortunately, standardized scores are often the natural metric used to interpret scores on psychometric instruments. Clinical interpretations for psychometric scales are often represented in terms of deviations from the average score produced by a particular normative group. Therefore, it is much easier to translate differences in standard deviation units into meaningful clinical judgements.

However, the heterogeneity among studies in the selection of psychometric instruments is a critical substantive issue that can limit our ability to combine standardized effect size measures into a single, meaningful estimate of a treatment's effectiveness. The researcher must critically appraise the psychometric quality and substantive content of the measures in order to determine whether it is possible to combine the standardized scores into a single meaningful estimate. Combining standardized effect size measures without regard to their psychometric quality and substantive content at best yields meaningless results. It is just as likely, however, to yield very misleading, non-replicable results.

13.2.3   Categorical effect size measures

Categorical outcomes are scaled either as *dichotomous* or *multi-level ordinal* responses. Effect size measures for dichotomous categorical outcomes are well developed, but robust or categorical effect size measures for multi-level ordinal outcomes are not well developed and are the subject of ongoing research. One approach to computing effect size measures for ordered categorical responses redefines the response measure by collapsing the multi-level ordinal response categories into two clinically meaningful mutually exclusive and exhaustive categories. This approach permits us to use effect size measures for dichotomous outcomes to estimate and combine effect sizes for ordered categorical responses but it also assumes that a proportional odds model fits the ordered categorical responses.

	Event	No Event	
Treatment	a_i	b_i	$n_{ti} = a_i + b_i$
Control	c_i	d_i	$n_{ti} = c_i + d_i$
	$m_{1i} = a_i + c_i$	$m_{0i} = b_i + d_i$	$N = n_{ti} + n_{ci}$

Table 13.3: Summary 2×2 table for dichotomous categorical outcomes.

Effect size measures for dichotomous categorical outcomes represent either absolute or relative measures of a treatment's effectiveness. These indices are easily calculated from 2×2 tables, like the one displayed in Table 13.3[2]. Absolute measures are based on the simple difference between the proportion of clinical events observed in the treatment (p_{ti}) and control (p_{ci}) group, respectively. Relative measures are derived as ratio between some function of p_{ti} and some function of p_{ci}. These relative measures include the *relative risk*, the *relative risk reduction*, and the *odds ratio*. Computational definitions for our absolute and relative effect size measures and their variances are shown in Table 13.4. Interpretation of the risk dif-

Measure	Effect Size	Variance
Risk Diff.	$RD_i = p_{ti} - p_{ci}$	$Var(RD_i) = \frac{p_{ti}(1-p_{ti})}{n_{ti}} + \frac{p_{ci}(1-p_{ci})}{n_{ci}}$
Rel. Risk	$RR_i = \frac{p_{ti}}{p_{ci}}$	$Var(\ln RR_i) = \frac{1-p_{ti}}{n_{ti}p_{ti}} + \frac{1-p_{ci}}{n_{ci}p_{ci}}$
Odds Ratio	$OR_i = \frac{p_{ti}(1-p_{ci})}{p_{ci}(1-p_{ti})}$	$Var(\ln OR_i) =$ $\frac{1}{n_{ti}p_{ti}(1-p_{ti})} + \frac{1}{n_{ci}p_{ci}(1-p_{ci})}$
Peto Odds Ratio	$POR_i = \exp\left(\frac{O_i - E_i}{V_i}\right)$	$Var(\ln POR_i) = \frac{N^2(N_i-1)}{n_{ti}n_{ci}m_{1i}m_{0i}}$

Table 13.4: Measures of effect size for categorical outcomes.

ference is straightforward. A risk difference of zero indicated that there is no difference between the treatment and control group with respect to the proportion of clinical events observed in the study. Thus, the size of

---

[2]We write $p_{ti} = \frac{a_i}{n_{ti}}$ to represent the proportion of subjects in the treatment group who experience the clinical event in the ith study and $p_{ci} = \frac{c_i}{n_{ci}}$ to represent the proportion of subjects in the control group who experience the clinical event in the ith study.

the risk difference has a clear clinical meaning. Another clinically useful measure, the *number needed to treat (NNT)*, is easily obtained by taking the inverse of the absolute value risk difference (Cook & Sackett, 1995). NNT estimates the number of patients a physician may expect to treat over a specified period of time in order to prevent one clinical event. However, NNTs are meaningful only when study results are statistically significant. We typically standardized the NNT to some fixed follow-up period. The standardized NNT is computed as

$$stdNNT = NNT \left(\frac{\text{Observed Average Length of Follow-up}}{\text{Desired Standard Follow-up Interval}} \right)$$

Relative measures like the relative risk, relative risk reduction, and odds ratio are a bit more difficult to interpret. A relative risk or odds ratio of 1.00 indicates that there is no difference in the number of clinical events observed in the treatment or control group. Values less than 1.00 suggest a beneficial treatment effect, while values greater than 1.00 suggest that better outcomes are observed among control subjects. The relative risk is often expressed in terms of its complement, the relative risk reduction ($RRR_i = 1 - RR_i$). A zero value indicates that there appears to be no advantage to the treatment over the control intervention.

	Event	No Event	
Treatment	31	262	293
Control	40	249	289
	71	511	582

Effect Size Estimates:

Measure	Effect Size	95% *C.I.*
Risk Difference	−0.033	(−0.086, 0.021)
Relative Risk	0.764	(0.492, 1.186)
Odds Ratio	0.737	(0.447, 1.215)
Peto Odds Ratio	0.737	(0.449, 1.212)

Table 13.5: Effect size estimates for cardiovascular morbidity and mortality counts from the Australian National Blood Pressure Trial.

EXAMPLE 3

Table 13.5 displays the 2×2 table and effect size measures for morbid and mortal cardiovascular events observed in the Australian National Blood Pressure Trial (Australia, 1981) The risk difference (RD_i) is the simplest effect size measure to compute and interpret:

$$RD_i = p_{ti} - p_{ci} = \frac{31}{293} - \frac{40}{289} = 0.1058 - 0.1384 = -0.0326$$

The variance for the relative risk is also relatively easy to calculate. If the number of events in the treatment and control groups are sufficiently large, the normal approximation to the binomial distribution may be used to compute an approximate 95% $C.I.$ for the risk difference:

$$95\% \ C.I. = (p_{ti} - p_{ci}) \pm z_{0.975}\sqrt{\text{variance}}$$

This approximation is reasonable when $n_{ti}p_{ti} > 5$ and $n_{ci}p_{ci} > 5$. When the number of events in either the treatment or control group is less than 5, we need to compute exact confidence intervals directly from the binomial distribution. Notice that the approximate 95% $C.I.$ for morbid and mortal cardiovascular events in the ANBP trial includes zero, indicating that the proportion of morbid and mortal cardiovascular events observed in the treatment group is not statistically different from the proportion of events observed in the control group. Thus, it does not make sense to compute an NNT for this study result.

The sampling distribution of RR_i is seldom normally distributed, but the natural logarithm transformation of RR_i is often approximately normal. This allows us to use a large sample standard error to compute an approximate 95% $C.I.$ for this effect size measure. The square of the standard error gives us the standard error variance for the RR_i shown in Table 13.3. We obtain the 95% $C.I.$ by using the exponential function

$$95\% \ C.I. = e^{\ln RR_i \pm z_{.975}\sqrt{\text{variance}}}$$

to transform the upper and lower limits for the relative risk back into their original metric. Study results for the ANBP trial show an $RR_i = 0.764$, indicating that the pharmacotherapy group experienced a 23.6% reduction in the risk for cardiovascular morbidity and mortality relative to the placebo control group. The 95% $C.I.$ includes 1.00, however. Thus, we are unable to exclude the possibility that a placebo does just as well as pharmacotherapy in reducing cardiovascular morbidity and mortality among elderly patients with mild to moderate hypertension.

RD_i and RR_i are estimable only from randomized cross-sectional or prospective studies. It is improper to compute these effect size measures for retrospective or observational studies, such as case-control studies. Retrospective studies ask a different question, namely: *'What is the probability that the risk factor or intervention is present in the patient's history given that he or she experienced the clinical event?'* The odds ratio is estimable for all major clinical research designs, including randomized cross-sectional, prospective, and retrospective designs (Fleiss, 1994).

Two different approaches are used to compute odds ratio effect size estimates for dichotomous outcomes in medical research.

One is the maximum likelihood estimator of the population odds ratio

$$\omega = \frac{\pi_t(1 - \pi_c)}{\pi_c(1 - \pi_t)}$$

where π_t and π_c are the proportion of clinical events observed in the treatment and control populations, respectively. We refer to this estimator as the odds ratio, denoted OR_i in Table 13.4. The sampling distribution of $\ln OR_i$ is approximately normal. This fact allows us to compute a 95% $C.I.$ for OR_i based on the large sample standard error for $\ln OR_i$. As in the case of the relative risk, we use the exponential function to transform the upper and lower 95% $C.I.$ limits for $\ln OR_i$ back to the original units.

The second estimator first appeared in a meta-analysis by Yusuf, Peto, Lewis, Collins, & Sleight (1985) and is referred to as the *Peto odds ratio*, denoted POR_i in Table 13.4. The Peto estimator is

$$L_i = \frac{O_i - E_i}{V_i}$$

where $O_i = a$ is the number of clinical events observed in the treatment group for the ith study and $E_i = \frac{n_{ti}m_{1i}}{N_i}$ represents the number of clinical events we expect to observe by chance alone in the treatment group for the ith study. V_i is the exact hypergeometric variance of a_i:

$$V_i = \frac{n_{ti}n_{ci}m_{1i}m_{0i}}{N_i^2(N_i - 1)}$$

The standard error for L_i is

$$SE(L_i) = \frac{1}{\sqrt{V_i}}$$

L_i provides a good estimator of $\ln \omega$ when ω is close to unity. Unfortunately, L_i may overestimate or underestimate $\ln \omega$ and its standard error (Fleiss, 1994).

This bias appears greatest when there is serious imbalance in both margins of the 2×2 table or when the underlying odds ratio is large (Greenland & Salvan, 1990). Since L_i uses only the number of clinical events observed in the control group to compute the Peto odds ratio, it has a distinct advantage over OR_i in cases where we have zero clinical events in the control group. The typical solution to this 'sparse cell' problem with the standard method for computing the odds ratio is to add 0.5 to each cell of the 2×2 table. In the case where the numbers of events in the control group are well below an expected frequency of 5 or are zero, the standard odds ratio can produce very biased estimates of a treatment's efficacy. Otherwise, $\ln(OR_i)$ provides a simpler and statistically superior effect size estimate than does L_i.

Point estimates and 95% $C.I.$s for the maximum likelihood and Peto odds ratios for cardiovascular morbidity and mortality are nearly identical in the ANBP trial. These effect size estimates are also close to the value for the relative risk. The 95%$C.I.$ for both estimators includes 1.00. Thus, the study results fail to support an advantage for antihypertensive pharmacologic interventions in the reduction of cardiovascular morbidity and mortality among mild or moderately hypertensive elderly patients.

13.2.4 Selecting an effect size measure for categorical outcomes

As in the case of effect size measures for continuous outcomes, selection of an appropriate effect size measure for categorical outcomes depends upon substantive meaning, as well as statistical considerations. The risk difference and the relative risk reduction have intuitive appeal among clinicians. The odds ratio has better statistical properties, but its meaning, derived from a gambling setting, is more ambiguous within the clinical setting.

The risk difference has the greatest sampling variability among the effect size estimators for categorical outcomes, and its range of variation is limited by the values of p_{ti} and p_{ci}. The range of variation in the risk ratio is also constrained by the proportion of events in the control group. These qualities limit the value of these measures when the goal is to assess the relative efficacy of a treatment. The odds ratio is an unbiased and consistent estimator, and it is not constrained by either p_{ti} or p_{ci}. Thus, it assumes values between 0 and ∞ independent of the proportion of events in the control group. These statistical qualities make the logarithm of the maximum likelihood estimator for the odds ratio an ideal statistic for use in logistic regression and loglinear models.

Preference for the odds ratio among some meta-analysts is based on its convenient statistical properties. It is the only choice available for combining information from retrospective studies. Sinclair & Bracken (1994), however, question whether or not the odds ratio is a good choice for meta-analysis of randomized controlled clinical trials. Their main objection to the use of the odds ratio is that its clinical meaning is unclear to most clinicians. They point out that the odds ratio is neither a clinically intuitive measure of the relative size of a treatment effect as is the notion of relative risk reduction, nor does it convey information about the absolute size of a treatment effect. Moreover, because the odds ratio is independent of p_{ci}, the odds ratio tends to yield a larger value than does the relative risk. When p_{ci} is very small, the risk ratio is approximately equal to the odds ratio. The difference between the odds ratio and relative risk increases as p_{ci} increases. Since in published studies the odds ratio is often called a risk ratio, clinicians may mistakenly interpret the odds ratio as a relative risk; and, consequently, they may overestimate a treatment's actual clinical utility. The possibility of misinterpretation and overestimation of a treatment's relative efficacy is even greater when comparing results for subgroups with different baseline risks.

The relative risk, on the other hand, is commonly used when reporting results from randomized controlled clinical trials. Thus, the relative risk is more familiar to clinicians. A number of studies report that results presented as a relative risk reduction are more likely to influence physicians's acceptance of a treatment's efficacy than any other relative or absolute measure of treatment efficacy (see e.g., Cranney & Walley, 1996). On the surface, these findings suggest that the use of relative risk reduction optimizes communication of results to practicing clinicians. Relative measures do not convey information about the therapeutic yield a clinician can expect by using a treatment with his or her patients. We need to balance the information that relative measures provide with an absolute measure.

Sackett (1995) illustrates how important it is to supplement relative measures with an absolute measure. He used data from the Collins study on blood pressure, stroke, and coronary heart disease to demonstrate his point (Collins, 1990). The 5-year relative risk reduction for stroke, attributable to antihypertensive therapy, in patients with either mild or moderate hypertension is $RRR_i = 0.40$ for either group. The actual clinical yields were substantially different, however. The 5-year NNT for patients with moderate hypertension indicated that 13 patients need to be treated for 5 years to prevent one stroke, while a physician needs to treat 167 patients with mild hypertension for 5 years to prevent one stoke event.

Sackett's example illustrates the importance of describing results in terms of both relative and absolute measures. It also illustrates the importance of presenting results in terms of questions important to physicians. Clinically relevant questions address issues about relative impact therapeutic interventions have within specific subgroups of patients that differ with respect to clinically relevant variables such as age and baseline risk. Decision makers and clinicians need results that are based on clear, focused research questions. Moreover, the results need to be reported in terms of effect size measures that are clinically meaningful and convey information about treatment's absolute, as well as relative efficacy.

13.2.5   Ordered categorical effect size measures

Ordered categorical outcomes pose a number of significant problems for a meta-analyst. A common approach to estimating effect size measures for ordered categorical scales is to treat the responses as if they were measured on a continuous scale and use a standardized mean difference to assess a treatment's effectiveness. However, this approach ignores a fundamental problem with ordered categorical outcomes, their inherent heterogeneity. Multi-level ordinal measures are often heterogeneous with respect to both the number of levels used and the words used to describe or define the individual levels. With some exceptions, studies seldom use a consistent, well-established ordinal scale. Researchers tend to use scales either designed or adapted for their own specific purposes. Therefore, the inherent heterogeneity among ordered categorical outcome measures seriously undermines the validity of combining study results based on mean differences. Parametric effect size measures also assume that study results are normally distributed, so that the mean value provides a robust estimate of the study result. This assumption is seldom satisfied with ordered categorical outcomes.

Whitehead & Jones (1994) provide a simple and robust model for the analysis of multi-level ordinal measures. Their method collapses the multi-level categories into two clinically meaningful and mutually exclusive responses. Thus, it reduces the multi-level measure to a dichotomous one. This approach resolves the heterogeneous multi-level categories into dichotomous categories with comparable clinical meaning across studies. We can then use effect size measures derived from 2×2 tables to assess a treatment's effectiveness.

Application of their approach assumes, however, that a proportional odds model fits the data within a given study: i.e., that the odds ratio computed between any particular dichotomous split among the categories is approximately equal to the odds ratio computed for any other dichotomous split. They also demonstrate how to test the tenability of the proportional odds assumption using standard statistical packages. Thus, provided the proportional odds assumption is tenable, we can redefine the measure as a dichotomous response and apply readily available effect size measures for dichotomous outcomes to studies that use multi-level ordinal clinical measures.

13.3 Combining effect size measures

A single study rarely, if ever, provides a definitive answer about the effectiveness of a therapeutic intervention. In fact, studies often disagree with respect to the magnitude of the observed treatment effect and/or its statistical significance. If we assume, however, that each study represents a sample drawn from a population, then study level effect size measures are population values. Each individual study is considered either an identical replicate of the same experiment or exchangeable with respect to the other studies included in the meta-analysis. Studies are exchangeable in the sense that each study, while it may produce somewhat different results from the other studies included in the meta-analysis, yields information pertinent to the research question. Exchangeability assumes, however, that variation in results from trial to trial are not expected, *a priori*, to favor one study over another. Thus, we can use the sampling distribution for the effect size statistic to estimate the true treatment effect.

Meta-analysis attempts estimate or predict the true treatment effect based on the combined strength of the information contained in a set of comparable studies that provide evidence relevant to the research question under investigation. Given the observed variability among study results, however, it is reasonable to ask whether the collection of study results estimates a single true population value or whether the true population value itself varies with patient or study characteristics. Are the study results, in spite of their variability, relatively homogeneous with respect to their estimate of the true population value; or is the variability among study results so large that it suggests that the true population value may vary significantly with patient or study characteristics? The answer to this question determines whether we use a fixed-effects or a random-effects model to combine effect size estimates.

Fixed-effect models assume that study results are relatively homogeneous. Variation in effect size estimates is attributable only to sampling variability. Thus, a simple model based on the sampling distribution of the effect size statistics may be used to estimate the true effect size for a given treatment comparison. *Random-effect models* assume that the true population effect varies from study to study, so that we have a distribution of true population effects. The observed variation may be due to differences in specific patient or study characteristics that influence a treatment's effectiveness. In this case, we have two independent sources of variation – within-study sampling variability and between-study sampling variability – that we need to take into account when estimating the true treatment effect.

13.4   Fixed-effects models

A simple weighted average is the basic model for combining effect sizes for categorical or continuous outcomes. This approach is often referred to as the *direct method for pooling effect sizes*. The pooled estimate of a treatment's effect is estimated by computing the weighted average of the effect size across the k trials:

$$d_+ = \frac{\sum_{i=1}^{k} w_i d_i}{\sum_{i=1}^{k} w_i}$$

The best choice for a weight (w_i) is the inverse of the variance for the trial's effect size measure:

$$w_i = \frac{1}{v_i}$$

where v_i is the variance for the effect size statistic.

This approach gives the largest weights to the studies with the smallest variance and the greatest degree of precision for the effect size measure. It is also the best choice for w_i to reduce the variance of the pooled effect size estimate. Defining w_i in this manner also simplifies computation of the variance of the pooled effect size. It is simply the inverse of the sum of the weights:

$$Var(d_+) = \frac{1}{\sum_{i=1}^{k} w_i}$$

Application of this method with continuous measures is relatively straightforward. With categorical outcomes, the *direct* or *weighted average* method uses the risk difference (RD), the natural logarithm of the odds ratio $(\ln OR)$, or the natural logarithm of the relative risk $(\ln RR)$ to pool the effect sizes across trials. We transform the OR and RR effect size measures to the natural logarithm scale before pooling the values. This transformation allows us to sum the measures; and, since the $\ln(1.0) = 0.0$, it assigns a value of zero to those trials that show no advantage to the treatment group over the control group.

Study	Author (Year)	Frequencies	
		a_i/n_{ti}	c_i/n_{ci}
ANBP	The Management Committee (1981)	31/293	40/289
HNT Coop	Hypertension-Stroke Cooperative Study (1982)	28/101	34/9
Kuramoto	Kuramoto (1981)	4/44	9/47
MRCOA	MRC Working Party (1992)	258/2183	309/2213
SHEP	SHEP Cooperative Research Group (1991)	346/2365	519/2371
SHEP-PS	Perry et al. (1986)	33/443	14/108
STOP	Dahlof et al. (1991)	84/812	152 / 815
SYS-EUR	Amery, et al. (1991)	160/2398	216 / 2297
VA Coop	VA Cooperative Group on Antihypertensive Agents (1972)	9/38	25/43

Table 13.6: Cardiovascular morbidity and mortality data for nine blinded placebo controlled randomized trials of antihypertensive drug therapy in the elderly.

EXAMPLE 4

Let us use the cardiovascular morbidity and mortality outcomes from the blinded, placebo controlled trials on antihypertensive drug therapy in the elderly to illustrate computation of the pooled estimate of treatment benefit. Table 13.6 displays the count data from the nine randomized controlled trials that provide data on cardiovascular morbidity and mortality. The pooled $\ln RR$ for cardiovascular morbid and mortal events is -0.354, so that $RR = e^{-0.354} = 0.702$. The 95% $C.I.$ for the RR is $(0.650, 0.759)$. These results suggest that antihypertensive drug therapy may reduce the risk of a cardiovascular morbid or mortal event by nearly $100(1 - RR_i) = 30\%$ with a potential benefit that ranges from a 24% to a 35% reduction in risk.

Meta-analysis results are usually displayed in graphical form. Figure 13.1 shows a typical *forest plot* for the relative risk of cardiovascular morbidity and mortality among elderly hypertensive patients treated with antihypertensive medications. Effect sizes for individual studies are represented boxes of varying size. The size of each box is proportional to the weight assigned to the effect size estimate in the analysis. The line through the box indicates the 95% confidence interval for the effect size estimate. A diamond, drawn at the bottom of the graph, represents the mean and 95% confidence interval for the combined estimate of the treatment effect. The vertical axis of the diamond is then centered at the mean value, and the horizontal axis spans its 95% confidence interval. The broken vertical line allows you to see how much the effect size for the individual studies varies from the combined estimate. A solid vertical line is drawn at the point where the effect size indicates that the antihypertensive medication has no effect on cardiovascular morbidity and mortality.

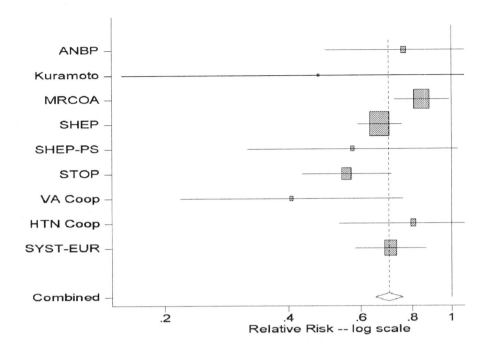

Figure 13.1: Forest plot of the Relative Risk for cardiovascular morbidity and mortality for nine randomized controlled trials investigating the effect of antihypertensive drug therapy with elderly hypertensive patients.

In our example, the summary diamond's vertical axis is centered near a relative risk equal to approximately 0.70, and the vertical axis does not cross the solid line. Values falling to the left of the solid line indicate that fewer cardiovascular morbid or mortal events are observed in the patients treated with antihypertensive medications. Thus, the combined results suggest that antihypertensive medications may be beneficial in reducing cardiovascular morbid and mortal events among elderly hypertensive patients. The 5-year standardized $NNT \approx 15$ indicates that a physician needs to treat 15 patients for 5 years in order to prevent one cardiovascular morbid or mortal event.

Meta-analysis is equally concerned with revealing and analysing the pattern of results across studies, as it is with estimating the combined effect size for a treatment. The forest plot provides a visual profile of the pattern of results relative to the combined effect size. A causal glance at Figure 13.1 reveals that, while all the point estimates appear to indicate a treatment benefit, there is considerable variability in the effect sizes across studies. This pattern suggests that significant variability may exist in the true treatment among the studies, a hypothesis that we must formally test and investigate.

The direct method is only one of several methods used to pool effect sizes for categorical outcomes. Other computationally convenient methods include the *Peto Method for pooling odds ratios* (Yusuf et al., 1985) and the Mantel-Haenszel method for pooling odds ratios, relative risk ratios, and risk differences. Maximum likelihood methods, exact methods, and Bayesian methods are also used to pool categorical outcomes. These latter methods are computationally complex and require approximate methods to obtain a numeric solution.

The summary estimate and variance for the Peto Method (OR_{Peto}) is computed as

$$\ln OR_{Peto} = \frac{\sum_{i=1}^{k}(O_i - E_i)}{\sum_{i=1}^{k} V_i}$$

$$Var(\ln OR_{Peto}) = \frac{1}{\sum_{i=1}^{k} V_i}$$

The pooled $\ln OR_{Peto}$ for the above example trials is $\ln OR_{Peto} = -0.4222$ and the OR_{Peto} is $\exp(-0.4222) = 0.656$ with a 95% C.I. of $(0.594, 0.724)$.

The Mantel-Haenszel pooled odds ratio (OR_{MH}) is computed as

$$OR_{MH} = \frac{\sum_{i=1}^{k} \frac{a_i d_i}{N_i}}{\sum_{i=1}^{k} \frac{b_i c_i}{N_i}}$$

The Mantel-Haenszel OR for our trials is $OR_{MH} = 0.654$.

There are several different approaches to estimating the variance for the OR_{MH}. A general estimator for the variance of the OR_{MH} that is easy to compute and provides a consistent estimate under a sparse data is the Robins, Breslow, & Greenland (1986) or *RBG* estimator.

$$Var(\ln OR_{MH}) = \frac{\sum_{i=1}^{k} P_i R_i}{2\left(\sum_{i=1}^{k} R_i\right)^2} + \frac{\sum_{i=1}^{k}(P_i S_i + Q_i R_i)}{2\sum_{i=1}^{k} R_i \cdot \sum_{i=1}^{k} S_i} + \frac{\sum_{i=1}^{k} Q_i S_i}{2\left(\sum_{i=1}^{k} S_i\right)^2}$$

where $R_i = \frac{a_i d_i}{N_i}, S_i = \frac{b_i c_i}{N_i}, P_i = \frac{a_i + d_i}{N_i}$ and $Q_i = \frac{b_i + c_i}{N_i}$. In our case, the $Var(\ln OR_{MH})$ is 0.0026, and the 95% C.I. is $(0.592, 723)$.

In contrast to the relative risk, interpretation of an odds ratio is not straightforward. We do know that the fewer CM&M events experienced by a patient group indicates a possible benefit associated with the assigned treatment. Thus, a value less than 1.00 indicates a treatment benefit; and, since the confidence interval exclude 1.00 the pooled result suggests that antihypertensive drugs may have a beneficial effect on CM&M events with elderly hypertensive patients. It is not appropriate, however, to compute the simple complement, as we did with the risk ratio, and interpret the results as a reduction in the relative odds of experiencing a cardiovascular morbid or mortal (CM&M) event. We can compute the relative odds that an event is more likely in the control group by taking its inverse.

Thus, in our example, an elderly hypertensive patient in the placebo control group is $1/OR_i = 1.53$ times more likely to experience a CM&M event than an elderly hypertensive patient taking antihypertensive medication. However, the practical importance of an odds ratio of 1.5 is less clear to clinicians than a relative risk reduction of 30%.

13.5   Random-effects models

The direct weighted average, Peto, and Mantel-Haenszel methods for pooling data essentially assume that each observed value represents a measurement drawn from a single population, so that the weighted sample mean provides an unbiased estimate of its true population value. Any observed differences in the treatment measure among studies represent chance variation due to measurement error. If this homogeneity assumption is reasonable, then we only need to take the within-study variance into account when we pool data across studies. However, if the homogeneity assumption is suspect, we need to factor the variance between studies into our pooled estimate of the treatment effect. Essentially, we must assume that there is a population of possible treatment effects, as opposed to a single true treatment effect, that may vary from patient group to patient group. Our studies, then, represent a random sample of possible treatment effects among patient populations. In this case we have a *random-effects model.*

We use a χ^2 test to evaluate the validity of the fixed-effects model. The test statistic for homogeneity (Cochran, 1954) is

$$Q = \sum_{i=1}^{k} w_i (d_i - d_+)^2$$

where $w = \frac{1}{v_i}$ and $d_+ = \frac{\sum_{i=1}^{k} w_i d_i}{\sum_{i=1}^{k} w_i}$. When the number of patients in the treatment and control group are large, Q has an approximate χ^2 distribution with $k - 1$ degrees of freedom. The test for heterogeneity is relatively insensitive to moderate levels of heterogeneity. Therefore, the hypothesis that the studies are homogeneous is rejected if the Q statistic is larger than the 0.10 or 0.20 critical value for the central χ^2 distribution with $k - 1$ degrees of freedom (Berlin, Laird, Sacks, & Chalmers, 1989).

For the nine trials in our cardiovascular morbidity and mortality example, the tabled critical values for a statistic with $k - 1 = 9 - 1 = 8$ degrees of freedom are 13.36 at the 0.10 level and 10.22 at the 0.20 level. The result for our CM&M data is $Q = \sum_{i=1}^{k} w_i (d_i - d_+)$. When we compare Q = 14.144 against the critical value for the central χ^2 distribution with $k - 1 = 8$ degrees of freedom at the 0.10 level, we notice that $Q = 14.144$ is larger than the critical value of 12.017. This result suggests that the effect size is not consistent across the nine trials. It means that differences among the trials, other than the treatment, contribute to variation in the effect size.

13.5.1 DerSimonian-Laird random-effects models

DerSimonian & Laird (1986) offer a relatively simple computational solution to estimating the between-study variance. When the between-study variance is not equal to zero, the Q statistic is used to derive a computationally convenient estimator for the between-study variance:

$$\hat{\tau}^2 = \frac{Q - k - 1}{\sum_{i=1}^{k} w_i - \frac{\sum_{i=1}^{k} w_i^2}{\sum_{i=1}^{k} w_i}}.$$

The between-study variance estimate in our case is 0.013. The DerSimonian-Laird (DL) random-effects estimator is computed as

$$d_+ = \frac{\sum_{i=1}^{k} w_i^* d_i}{\sum_{i=1}^{k} w_i^*}$$

where $w_i^* = \frac{1}{v_i + \hat{\tau}^2}$.

Here, the pooled random-effects estimate for the $\ln RR_i$ is -0.39216, and its variance is $Var(d_+) = \frac{1}{\sum_{i=1}^{k} w_i^*} = \frac{1}{136.654} = 0.0061$. The random-effects relative risk is $\exp(-0.39216) = 0.6756$ and the 95% $C.I.$ is $\exp(-0.3926 \pm 1.96\sqrt{0.0061}) = (0.5796, 0.7875)$.

In comparison with the fixed-effect direct method or $MHRR$ method, the DerSimonian-Laird random-effects estimator for the pooled cardiovascular morbidity and mortality risk ratio yields a slightly lower relative risk ratio and a larger confidence interval. All three pooled estimators indicate that there is a statistically significant benefit to the use of antihypertensive therapy with elderly hypertensives.

13.5.2 Empirical Bayes and full Bayesian random-effect estimates

In the Bayesian paradigm for meta-analysis, all pooled point estimates and their variances are treated as random quantities. Each random quantity is related to a probability distribution. The combined treatment effect in the Bayesian paradigm is estimated as the mean of the posterior distribution or as a predicted effect that represents an effect that is exchangeable with those observed in the data. It can be understood as the effect we might expect to observe in a new $(k+1)^{st}$ study. The basic Bayesian model is

Posterior $\propto$ Prior $\times$ [Data].

Estimates of the predicted effect and its standard error are derived from a prior probability distribution assumed for the random quantity being estimated and information contained in the data. The information contained in the 'Data' is represented by a likelihood function.

Suppose we assume that the effect size estimates are normally distributed. The natural prior for the predicted effect is then a normal distribution. Empirical Bayes and Full Bayesian approaches differ with respect to how much information about the unknown parameters of the prior distribution are assumed to be estimatable from the data.

To understand this, let us suppose that the true treatment effect for an individual study is Δ_i. The exchangeable normal prior is

$$\Delta_i | \mu_\Delta, \tau^2 \sim N(\mu_\Delta, \tau^2)$$

where μ_Δ and τ^2 are unknown random quantities that represent the mean value of the distribution of true treatment effect and a measure of the variability among the true treatment effects. These unknowns are referred to as *hyperparameters* in the Bayesian paradigm. In a full Bayesian analysis these hyperparameters are assumed to be stochastic, each following a probability distribution. A simple empirical Bayes meta-analysis assumes that μ_Δ is either normally distributed or is drawn from a locally uniform (a noninformative prior) distribution, and it substitutes a point estimate for τ^2 that is derived from the data. This point estimate is usually a method of moments estimator, such as the DerSimonian-Laird estimate, or a maximum likelihood estimator (Carlin, 1992) or even an empirical Bayes estimator (Morris, 1983).

Empirical Bayes estimators are particularly suited for relatively small samples ($n = 10$ trials) and allow a more complete accounting for the uncertainty involved in the estimation process than does the random-effect method of DerSimonian and Laird. If there is no substantial heterogeneity among the trials the empirical Bayes estimator reduces to the class fixed-effects estimate.

Pooled effect size estimates (d_+) are calculated as a weighted average of the effect size estimates for each trial:

$$d_+ = \frac{\sum_{i=1}^{k} w_i d_i}{\sum_{i=1}^{k} w_i}$$

where $w_i = 1/v_i$ the inverse of the variance of d_i. The empirical Bayes estimator for each study is

$$e_i = \frac{\frac{d_i}{v_i} + \frac{d_+}{\widehat{\tau}^2}}{\frac{1}{v_i} + \frac{1}{\widehat{\tau}^2}}$$

where d_+ is the DerSimonian-Laird or empirical Bayes random-effects estimate for the overall treatment effect and $\widehat{\tau}^2$ is the commonly used moment estimator for the between-studies variance. Its variance is

$$v_{e_i} = \frac{\widehat{\tau}^2 v_i}{\widehat{\tau}^2 + v_i} + \frac{\frac{v_i}{\widehat{\tau}^2 + v_i}}{\sum_{i=1}^{k} w_i^*}$$

where $w_i^* = 1/(v_i + \widehat{\tau}^2)$. Pooled empirical Bayes random-effects estimates are obtained via iterative least squares regression with an intercept-only model (Berkey, Hoaglin, Mosteller, & Colditz, 1995). Details of this computational procedure are given in Section 13.7 on Meta-Regression.

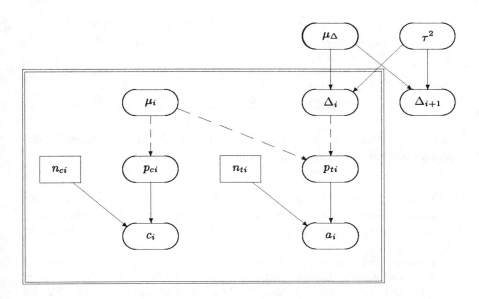

Figure 13.2: Graphical model for the Smith, Spiegelhalter, and Thomas full Bayesian random-effects model[4].

Full Bayesian meta-analysis models take into account the full uncertainty we have in estimating μ_Δ and τ^2 by replacing point estimates with probability distributions for these hyperparameters. Figure 13.2 is a graphical representation for a full Bayesian random-effects meta-analysis (Smith, Spiegelhalter, & Thomas, 1995). In this example, the true treatment effect Δ_i is measured on the logit scale. The data and parameters are represented as nodes in the graph. Square nodes represent stochastic variables that are fixed by design. Elliptical nodes represent stochastic variables that may be observed data or unobserved parameters. Arrows are drawn from the parent nodes to their descendant nodes. Solid arrows represent stochastic (probabilistic) dependence and dotted arrows represent logical functions that link the parent node to the descendant node. In this model for example, the logit(p_{ti}) is represented as a logical function of parameters that represent the true value for the placebo effect, μ_i, and the true treatment effect: i.e., logit(p_{ti}) $= \mu_i + \Delta_i$. The links between Δ_i and the hyperparameters μ_Δ and τ^2 are stochastic determined. The choice of prior probability distributions for μ_Δ and τ^2 is not always simple. Carlin prefers non-informative locally uniform distributions for μ_Δ and τ^2, while Smith et al. assume that μ_Δ is normally distributed and τ^2 follows a gamma distribution. A full discussion of choice of priors is beyond the scope of this chapter. The interested reader is referred to the prior references for an in-depth discussion of this issue.

Table 13.7 compares the results of the classical fixed-effect estimate for the log odds ratio with random-effect estimators based on the DerSimonian-Laird method of moment estimator, an empirical Bayes estimator (Morris, 1983), and a full Bayesian estimator. The empirical Bayes random-effect

	d_+	95% Confidence Interval
Fixed-Effect	0.661	(0.604, 0.724)
Random-Effect		
DerSimonian-Laird	0.638	(0.542, 0.751)
Empirical Bayesian	0.635	(0.534, 0.755)
Full Bayesian	0.635	(0.513, 0.750)

Table 13.7: Comparison of fixed- and random-effects estimators for the pooled odds ratio for the CM&M in the elderly studies.

estimate is computed via an iterative least-squares procedure. The full Bayesian random-effects estimate is computed via a Markov chain Monte Carlo method known as Gibbs sampling (Gilks, Thomas, & Spiegelhalter, 1994).

Random-effect models produce wider confidence intervals or regions (in Bayesian terminology) than comparable fixed-effects models. In this case, the random-effects models produce fairly consistent point estimates for the pooled odds ratio that are a little lower than the fixed-effects estimator. The Bayesian estimators, because they incorporate uncertainty about the estimates d_+ and τ^2, produce wider confidence regions than the DerSimonian-Laird method, with the full Bayesian random-effects model yielding the widest confidence region. All four methods produce estimates that are less than 1 with confidence intervals/regions that do not include 1. Thus, the results suggest that antihypertensive drug therapy does reduce CM&M events among elderly hypertensive patients.

13.5.3   Robustness and publication bias

Given the retrospective nature of a meta-analysis, meta-analysts are acutely aware of how analytic results are influenced by methodological decisions they make and limitations in the data sources for a meta-analysis. They make a number of methodological decisions in the design and conduct of a meta-analysis. At the outset of the meta-analysis they:

1. establish inclusion criteria for studies,

2. set rules about whether to include studies where ambiguity exists about their eligibility,

3. decide whether to include unpublished studies or studies with methodological flaws,

4. determine which outcome measures to abstract and assess their comparability, and

5. set rules for imputing values for missing information.

Each decision can substantially influence the internal and external validity of our meta-analysis. Consequently, we must evaluate the *robustness* of our results and their *generalizibility*.

	d_+	95% Confidence Interval
Fixed-Effect	0.674	(0.622, 0.731)
Random-Effect		
DerSimonian-Laird	0.666	(0.589, 0.754)
Empirical Bayesian	0.664	(0.582, 0.759)
Full Bayesian	0.667	(0.582, 0.754)

Table 13.8: Comparison of fixed- and random-effects estimators for the pooled odds ratio for all 12 randomized controlled trials.

Sensitivity analysis. Sensitivity analysis examines how robust our results are with respect to the different assumptions and decisions we use to guide our literature search, study selection, data abstraction, and statistical analysis in a meta-analysis. In a sensitivity analysis, we re-analyse our data under different assumptions and decisions; and we compare the results obtained against those of our primary analysis. We may, for example, change the inclusion criteria for the studies used in our meta-analysis on the effect antihypertensive drug therapy has on CM&M events among elderly hypertensive patients. Three randomized controlled trials were excluded from our primary analysis because some ambiguity existed about their eligibility or comparability with the nine studies included in our primary analysis. The results of our analysis of the pooled odds ratio for the fixed- and random-effects models are presented in Table 13.8. Inclusion of the three additional trials has little effect on our results. Thus, our results appear to be robust with respect to our application of inclusion criteria.

We could use sensitivity analysis to examine the effects of other assumptions and decisions, as well. For example, all 12 studies in our meta-analysis on the efficacy of antihypertensive drug therapy in the elderly are randomized controlled trials. What impact would the inclusion of non-randomized trials have on our results? In order to answer this question, we need to abstract all available non-randomized trials and re-analyse the data with these trials included. Each of the fixed- and random-effects models we examined make different assumptions about the nature of the true treatment effect and the importance of between-study variation in our meta-analysis. Re-analysing the data under different statistical models is another example of a sensitivity analysis. With the full Bayesian random-effects models, we should also examine the model's sensitivity to our choice of a prior distribution for the hyperparameters. Suppose we assume non-informative priors for μ_Δ and τ^2; or, suppose we assume that μ_Δ is drawn from a distribution with heavier tails, such as a t distribution with few degrees of freedom. Are our results substantively dependent on our choice of prior distributions?

The point we are making is that meta-analytic results may be substantially influenced by the assumptions and decisions we use to guide our collection, appraisal, and analysis of the data. At the outset of our meta-analysis, we must identify the key assumptions and decisions that may be open to question. We also need to conduct our literature search, plan our data abstraction, and plan our data analysis so that we capture and present the information needed to allow us to explicitly evaluate the impact these key decisions and assumptions have on our results.

Publication Bias. Publication bias refers to a tendency on the part of researchers, reviewers, and editors to submit, accept, and publish studies that report statistically significant results consistent with theoretical or previously established empirical expectations. The factors shown to influence publication include reporting significant results, type of research design, rating of scientific importance, and external funding (Dickersin, Min, & Meinert, 1992). In the cases where studies with negative results are published, there appears to be a substantial delay in publication (Stern & Simes, 1997). The reluctance to publish non-significant or contradictory results can not be attributed solely to editorial practices. Researchers themselves are reluctant to submit manuscripts for review unless the results are statistically significant. There is evidence that publication bias is not as serious a problem with randomized controlled clinical trials, as it is with observational or laboratory-based studies (Easterbrook, Berlin, Gopalan, & Matthews, 1991). However, a majority of meta-analysts believe that validity of a meta-analysis is strengthened by the inclusion and critical appraisal of unpublished studies (Cook, 1993).

Our chief concern is that a selection bias is introduced into the analysis that may produce spurious positive results that compromise the internal and external validity of our meta-analysis results. Well-designed unpublished studies may exist that contradict the results of our meta-analysis. The burden of proof is on meta-analysts to assess the presence of publication bias and estimate the extent to which it may or may not impact their results.

Graphical and quantitative methods are available to assess the presence of publication bias. The funnel plot, for example, is a simple graphical method used to assess publication bias. It is based on the notion that, in the absence of publication bias, a plot of effect sizes against a measure of precision (sample size, standard error, or the inverse of the standard error) should be symmetrically distributed in a funnel shape with high precision studies at the apex. We assume smaller studies produce less precise and more variable results; and, thus, distribute themselves symmetrically about a line drawn from the apex perpendicular to the base. Asymmetry in the observed funnel plot indicates the extent of publication bias. Figure 13.3 is a funnel plot of the log Odds Ratio for each of the 12 randomized controlled trials against its standard error. The outer lines represent pseudo 95% confidence limits for the distribution of studies at each level of precision. It

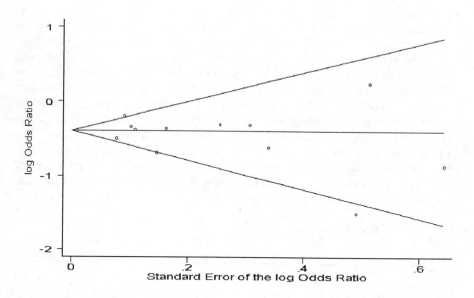

Figure 13.3: Funnel plot with pseudo 95% confidence limits for the 12 randomized controlled trials evaluating the efficacy of antihypertensive drug therapy among elderly hypertension patients.

is difficult to determine a definitive pattern with a small number of studies. However, there is some trend toward a positive publication bias among the smaller, less precise studies.

Begg & Mazumdar (1994) developed a formal test for publication bias based on the normalized Kendall rank correlation test statistic. A significant rank correlation between the standardized effect sizes ($d_i^* = d_i/\sqrt{v_i}$) and their variance is evidence of publication bias. The Kendall rank correlation test is fairly powerful for large meta-analyses ($k \geq 75$ studies), but it is relatively insensitive to departures from symmetry when fewer than 25 studies are included in the meta-analysis.

In our case, the Kendall rank correlation test on the log odds ratios for our 12 randomized trials is $z = -0.69, p = 0.493$. Even given the low power of this test statistic for small numbers of studies, the relatively high p-value provides some evidence that publication may not be a serious problem in our meta-analysis.

Eggar, Smith, Schneider, & Minder (1997) developed a regression-based test for detecting asymmetry in the funnel plot. Their simple linear model regresses standardized effect size (d_i^*) onto our measure of precision, the square root of the weight ($\sqrt{w_i} = 1/\sqrt{v_i}$): $d_i = \alpha + \beta\sqrt{w_i}$. In theory, since precision is largely determined by sample size, effect size estimates for small studies will be close to zero on the x-axis. In the absence of publication bias, these smaller trials, because their standard errors are large, will produce standardized effect size estimates that distribute themselves near zero on the y-axis, as well. Thus, the points from a homogeneous set of trials, not distorted by publication bias, will scatter about a line that runs through the origin at standard normal deviate zero ($\alpha = 0$), with the slope β indicating the size and direction of the effect. Asymmetry produced by large discrepancies between standardized effect size estimates produced by larger versus smaller studies, shifts the intercept away from the origin. Thus, large deviations of the intercept from zero are indicative of publication bias. Little is known about the power of this regression-based test for publication bias. Eggar et al. suggest a p-value of $p < 0.10$ be used as the criterion for their test of asymmetry. A 90% confidence interval about the intercept that contains $\alpha = 0$ provides some evidence for the absence of publication bias.

	Reg. Coefficient	Std. Error	t	p-value	95% C.I.
Slope	−0.331	0.101	−3.273	0.008	(−0.556, −0.106)
Intercept	−0.532	0.718	−0.742	0.475	(−2.121, −1.066)

Table 13.9: Regression-test for publication bias for 12 randomized controlled trials on the efficacy of antihypertensive drug therapy among elderly hypertension patients.

EXAMPLE 5
Table 13.9 displays the regression-based test results for publication bias with respect to the log odds ratios observed in our 12 randomized controlled trials on the efficacy of antihypertensive drug therapy in reducing CM&M events among elderly hypertensive patients. Although the intercept is negative, indicating a positive bias among the smaller trials, the p-value for the hypothesis that $\alpha = 0$ is $p = 0.475$ with a 90% confidence interval of $(-1.71, 0.65)$. Again, the evidence suggests that publication bias may not be a substantial problem in our interpretation of results from our meta-analysis.

13.6   Exploring sources of heterogeneity

Random-effect models treat between-study variability as an additional source of error variance in computing and evaluating the true treatment effect. It is important, however, to move beyond simple adjustments for heterogeneity to identify those factors that contribute to heterogeneity among the studies. For example, what patient population characteristics or study design characteristics contribute to the observed heterogeneity? Important clinical information is often buried within the observed heterogeneity. Study results may vary with a patient's age or socioeconomic level, duration or severity of illness, or dropout and crossover rates for the groups. Clinicians and patients want to know how effective a particular intervention is for individuals whose profile has 'pertinent clinical relevance' to the patient being treated (Feinstein, 1995). Thus, heterogeneity is a scientifically and clinically important source of variance to be explained, rather than simply a nuisance factor to be controlled.

Potential sources of heterogeneity can be identified either *a priori* or empirically. At the initial conceptual stage in the development of a meta-analysis, we can often identify patient or study characteristics that may influence a therapeutic effect. Prior knowledge, experience, and empirical evidence help us identify these potential sources of heterogeneity. We also can use exploratory data analytic methods to identify subsets of studies with unique characteristics that may account for the observed heterogeneity among the studies. Prior knowledge or results from exploratory data analyses enable us to formulate specific hypotheses to test in our meta-analysis. Caution must be observed when testing hypotheses that arise from the data. Any hypotheses generated through application of exploratory data methods must make biological, psychological, or sociological sense. Empirically derived hypotheses must be plausible given what is known about the disease and the intervention (Mulrow & Oxman, 1997).

13.6.1   Exploratory data analysis: the Galbraith plot

There exists a special graphical method for identifying outliers in a meta-analysis. The so-called *Galbraith Plot* is a bivariate scatter plot of $y_i = d_i/\sqrt{v_i}$ against $x_i = \frac{1}{\sqrt{v_i}}$. The Galbraith plot for the natural logarithm of the relative risk is displayed in Figure 13.4. The slope of the regression line drawn through the origin is the common or pooled value for the effect size measure. If the studies are homogeneous, they should be distributed within ± 2 standard errors of the regression line through the origin. Studies that fall near or outside these boundaries are examined to identify unique characteristics that may plausibly account for their extreme deviation from the pooled estimate.

EXAMPLE 6
Inspection of Figure 13.4 reveals that one of the larger studies, MRCOA, deviates significantly from the common relative risk. A review of this study reveals that it had the largest number of patients either who withdrew from the study, were lost to follow-up, or crossed over from one treatment arm to another. At the end of the trial, 53% of those randomly assigned to the placebo group, 48% of those randomly assigned to the diuretic group, and 63% of those randomly assigned to the beta-blocker group were no longer on the assigned intervention.

On methodological grounds alone, we expect treatment effects to be strongly influenced when high proportions of patients who either withdraw from the assigned therapy or crossover from one therapeutic arm to another. It might be reasonable to test the hypothesis that the pooled relative risk is significantly lower for studies with 30% or more of the patients no longer

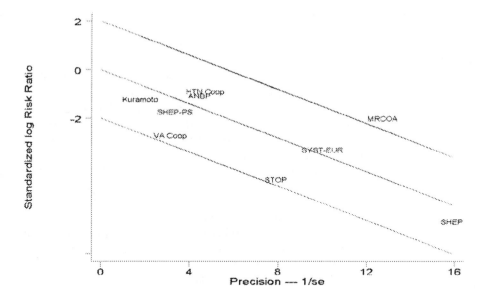

Figure 13.4: Galbraith plot of the Relative Risk for cardiovascular morbidity and mortality in nine controlled randomized trials of antihypertensive drug therapy with elderly hypertensive patients.

on the assigned therapy at the end of treatment compared with studies that do not experience large numbers of crossovers and withdrawals.

13.6.2   Subgroup analysis

One way to test this hypothesis is to stratify the studies based on the proportion of patients no longer on assigned therapy at the end of the trial. Suppose those studies with 30% or more no longer on assigned therapy at the end of the trial are assigned to the High Loss group and those with less that 30% no longer on assigned therapy at the end of the trial are assigned to the Low Loss group. Separate pooled effect size estimates are obtained for each group and compared. Figure 13.5 displays the stratified analyses in a single forest plot. The pooled relative risk and 95% confidence interval for the three trials in the High Loss group is 0.82 (95% $C.I$: $(0.71, 0.94)$). This value is substantially larger than the pooled relative risk for the Low Loss group, which is 0.66 (95% $C.I$: $(0.60, 0.72)$). We tested our initial hypothesis about the impact of proportion of patients no longer on assigned therapy at the end of the trial on the relative risk for CM&M using meta-regression. An indicator variable was created to represent the subgroup comparison. Studies in the High Loss group were assigned a value of 1 while studies in the Low Loss group were assigned a value of 0. The regression

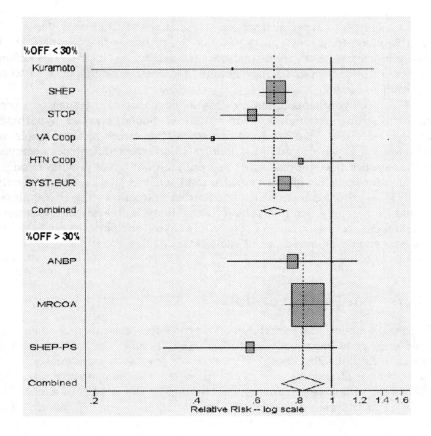

Figure 13.5: Stratified forest plot of the relative risk for cardiovascular morbidity and mortality in nine randomized controlled trials investigating the effect of antihypertensive drug therapy with elderly hypertensive patients.

coefficient for the indicator variable was statistically significant ($p \approx 0.032$). As predicted in our hypothesis, the pooled relative risk for the High Loss group is quite a bit closer to 1.00 compared to the Low Loss group.

Although the data appear to support our hypothesis, we need to exercise extreme caution in the conduct and interpretation of subgroup analyses. Remember meta-analysis is a retrospective research method. Even if our meta-analysis included only high quality randomized controlled trials, patients are not randomized to one study versus another study. Thus, between-study comparisons are based on non-equivalent groups. Studies may differ in many ways, all or some of which may influence a patient's response to the intervention. Patient populations may vary with respect to the underlying risk for the event, the prevalence of comorbid conditions, or other exposure variables that may affect the outcome. Studies may also vary with respect to specific drugs or combinations of drugs used, dose levels or scheduling, frequency and types of co-interventions that are permitted, and other treatment and non-treatment related factors. Interactions among any or all of these factors may account for observed differences between subgroups of studies.

A *priori* hypotheses based on data independent of the subgroup provide the strongest foundation for inference. Sound *a priori* hypotheses are derived either from a strong theoretical framework or from empirical evidence found within published studies. Consistent differences observed within studies that are confirmed in a subgroup analyses provide stronger evidence for the effect of a given factor than evidence that is supported only by between-groups comparisons. The bottom line is that subgroup analyses should be carefully planned prior to data analysis, the set of hypotheses should focus on small numbers of carefully chosen comparisons, and the hypotheses should be based on substantive knowledge about the disease and the intervention.

13.7   Meta-regression

Regression models are powerful analytic tools for exploration of sources of heterogeneity in meta-analytic studies. They permit us to simultaneously examine the influence several different study-level covariates may have on our estimate of treatment efficacy. However, the number of study-level covariates (p) in a regression model is limited by the number of studies (k) included in the analysis. At a minimum, regression models require that the number of studies exceeds the number of study-level covariates: $k > p$. The $k : p$ ratio also determines the model's sensitivity with respect to its ability to detect significant, meaningful associations between the study-level covariates and our measure of treatment effectiveness. We must, therefore, exercise careful scientific and clinical judgement in our selection of study-level covariates. Again, *a priori* hypotheses derived from a sound theoretical framework or empirical evidence are the best guides to selection of study-level covariates.

Meta-regression models violate the assumptions of ordinary regression analysis in that the variances for effect size estimates are proportional to the sample sizes of the studies. The solution to this problem is to use generalized least-squares to estimate the parameters in our regression models (Hedges & Olkin, 1985). Let us consider the simple linear model

$$d = X\beta + \varepsilon$$

where d is a $k \times 1$ vector of effect size measures, X is a $k \times (p+1)$ design matrix (p is the number of parameters estimated in the model), β is a $(p+1) \times 1$ vector of regression coefficients, and ε is a $k \times 1$ vector of residuals. The residuals are assumed to be normally distributed with mean 0 and a diagonal covariance matrix σ_d. The elements of σ_d are the population variances for the effect size estimators. The population variances are assumed to be independent but not identically distributed. In practice, we use the sample variances, v_i, to estimate this covariance matrix. The generalized least-squares estimator for the regression coefficients is

$$\beta = (X_T W X)^{-1} X^T W_d$$

where the weight matrix $W = \Sigma_d^{-1}$ is a diagonal matrix with elements $w_{ii} = 1/v_i$. Thus, β is a generalization of our fixed-effects estimator $d_+ = \sum_{i=1}^{k} w_i d_i / \sum_{i=1}^{k} w_i$. In fact, the intercept only model reduces to our *fixed-effects* estimator.

The weighted least-squares meta-regression model allows us to test two important hypotheses about how well the model fits the data (see Hedges & Olkin, 1985). The first hypothesis tests whether the weighted sum of squares due to regression is greater than would be expected if $\beta = 0$. This test statistic is distributed χ^2 with p degrees of freedom. Since meta-regression is performed on effect size estimates, we can also test whether or not the model is correctly specified. Estimates of regression coefficients are consistent when the study-level covariates included in the model actually determine the variability in our effect size estimates. The goodness-of-fit test for model specification is also distributed χ^2 with $k - p$ degrees of freedom.

The strength of meta-regression, however, is its ability to simultaneously model and evaluate the influence of several covariates on our effect size estimates.

At the outset of our meta-analysis on the effect pharmacological interventions have on CM&M events among the elderly hypertension patients, we hypothesized that the relative risk for CM&M events varies with several study-level covariates. The primary study-level covariates were mean age of study participants (AGE), the baseline mean arterial blood pressure (MAP), the percent of female patients enrolled in the study (%FEM), and the percent of patients no longer on assigned treatment at the end of the study (%OFF). Since proportions are not linear, we used a logit transformation of %FEM and %OFF in our meta-regression models. Average baseline mean arterial pressure was computed from the mean systolic (SBP) and diastolic (DBP) blood pressures reported at baseline:

$$MAP = \frac{\overline{X}_{SBP} + \overline{X}_{DBP}}{3} + \overline{X}_{DBP}.$$

We also recognized that studies were highly variable with respect to the number of years follow-up (LOF) upon which the CM&M counts were based.

Preliminary examination of the weighted bivariate associations showed that the covariates had moderate to high correlations with the natural logarithm of the relative risk ($0.40 \leq r \leq 0.84$). The correlation of the log relative risk with %OFF alone was $r = 0.84$. Clearly, the logit of the proportion of patients no longer on assigned treatment at study's end would dominate any meta-regression model. We also observed that the correlation of %OFF with LOF is also substantial with $r = 0.74$. Thus, we did not include %OFF in our full meta-regression model. The VA Coop study had no female participants. It also was not included in our meta-regression analysis.

	β	$s.e.\beta$	z	$p > |z|$	95% C.I.
AGE	−0.005	0.012	−0.468	0.640	(−0.028, 0.017)
% FEM	0.235	0.145	1.623	0.105	(−0.049, 0.519)
MAP	0.005	0.002	2.664	0.008	(0.001, 0.009)
LOF	0.080	0.028	2.896	0.004	(0.026, 0.134)
Intercept	−0.333	0.039	−8.519	0.000	(−0.410, −0.257)

Model: $\chi^2(4) = 23.17, p < 0.001$
Goodness-of-Fit: $\chi^2(6) = 8.24, p > 0.2207$

Table 13.10: Fixed-effects meta-regression results of the relative risk for CM&M events among elderly hypertensive patients receiving antihypertensive drug therapy.

EXAMPLE 7

Table 13.10 displays the results of our meta-regression model for the relative risk CM&M events among elderly hypertensive patients receiving antihypertensive drug therapy. Each covariate in the model is centered about its respective mean. Thus, the intercept is the log relative risk at the mean value for the covariates. Both MAP and LOF are significantly associated with the log relative risk. The adjusted relative risk for CM&M events is 0.72 (95% $C.I : (0.66, 0.77)$) which suggests that antihypertensive drug therapy may yield an average reduction of 28% in CM&M events among elderly hypertensive patients. The relative risk for a CM&M event within a patient population increases with their MAP. A patient population with a MAP = 195 mmHg, which is 10 mmHg higher than the average for the populations included in our analysis, has a 4% increase in the relative risk for a CM&M event. Each additional year of follow-up also increases the relative risk by about 6%. Our indices of model fit indicate that our model accounts for a significant proportion of the variance in the log relative risk ($p = 0.0001$), and the goodness-of-fit statistic suggests that the remaining residual variation probably represents random variation ($p = 0.2207$).

Suppose we suspect that some of the residual variation in our meta-regression may be due to excess between-study variance not accounted for by the covariates. The generalized least-squares estimator is easily generalized to the random-effects model by substituting $w_{ii}^* = 1/v_i + \tau^2$ for w_{ii} in the weight matrix. Methods of moment, maximum likelihood, restricted maximum likelihood, or empirical Bayes estimators are available for τ^2 (see Thompson & Sharp, 1998, for a review of these estimators). The empirical Bayes estimator (Berkey et al., 1995; Morris, 1983) is

$$\tau^2 = \frac{\sum_{i=1}^k w_i^* \left\{ \frac{k}{k-p+1}(d_i - \hat{d}_i)^2 - v_i \right\}}{\sum_{i=1}^k w_i^*}$$

where k is the number of studies, p is the number of parameters in the model, and d_i is the predicted value for the ith study. An iterative least-squares method is used to obtain estimates for the model parameters (Berkey et al., 1995; Morris, 1983). The method iterates between estimating the regression coefficients and estimating between-study variance until a convergence criterion is reached. The method can also be generalized to handle multiple outcome data. Iterative generalized least-squares methods extend the basic meta-regression to include multiple response measures such as repeated measures (Berkey, Anderson, & Hoaglin, 1996) and survival data (Dear, 1994).

	β	$s.e.\beta$	z	$p > |z|$	95% $C.I.$
AGE	−0.005	0.016	−0.334	0.738	(−0.036, 0.025)
% FEM	0.196	0.180	1.095	0.273	(−0.155, 0.549)
MAP	0.005	0.003	1.752	0.080	(0.001, 0.010)
LOF	0.078	0.036	2.167	0.030	(0.007, 0.147)
Intercept	−0.328	0.050	−6.499	0.000	(−0.427, −0.229)
Model: $\chi^2(4) = 9.96, p = 0.0411$					
Goodness-of-Fit: $\chi^2(6) = 5.99, p > 0.4239$					

Table 13.11: Empirical Bayes random-effects meta-regression results of the relative risk for CM&M events among elderly hypertensive patients receiving antihypertensive drug therapy.

EXAMPLE 8

Table 13.11 gives the results for the empirical Bayes random-effects meta-regression model for our CM&M example. Although the point estimates for the regression coefficients are similar to those observed for the fixed-effects model, the standard errors are larger. Consequently, MAP is now no longer significantly associated with the relative risk for CM&M events. The restricted maximum likelihood estimator is obtained by substituting $w_i'^2$ for w_i' in the previous equation, and yields results similar to those obtained with the empirical Bayes estimator. So, which model do we believe?

A random-effect meta-regression is justified when we have evidence that sufficient, non-random between-study variance remains over and above the variance accounted for by the covariates. The goodness-of-fit test provides some evidence for or against this hypothesis. A non-significant goodness-of-fit test suggests that the model is specified correctly, so that the remaining residual variation represents non-systematic, random variation. Thus, the data suggests that our original fixed-effect model adequately accounts for the heterogeneity in the relative risk among the studies included in our meta-analysis.

Ideally, meta-regression models employ study-level covariates that have substantive clinical or scientific meaning. Such covariates address specific concerns that physicians and patients have about a treatment's relative efficacy with respect to characteristics of the patient. However, since study-level covariates are only measured as aggregate values, these values often tend to show little between-study variation. Restriction in the range of variation for a study-level covariate tends to attenuate its association with the treatment outcome; thus, reducing the sensitivity of the analysis. We also lose information about the within-study, patient-level, covariation between a study-level covariate and our measure of treatment efficacy (Schmid, Lau, McIntosh, & Cappelleri, 1998).

When insufficient data are available on key study-level covariates, control-rate meta-regression is used in meta-analyses on randomized controlled trials to explore the relationship between population risk and treatment efficacy. The proportion of events in the control group is used as a proxy for the collection of patient risk factors associated with between-study variation in treatment efficacy. A fundamental problem with control-rate meta-regression is the fact that variation in the covariate is represented on both sides of the equation. Consider the natural logarithm of the relative risk. The control-rate meta-regression model for the $\ln RR_i$ is

$$\ln RR_i = \ln(\frac{p_{ri}}{p_{ci}}) = \widehat{\alpha} + \widehat{\beta} \ln(\frac{p_{ci}}{1 - p_{ci}})$$

The presence of p_{ci} in the definitions of both $\ln RR_i$ and $logit(p_{ci})$ induces a natural correlation between the control rate and the treatment effect. Thus, it violates the assumption of independence in the error variation between a covariate and the measure of treatment efficacy (Senn, 1994; Sharp, Thompson, & Altman, 1996). The result is biased estimates for the model parameters and their respective standard errors.

Although we can remove the correlation by simply regressing p_{ti} onto p_{ci} or by regressing the risk difference on to the average of the treatment and control rates, neither approach takes into account of error variation in p_{ci} (McIntosh, 1996). The presence of measurement error in our estimate of p_{ci} results in an underestimate the standard error for the regression coefficient and yields a stronger estimate of the association between p_{ci} and our measure of treatment efficacy than is warranted. McIntosh proposes that we use a hierarchical Bayesian model to explicitly model both the correlated error variances and measurement error in control-rate meta-regression. Theoretical and empirical evidence suggests that a hierarchical Bayesian model provides unbiased estimates for the model parameters and their respective standard errors.

The aggregate nature of study-level data limits the meta-analyst ability to explain heterogeneity. Important patient-level information is lost in aggregate values. Yet, it is this patient-level data that contains the information about a treatment's efficacy that is of most interest to patients and clinicians. One solution to this problem is to invest time and effort in a patient-based meta-analysis (Stewart & Clarke, 1995). A patient-based meta-analysis attempts to secure the original data used to produce the published report from each of the trials to be included in the analysis. The time and effort involved in a patient-based meta-analysis is considerably greater than the time and effort required for a study-level meta-analysis. The statistical tools required for patient-based data are more complex: e.g., random-effects generalized linear models and random-coefficient models. The chief reward, however, is the ability to answer patient-specific questions about a treatment's effectiveness that are not accessible from aggregate data (Clarke & Stewart, 1995). Keep in mind, however, that even a patient-based meta-analysis is still a retrospective study.

Meta-regression is a useful tool for exploring sources of heterogeneity among study outcomes. We must keep in mind, however, that patients, though they may be randomized to treatment and control groups, are not randomized to one study versus another study. Caution must be observed in drawing inferences about the relationship between-study-level covariates and outcomes. The results must be consistent with methodologic, biologic, sociologic, and/or psychologic factors that we may reasonably expect, *a priori*, to influence the treatment outcome.

13.8   Meta-analysis: promises and pit-falls

Our premise going into this chapter was that meta-analysis is more than a collection of statistical techniques; it is a realization of the scientific method applied to the literature review process. Its goals are three-fold. First, meta-analysis efficiently integrates results of previous research to provide a rational basis for decision making. Second, meta-analysis establishes whether treatment effects are consistent across populations, settings, and differences in treatments. And, third, meta-analysis employs methods that minimize bias and random errors in the abstraction, summarization, and presentation of all available data that address the research question.

The value of a meta-analysis, however, depends on the care and rigor with which it is executed. Its retrospective nature opens the research process to many potential sources of bias that must be carefully dealt with in the design and conduct of a meta-analysis (Felson, 1992). Critics of meta-analysis complain that many published systematic reviews not only incorporate the biases and flaws contained in the original studies, but they also introduce new sources of bias that may lead physicians and patients to over- or underestimate the effectiveness of a healthcare intervention (Feinstein, 1995; Bailar, 1995). Failure to exercise scientific rigor and thoroughness in a meta-analysis produces misleading results (Jadad & McQuay, 1996; Khan, Daya, & Jadad, 1996). It also contributes to the observed discrepancies between meta-analysis results and large randomized controlled trials (1000 or more patients) results (see LeLorier, Grégoire, Benhaddad, Lapierre, & Dedrian, 1997; Ioannidis, Cappelleri, & Lau, 1998).

A well-designed and executed meta-analysis, whether study-level or patient-based, has the following characteristics (Moher & Olkin, 1995; Pogue & Yusuf, 1998):

1. It is based on a prospective protocol with well-described *a priori* hypotheses.

2. It uses a broad enough search strategy to identify all possible trials (published and unpublished, English-language and non-English-language).

3. It assesses the quality of the individual trials.

4. It assesses and tries to explain trial heterogeneity.

5. It evaluates the robustness of the findings relative to the key assumptions and decisions used to guide the selection and inclusion of trials in the analysis.

6. It evaluates the extent to which publication bias influences the results.

It is imperative that meta-analysts exercise the same level of scientific rigor in the design and execution of a meta-analysis as he or she would a randomized controlled trial (Pogue & Yusuf, 1998).

We must recognize the retrospective nature of the data and critically evaluate the limitations in our data sources, the individual studies. Individual study results are influenced by several factors. Some key factors are the selection criteria and rules used to assign treatments to patients, the amount and quality of adjuvant care and co-interventions provided to participants across groups, differences in crossover and attrition rates among the groups, and systematic differences in the timing and accuracy of outcome assessments. A number of scales and checklists are available to measure the quality of randomized control trials. Unfortunately, the vast majority of these instruments lack sufficient validity and reliability to recommend their use (Moher et al., 1995). So, what are we to do?

With respect to randomized controlled trials, concealment of allocation is the most influential factor in study quality. An empirical study of the effects of study quality on pooled effect sizes found that trials with inadequate or unclear concealment of allocation yielded odds ratios whose magnitude favored the target intervention by as much as 41% more than pooled estimates based on trials with clearly adequate concealment of randomization. Pooled results based on studies that were not double-blinded yield pooled estimates that were 17% more favorable than double-blinded trial (Schulz, Chalmers, Hayes, & Altman, 1995). Adequate concealment of randomization and blinding are the key criteria for assessing the quality of randomized controlled trial.

Little consensus or data is available on how to assess study quality with respect to non-randomized studies (e.g., case series, longitudinal, cohort, or case-control studies). The most comprehensive approach to evaluation of non-randomized studies is outlined in a document on conducting systematic reviews produced by the NHS Center for Reviews of Research and Dissemination (1996). The proposed guidelines and checklists use a hierarchical classification system for study designs based on potential sources of bias that threaten the study's internal and external validity. Study quality within each class is evaluated according to the methodological steps taken by the author(s) to minimize or control for the bias that poses the greatest threat to the study's internal and external validity. Recognition of the level, strength, and quality of the evidence is essential in making decisions about whether and how to combine study results in a meta-analysis. It is also critical to drawing scientifically sound and clinically appropriate conclusions from the data.

Meta-analysis is a quantitative approach to integrating findings from a set of related studies. It introduces a level of scientific rigor to the review process that limits bias and reduces random error in the selection, critical appraisal, and synthesis of published information relevant to an important clinical or research question. Meta-analysis provides graphic and analytic tools that assist clinicians and researchers to efficiently integrate research findings and establish whether treatment effects are consistent across populations, settings, and differences in treatments. A well-designed meta-analysis also identifies significant limitations in our data and gaps in our knowledge that patients and clinicians can use to make rational, informed decisions about whether to initiate or maintain a course of treatment with a patient. Researchers can use this information to plan new research initiatives to address the methodological limitations and fill in critical gaps in our current knowledge. Thus, a properly designed and conducted meta-analysis provides a rational basis for decision making.

Chapter 14

Discussion

Gideon J. Mellenbergh
with comments by:
David J. Hand, Jan B. Hoeksma, D. Joop Kuik,
P. Dick Bezemer, Judea Pearl and Herman J. Adèr

The methodology of the empirical life, behavioural, and social sciences is a broad field. It covers both methods, which are typical for the humanities, and methods typical for the sciences. It is bounded on one side by philosophy of science and on the other side by mathematics. The editors of this volume take the position that methodology is a field of its own. It gratefully borrows from other disciplines, such as statistics and computer science, but it is an independent field having its own concepts and developments. The methods used in different substantive disciplines, such as epidemiology, psychology, and sociology, widely differ among each other. The diversity, however, mainly occurs in the use of highly different techniques and procedures. For example, sociometrical methods for the analysis of verbal interview protocols are very different from psychometrical methods for the analysis of tests and questionnaires. In spite of this diversity, methodology shows far more unity in its objectives and concepts. The general objective of methodology is the improvement of the quality of substantive empirical research. Four subfields of methodology are distinguished:

1. Hypothesis- and Theory construction,

2. Data collection,

3. Measurement, and

4. Data analysis.

More specific objectives of methodology are, therefore, the improvement of hypothesis- and theory construction, data collection, measurement, and data analysis of substantive empirical research.

The quality of empirical research can be considered from the validity point of view. *Validity* is a general key-concept of methodology. In empirical studies, substantive hypotheses and theories are investigated. A study is said to be *valid* if the statements on the investigated hypotheses and theories can be justified by the empirical results of the study. A study is, however, invalid if flaws in the study are detected, which raise doubts on the justification of these statements. The validity concept is very general and applies to all subfields of methodology, whereas other, less general, concepts only apply to a specific methodological subfield or substantive research area. At the conceptual level, methodology is a reasonably united field, because identical or similar concepts are used in a wide variety of subfields and substantive areas. An example of a specific concept, which applies to a wider variety of situations, is *measurement precision*. Although the methods for assessing the reliability of, for example, verbal interview protocol data and cognitive tests are very different, the concept of precision applies to both types of data. The conceptual unity is, however, often obscured by the use of different terminology, for example, in epidemiology the concepts *sensitivity* and *specificity* are used and in psychometrics the concept of *information*, but these concepts are related to each other (see Chapter 9 of this volume).

In this final chapter, the contributions to this volume are discussed. The discussion is not in the form of detailed comments, but is at a conceptual level. First, in Section 14.1 the contributions are put in a context. The validity concept and the four methodological subfields mentioned above are used to provide a context for the different contributions. Second, three methodological topics are discussed, which recur in several contributions: *graphical representation*, the *model* concept, and *causal explanation*.

14.1   Context

The contributions to this volume are embedded in the context of (a) the validity concept, and (b) the four methodological subfields.

14.1.1   Validity

Validity is a very general concept, which must be specified to be of practical use. Cook & Campbell (1979, Chapter 2) divided the validity concept into four subconcepts:

1. Statistical conclusion validity,

2. Internal validity,

3. Construct validity, and

4. External validity.

Statistical conclusion validity refers to the relation between variables in empirical research. Statistics, such as a correlation coefficient or t-value, quantify the relation between two variables. Statistical conclusion validity refers to the correctness of relations between variables. Statistical conclusion validity is threatened by, for example, a low power or assumption violation of statistical procedures.

If a relation between two variables is found, the next question concerns the causality of the relation. *Internal validity* refers to the plausibility and nature of a causal relation. If variables X and Y are statistically related, it is not known whether the relation is causal; and if the relation is causal, the direction of the relation is not always obvious (X a cause of Y or Y a cause of X). The main problem for a causal interpretation of a relation between X and Y is that another variable (Z) is a cause of both X and Y, for example, a positive correlation between the number of fire engines (X) and fire damage (Y) is not causal but is completely explained by the size of the fire (Z). Threats to the internal validity of a study are possible variables Z which explain the statistical relation between X and Y.

Cook & Campbell (1979, p. 38) used Cronbach & Meehl's (1955) concept of *construct validity ('to refer to the approximate validity with which we can make generalizations about higher-order constructs from research operations')*, and they applied this concept to both independent and dependent variables. A measured variable is said to be *construct valid* if it is an adequate representation of the theoretical construct of interest.

Finally, *external validity* concerns the validity of generalization of research conclusions. Cook & Campbell (1979, p. 71) distinguished between three different sources of generalizations: *persons, settings*, and *times*. Moreover, they distinguished between generalizations *to* and generalizations *across* persons, settings, and times. 'Generalizations to' means that conclusions based on a sample of persons, settings, or times can be generalized to a population of persons, settings or times. 'Generalization across' means that conclusions apply to different subpopulations of persons, settings, or times, such as males and females, school and home settings, or summer and winter time.

The contributions to this volume do not explicitly discuss the validity concept, but they address many issues which are highly relevant for validity. Some chapters concentrate on one of the four validity subconcepts, while other chapters are relevant for different subconcepts or general aspects of validity.

Chapters 4, 8, 10, 11, and 13 are relevant for statistical conclusion validity. Chapter 4 (De Greef) discusses methods to construct meta data from data sets. Meta data represent, summarize, or specify the original data. The construction of meta data is relevant for statistical conclusion validity if the statistical analysis of the meta data is more appropriate or convenient than the analysis of the original data. Chapter 8 (Molenaar) describes statistical methods for the analysis of change. Chapter 10 (Whittaker and Sewart) discusses graphical models for the analysis of the independence of variables conditional on values of other variables. Saris's Chapter 11 gives, among others, estimation and testing methods of structural equation models. Chapter 13 (Cornell and Mulrow) is on meta-analysis, and reports statistical methods which can be used in this type of research.

Chapters 5 (Darius and Portier) and 6 (Pocock) report on designs and procedures for doing experimental studies and clinical trials, respectively. These methods are relevant for the internal validity of experimental research. Chapter 12 (Pearl) is on causal models in observational studies, and is relevant for the internal validity of non-experimental research. Chapter 11 (Saris) on structural relation models also addresses causal interpretations of non-experimental data and, therefore, also fits in the internal validity aspect. Molenaar (Chapter 8) makes a distinction between the time-dependent change of one single subject (within-subject change) and a population of subjects (between-subjects change). He demonstrates that a sample of subjects following completely different within-subject time series models yields one, rather simple, between-subjects model. Therefore causal interpretations at the between-subject level do not apply to the individual subjects.

Measurement models are needed for making valid generalizations from research operations to theoretical constructs. Chapter 9 (Mellenbergh) gives an overview of measurement models and fits the construct validity aspect.

Chapter 7 (Bethlehem) is on the generalization of sample survey data to a population of subjects. This topic belongs to the external validity aspect. Molenaar's (Chapter 8) demonstration of the discrepancy between within-subject and between-subject change models has also consequences for external validity: Using a within-subject model, generalization is from a sample of time points to a population of time points for a given subject, and using a between-subjects change model the generalization is from a sample of subjects to a population of subjects at fixed time points.

Chapter 2 (Van Heerden) and 3 (Adèr) do not address particular aspects of the validity concept, but these chapters relate to validity in a more general sense. Van Heerden (Chapter 2) discusses the historical context of methodological concepts which is important for understanding the development of these concepts and their contribution to validity. Adèr (Chapter 3) describes formal systems for the representation of methodological concepts. Formal representation can show flaws and omissions in, for example designs and procedures, and clarifies the validity of empirical research.

14.1.2 Subfields

Four methodological subfields were distinguished. The contributions to this volume are put into the context of this distinction.

The first methodological subfield is on the construction of hypotheses and theories. Chapters 2 (Van Heerden) and 3 (Adèr) belong to this subfield: The history of methods (Chapter 2) and the formal representation of methodological concepts (Chapter 3) mainly contribute to this theoretical subfield. Pearl's contribution (Chapter 12) is on causal models. It discusses relations between theoretical constructs and also fits within this subfield.

The data collection subfield includes, among others, designs for experimental and non-experimental research. Chapters 5 (Darius and Portier), 6 (Pocock), and 7 (Bethlehem) belong to this subfield: Darius and Portier (Chapter 5) and Pocock (Chapter 6) discuss designs for experimental studies, while Bethlehem (Chapter 7) is on sample survey research, that is, on design procedures for observational (non-experimental) research.

The measurement subfield deals with measurement models and procedures, such as, classical test theory for scores and item response theory for answers to items. Mellenbergh's Chapter 9 is on measurement models, which topic belongs to this subfield.

The data analysis subfield is represented by Chapters 4 (De Greef), 8 (Molenaar), 10 (Whittaker and Sewart), 11 (Saris) and 12 (Cornell and Mulrow). Most of these chapters have parts, which can be subsumed under one of the other three subfields, for example Saris (Chapter 11) discusses structural relations between variables, which can be subsumed under the theoretical subfield; and Molenaar (Chapter 8) emphasizes the difference between within-subject and between-subjects models, which can be subsumed under the design aspect of the data collection subfield.

14.2   Topics

The topics of graphical representation, modelling, and causality criss-cross this volume. They are important issues in modern methodology and are shortly discussed in this section.

14.2.1   Graphical representation

In Chapters 3 (Adèr), 9 (Mellenbergh), 10 (Whittaker and Sewart), 11 (Saris), and 12 (Pearl) graphical representations are used. Although all of these representations are of a graphical nature, they differ among each other in scope and status.

Adèr's F-graphs fit into a comprehensive representational system (Chapter 3), which consists of graphical representations of objects, sets, and time-independent as well as time-dependent relations. It has a very broad scope because it can represent all possible methodological concepts, such as, designs, data collection procedures, measurement, theoretical relations, and so on. The F-graph can easily subsume more limited graphical systems, such as used in other chapters of this volume. Another feature of this representational system is that it corresponds to an algebraic notational system (F-notation), which implies that algorithmic operations can be applied to the graphical system.

The scope of the graphical systems used in the other chapters is more limited. In these chapters, graphical representations are used which are common in factor- and path analysis. These graphs only represent the relations among and between latent and observed variables. These graphical systems are mainly used for the description of theoretical relations between variables. However, the interpretational status of a graphical representation of a relation between variables can be very different. On one hand, this graphical representation is interpreted as a causal relation between variables (see, for example, Pearl's Chapter 12), whereas on the other hand this graphical representation is interpreted as (conditional) dependence between variables, without any connotation of a causal relation between them (see Whittaker & Sewart's Chapter 10).

14.2.2 Models

In the scientific literature, the term model is extensively used, but the context wherein it is used, may widely differ, for example, a small-scale physical system (e.g. a wind-tunnel) as a model for a large-scale system (e.g. the air); a computer simulation system as a model for a real system; a system of linear equations as a model for behaviour; or graph theory as a model for human interactions. In general, the term *model* refers to the theoretical aspects of a research problem, and it seems that the terms theory and model are used interchangeably. The term *theory* refers to a system consisting of three major components (Nagel, 1961, Chapter 5):

1. a *calculus* which defines the basic notions of the system,

2. a *set of rules* which relate the calculus to empirical observations, and

3. an *interpretation* for the calculus.

The authors of the volume seem to use 'model' for a system which consists of Nagel's three components. For example, Saris (Chapter 11) describes a model for causal relations between Education, Age, Income, and Satisfaction. The assumed causal relations between the four variables are expressed in a system of linear equations. These equations imply that the correlations between the four variables can be expressed as functions of the equation parameters. Using precise measurements of the four variables, their intercorrelations can be estimated in a sample of subjects. From these estimates, the parameters of the linear equations can be estimated, and using these estimates the fit of the model can be tested. The linear equations of the model are visualized by a path diagram, where a one-directional arrow represents an assumed causal relation between two variables and a two-directional arrow a non-causal relation. This example has all three major components of a theory: (a) The set of linear equations is the calculus part, (b) the model parameters expressed as correlations relate the calculus to observable (sample) correlations, and (c) the path diagram interprets the calculus of linear equations. Although Saris describes a theory in Nagel's sense, he uses the term 'model' and not 'theory'.

Not only Saris, but most of the authors of this volume as well as other methodologists, prefer model above theory. This raises the question whether theory and model can be distinguished on other grounds than Nagel's three components. Van Heerden (1982, Chapter 5) remarks that model and theory can be distinguished in their pretension to explain phenomena. A model is a heuristic and preliminary approximation of reality. It is not pretentious and can easily be replaced by another, better fitting, model. In contrast, a theory pretends to give a true explanation of phenomena. In general methodologists do not pretend to truly explain social and behavioural phenomena, but they are quite satisfied by reasonable approximations, which might explain their preference for model above theory.

14.2.3   Causal explanation

Brand (1979) and Cook & Campbell (1979, Chapter 1) discuss several philosophy of science views on *causation*. At least three criteria seem to be needed for the plausibility of the statement that an event A is a cause of event B (in a probabilistic sense):

1. A must precede B in time;

2. The conditional probability of B given A must be larger than the unconditional probability of B, that is,

$$P(B|A) > P(B);$$

3. There is no other event C such that C occurs earlier than or simultaneous with A and C makes B statistically irrelevant to A which means that:
$$P(B|A, C) = P(B|C).$$

These criteria are routinely applied in experimental research. For example, suppose that it is known that 50% of a certain type of patient spontaneously recover, that is, the probability of recovery (event B) is $P(B) = 0.5$. A group of patients is treated with a drug, which has a chemical active part, and 90% of these patients recover. The probability of recovering given the treatment by the chemical active part of the drug (event A) is $P(B|A) = 0.9$. The administration of the chemical active part of the drug precedes the recovery, and the conditional probability of recovery given administration of the chemical active part, $P(B|A) = 0.9$, is higher than the unconditional probability of recovery, $P(B) = 0.5$. Therefore, the first two conditions of the probabilistic explanation of recovery caused by the active part of the drug are fulfilled. A rival explanation is that the setting of the medical treatment induces cognitive processes in the patients, which stimulate biological recovery processes. In other words, not the chemical active part but cognitive processes cause recovery. Therefore, the induction of the cognitive processes by the treatment is an event (C), which is simultaneous to the administration of the chemical active part of the drug (A).

To investigate the third condition for a probabilistic causal explanation, a placebo treatment is administered to another group of patients. The placebo treatment seems identical to the medical treatment, but the chemical active part of the drug is replaced by a chemical inactive part. In the medical treatment group both events occur, that is, the active part of the drug (A) and the induction of patients's cognitive processes (C). The probability of recovery given these two events is $P(B|A, C) = 0.9$. In the placebo group only the patient's cognitive processes are stimulated, which means that the probability of recovery in this group is $P(B|C)$. If $P(B|A, C) = P(B|C) = 0.9$, the stimulation of patients' cognitive processes (C) makes recovery (B) statistically irrelevant to the chemical active part of the drug (A), that is, the chemical active part cannot be considered a cause of recovery.

A problem of the third condition of a probabilistic causal explanation is that many different rival events (C's) are possible and that each of them must be checked in empirical research. In experimental studies, special designs are used to investigate frequently occurring rival events, for example, the random and double-blind assignment of patients to treatment and placebo groups. The weakness of the third condition is, however, that always a new rival event C could be found in the future.

The investigation of the third condition is hard, but usually it is even harder in non-experimental research than in experimental research. For example suppose that in a retrospective epidemiological study an association is found between smoking and heart affections: People having heart affections more frequently report to have been smokers in the past than people without heart affections. The first two conditions for the probabilistic explanation of heart affections by smoking are fulfilled: smoking precedes heart affections and the conditional probability of heart affections given smoking is higher than the unconditional probability of heart affections. It is, however, very difficult to fulfill the third condition, because many rival explanations can be considered. For example, stress or personality type may make heart affections statistically irrelevant to smoking.

In some non-experimental studies, probabilistic causal explanations are very plausible, whereas they are doubted in other ones. In, for example, measurement research probabilistic causal explanations are very common: It is assumed that an examinee's achievement test score is explained by his or her true test score, and that a subject's responses to intelligence test items are explained by his or her latent trait (see Chapter 9). These causal interpretations are usually beyond doubt. However, the opinions on the validity of probabilistic causal explanations in non-experimental research diverge. In this volume, Pearl (Chapter 12) holds that causal explanations can be made, whereas Whittaker and Sewart (Chapter 10) do not seem to share this opinion.

In our opinion, the plausibility of probabilistic causal interpretations is mainly determined by the possibility to eliminate the rival explanations of the third condition. Experimental designs eliminate a large number of rival explanations in experimental research, and psychometric methods eliminate them in non-experimental measurement research. The plausibility of a causal explanation in a non-experimental study is considerably increased if an appeal can be made on a general *principle* or *mechanism*. For example, it is very plausible that smoking is a probabilistic cause of heart affections if the biological mechanism, which leads from smoking to heart affections, is known. The law or mechanism increases the plausibility of the probabilistic causal explanation because it eliminates most of the rival explanations of the third condition.

14.3   Conclusions

Methodology of the life, social, and behavioural sciences is an independent field of research. It has its own theoretical and practical development, and it has important implications for and influence on substantive research via methodological teaching and consultation.

The field is broad, and ranges from philosophy of science to mathematics. It diverges at the technical and procedural level: Some techniques and procedures are typical for the humanities, whereas others are typical for the sciences. As shown by the contributions to this volume, there is more unity at the conceptual level.

The same types of concepts are used in different methodological subfields, although frequently different terms are used for similar concepts. This volume also demonstrates that methodologists's opinions diverge on philosophical issues, such as the status of graphical representations and causal explanations. It cannot be expected that opinions on these matters will converge in the near future, but the editors hope that this volume contributes to a better understanding of the different issues.

References

Brand, M. (1979). Causality. In P. D. Asquith & H. E. Kyburg Jr. (Eds.), *Current research in philosophy of science* (pp. 252–281). Ann Arbor: Philosophy of Science Association.

Cook, T. D., & Campbell, D. T. (1979). *Quasi-experimentation: Design and analysis issues for field settings.* Chicago: RandMcNally.

Cronbach, L. J., & Meehl, P. E. (1955). Construct validity in psychological tests. *Psychological Bulletin, 52,* 281–302.

Nagel, E. (1961). *The structure of science: Problems in the logic of scientific explanation.* London: Routledge and Kegan Paul.

Van Heerden, J. (1982). *De zorgelijke staats van het onbewuste* [The critical condition of the unconscious]. Amsterdam: Boom. (Dissertation. University of Amsterdam)

Comments
by David J. Hand
Imperial College, London, UK

The editors of this book hold the view that there is, or should be, a distinct field – *methodology* – consisting of the common ground of ideas and methods of substantive empirical research adopted by different domains of scientific enquiry. The ideas and principles of methodology are held to lie between the ideas and principles of the scientific domains on the one hand and those of statistics and data analysis on the other. By identifying methodology as a distinct field, the editors hope that researchers may focus on it, and refine it, as well as using the insights derived from it more widely across scientific disciplines. In an effort to promote this, they have put together a collection of articles, written by experts in the respective fields, so that the common ground can be discerned.

It is certainly true that the methodological developments in one field can benefit others - and many historical examples exist. One example not treated in the book is measurement theory. In response to the revolutions in physics which occurred at the turn of the century, with the development of quantum mechanics and relativity, the American physicist P. W. Bridgman developed a philosophical approach to scientific measurement which took the concepts under study as being defined by the procedures used to measure them. Later this was adopted by psychologists as legitimising the study of concepts lacking crisp definitions (e.g. as E. G. Boring wrote of intelligence: "Intelligence is what tests test," Boring, 1945).

The present volume focuses on certain key, but inevitably interwoven issues, and discusses them in different chapters. These issues include such things as causality, the role of time and change over time, relationships between variables, the design of studies so as to tease out causal and other kinds of relationships, the fundamental importance of context in stating research questions, and broader issues of integrating conclusions, often contradictory, from different researchers and different studies. This division of the different topics, into chapters written by different authors, is unfortunate in some ways. Although it permitted experts to discourse on each separate domain, it means that the links between the different domains are less developed than they might be. Causality is fundamentally about relationships between different variables, design is about the best way to investigate what influences what, relationships between variables define the context in which questions are asked, and so on. Perhaps the editors of the volume will develop further work in this direction, showing more clearly how the different topics are related.

There have been very substantial advances in methodological work over the last decade. Within statistics, many of these have been stimulated by advances in computer power (for example, bootstrap methods and generalized linear models). It is true that many of these have not yet permeated through to practical application (as just one illustration, much work in psychology continues to use univariate and multivariate analysis of variance methods for analysing repeated measures data, despite the fact that more satisfactory general methods have been well developed (e.g. Crowder & Hand, 1990; Hand & Crowder, 1996) and that software is now readily available. There are at least two reasons for this. One is that the methods are often fairly mathematical, at least in their initial formulations. (An important stage in methodological progress is the process of 'digestion' and restatement of theoretical advances into more practically oriented terms.) Another is simply the time it takes for developments to move from the laboratory (in this case, the statistician's 'laboratory') to the workbench (in this case, the psychologist's 'workbench'). 'The last decade', to which the editors refer, does not seem too long to me. It would be interesting to see some quantitative assessment of how long it takes for theoretical advances to become integrated into practical use, and of whether things have deteriorated or improved over time.

Adèr and Mellenbergh also refer to the unfortunate fact that much material published in the statistical literature is irrelevant to practical researchers. This is true and is a severe criticism of modern statistics. Statistics is (or, at least, should be), above all about solving real problems. To pursue the mathematics at the expense of these applications endangers the discipline as well as all those other disciplines which might benefit from it. (For a discussion of these issues, see the series of papers by Sprent, Hand, Senn, and Bailey, and the ensuing discussion in *Journal of the Royal Statistical Society, Series D (The Statistician), 47*, 1998, 239–290.)

The authors say that researchers often adopt a data analytic, 'technique-driven' view of practical statistical applications. This is certainly true, and it is presumably as a way of coping with the need to know something about statistics as well as much about their own discipline. But it is at odds with the modern statistical perspective, which is essentially model driven. (It is interesting to note, however, that the new domain of *data mining* puts equal emphasis on an algorithm-driven perspective. This reflects its shared roots in statistics and machine learning, and the necessity for heavy usage of computers in analysing large data sets (see Hand, Mannila, & Smyth, 1999, (forthcoming)). The fact that researchers in some disciplines often adopt a technique-driven view of statistics has often been disparaged. Indeed, it has been mocked, by referring to it as the 'cookbook' approach, based on the notion that one simply draws an appropriate data analytic recipe from a collection. The truth of the matter is that statistical methods of data analysis are not simply a disparate 'collection', but rather provide a unified set of ideas, with complex interrelations. The cookbook approach impoverishes one's perspective on research methodology, the questions which can be answered, and the progress which can be made.

The editors note that this book has its origins in work on statistical expert systems. Research in that area, carried out in the 1980s, led to some interesting software tools, but seems to have had little practical impact. Perhaps it was premature, and required the development of more sophisticated computational tools before it could be applied in practice. Having said that, it is rewarding to see that that work has had a longer term impact, as this book illustrates, on ideas about research strategies and research methodology in general.

References

Boring, E. G. (1945). The use of operational definitions in science. *Psychological Review, 52*, 243–245.

Crowder, M. J., & Hand, D. J. (1990). *Analysis of Repeated Measures.* London: Chapman & Hall.

Hand, D. J. (1994). Deconstructing Statistical Questions. *Journal of the Royal Statistical Society, Series A, 157*, 65–76.

Hand, D. J., & Crowder, M. J. (1996). *Practical longitudinal data analysis.* London: Chapman & Hall.

Hand, D. J., Mannila, H., & Smyth, P. (1999). *Principles of Data Mining.* Cambridge, Massachusetts. (forthcoming)

On models and theories
Jan B. Hoeksma
Vrije Universiteit, The Netherlands

It is striking that in everyday parlour of researchers the terms 'model' and 'theory' are used as if they refer to the same thing. Mellenbergh offers a similar observation in his concluding chapter. He notes that "the terms model and theory are used interchangeably" (page 329). Pondering on this issue, he further notes that the models presented in the present volume would qualify as theories. Saris for instance describes the causal relations between Education Age, Income and Satisfaction. Mellenbergh carefully explains that the structural equation model presented by Saris complies with the three definitional characteristics of a theory, as they were put forward by Nagel (1961). In other words Saris' model and the models of other authors in the present volume resemble theories. After this has been said, Mellenbergh appears to be willing to give some special meaning to theories. Fortunately, methodologists appear to be sensible people (they are indeed), they prefer models above theories, they prefer to give a reasonable description of the world.

In this comment I would like to argue that methodologist should keep a clear conceptual distinction between model and theory. The argument is not based on philosophical but on pragmatic grounds. I heartily agree with the editors' notion that methodology is a distinct discipline within the field of life, social and behavioural sciences. In my view this position of methodology as a discipline is largely based on the distinction between models and theories. If theory and model are to be used interchangeably, methodology, as a discipline would disappear.

The argument runs as follows. First the relationship between model and theory will be considered from a philosophical and a natural science perspective. Then a few words will be spent on theories in the behavioural sciences. Next I shortly discuss two models. It will be shown that models may have very different meanings, depending on their use.

Models versus theories

Is there a difference between models and theories? A well-known Dutch introduction into the philosophy of science by Koningsveld (1976) clearly suggests a difference. A model should be seen as part of a theory. For that reason Koningsveld warns that model and theory should not be identified with each other. A model pictures the world, but does not go beyond it. A theory offers an explanation, often by introducing theoretical (unobservable) concepts and mechanisms. A nice example is found in Mellenbergh's conclusion (page 332), where he notes that ruling out alternative explanations in observational studies regarding the relationship between smoking and heart affections (a probabilistically modelled relationship) is remarkably facilitated if the biological mechanism (theoretical notion) is known.

Natural scientists are rarely bothered by questions regarding differences between models and theories. Casti (1992) elaborates on the theory-model issue in his book on mathematical modelling. He argues that the (philosophical) distinction between model and theory blurs if one is interested in mathematical models at a practical level. When one tries to model some natural system, model and theory are hard to separate. Models can be seen as mathematical manifestations of theories. At a practical level, that is when making models, there is no distinction. For that reason Casti is happy to leave the question about what is the theory and what is the model to the philosophical literature.

What about theories and models in the medical social and behavioural sciences? The theories in this broadly defined area characteristically range from strictly mathematical to fully verbal. The majority of theories only contain non-mathematical, lexical, statements. Nevertheless, as every methodologist will agree, models play, tacitly or explicitly, an important part in almost every theory. But what role do they play? To give answers to this question we discuss some models and their uses under different circumstances. An oldie and a more fashionable model will be discussed.

Models and methods

Fisher & Mackenzie (1923) published an important study regarding the manurial response of different potato varieties. They argued that the yield of a given variety of potatoes and a given manurial treatment was the sum of two quantities, one depending on the potato and one depending on the fertilizer (Fisher Box, 1978). Besides these two effects an interaction of manure and potato was distinguished. The results of the study were summarized in a table containing the sum of squares of the effects.

Fisher and Mackenzie used a simple linear additive model to analyse their data. The model is easily recognized by the present reader as Analysis of Variance. The results about the manurial responses of potatoes are forgotten by now. The model, however, has become the principle method for analysing experiments in almost every field of research. As Joan Fisher Box (1978), Sir Ronald Fisher's daughter, notes in his biography: setting up an Anova table in one case suggests its use in others.

When Anova is used nobody would be inclined to call the linear model a theory even if we could show that Nagel's criteria would apply. Of course Anova is part of the general statistical theory and when it is used to analyse experimental data the assumptions of Anova have to be dealt with in the substantial theory. But the model and the theory can't be interchanged, nor can they be identified with each other. Methodologists prefer to call Anova a model or a method, not a theory.

Models and metaphors

One and the same model may be used in rather different ways. The same model may be used as a mathematical tool in one application and as an abstract metaphor in another. Recent (non-linear) models derived from catastrophe theory offer a good example. René Thom created catastrophe theory. As commonly known, he endeavoured to model embryonic growth. Within the confines of mathematics the theory offers classification theorems of elementary smooth functions and manifolds (see Castrigiano & Hayes, 1993; Thom, 1975). Within other fields it helps to understand sudden changes, or transitions, in slowly changing environment. The mathematical properties of catastrophe theory are beyond dispute, its applications in biological, social and behavioural sciences are not (Thom, 1993). One of the models is designated the cusp catastrophe model. The model has been applied in at least three different ways.

In physics and engineering it is used to study local instabilities of known dynamical systems. A typical application, including its mathematical details, can be found in Casti (1992). The natural system to be modelled consists of two electronic power generators. The mathematical description, the model, is known. Using the model it can be shown how slow changes in angular momentum and damping lead to an abrupt breakdown of the supply of electricity or in other words to a catastrophe.

In the social and behavioural sciences the cusp catastrophe model is used to analyse transitions. It can be used with observed data in a similar way as the regression model. (The main difference with the regression model is that response surface is not flat but folded). Cobb (1980) gave a first application. He used the cusp catastrophe model to predict the transitions from low to high birth rates on basis of slow changes in literacy and death rate. Another kind of application can be found in developmental psychology.

Van der Maas (1992) used characteristics derived from the model (not the model itself) to detect sudden cognitive changes. He checked his data to see whether they show bi-modality, anomalous variance etc. to decide whether or not a sudden change is to be designated a developmental transition or not.

How is the cusp catastrophe model used in these examples? In engineering, the model including its parameters is fully known. In the birth-rate example the model is estimated on data. In the example from developmental psychology, it is only decided whether or not the model would apply (in this case the parameters in the model can't be traced). One step further is to use the model without data. The model then becomes a metaphor to come to grips with transitions.

Conclusion

The examples show that the same model may be used in diverse ways and in distinct fields of research. This is precisely what models offer us. Models, as methodologists know them, are widely applicable. Theories are restricted to certain classes of phenomena. The majority of models, Anova is one of them, are used as analytic tools. These models are methods for data analyses. They are used to answer all kind of research questions in a more or less routine way. One can only wish that many of the models presented in this volume will follow the same road as Fisher's original Anova-table. That is, that the models become methods (not theories).

Models serve theories, they affect theories to a large extent. In some cases the formal model coincides with the conceptual theory. The physical sciences offer many examples. Somewhat paradoxically if one starts making models that fully explain specific phenomena, the model becomes quite specific too. In that case the model may lose its function as a model to analyse and understand other seemingly unrelated phenomena.

Methodology is an independent field of research. What unites methodologists from different fields of research, are the models they use. Of course the models may diverge at a technical or procedural level as Mellenbergh notes. The diversity is also to be found in what theories the models serve and *how* they serve them. In my view, methodology as a discipline is based on common models, not on common theories. Would it not be better then to keep a clear distinction between model and theory?

One question remains. Is the model presented by Saris a theory? His personal answer was: 'no'. However, his intention is to create models that are theories, not just models!

References

Casti, J. L. (1992). *Reality rules I & II, Picturing the world in mathematics.* New York: Wiley.

Castrigiano, D. P. L., & Hayes, S. A. (1993). *Catastrophe Theory.* Reading, Massachusetts: Addison-Wesley.

Cobb, L. (1980). Estimation theory for the cusp catastrophe model. In *Proc. section on survey research methods* (pp. 772–776). American Statistical Association.

Fisher Box, J. (1978). *R. A. Fisher: The life of a scientist.* New York: Wiley.

Fisher, R. A., & Mackenzie, W. A. (1923). Studies in crop variation II. The manurial response of different potato varieties. *J. Agric. Sci, 13,* 311–320.

Koningsveld, H. (1976). *Het verschijnsel wetenschap: een inleiding tot de wetenschapsfilosofie* [Phenomenon science: an introduction to the philosophy of science]. Meppel.

Nagel, E. (1961). *The structure of science: Problems in the logic of scientific explanation.* London: Routledge and Kegan Paul.

Thom, R. (1975). *Structural Stability and Morphogenesis.* Reading, Massachusetts: Benjamin.

Thom, R. (1993). Foreword to Catastrophe theory. In D. P. L. Castrigiano & S. A. Hayes (Eds.), *Catastrophe Theory (ix-x).* Reading, Massachusetts: Addison-Wesley.

Van der Maas, H. (1992). Stagewise cognitive development: an application of catastrophe theory. *Psychological Review, 99*(3), 395–417.

Methodology in practice and research thereupon
by Dirk J. Kuik
Vrije Universiteit, The Netherlands

A book, completely devoted to research methodology, is a daring enterprise. Many challenges await the intrepid author who has to define a corner of that vast field. And in the book in front of us, a courageous mapping of the territory has been done. But one area has not been explored. Or, rather, only half of the subject has been addressed. To illuminate this point, let us consider what using methodology implies in practice.

One of the essential facts in using methodology is that there exist two other fields, that are of primary interest, namely the 'Subject Matter Field' and 'Statistics'. And in practice the first knowledge domain often rests with a researcher, consulting the statistician on his/her expertise in the latter domain. And, as all statisticians and most researchers know, there must be an intermediator, a knowledge domain of translating research hypotheses into data collections and resulting statistics into relevant answers. This intermediator is called 'Methodology'. And it plays its role twice, as we will see.

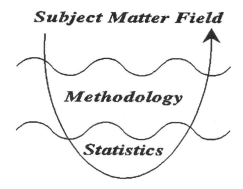

Figure 14.1: Relation between Subject Matter Field, Methodology and Statistics.

To illustrate this point, let us consider Figure 14.1. There are two characteristic properties of the implementation of methodology that can be read from it. One is the fact that there are three domains of knowledge. The other is the mirror order repetition of the course of the research through the domains. As we have seen, the three domains each have their own role in scientific research. The subject matter field gives rise to the interesting questions to be researched. Methodology then translates these into research hypotheses and study designs. Statistics organizes the data and extracts the appropriate statistics. Then, methodology applies the probability models as implicated in the designs, and produces significancies and other data-derived verdicts. And, finally, the subject matter field interprets the relevancy of these findings to produce new knowledge in the field. The existence of three knowledge domains implies automatically the existence of two interfaces, each with its own issues. The upper interface is concerned with discussing the research questions in terms of admissible designs, the lower with relating design structures to computable analysis techniques. As can be seen in the scheme, there is not only a translation problem in space (the domains), but also in time. In the two top domains the problem of getting from the question to the correct answer arises. This is in no way a trivial problem.

Usually, the domain knowledge for Methodology is residing with the statistician. Therefore, (s)he has a two-fold role: to discuss the research questions in terms of admissible designs and to relate design structures to computable analysis techniques. The second role is completely within the area of the statistician's competence, and therefore it is entirely understandable that this is also the subject addressed by this book: the subject of representing and translating developed designs, i.e.the implementations of the activities along the lower interface. This is a technical area, with even some overlap into the Statistics domain. Now we can also see which area is not addressed: the activities around the first interface, with its considerations for translating research questions into designs and extracting relevancies from significancies, are not discussed.

If one intends to research 'Methodology' in this area, then what questions can be raised? In my view, these should be related to the activities in the two timepoints as mentioned. The first, translating questions into designs, centres around the fact that knowledge here not only is found in two domains, but also rests with two research partners: the 'scientist' and the 'statistician'. In which the former seldom has knowledge of the domain of the latter. So, the onus of translating falls to the statistician, and research in this area should address questions like: "what does (s)he mean", "what can we do" and "how do I tell her(him) what we are doing". The second activity has the mirror image problems of the first and the central questions that could be addressed are "why is 'significant' not the same as 'relevant'", "what does the value of this number mean in terms of the paradigms of the subject matter field", "what did we prove" and "how certain are we of our results".

Due to the central themes of the methodology-subject matter field interface, research in these areas will take a more non-technical form and maybe should be driven by paradigms from Psychology and related fields. Research topics could be found in several areas. We might think of Context Analysis, to investigate the interrelated roles of concepts and paradigms within a specific or a generalized subject matter field. Or about Chomsky's Generic Grammars and how to translate and describe these in generic terms. We might think of Cognitive Processes and the way in which researchers tend to formulate concepts and interpret results. And, related to this, how humans perceive values of measure and number and their relative and absolute magnitudes. We might think of Perception Research and the fact that the human animal is driven by a pattern recognizing concept of the outer world and tends to impress structures on it, whether they are there or not. Which means that we could investigate the role of stochasticity on the way researchers perceive probabilistic results. And the means whereby a statistician might influence these perceptions of the world.

Investigation of all these questions could be the subject of another book and would have the scope to be so. This book would be well worth written, the more since it could lay the founding stones of the practical part of a course or handbook in how to practise methodology. The technical part of such a handbook has been laid by this book, while the theoretical part could be found in any adequate book on statistics.

Summarizing, we may say that this book fills an important lacuna in the way we think about methodology, but that we need another like this to complete the picture.

Comment: a unified theory?
P. Dick Bezemer
Vrije Universiteit, The Netherlands

Amongst methodologists

This book is born out of idealism, and I appreciate that very much. Idealists, including methodologists, tend to bend reality into their conceptual framework; which may be irritating but also stimulating. The conception of this book, as I understand, had to do with a worry or even frustration about the diversity amongst methodologists. The editors have the idealistic view that there is far more unity in concepts than is apparent from the language of methodologists in different fields. They seek, so to say, a unified theory of fundamental concepts, without confounding language.

At first sight, this book adds to the diversity. Authors working in various substantive empirical disciplines discuss methodological topics in their field. But, especially in the general discussion, there is an emphasis on what is common. Besides, assessment of diversity is the first step towards understanding of unity. With the editors, I consider methodology as a field on its own, for which it is rewarding to seek the fundamental concepts.

Applied methodologists often have the inclination to adapt study objectives or empirical data to their framework. They reformulate hypotheses and transform or even fill in data. And, of course, a proper analysis asks for modelling reality. However, at least two principles should be borne in mind: the object of study is of prime importance and the data themselves are conclusive. The first principle implies involvement in the substantive field and translation of results of analyses, the second principle means that data analysis is the art of staying close to the data, without playing dark tricks.

As a biostatistician and epidemiologist, I feel the tension between generality (the abstract concepts of a unified theory) and specificity (the operational concepts of applications). Perhaps this tension is strongest in medicine, with its urgency of bringing new knowledge into practice. Not only on the conceptual level, but also in choosing methods of (statistical) analysis this tension is present. Nevertheless, a clear view of what one is doing within a broader framework is rewarding. I hope the evolving field of methodology will be fruitful as a means of improving quality of research in substantive empirical disciplines. It may do so, but only when it does not drift away from applicability into abstract technicalities. In the remainder I ask attention for the operationalization of two general concepts, *validity* and *causal explanation*, in epidemiology.

Amongst epidemiologists

Validity (Ref. 14.1.1, this book). Perhaps validity is the most general concept in methodology. In epidemiology, especially in clinical research, attention is focussed on internal validity. Without being explicit, most books consider statistical conclusion validity as a part of it. Bias is seen as a form of invalidity, sometimes repairable in the statistical analysis, and is subdivided into three broad categories: selection-, information- and confounding-bias. Selection refers to persons and confounding to variables, but sometimes these two biases coincide (e.g., different ages in two treatment groups). A lengthy catalogue of biases, to be used as a checklist, has been made by Sackett (1979). An interesting recent development is meta-analysis, especially applied to studies on effects of treatment: studies are assessed to judge internal validity and pooled to ensure external validity (this book, Chapter 13). To conclude these short remarks on a broad topic, validity plays a key role in epidemiology, but distinctions are not always very clear. A general theory, as the controversial one developed by Miettinen (1985), could enhance the discipline of epidemiology.

Causality (Ref. 14.2.3, this book). In epidemiology the general object of study is the frequency and determinants of disease in human beings. There is some debate about the causal content of the concept 'determinant', but it is clear that causality is important. The relation between risk factor and disease, or between treatment and outcome, should be causal to be of real value in practice. To facilitate judgement of causality, nine criteria have been proposed by Bradford Hill (Rothman, 1988), in short: Temporality, Strength, Dose-response, Experimental, Coherence, Consistency, Biologic plausibility, Specificity, Analogy. The three minimum-criteria of 14.2.3 may be recognized in this list. Of course several modifications have been proposed. For instance, it is curious that statistical significance is not explicitly present. Nevertheless, it is an example of a useful operationalization in epidemiology of a general concept.

References

Miettinen, O. S. (1985). *Theoretical epidemiology*. New York: Wiley.

Rothman, K. J. (Ed.). (1988). *Causal Inference*. Chestnut Hill: Epidemiology Resources Inc.

Sackett, D. L. (1979). Bias in analytic research. *Journal of Chronic Disease*, *32*, 51–63.

Comments on Causal Explanation by Judea Pearl, University of California at Los Angeles, USA

Dr Mellenbergh's discussion of causal explanation offers a golden opportunity for readers to witness the vast progress that causal analysis has made over the past ten years. It also raises important questions as to why scholars like Dr Mellenbergh would remain captive of outdated conceptions of the 1970s, instead of embracing the benefits of current developments in the logic of causation.

My chapter opens with a statement and a demonstration that causal relationships cannot be expressed in the language of probabilities. Dr Mellenbergh's discussion opens with a diametrically opposed statement (based on Brand (1979) and Cook & Campbell (1979)), claiming that "At least three criteria seem to be needed for the plausibility of the statement that an event A is a cause of event B", two of the three criteria are probabilistic. Readers of Chapter 12 should have no difficulty demonstrating that conditions (2) and (3) are plain false. For example, an event A can be a genuine cause of B and yet $P(B|A)$ can be lower than $P(B)$. My speeding on the freeway today (A) was unquestionably the cause of my getting to work on time (B). Yet anyone who examines my driving record would note that the probability of being late to work is much higher on days that I speed, compared with days in which I drive slowly, simply because I speed only when I over-sleep. One does not need to be particularly imaginative to construct counterexamples to (2), a quick glance at the graph of Figure 12.13 would reveal that Z can be a genuine positive cause of Y and, still, the conditional expectation of Y given Z can be negative. Condition (3) can also be shown false using graphs like that of Figure 12.13; Z may be a genuine cause of Y and, yet, if we choose the parameters properly, the partial correlation of $ZY.X$ can be zero.

The choice of Condition (3) is particularily unfortunate, as it is a relic of the outdated 'collapsibility' literature, which has taken heavy toll before recognized as irrelevant. Many statisticians in the 1970s came to believe that the non-collapsibility condition $P(B|A, C) \neq P(B|A)$ provides evidence for the existence of confounding (or 'effect bias'), and a whole literature on collapsibility has emerged, aiming at finding assurances against the 'perils' of non-collapsible events such as C. Today we know that this condition is neither necessary nor sufficient for confounding (Pearl, 1998), that confounding is a causal concept hence it cannot be tested by any statistical means, and that some causal assumptions (e.g., graphs) are needed before one can secure unbiased effect estimates (see Theorems (6)–(7), Chapter 12).

I urge Dr Mellenbergh to study the modern conception of causality, according to which causation predicts behaviour under interventions and changes of mechanisms (see Section 12.3.3, Chapter 12), and to succumb to the realization that causality is no longer a metaphysical concept left to the mercy of personal opinion – it has turned into a mathematical object with well-defined logic and well-defined empirical semantics (see Section 12.4, Chapter 12). Divergence of opinions, such as the one Dr Mellenbergh attributes to me vs. Whittaker and Sewart (Chapter 10) have no place in the new conception of causality, for such differences can be resolved by mathematical analysis. And although we still have many unsolved problems in causal analysis, we know precisely what causal assumptions are needed for resolving differences of opinion, when such exist. As a side remark, I should note that I could not find any opinion about causality in Chapter 10.

I am hopeful that young readers of this book will be introduced to causality through its modern conception, and that they will seize upon the opportunity to benefit from insights and techniques now emerging in the field of causal analysis.

Additional comments
by Herman J. Adèr,
Vrije Universiteit, The Netherlands

Now that we have an overall view of the contents of this book, it becomes apparent what has *not* been discussed. Clearly, at several points additions and extensions can be made. I give a few suggestions here, but I suspect that to completely discuss even the ones mentioned, another volume would be needed.

In the present book a more or less technique-centred position is taken as a starting point to reflect on more fundamental methodological issues. But in most cases the original starting point stays visible. An even broader view could be taken: I can think of several points where this unification is possible:

- *'To find means to explore and represent subject matter information.'*

  Research design could generally benefit from this, since it would be easier to formalize and find bottlenecks in the design. To open up this potentially large and interesting subfield, one could consult techniques for knowledge elicitation as have been developed in Artificial Intelligence research.

- *'To make the ART of research design into a SCIENCE aimed to systematically extend our knowledge.'*

  Agreed, much has been written about this, but I find Judea Pearl's comment in this discussion provoking at this point. It seems that much is lacking in the way those working in everyday research *reason* about what they are doing and about the outcomes they are getting, in particular when it comes to causality issues. Methods from formal logic seem to have much wider applicability than we, methodologists, are aware of. It would be a worthwhile effort to directly apply Judea's ideas in a practical research setting.

- *'To make the ART of statistical model formulation into a SCIENCE.'*

  Much is written about how to find a statistical model corresponding to a particular research question but since the description of related subject matter information is often quite vague, statistical modelling usually remains an activity based on common sense. It is time to try to formalize this art and try to find the basic rules for it. The contents of this volume may serve as a first step in that direction.

As pointed out by David Hand in this discussion, we did not systematically compare between fields, although this seems to be a potential gold mine of future research. To give an example, the **aim** of psychological research seems to be different from the aim of mainstream medical research:

in psychology, research often centres around the question how a certain phenomenon is *structured*. For instance, in research on the development of reading skills of young children we want to know what the underlying *mechanisms* of learning are, much more than we want to find better ways to teach children how to read, although at a later stage that may be the only tangible outcome.

In medicine, the aim is often more pragmatic and directed towards optimization of the treatment of a disease. It focuses on the question: *'How can I improve treatment[1] in respect to: (a) effect; (b) cost, and (c) quality of life of the patient.'*

By the same token, we did not compare between design methods, modelling methods, and analysis techniques. To exemplify how one could go about here, I will bring up some points that could be made in comparing between the design of **Clinical Trials** and **Experimental Design**[2]: It is striking how many differences there are in emphasis and terminology between these seemingly related fields.

Ethical issues. In most countries there is some regulation on what can be asked from respondents when they undergo psychological testing and what experimental situations are acceptable or unacceptable.

But the situation that an experiment has to be stopped when a new treatment turns out unsatisfactory as it is unethical to deprive patients from better treatment, is uncommon in the social sciences. Thus, results of the intensive research on statistical techniques to determine stopping rules and on sequential testing are considered less relevant in that field.

Randomization. In the social sciences, the population from which respondents are recruited is usually known beforehand and random sampling takes place once and for all at the beginning. Even if subjects are tested one after another, determination of their inclusion has been done before and not dependent on the experimental situation. In contrast, randomization in medicine is an activity that is conducted for each patient anew. Inclusion of patients goes on until a number of patients, fixed beforehand, is reached (or, if some stopping criterion is met).

More importantly, the rationale behind random sampling and randomization is different. In the first case the motivation is **generalization**: being able to extend the findings of the study to the whole of the population of which the sample is a part. In the case of randomization in a clinical trial, the underlying idea is to neutralize disturbing, **confounding** influences that are of no interest to the study itself but that

---

[1]Similar remarks could be made on research that aims at improving *diagnosis*.

I *am* aware that for those working in fundamental medical research like Genetics, the mechanism of things *is* at the centre.

[2]And, to a lesser extent, **Survey Analysis**.

have to be controlled for. Here generalization is not so much an issue since the study often concerns a very specific, well determined group of patients.

Trial size calculations. These are so important in medicine since treatment can be extremely expensive and funding bodies require a justification of sample size to judge cost-effectiveness.

In social science research this is often considered less of an issue.

Intention-to-treat principle. Consider the situation in which patients are randomized according to protocol to either of two treatments, the treatments consisting of two different regimes of the same medication in different doses. During treatment some patients may have switched to a dose that corresponds to the alternative treatment. They have 'crossed over' to the other treatment. Now the question arises to which group those patients should be assigned during analysis: (a) To the treatment group they were initially assigned to; (b) To the treatment group they switched to, or (c) To a newly defined group consisting of 'crossover' cases; (d) To the group of patients that is missing or 'lost to follow-up'.

The intention-to-treat principle says that we should stick to the first option during analysis, the justification being that this kind of deviations often occur during real-life treatment. Choosing the second or the third option above is called the 'explanatory attitude' in Chapter 6 on clinical trials where this point is discussed. Obviously, the fourth option is methodologically unsound.

This whole idea may sound very peculiar to the social scientist. It has much to do with the difference in research aim between the social sciences and medicine brought up earlier: Medical research is conducted with an eye to the later application of the results.

Non-compliance. This indicates the phenomenon that patients, although assigned to one of several conditions do not precisely follow the protocol for that condition: for instance, by not taking the prescribed treatment medication from time to time. This may be very difficult to find out, although, when known, correction at the analysis level is possible.

This is different from the non-response that may occur in survey research: the situation where subjects, for whatever reason, do not hand in the questionnaires they were asked to fill out. This is easy to find out but difficult to properly correct for at the analysis level (compare the interesting treatment of non-response in section 7.4).

Pragmatic and **Socially determined** influences on research methodology have been mentioned here and there, but were not thoroughly discussed. Obvious themes are:

o *Publication bias.* In the chapter on Meta-analysis (Chapter 13) it has been discussed how to correct for this. The methodological consequences of this issue seem very worthwhile to pursue.

o *Publication 'lore'.* Research fields differ in the level of methodological sophistication that is accepted by journal reviewers and editors. Thus, the reaction to a statistical consultant's suggestion to use multi-level analysis, may be 'You may find MLA appropriate in this case, but I find it difficult to describe the results, let alone that I can properly justify it in my article against straightforward multiple regression analysis.'

o *Cost-effectiveness analysis.* This is referred to in section 6.7 where *Economic analysis* is discussed. At the moment this field is in full development in the realm of medicine and health care.

From a methodological point of view, considerations on Cost-effectiveness are very interesting since they require proper weighting of clinical outcome and cost considerations while until recently only interpretation of outcome effects seemed important. Technically, this may require invoking approaches from Decision Theory.

o *Requirements of Decision and Policy making.* As exemplified by the previous point, research that is done to support this kind of activity may have aims different from what we are accustomed to in 'normal' research. These differences should be made explicit and the consequences for research and methodology investigated.

In sum, it seems that the production of this book has resulted in the generation of a host of new questions and in bringing up a range of new issues to explore.

A Rejoinder
Gideon J. Mellenbergh,
University of Amsterdam, The Netherlands

My Discussion chapter provoked a number of interesting comments. Because of time and space limitations, I will only respond in brief to some of these comments.

Adèr, Bezemer, Hand, and Kuik mentioned a large number of issues, which were not discussed in this volume. I agree with most of their comments, and I hope that this volume will stimulate further methodological research on these topics.

Hoeksma discussed the difference between the concepts of model and theory. I am always a bit puzzled why I and my methodological colleagues prefer the term model, whereas my substantive colleagues prefer theory.

Van Heerden (1982) gave me a plausible explanation: A model is a heuristic and preliminary approximation of reality, whereas a theory pretends to give a true explanation of phenomena. Hoeksma gave me another plausible explanation: A model is widely applicable, whereas a theory is restricted to a certain class of phenomena. These two distinctions do not coincide, but they seem to be related. A model, such as a regression model, is widely applicable, and is at the same time a heuristic approximation of reality. On the other hand, a theory, for example, on human problem solving, applies to a restricted type of behaviour, and is also considered to be a true explanation of this behaviour. Nagel's (1961) three components of a theory ((1) a calculus, (2) a set of rules to relate the calculus to empirical observations, and (3) an interpretation of the calculus) do not separate the concept of theory from model. Van Heerden's and Hoeksma's remarks give me some grip to distinguish the concepts on two dimensions: approximation versus truth of reality, and widely versus narrowly applicable. It might be that other dimensions can be found, which distinguish the two concepts. It is, therefore, worthwhile to further explore properties and dimensions which distinguish model and theory.

Pearl is very critical on my view on causality. His main criticism is that I adhere to an outdated and metaphysical concept of causality. He presents, among others, a counterexample to Brand's (1979) second criterion for the plausibility that an even A is a cause of event B, that is, $P(B|A) > P(B)$. The speeding on the freeway today (A) is a cause of getting to work on time (B), but in general $P(B|A)$ will be smaller than $P(B)$ because speeding on the freeway is done in case of over-sleep. This situation is not a counterexample of Brand's second criterion because a third event of over-sleep (C) is introduced, and C must be accounted for. The probability of getting to work on time given speeding on the freeway and over-sleep is larger than the probability of getting to work on time given only over-sleep, that is, $P(B|A,C) > P(B|C)$, which satisfies Brand's second criterion.

Moreover, Pearl states that causality *'has turned into a mathematical object with well-defined logic and well-defined empirical semantics'*. I agree with Pearl and Adèr that much can be learned from logical and mathematical analysis, but a mathematical object does not coincide with empirical phenomena. A mathematical structure is a representation of an empirical structure. Proofs are valid within the mathematical structure, but mathematical proofs do not prove empirical relations. A conjectured empirical causal relation can be represented by a mathematical model, such as, a structural equation model. A good fit of the model to empirical data supports the causal interpretation, but it does not prove the causality of the empirical relation. Mathematical models, empirical studies, logical arguments, and thought-experiments effect the plausibility of a causal explanation. Plausibility is not a metaphysical concept because it can be described in operational terms, although methodologists have different views on these operational terms. For example, De Groot (1969, Section 1;3;5) operationalizes the plausibility of a hypothesis as *consensus among the forum of researchers*, Hofstee (1980, Chapter 6) as *the researcher's scientific status stake by betting on the correctness of a hypothesis*, and Royall (1997, Chapter 1) as the *likelihood of a hypothesis with respect to another hypothesis*.

In my view, causal relations are hypotheses which can be rejected or supported by empirical and logical arguments. If my view on causality is outdated and metaphysical, then the bulk of scientific research is outdated and metaphysical.

References

Brand, M. (1979). Causality. In P. D. Asquith & H. E. Kyburg Jr. (Eds.), *Current research in philosophy of science* (pp. 252–281). Ann Arbor: Philosophy of Science Association.

De Groot, A. D. (1969). *Methodology*. The Hague, The Netherlands: Mouton.

Hofstee, W. K. B. (1980). *De empirische discussie* [The empirical discussion]. Amsterdam, The Netherlands: Boom.

Nagel, E. (1961). *The structure of science: Problems in the logic of scientific explanation*. London: Routledge and Kegan Paul.

Royall, R. (1997). *Statistical evidence*. London: Chapman and Hall.

Van Heerden, J. (1982). *De zorgelijke staats van het onbewuste* [The critical condition of the unconscious]. Amsterdam: Boom. (Dissertation. University of Amsterdam)

References

Adèr, H. J. (1995). *Methodological knowledge: Notation and Implementation in Expert Systems.* Phd thesis, University of Amsterdam.

Adèr, H. J. (1998). Diagramming Research designs. In P. Olivier (Ed.), *TWD98, Thinking with Diagrams 98. Is there a Science of Diagrams?* (pp. 122–128). Aberystwyth. (August 22–23, 1998)

Adèr, H. J., & Bramsen, I. (1998). Representation of a Structural Model as a Neural Network. In W. Liebrand (Ed.), *Computer modeling and the study of dynamic social processes.* London: Sage.

Agresti, A. (1990). *Categorical data analysis.* New York: Wiley.

Allen, J. F. (1983). Maintaining knowledge about temporal intervals. *Communications of the ACM, 26*(1), 832–843.

Allen, M. J., & Yen, W. M. (1979). *Introduction to measurement theory.* Monterey, CA: Brooks /Cole.

Alwin, D., & Krosnick, J. (1991). The reliability of survey attitude measurement: the influence of question and respondent attributes. *Sociological Methods and Research, 20,* 139–181.

Amery, A., Birkenhager, W., Brixko, P., Bulpitt, C., Clement, D., Deruyttere, M., et al. (1986). Mortality and morbidy results from the European Working Party on High Blood Pressure in the Elderly Trial. *Lancet, 1,* 1349–1354.

Andersen, P. K., Borgan, Ø., Gill, R. D., & Keiding, N. (1993). *Statistical models based on counting processes.* New York: Springer-Verlag.

Anderson, M. (1992). *Intelligence and development: A cognitive theory.* Oxford: Blackwell.

Andersson, S. A., Madigan, D., Perlman, M. D., & Richardson, T. S. (1998). Graphical markov models in multivariate analysis. In S. Ghosh (Ed.), *Multivariate analysis, Design of Experiments, and Survey Sampling.* Marcel Dekker, Inc.

Andrews, F. M. (1984). Construct validity and error components of survey measures: a structural modelling approach . *Public opinion quarterly, 48,* 409–422.

Armitage, P. (1975). *Sequential Medical Trials.* Oxford: Blackwell Scientific Publications.

Armitage, P. (1985). The search for optimality in clinical trials. *International Statistical Review, 3,* 5–24.

Armitage, P. (1992). Bradford Hill and the randomized controlled trial. *Pharmaceutical Medicine, 6,* 23–37.

Atkinson, A. C., & Donev, A. N. (1992). *Optimum Experimental Designs.* Oxford: Clarendon Press.

Australia, N. H. F. of. (1981). Treatment of mild hypertension in the elderly. *The Medical Journal of Australia, 2*, 398–402.

Bagozzi, R. P., & Burnkrant, R. E. (1979). Attitude organization and the attitude-behavior relationship. *Journal of Personality and Social Psychology, 37*, 913–929.

Bailar, J. C. (1995). The practice of meta-analysis. . *Journal of Clinical Epidemiology , 48*, 149–157.

Balke, A., & Pearl, J. (1995). Counterfactuals and policy analysis in structural models. In P. Besnard & S. Hanks (Eds.), *Uncertainty in artificial intelligence* (Vol. 11, pp. 11–18). San Francisco: Morgan Kaufmann.

Balke, A., & Pearl, J. (1997). Nonparametric bounds on causal effects from partial compliance data. *Journal of the American Statistical Association, 92*(439), 1–6.

Baltes, P. B., Reese, H. W., & Nesselroade, J. R. (1977). *Life-span developmental psychology: Introduction to research methods.* Monterey: Brooks/Cole.

Bangert-Drowns, R. L. (1995). Misunderstanding meta-analysis. *Evaluation and the Health Professions, 18*, 304–314.

Barr, M., & Wells, C. (1990). *Category Theory for Computing Science.* Englewood Cliffs, New Jersey: Prentice-Hall.

Bartlett, R. H., Roloff, D. W., Cornell, R. G., Andrews, A. F., Dillon, P. W., & Zwischenberger, J. S. (1985). Extracorporeal circulation in neonatal respiratory failure: a prospective randomized study. *Pediatrics, 76*, 479–487.

Begg, C. B. (1990). On inferences from Wei's biased coin design for clinical trials. *Biometrika, 77*, 467–484.

Begg, C. B., & Mazumdar, M. (1994). Operating characteristics of a rank correlation test for publication bias. *Biometrics, 50*, 1088–1101.

Belson, W. A. (1981). *Design and understanding of survey questions.* London: Gower.

Berkey, C. S., Anderson, J. J., & Hoaglin, D. C. (1996). Multiple-outcome meta-analysis of clinical trials. *Statistics in Medicine, 15*, 537–557.

Berkey, C. S., Hoaglin, D. C., Mosteller, R., & Colditz, G. A. (1995). A random-effects regression model for meta-analysis . *Statistics in Medicine, 14*, 395–411.

Berkson, J. (1946). Limitations of the application of fourfold table analysis to hospital data. *Biomet. Bull., 2*, 47–53.

Berlin, J. A., Laird, N. M., Sacks, H. S., & Chalmers, T. C. (1989). A comparison of statistical methods for combining event rates from clinical trials. *Statistics in Medicine, 8*, 141–151.

Berzuini, C. (1990). Modeling temporal processes via Belief Networks and Petri Nets, with application to Expert Systems. *Annals of Mathematics and Artificial Intelligence, 2*, 39–64.

Bethlehem, J. G. (1988). Reduction of Nonresponse Bias through Regression Estimation. *Journal of Official Statistics*(4), 251–260.

Bethlehem, J. G., & Keller, W. J. (1987). Linear weighting of sample survey data. *Journal of Official Statistics*(3), 141–154.

Bethlehem, J. G., & Kersten, H. M. P. (1985). On the treatment of non-response in sample surveys. *Journal of Official Statistics*(1), 287–300.

Bethlehem, J. G., & Kersten, H. M. P. (1986). *Werken met non-respons* (Statistische Onderzoekingen No. M30). Statistics Netherlands.

Bethlehem, J. G., & Kersten, H. M. P. (1987). The Non-response Problem. *Survey Methodology*(7), 130–156.

Bickel, P. J., Hammel, E. A., & O'Connell, J. W. (1975). Sex bias in graduate admissions: Data from Berkeley. *Science, 187*, 398–404.

Birnbaum, A. (1968). Some latent trait models and their use in inferring an examinee's ability. In F. M. Lord & M. R. Novick (Eds.), *Statistical theories of mental test scores* (pp. 397–424). Reading, MA: Addison-Wesley.

Bishop, C. M. (1995). *Neural networks for pattern recognition.* Oxford: Clarendon Press.

Blalock, Jr., H. M. (1962). Four-variable causal models and partial correlations. *American Journal of Sociology, 68*, 182–194.

Blalock, H. M. (1964). *Causal Inferences in non experimental research.* Chapel Hill: University of North Carolina Press.

Boddy, M. (1993). Temporal Reasoning for Planning and Scheduling. *SIGART Bulletin, 4*(3), 17–20.

Bollen, K. A. (1989). *Structural Equations with Latent Variables.* New York: John Wiley and Sons.

Boomsma, D. I., Molenaar, P. C. M., & Orlebeke, J. F. (1990). Estimation of individual genetic and environmental factor scores. *Genetic Epidemiology, 7*(1), 83–92.

Borgatta, E. F., & Bohrnstedt, G. W. (1981). Level of measurement , Once over again . In G. W. Bohrnstedt & E. F. Borgatta (Eds.), *Social Measurement: Current Issues* (pp. 23–37). Beverly Hills: Sage.

Boring, E. C. (1954). The Nature and History of Experimental Control. *The American Journal of Psychology, 67*(4), 573–589.

Bouvier, A., & George, M. (1983). *Dictionnaire des mathématiques.* Presses Universitaires de France.

Bowden, R. J., & Turkington, D. A. (1984). *Instrumental variables.* Cambridge, England: Cambridge University Press.

Bowley, A. L. (1906). Adress to the Economic Science and Statistics Section of the British Association of the Advancement of Science. *Journal of the Royal Statistical Society*(69), 548–557.

Bowley, A. L. (1926). Measurement of the Precision Attained in Sampling. In *Bulletin of the International Statistical Institute* (Vol. Book 1).

Box, G. E. P., Hunter, W. G., & Hunter, J. S. (1978). *Statistics for Experimenters.* Wiley: New York.

Breckler, S. J. (1990). Applications of covariance structure modeling in psychology: Cause for concern? *Psychological Bulletin, 107*(2), 260–273.

Brennan, R. L. (1983). *Elements of generalizability theory.* Iowa City: ACT.

Brown, B. (1980). The cross-over experiment for clinical trials. *Biometrics, 36*, 69–79.

Byar, D. P., & Piantadosi, S. (1985). Factorial designs for randomized clinical trials. *Cancer Treatment Reports, 69*, 1055–1063.

Campbell, D. T., & Fiske, D. W. (1959). Convergent and discriminant validation by the multitrait-multimethod matrix. *Psychological Bulletin*(56), 81–105.

Campbell, M. J., Julious, S. A., & Altman, D. G. (1995). Estimating sample sizes for binary, ordered categorical, and continuous outcomes in two group comparisons. *British Medical Journal, 311*, 1145–1148.

Carlin, J. B. (1992). Meta-analysis for 2x2 tables: A Bayesian approach. *Statistics in Medicine, 11*, 141–158.

Cartwright, N. (1989). *Nature' s capacities and their measurement.* Oxford: Oxford University Press.

Cartwright, N. (1995). Probabilities and experiments. *Journal of Econometrics, 67*, 47–59.

Chalmers, I. (1993). The Cochrane Collaboration: preparing, maintaining and disseminating systematic reviews of the effects of health care. *Annals of the New York Academy of Science , 703*, 156–165.

Chalmers, T. C. (1991). Problems induced by meta-analyses. *Statistics in Medicine, 10*, 971–980.

Chalmers, T. C., Levin, H., Sacks, H. S., Rettman, D., Berrier, J., & Nagalingam, R. (1987). Meta-analysis of clinical trials as a scientific discipline: I: Control of bias and comparison with large co-operative trials. *Statistics in Medicine, 6*, 315–325.

Chambers, J. M., Kleiner, W. S., & Tukey, P. A. (1983). *Graphical Methods for Data Analysis.* Belmont, California: Wadsworth.

Chandrasekaran, B., Glasgow, J., & Hari Narayanan, N. (1995). *Diagrammatic Reasoning. Cognitive and Computational Perspectives.* Menlo Park, California: AAAI Press / The MIT Press.

Chatellier, G., Zapletal, E., Lamaitre, D., Menard, J., & Degoulet, P. (1996). The number needed to treat: A clinically useful nomogram in its proper context. *British Medical Journal, 312,* 426–429.

Chickering, D. M. (1995). A transformational characterization of Bayesian network structures. In P. Besnard & S. Hanks (Eds.), *Uncertainty in artificial intelligence 11* (pp. 87–98). San Francisco: Morgan Kaufmann.

Chou, C. P., & Bentler, P. (1995). Estimations and tests in structural equation modeling. In R. H. Hoyle (Ed.), *Structural equation modeling* (pp. 37–55). Thousand Oaks, CA: Sage.

Christ, F. S. (1966). *Econometric models and methods.* New York: Wiley.

Clancey, W. J. (1985). *Heuristic Classification* (Report KSL 85–5). New York: Stanford Knowledge Systems Laboratory, Department of Computer Science, Palo Alto, CA.

Clarke, M. J., & Stewart, L. A. (1995). Systematic reviews of randomized controlled trials: the need for complete data. *Journal of Evaluation in Clinical Practice , 1,* 119–126.

Clogg, C. C. (1995). Latent Class models. In G. Arminger, C. C. Clogg, & M. E. Sobel (Eds.), *Handbook of statistical modeling for the social and behavioral sciences* (pp. 311–360). New York: Plenum Press.

Cochrane, A. L. (1972). Effectiveness and Efficiency: Random Reflections on Health Services.

Cochran, W. G. (1954). The combination of estimates from different experiments. *Biometrics, 3,* 177–188.

Cochran, W. G. (1977). *Sampling Techniques* (3rd ed.). New York: Wiley.

Codd, E. (1979). Extending the database relational model to capture more meaning. *Transactions on Database Systems, 4*(4), 397–434.

Coenders, G., Satorra, A., & Saris, W. E. (1997). Alternative approaches to structural modeling of ordinal data: A monte carlo study. In *Structural Equation Modeling .*

Collaboration, T. C. (1998). *The Cochrane Library (Issue 2)* (Tech. Rep.). Oxford, UK.

Collins, R., *et al.* (1990). Blood pressure, Stroke, and coronary heart disease. Part 2: Short-term reductions in blood pressure: Overview of randomized drug trials in their epidemiologic context. *Lancet, 335,* 827–838.

Concorde Coordinating Committee. (1994). Concorde: MRC/ANRS randomised double-blind controlled trial of immediate and deferred zidovudine in symptom-free HIV infection. *Lancet, 343,* 871–881.

Cook, D. J., *et al.* (1993). Should unpublished data be included in meta-analyses? *Journal of the American Medical Association, 269,* 2749–2753.

Cook, D. J., Mulrow, C. D., & Haynes, R. B. (1997). Systematic reviews: Synthesis of best evidence for clinical decisions. *Annals of Internal Medicine, 126,* 376–380.

Cook, D. J., & Sackett, D. L. (1995). The number needed to treat: A clinically useful measure of treatment effect. *British Medical Journal, 310,* 452–454.

Cook, D. J., Sackett, D. L., & Spitzer, W. O. (1995). Methodologic guidelines for systematic reviews of randomized control trials in health care from the Potsam Consultation on Meta-Analysis. *Journal of Clinical Epidemiology,, 48,* 167–171.

Cook, R. J., & Farewell, V. T. (1995). Multiplicity considerations in the design and analysis of clinical trials. *Journal of the Royal Statistical Society, 159,* 93–110.

Cook, T. D., & Campbell, D. T. (1979). *Quasi-experimentation: Design and analysis issues for field settings.* Chicago: RandMcNally.

Cooper, H. M. (1984). *The intergrative research review: A systematic approach.* Newbury Park, CA: SAGE Publications.

Cooper, H. M., & Hedges, L. V. (1994). *The handbook of research systhesis.* NY: Russell Sage Foundation.

Copi, I. M. (1953). *Introduction to logic.* New York: MacMillan.

Cornell, J. A. (1990). *Experiments with Mixtures: Designs, Models, and the analysis of Mixture Data.* New York: Wiley.

Couper, M., Baker, R. P., Bethlehem, J. G., Clark, C. Z. F., Martin, J., Nicholls, W. L., & O'Reilly, J. M. (Eds.). (1998). *Computer Assisted Survey Information Collection.* New York: Wiley.

Cox, D. R., & Wermuth, N. (1996). *Multivariate Dependencies.* London: Chapman Hall.

Cranney, M., & Walley, W. (1996). Same information, different decisions: The influence of evidence on the management of hypertension in the elderly. *British Journal of General Practice, 46,* 661–663.

Crocker, L., & Algina, J. (1986). *Introduction to classical and modern test theory.* New York: Holt, Rinehart and Winston.

Cronbach, L. J., Gleser, G. C., Nanda, H., & Rajaratnam, N. (1972). *The dependability of behavioral measurements: Theory of generalizability for scores and profiles.* New York: Wiley.

Crowder, M. J., & Hand, D. J. (1990). *Analysis of Repeated Measures.* London: Chapman & Hall.

Crutchfield, J. P. (1994). The calculi of emergence: Computation, dynamics and induction. *Physica D*, *75*, 11–54.

Darius, P. L., Coucke, W. J., & Portier, K. M. (1998). A Visual Environment for Designing Experiments. In *COMPSTAT98. Proceedings in Computational Statistics*. Heidelberg: Physica Verlag.

Darius, P., Boucneau, M., De Greef, P., De Feber, E., & Froeschl, K. (1993). Modelling meta data. *Statistical Journal of the United Nations ECE*, *10*(2), 171–179. (also in: Statistical Meta Information Systems, Proceedings of the Workshop, Luxembourg, 2–4 February 1993. Eurostat)

Darroch, J. N., Lauritzen, S. L., & Speed, T. P. (1980). Markov-fields and log-linear models for contingency tables. *Ann. Statist*, *8*, 522–539.

Dawid, A. P. (1979). Conditional independence in statistical theory. *Journal of the Royal Statistical Society, Series B*, *41*(1), 1–31.

Dean, K. E. (1993). *Population Health Research: Linking Theory and Methods.* London: Sage Press.

Dear, K. B. G. (1994). Iterative generalized least squares for meta-analysis of survival data at multiple times. *Biometrics*, *50*, 989–1002.

Dehue, T. (1997). Deception, Efficiency, and Random Groups. *Isis*, *88*, 653–673.

Dempster, A. P., Laird, N. M., & Rubin, D. B. (1977). Maximum likelihood from incomplete data via the EM algorithm (with discussion). *Journal of the Royal Statistical Society*, *39*, 1–38.

DerSimonian, R., & Laird, N. (1986). Meta-analysis in clinical trials. *Controlled Clinical Trials*, *7*, 177–188.

De Feber, E., & De Greef, P. (1992). Toward a formalised meta-data concept. In Y. Dodge & J. Whittaker (Eds.), *Proceedings of Compstat 1992* (pp. 351–356). Wuerzburg, Germany: Physica Verlag.

Dickersin, K., Min, Y.-I., & Meinert, C. L. (1992). Factors influencing publication of research results. *Journal of the American Medical Assoication*, *267*, 374–378.

Diggle, P. J., Liang, K.-Y., & Zeger, S. L. (1994). *Analysis of Longitudinal Data.* Oxford: Clarendon Press.

Dijksterhuis, E. J. (1961). *The Mechanization of the World Picture.* Oxford: Clarendon Press.

Doll, R. (1991). Development of controlled trials in preventive and therapeutic medicine. *Journal of Biosocial Science*, *23*, 365–378.

Dougherty, E. R., & Giardina, C. R. (1988). *Mathematical methods for artificial intelligence and autonomous systems.* Englewood Cliffs, NJ: Prentice-Hall International.

Drummond, M. F., O'Brien, B. J., Stoddart, G. L., & Torrance, G. W. (1997). *Methods for the Economic Evaluation of Health Care Programmes* (2nd ed.). Oxford New York Toronto: Oxford University Press.

Drummond, M., & Davies, L. (1991). Economic analysis alongside clinical trials. *International Journal of Technological Assessment in Health Care, 7*, 561–573.

Dube, R., & Weiss, S. M. (1989). A State Transition Model for Building Rule-based Systems. *Int. J. Expert Systems, 2*(3/4), 291–329.

Duchateau, L. (1995). *A Strategy-based Approach to Computer aided Analysis of Experiments*. Phd thesis, Katholieke Universiteit te Leuven.

Duncan, O. D. (1966). Path analysis: Sociological examples. *American Journal of Sociology, 72*, pp. 1–16.

Duncan, O. D. (1975). *Introduction to Structural equation models*. New York: Academic Press.

Easterbrook, P. J., Berlin, J. A., Gopalan, R., & Matthews, D. R. (1991). Publication bias in clinical research. *The Lancet, 337*, 867–872.

Edgeworth, F. Y. (1888). The statistics of examinations. *The Journal of the Royal Statistical Society*(51), 599–635.

Edwards, D. (1995). *An Introduction to Graphical Modelling*. New York: Springer Verlag.

Efron, B., & Feldman, D. (1991). Compliance as an explanatory variable in clinical trials (with Comments). *Journal of the American Statistical Association, 86*, 9–26.

Eggar, M., Smith, G. D., Smith, Schneider, M., & Minder, C. (1997). Bias in meta-analysis detected by a simple, graphical test. *British Medical Journal, 315*, 629–634.

Elliott, R. J., Aggoun, L., & Moore, J. B. (1995). *Hidden Markov models: Estimation and control*. New York: Springer-Verlag.

Engle, R. F., Hendry, D. F., & Richard, J. F. (1983). Exogeneity. *Econometrica, 51*, 277–304.

Epstein, R. J. (1987). *A history of econometrics*. New York: Elsevier Science.

Fahrmeir, L., & Tutz, G. (1994). *Multivariate statistical modeling based on generalized linear models*. New York: Springer-Verlag.

Family Heart Study Group. (1994). Randomised controlled trial evaluating cardiovascular screening and intervention in general practice: principal results of British family heart study. *British Medical Journal, 308*, 313–320.

Fayyad, U., Piatetsky-Shapiro, G., & Smyth, P. (1996). The KDD process for Extracting Useful Knowledge from Volumes of Data. *Communications of the ACM, 39*(11), 27–34.

Feinstein, A. R. (1995). Meta-analysis: Statistical alchemy for the 21st century. *Journal of Clinical Epidemiology, 48*, 71–79.

Fellegi, I. P., & Holt, D. (1976). A Systematic Approach to Automatic Edit and Imputation. *Journal of the American Statistical Association*(71), 17–35.

Felson, D. T. (1992). Bias in meta-analytic research. *Journal of Clinical Epidemiology, 45*, 885–892.

Fibrinolytic Therapy Trialists Collaborative Group. (1994). Indications for fibrinolytic therapy in suspected acute myocardial infarction: collaborative overview of early mortality and major morbidity results from all randomised trials of more than 1000 patients. *Lancet, 343*, 311–322.

Fisher, F. M. (1970). A correspondence principle for simultaneous equations models. *Econometrica, 38*(1), 73–92.

Fisher, R. A. (1932). *Statistical methods for research workers* (4th ed.). London: Oliver and Boyd.

Fleiss, J. L. (1993). The statistical basis of meta-analysis. *Statistical Methods in Medical Research* , *2*, 121–145.

Fleiss, J. L. (1994). Measures of effect size for categorical data. In H. Cooper & L. V. Hedges (Eds.), *The handbook of research synthesis*. NY: Russell Sage Foundation.

Fleming, T. R., Prentice, R. L., Pepe, M. S., & Glidden, D. (1994). Surrogate and auxiliary endpoints in clinical trials, with potential applications in cancer and AIDS research. *Statistics in Medicine, 13*, 955–968.

Fleming, T. R., & Watelet, L. F. (1989). Approaches to monitoring clinical trials. *Journal of the National Cancer Institute, 81*, 188- 193.

Fletcher, A., Gore, S., Jones, D., Fitzpatrick, D., R. Spiegelhalter, & Cox, D. (1992). Quality of life measures in health care II: Design, analysis, and interpretation. *British Medical Journal, 305*, 1145–1148.

Flury, B. (1997). *A First Course In Multivariate Statistics*. New York: Springer Verlag.

Fox, J. (1984). *Linear Statistical models and related methods*. New York: Wiley.

Frederiks, P. J. M., Hofstede, A. H. M. ter, & Lippe, E. (1994). *A Unifying Framework for Conceptual Data Modelling Concepts* (Report CSI-R9410). Katholieke Universiteit Nijmegen: Computing Science Institute, Faculty of Mathematics and Informatics.

Freedman, D. (1987). As others see us: A case study in path analysis (with discussion). *Journal of Educational Statistics, 12*(2), 101–223.

Freiman, J. A., Chalmers, T., Smith, H. J., & Kuebler, R. R. (1978). The importance of beta, the type II error and sample size in the design and interpretation of the randomized control trial Survey of 71 'negative' trials. *New England Journal of Medicine, 299*, 690–694.

Froeschl, K. A. (1997). *Metadata management in statistical information processing.* Wien, New York: Springer.

Galles, D., & Pearl, J. (1995). Testing identifiability of causal effects. In P. Besnard & S. Hanks (Eds.), *Uncertainty in artificial intelligence* (Vol. 11, pp. 185–195). San Francisco: Morgan Kaufmann.

Galles, D., & Pearl, J. (1997). Axioms of causal relevance. *Artificial Intelligence, 97*(1–2), 9–43.

Galles, D., & Pearl, J. (1998). An axiomatic characterization of causal counterfactuals. *Foundation of Science, 3*(1), 151–182.

Galton, F. (1865). Hereditary Talent and Character. *MacMillan's Magazine.* (also collected in: R. Jacoby and N. Glauberman (Eds.), The Bell Curve Debate (1995). New York: Random House.)

Geach, P. T. (1972). *Logic matters* (2nd ed.). Oxford: Blackwell.

Geiger, D., Verma, T. S., & Pearl, J. (1990). Identifying independence in Bayesian networks. *Networks, 20,* 507–534.

Genesereth, M. R., & Nilsson, N. J. (1987). *Logical Foundations of Artificial Intelligence.* Los Altos: Morgan Kaufmann Publishers, Inc.

Gilks, W. R., Thomas, A., & Spiegelhalter, D. J. (1994). A language and program for complex Bayesian modeling. *The Statistician, 43,* 169–178.

Glass, G. V. (1976). Primary, secondary, and meta-analysis of research. *Education Researcher, 5,* 3–8.

Goldberger, A. S. (1972). Structural equation models in the social sciences. *Econometrica: Journal of the Econometric Society, 40,* 979–1001.

Goldberger, A. S. (1973). Structural equation models: an Overview. In A. S. Goldberger & O. D. Duncan (Eds.), *Structural equation models in the social sciences* (pp. 1–18). New York:: Seminar Press.

Goldberger, A. S. (1992). Models of substance; comment on N. Wermuth, 'on block-recursive linear regression equations'. *Brazilian Journal of Probability and Statistics, 6,* 1–56.

Goldberger, A. S., & Duncan, O. D. (1973). *Structural equation models in the social sciences.* New York: Seminar Press.

Goldblatt, R. (1986). *Topoi, The Categorial Analysis of Logic* (Vol. 98, Revised ed.). Amsterdam, New York, Oxford, Tokyo: North-Holland Publ.

Goldstein, H., Healy, M., & Rasbash, J. (1994). Multilevel time series models with applications to repeated measures data. *Statistics in Medicine, 13,* 1643–1655.

Goldszmidt, M., & Pearl, J. (1992). Stratified rankings for causal modeling and reasoning about actions. In *Proceedings of the fourth international workshop on nonmonotonic reasoning* (pp. 99–110). Vermont.

Gomes, J., & Velho, L. (1997). *Image processing for computer graphics.* New York: Springer.

Goodwin, G. C., & Sin, K. S. (1984). *Adaptive filtering, prediction and control.* Englewood Cliffs, NJ: Prentice Hall.

Gould, A. L. (1980). A new approach to the analysis of clinical drug trials with withdrawals. *Biometrics, 36,* 721–727.

Gould, S. J. (1981). *The mismeasure of man.* New York: W. W. Norton & Company.

Grayson, D. A. (1987). Confounding confounding. *American Journal of Epidemiology, 126,* 546–553.

Greenland, S., Pearl, J., & Robins, J. M. (1999). Causal diagrams for epidemiologic research. *Epidemiology, 10*(1), 37–48.

Greenland, S., & Robins, J. (1986). Identifiability, exchangeability, and epidemiological confounding. *International Journal of Epidemiology, 15,* 413–419.

Greenland, S., & Salvan, A. (1990). Bias in the one-step method for pooling study results. *Statistics in Medicine, 9,* 247–252.

Gulliksen, H. (1950). *Theory of mental tests.* New York: Wiley.

Guttman, L. (1950). The basis for scalogram analysis. In S. A. Stouffer, L. Guttman, E. A. Suchman, P. L. Lazarsfeld, S. A. Star, & J. A. Clausen (Eds.), *Measurement and prediction* (Vol. IV, pp. 60–90). Princeton, NJ: Princeton University Press.

Haavelmo, T. (1943). The statistical implications of a system of simultaneous equations. *Econometrica, 11,* 1–12. (Reprinted in D. F. Hendry & M. S. Morgan , *The Foundations of Econometric Analysis*, Cambridge University Press, 477–490, 1995)

Hagenaars, J. (1990). *Categorical Longitudinal data: Log-linear panel, trend and Cohort analysis .* Newbury Park, CA-New York: Sage.

Hagenaars, J. (1993). Loglinear models with Latent variables. In *Quantitative Applications in the Social Sciences BN 94.* Sage.

Hambleton, R. K. (1989). Principles and selected applications of item response theory. In R. L. Linn (Ed.), *Educational Measurement* (3rd ed., pp. 147–200). New York: Macmillan.

Hambleton, R. K., & Swaminathan, H. (1985). *Item response theory: Principles and applications.* Boston: Kluwer-Nijhoff.

Hambleton, R. K., Swaminathan, H., & Rogers, H. J. (1991). *Fundamentals of item response theory.* Newbury Park, CA: Sage.

Hamblin, R. (1974). Social attitudes: Magnitude measurement and theory . In H. M. Blalock (Ed.), *Measurement in the social sciences* (pp. 61–121). New York: Wiley.

Hand, D. J. (1994). Deconstructing Statistical Questions. *Journal of the Royal Statistical Society, Series A, 157*, 65–76.

Hand, D. J. (1996). Statistics and the theory of measurement. *Journal Royal Statistical Society Series A*(159), 445–492.

Hand, D. J., & Crowder, M. J. (1996). *Practical longitudinal data analysis.* London: Chapman & Hall.

Hand, D. J., & Jacka, S. D. (Eds.). (1997). *Statistics in finance.* London: Arnold.

Hand, D. J., McConway, K. J., & Stanghellini, E. (1996). Graphical models of applicants for credit. *IMA J. Math. Appl. in Business & Industry, 8,* 143–155.

Hassoun, M. H. (1995). *Fundamentals of artificial neural networks.* Cambridge, Massachusetts: The MIT Press. (A Bradford Book)

Hays, W. L. (1974). *Statistics for the Social Sciences.* London: Holt, Rinehart and Winston.

Hedges, L. V., & Olkin, I. (Eds.). (1985). *Statistical methods for meta-analysis.* Orlando: Academic Press.

Heinen, A. G. J. H. (1996). *Latent clas and discrete latent trait models.* Newbury Park, CA: Sage.

Hellman, S., & Hellman, D. S. (1991). Of mice but not men: problems of the randomized clinical trial. *New England Journal of Medicine, 324,* 1585–1589.

Hendry, D. F. (1995). *Dynamic econometrics.* New York: Oxford University Press.

Hill, A. B. (1977). *Principles of Medical Statistics* (10th ed.). London.

Hill, A. B. (1990). Memories of the British streptomycin trial in tuberculosis: the first randomized clinical trial. *Controlled Clinical Trials, 11,* 77–79.

Holland, P. W. (1986). Statistics and causal inference. *Journal of the American Statistical Association, 81*(396), 945–960.

Holland, P. W. (1988). Causal inference, path analysis, and recursive structural equations models. In C. Clogg (Ed.), *Sociological methodology* (pp. 449–484). Washington, D. C.: American Sociological Association.

Holland, P. W. (1995). Some reflections on Freedman's critiques. *Foundations of Science, 1,* 50–57.

Holland, P. W., & Rubin, D. B. (1983). On Lord's paradox. In H. Wainer & S. Messick (Eds.), *Principals of modern psychological measurement* (pp. 3–25). Hillsdale, NJ: Lawrence Earlbaum.

Holly, S., & Hallett, A. H. (1989). *Optimal control, expectations and uncertainty.* Cambridge: Cambridge University Press.

Homer, P., & O'Brien, R. M. (1988). Using Lisrel models with crude and category measures. *Quality and Quantity*(22), 191–201.

Horvitz, D. G., & Thompson, D. J. (1952). A generalization of sampling without replacement from a finite universe. *Journal of the American Statistical Association*(47), 663–685.

Hox, J. J., & Mellenbergh, G. J. (1990). The interplay of substantive and auxiliary theory. In J. J. Hox & J. de Jong-Gierveld (Eds.), *Operationalization and research strategy* (pp. 123–136). Amsterdam, The Netherlands: Swets and Zeitlinger.

Hsu, J. E. (1996). *Multiple Comparisons. Theory and Methods.* London: Chapman & Hall.

Ioannidis, J. P. A., Cappelleri, J. C., & Lau, J. (1998). Issues in comparisons between meta-analyses and large trials. *Journal of the American Medical Association, 279,* 1089–1093.

Isidori, A. (1989). *Nonlinear control theory* (2nd ed.). New York: Springer-Verlag.

ISIS-2 Collaborative Group. (1988). Randomized trial of intravenous streptokinase oral aspirin, both, or neither among 17187 cases of suspected acute myocardial infarction: ISIS-2. *Lancet, 2,* 349–360. (Second International Study of Infarct Survival)

Jaccard, J., Turrisi, R., & Wan, C. K. (1990). *Interaction effects in multiple regression.* Newbury Park, CA: Sage.

Jadad, A. R., & McQuay, H. J. (1996). Meta-analyses to evaluate analgesic interventions: A systematic qualitative review of their methodology. *Journal of Clinical Epidemiology, 49,* 235–243.

James, L. R., Mulaik, S. A., & Brett, J. M. (1982). *Causal analysis: Assumptions, models, and data.* Beverly Hills: Sage.

Jensen, F. V. (1996). *An Introduction to Bayesian Networks.* London: UCL Press.

Jones, B., & Kenward, M. G. (1989). *Design and analysis of cross-over trials.* London: Chapman and Hall.

Jones, D. R. (1995). Meta-analysis: Weighing the evidence. *Statistics in Medicine, 14,* 137–149.

Jöreskog, K. G. (1973). A general method for estimating a linear structural equation system . In A. S. Goldberger & O. D. Duncan (Eds.), *Structural equation models in the social sciences* (pp. 85–112). New York: Seminar Press.

Jöreskog, K. G. (1974). Analyzing psychological data by structural analysis of covariance matrices. In D. H. Krantz, R. C. Atkinson, R. D. Luce, & P. Suppes (Eds.), *Contemporary developments in mathematical psychology: Measurement, psychophysics, and neural information processing* (Vol. II, pp. 1–56). San Francisco: W. H. Freeman.

Jöreskog, K. G. (1979). Statistical estimation of structural models in longitudinal developmental investigations. In J. R. Nesselroade & P. B. Baltes (Eds.), *Longitudinal research in the study of behavior and development* (pp. 303–351). New York: Academic Press.

Jöreskog, K. G., & Sörbom, D. (1989). *Lisrel 7: Users reference guide* . Mooresville.

Jöreskog, K. G., & Sörbom, D. (1993). *LISREL 8 User's reference guide.* Chicago: Scientific Software International.

Judd, C. M., Smith, E. R., & Kidder, L. H. (1991). *Research Methods in Social Relations* (6-th Edition ed.). New York: Holt, Rinehart and Winston, Inc.

Kalton, G., & Kasprzyk, D. (1986). The Treatment of Missing Survey Data. *Survey Methodology*(12), 1–16.

Kenny, D. A., & Judd, C. M. (1984). Estimating the nonlinear and interactive effects of latent variables. *Psychological Bulletin*(96), 201–210.

Kersten, H. M. P., & Bethlehem, J. G. (1984). Exploring and reducing the nonresponse bias by asking the basic question. *Statistical Journal of the United Nations ECE*(2), 369–380.

Khan, K. S., Daya, S., & Jadad, A. R. (1996). The importance of quality of primary studies in producing unbiased systematic reviews. *Archives of Internal Medicine* , *156*, 661–666.

Khuri, A. I., & Cornell, J. A. (1987). *Response Surfaces: Designs and Analysis.* New York: Dekker.

Kiaer, A. N. (1895). Observations et expériences concernant des dénombrements réprésentatifs. In *Bulletin of the International Statistical Institute* (Vol. Book 2, pp. 176–183).

Kim, J. H., & Pearl, J. (1983). A computational model for combined causal and diagnostic reasoning in inference systems. In *Proceedings IJCAI-83, (Karlsruhe, Germany)* (pp. 190–193). San Francisco, CA: Morgan Kaufman Publishers.

Kish, L. (1967). *Survey Sampling.* New York: Wiley.

Kish, L. (1987). *Statistical Design for Research.* New York: Wiley.

Kolk, H. (1994). *Actief en passief bewustzijn* [Active and passive consciousness]. Rotterdam: Ad Donker.

Költringer, R. (1993). *Messqualität in der sozialwissenschaftlichen Umfrageforschung* (Endbericht Project P8690-SOZ). Wien: Fonds zur Förderung der wissenschaftlichen Forschung FWF.

Koopmans, T. C. (1953). Identification problems in econometric model construction. In W. C. Hood & T. C. Koopmans (Eds.), *Studies in econometric method* (pp. 27–48). New York: Wiley.

Koopmans, T. C., Rubin, H., & Leipnik, R. B. (1950). Statistical inference in dynamic economic models. In T. C. Koopmans (Ed.), (pp. 53–237). New York: John Wiley.

Koster, J. T. (1996). Markov properties of nonrecursive causal models. *The Annals of Statistics, 24*(5), 2148–2177.

Krzanowski, W. J. (1988). *Principles of Multivariate Analysis.* Oxford University Press: Oxford.

Kuhn, T. (1977). Chapter 8, The Function of Measurement in Modern Physical Science. In *The Essential Tension.* Chicago: University of Chicago Press.

Langefors, B. (1977). Information systems theory. *Inf. Syst., 2*, 207–219.

Langeheine, R. (1994). Latent variables Markov models. In A. von Eye & C. C. Clogg (Eds.), *Latent variables analysis: Applications for developmental research* (pp. 373–395). Thousand Oaks: Sage.

Lanzing, J. W. A. (1996). *Everything you always wanted to know about ... Concept Mapping.* (WWW document. http://utto1031.to.utwente.nl/artikel1/)

Lauritzen, S. (1996). *Graphical Models.* Oxford University Press: Oxford.

Läuter, J., Glimm, E., & Kropf, S. (1996). New Multivariate Tests for Data with an Inherent Structure. *Biometrical Journal, 38*(1), 5–23.

Leamer, E. E. (1985). Vector autoregressions for causal inference? *Carnegie-Rochester Conference Series on Public Policy, 22*, 255–304.

Lee, S., & Hershberger, S. A. (1990). A simple rule for generating equivalent models in covariance structure modeling. *Multivariate Behavioral Research, 25*(3), 313–334.

LeLorier, J., Grégoire, G., Benhaddad, A., Lapierre, J., & Dedrian, F. (1997). Discrepancies between meta-analyses and subsequent large randomized controlled trials. *The New England Journal of Medicine, 337*, 536–542.

LeRoy, S. F. (1995). Causal orderings. In K. D. Hoover (Ed.), *Macroeconometrics: Developments, tensions, prospects* (pp. 211–227). Boston: Kluwer Academic.

Letzel, H. (1995). Best-evidence synthesis: An intelligent alternative to meta-analysis: Discission. A case of 'either-or' or 'as well'. *Journal of Clinical Epidemiology, 48*, 19–21.

Lewis, D. (1973). Causation. *The Journal of Philosophy, 70*, 556–567. (Reprinted with postscript in D. Lewis, *Philosophical Papers*, vol. II. New York: Oxford, 1986)

Lewis, E. M. (1992). *An Introduction to Credit Scoring.* Athena Press.

Lewis, J. A., Jones, D. R., & Rohmel, J. (1995). Biostatistical methodology in clinical trials - a European guideline. *Statistics in Medicine, 14*, 1655–1657.

Light, R. J., & Pillemer, D. B. (1984). *Summing up: The science of reviewing research.* Cambridge, MA: Harvard University Press.

Likert, R. (1932). A technique for the measurement of attitudes. *Archives of Psychology*(140), 5–55.

Lindgren, B. W. (1976). *Statistical theory* (3rd ed.). New York: Macmillan.

Littell, R. C., Milliken, G. A., Stroup, W. W., & Wolfinger, R. D. (1996). *SAS System for Mixed Models.* Cary, NC, USA: SAS Institute.

Little, R. J. A., & Rubin, D. B. (1987). *Statistical Analysis with Missing Data.* New York: Wiley.

Little, R. J. A., & Rubin, D. B. (1990). The Analysis of Social Science Data with Missing Values. *Sociological Methods & Research, 18*(2–3), 292–326.

Little, R., & Yau, L. (1996). Intent-to-treat analysis for longitudinal studies with drop-outs. *Biometrics, 52*(4), 1324–1333.

Lord, F. M. (1980). *Applications of item response theory to practical testing problems.* Hillsdale, NJ: Lawrence Erlbaum.

Lord, F. M., & Novick, M. R. (1968). *Statistical theories of mental test scores.* Reading, MA: Addison-Wesley.

Lucas Jr., R. E. (1976). Econometric policy evaluation: a critique. In K. Brunner & A. H. Meltzer (Eds.), *The phillips curve and labor markets* (Vols. CRCS, Vol. 1, pp. 19–46). Amsterdam: North-Holland.

Lütkepohl, H. (1991). *Introduction to multiple time series analysis.* Berlin: Springer-Verlag.

MacCallum, R. C., Wegener, D. T., Uchino, B. N., & Fabrigar, L. R. (1993). The problem of equivalent models in applications of covariance structure analysis. *Psychological Bulletin, 114*(1), 185–199.

MacCallum, R., & Ashby, F. G. (1986). Relationships between linear systems theory and covariance structure modeling. *Journal of Mathematical Psychology, 30*, 1–27.

Macready, G. B., & Dayton, C. M. (1980). The nature and use of state mastery models. *Applied Psychological Measurement*(4), 493–516.

Maki, D. P., & Thompson, M. (1973). *Mathematical models and applications.* Englewood Cliffs, New Jersey: Prentice Hall.

Marschak, J. (1950). Statistical inference in economics. In T. Koopmans (Ed.), *Statistical inference in dynamic economic models* (pp. 1–50). New York: Wiley. (Cowles Commission for Research in Economics, Monograph 10)

Marshall, K. T., & Oliver, R. M. (1995). *Decision Making and Forecasting.* USA.: McGraw-Hill.

McArdle, J. J., & Epstein, D. (1987). Latent Growth Curves within Developmental Structural Equation Models. *Child Development, 58*, 110–133.

McCullough, P., & Nelder, J. A. (1989). *Generalized Linear Models* (2nd ed.). New York: Chapman & Hall.

McDonald, R. P. (1997). Haldane's lungs: A case study in path analysis. *Multivariate Behavioral Research, 32*(1), 1–38.

McIntosh, M. (1996). The population risk as an explanatory variable in research synthesis of clinical trials. *Statistics in Medicine, 15*, 1713–1728.

Meek, C. (1995). Causal inference and causal explanation with background knowledge. In P. Besnard & S. Hanks (Eds.), *Uncertainty in artificial intelligence 11* (pp. 403–410). San Francisco: Morgan Kaufmann.

Mellenbergh, G. J. (1989). Item bias and item response theory. *International Journal of Educational Research*(13), 127–143.

Mellenbergh, G. J. (1994a). A unidimensional latent trait model for continuous item responses. *Multivariate Behavioral Research*(29), 223–236.

Mellenbergh, G. J. (1994b). Generalized linear item response theory", JOURNAL="Psychological Bulletin. (115), 300–307.

Mellenbergh, G. J. (1995). Conceptual notes on models for discrete polytomous item responses. *Applied Psychological Measurement*(19), 91–100.

Mellenbergh, G. J. (1996). Measurement precision in test score and item response models. *Psychological Methods*(1), 293–299.

Miettinen, O. S. (1985). *Theoretical epidemiology.* New York: Wiley.

Millsap, R. E., & Everson, H. T. (1993). Methodology review: Statistical approaches for assessing measurement bias. *Applied Psychological Measurement*(17), 297–334.

Mill, J. (1862). *System of Logic.* London: Parker.

Moher, D., Jadad, A. R., Nichol, G., Penman, M., Tugwell, P., & Walsh, S. (1995). Assessing the quality of randomized controlled trials: An annotated bibliography of scales and checklists. *Controlled Clinical Trials, 16*, 62–73.

Moher, D., & Olkin, I. (1995). Meta-analysis of randomized controlled trials: A concern for standards [Commentary]. *Journal of the American Medical Association, 274*, 1962–1964.

Mokken, R. J. (1970). *A theory and procedure of scale analysis.* The Hague, The Netherlands: Mouton.

Molenaar, I. W. (1982). Mokken scaling revisited. *Kwantitatieve Methoden*(3), 145–164.

Molenaar, P. C. M. (1985). A dynamic factor model for the analysis of multivariate time series. *Psychometrika, 50*, 181–202.

Molenaar, P. C. M. (1987). Dynamic assessment and adaptive optimisation of the therapeutic process. *Behavioral Assessment, 9*, 389–416.

Molenaar, P. C. M. (1994). Dynamic latent variable models in developmental psychology. In A. von Eye & C. C. Clogg (Eds.), *Analysis of latent variables in developmental research* (pp. 155–180). Newbury Park, CA: Sage.

Molenaar, P. C. M. (1997). Time series analysis and its relationship with longitudinal analysis. *International Journal of Sports Medicine, 18*, 232–237.

Molenaar, P. C. M., & Nesselroade, J. R. (1998). A comparison of pseudo-maximum likelihood and asymptotically distribution-free dynamic factor analysis parameter estimation in fitting covariance-structure models to block-Toeplitz matrices representing single-subject multivariate time-series. *Multivariate Behavioral Research, 33*, 313–342.

Montgomery, D. C. (1991). *Design and Analysis of Experiments* (3rd ed.). New York: Wiley.

Morris, C. N. (1983). Parametric empirical Bayes inference: theory and applications. *Journal of the American Statistical Association, 78*, 47–55.

Mulrow, C. D. (1995). Rationale for systematic reviews. In I. Chalmers & D. G. Altman (Eds.), *Systematic reviews* (pp. 1–8). London, United Kingdom: BMJ Publishing Group.

Mulrow, C. D., Cook, D. J., & Davidoff, F. (1997). Systematic reviews: Critical links in the great chain of evidence. *Annals of Internal Medicine, 126*, 389–391. (Editorial)

Mulrow, C. D., Langhorne, P., & Grimshaw, J. (1997). Integrating heterogeneous pieces of evidence in systematic reviews. *Annals of Internal Medicine.*

Mulrow, C. D., & Oxman, A. D. (1997). Cochrane Collaboration Handbook. In *The Cochrane Library.* Oxford Update Software: The Cochrane Collaboration. (Issue 4, database on disk and CDROM)

Muthen, B. (1984). A general structural equation model dichotomous, ordered categorical and continuous latent variables indicators . *Psychometrika*(43), 241–250.

Muthen, B. (1987). Response to Freedman's critique of path analysis: Improve credibility by better methodological training. *Journal of Educational Statistics, 12*(2), 178–184.

Nelder, J. (1974). Genstat, a statistical system. In G. Bruckman *et al.* (Ed.), *Proceedings compstat'74* (pp. 499–506). Wien: Physica verlag.

Nesselroade, J. R., & Molenaar, P. C. M. (1999). Pooling lagged covariance structures based on short, multivariate time series for dynamic factor analysis. In R. H. Hoyle (Ed.), *Statistical strategies for small sample research.* Thousand Oaks, CA: Sage Publications, Inc.

Neter, J., Kutner, M. H., Nachtsheim, C. J., & Wasserman, W. (1996). *Applied Linear Statistical Models* (4th ed.). Chicago: Irwin.

Neyman, J. (1934). On the two different aspects of the representative method: the method of stratified sampling and the method of purposive selection. *Journal of the Royal Statistical Society*(97), 558–625.

NHS Center for Reviews of Research and Dissemination. (1996). *Undertaking systematic reviews of research on effectiveness. CRC guidelines for those carrying or commissioning reviews* (Tech. Rep.). York, United Kingdom:.

Novak, J. D. (1990). How do we learn our lesson: Taking students through the process. *The science teacher, 60*(3), 50–55.

O'Brien, P. C. (1984). Procedures for comparing samples with multiple endpoints. *Biometrics, 40*, 1079–1087.

O'Brien, P. C., & Fleming, T. R. (1979). A multiple testing procedure for clinical trials. *Biometrics, 35*, 549–556.

Oldford, R. W. (1990). Software abstraction of elements of Statistical Strategy. *Annals of Mathematics and Artificial Intelligence, 2*, 291–308.

Olkin, I. (1990). History and goals. In K. W. Wachter & M. L. Straf (Eds.), *The future of meta-analysis* (pp. 3–10). NY:: Russell Sage Foundation.

Oort, F. J. (1996). *Using restricted factor analysis in test construction*. Phd thesis, University of Amsterdam, The Netherlands.

Orchard, R., & Woodbury, M. A. (1971). A missing information principle: Theory and application. In L. M. LeCam, J. Neyman, & E. L. Scott (Eds.), *Proceedings of sixth Berkeley symposium on mathematical statistics and probability* (pp. 697–715). Berkeley: University of California Press.

Oxman, A. D. (1993). Meta-statistics: Help or hindrance?

Pascal, B. (1954). *Oeuvres Complètes*. Paris: Gallimard.

Pearl, J. (1988). *Probabilistic Reasoning in Intelligent Systems*. San Mateo: Morgan Kaufman.

Pearl, J. (1993a). Belief networks revisited. *Artificial Intelligence, 59*, 49–56.

Pearl, J. (1993b). Comment: Graphical models, causality, and intervention. *Statistical Science, 8*, 266–269.

Pearl, J. (1993c). From Bayesian networks to causal networks. In *Proceedings of the adaptive computing and information processing seminar* (pp. 25–27). Brunel Conference Centre, London. (See also *Statistical Science*, 8(3), 266–269, 1993.)

Pearl, J. (1995). Causal diagrams for experimental research. *Biometrika, 82*, 669–710.

Pearl, J. (1996). Structural and probabilistic causality. In D. R. Shanks, K. J. Holyoak, & D. L. Medin (Eds.), *The psychology of learning and motivation* (Vol. 34, pp. 393–435). San Diego, CA: Academic Press.

Pearl, J. (1998). *Why there is no statistical test for confounding, why many think there is, and why they are almost right* (Tech. Rep. No. R-256). Los Angeles, CA: Department of Computer Science, University of California, Los Angeles.

Pearl, J. (1999). *Causality.* (forthcoming)

Pearl, J., & Meshkat, P. (1998). On testing regression models with fewer regressors. In J. Whittaker & Heckerman (Eds.), *Proceedings of the 7th international workshop on AI and statistics* (pp. 255–259). Fort Lauderdale, Florida: Morgan Kaufmann.

Pearl, J., & Robins, J. M. (1995). Probabilistic evaluation of sequential plans from causal models with hidden variables. In P. Besnard & S. Hanks (Eds.), *Uncertainty in artificial intelligence 11* (pp. 444–453). San Francisco: Morgan Kaufmann.

Pearl, J., & Verma, T. (1987). The Logic of Representing Dependencies by Directed Acyclic Graphs. In *Proc., 6th National Conference on AI (AAAI-87)* (pp. 374–379). Seattle, WA.

Pearl, J., & Verma, T. (1991). A theory of inferred causation. In J. A. Allen, R. Fikes, & E. Sandewall (Eds.), *Principles of knowledge representation and reasoning: Proceedings of the second international conference* (pp. 441–452). San Mateo, CA: Morgan Kaufmann.

Pearson, K. (1903). On the Inheritance of the Mental and Moral Characters in Man, and its comparison with the inheritance of the Physical characters. *Journal of the Royal Anthropological Institute of Great Britain and Ireland.* (also collected in: R. Jacoby and N. Glauberman (Eds.), The Bell Curve Debate (1995). New York: Random House.)

Pearson, K. (1904). Report on certain enteric fever inoculation statistics. *British Medical Journal, 3,* 1243–1246.

Pearson, K. (1933). On a method of determining whether a sample of size n supposed to have been drawn from a parent population having a known probability integral, has probably been drawn at random. *Biometrika, 25,* 379–410.

Peirce, C. S. (1933). *Collected papers of Charles Sanders Peirce.* Cambridge, Mass.: Harvard University Press.

Petersen, K. (1983). *Ergodic theory.* New York: Cambridge University Press.

Peto, R. (1987). Why do we need systematic overviews of randomized trials? *Statistics in Medicine, 6,* 233–240.

Peto, R., Pike, M. C., Armitage, P., Breslow, N., Cox, D. R., Howard, S. V., Mantel, N., McPherson, K., Peto, J., & Smith, P. G. (1976). Design and analysis of randomized clinical trials requiring prolonged observation of each patient I Introduction and design. *British Journal of Cancer, 34,* 585- 612.

Physicians' Health Study Research Group, S. C. of the. (1989). Final report on the aspirin component of the ongoing Physicians' Health Study. *New England Journal of Medicine, 321*, 129–135.

Pierce, B. C. (1991). *Basic Category Theory for Computer Scientists*. Cambridge, Massachusetts London, England: The MIT Press.

Pocock, S. J. (1992). When to stop a clinical trial. *British Medical Journal, 305*, 235–240.

Pogue, J., & Yusuf, S. (1998). Overcoming the limitations of current meta-analysis of randomized controlled trials . *Lancet, 351*, 47–52.

Pol, F. van de, & Bethlehem, J. G. (1997). Data Editing Perspectives. *Statistical Journal of the United Nations ECE*(14), 153–171.

Pratt, J. W., & Schlaifer, R. (1988). On the interpretation and observation of laws. *Journal of Econometrics, 39*, 23–52.

Prentice, R. L. (1989). Surrogate endpoints in clinical trials: definition and operational criteria. *Statistics in Medicine, 8*, 431–440.

Press, J. S. (1972). *Applied multivariate analysis*. New York: Holt, Rinehart & Winston.

Priestley, M. B., & Subba Rao, T. (1969). A test for stationarity of time series. *Journal of the Royal Statistical Society, 31*, 140–149.

Psaty, B. M., Heckbert, M. D., Koepsell, T., Siscovick, D. S., Raghunathan, T. E., Weiss, N. S., Rosendaal, F. R., Lemaitre, R. N., Smith, N. L., Wahl, P. W., Wagner, E. H., & Furberg, C. D. (1995). The risk of myocardial infarction associated with antihypertensive drug therapies. *Journal of the American Medical Association, 274*, 620- 625.

Pukelsheim, F. (1993). *Optimal Design of Experiments*. New York: Wiley.

Quillian, M. (1968). Semantic Memory. In M. Minsky (Ed.), *Semantic Information Processing* (pp. 216–270). Cambridge, Massachusetts: MIT Press.

Rabiner, L. R. (1989). A tutorial on hidden Markov models and selected applications in speech recognition . *Proceedings of the IEEE, 77*, 257–286.

Rajkumar, S. V., Sampathkumar, P., & Gustafson, A. B. (1996). Number needed to treat is a simple measure of treatment efficacy for clinicians. *Journal of General Internal Medicine, 11*, 357–359.

Rasch, D., & Darius, P. (1994). Computer aided design of experiments. In P. Dirschedl & R. Ostermann (Eds.), *Computational Statistics*. Heidelberg: Physica Verlag.

Rasch, G. (1960). *Probabilistic models for some intelligence and attainment tests*. Copenhagen: University of Chicago Press; Danish Institute for Educational Research. (Expanded edition)

Richardson, T. (1996). A discovery algorithm for directed cyclic graphs. In E. Horvitz & F. Jensen (Eds.), *Proceedings of the twelfth conference on uncertainty in artificial intelligence* (pp. 454–461). San Francisco, CA: Morgan Kaufmann.

Richard, J. F. (1980). Models with several regimes and changes in exogeneity. *Review of Economic Studies, 47*, 1–20.

Ripley, B. D. (1993). Statistical aspects of neural networks. In *Networks and Chaos - Statistical and Probabilistic Aspects* (pp. 40–123). London-Glasgow-New York-Tokyo-Melborne-Madras: Chapman and Hall.

Ripley, B. D. (1996). *Pattern recognition and neural networks.* Cambridge: Cambridge University Press.

Robins, J. M. (1986). A new approach to causal inference in mortality studies with a sustained exposure period – applications to control of the healthy workers survivor effect. *Mathematical Modeling, 7*, 1393–1512.

Robins, J. M. (1995). Discussion of "Causal diagrams for empirical research" by J. Pearl. *Biometrika, 82*(4), 695–698.

Robins, J. M., & Greenland, S. (1992). Identifiability and exchangeability for direct and indirect effects. *Epidemiology, 3*(2), 143–155.

Robins, J., Breslow, N., & Greenland, S. (1986). Estimators of the Mantel-Haenszel variance consistent in both sparse data and large-strata limiting models. *Biometrics, 42*, 311–323.

Rosenbaum, P., & Rubin, D. (1983). The central role of propensity score in observational studies for causal effects. *Biometrica, 70*, 41–55.

Rosenthal, R. (1991). *Meta-analytic procedures for social research.* Newbury Park, CA: Sage Publications, Inc. (Rev. ed.)

Rosenthal, R. (1994). Parametric measures of effect size. In H. Cooper & L. V. Hedges (Eds.), *The handbook of research synthesis* (pp. 231–244). NY: Russell Sage Foundation.

Rosen, R. (1991). *Life itself: a comprehensive enquiry into the nature, origin and fabrication of life.* Columbia University Press.

Rovine, M. J., & Molenaar, P. C. M. (1998). A Lisrel model for the analysis of repeated measures. *Structural Equation Modeling.* (to appear)

Rubin, D. B. (1974). Estimating causal effects of treatments in randomized and nonrandomized studies. *Journal of Educational Psychology, 66*, 688–701.

Rubin, D. B. (1979). Illustrating the use of multiple imputations to handle non-response in sample surveys. In *Bulletin of the International Statistical Institute* (Vol. Book 2, pp. 517–532).

Rubin, D. B. (1990). Neyman (1923) and causal inference in experiments and observational studies. *Statistical Science, 5*, 472–480.

Rydeheard, D. R., & Burstall, R. M. (1988). *Computational Category Theory*. New York: Prentice-Hall.

Sackett, D. L. (1995). Applying overviews and meta-analyses at the bedside. *Journal of Clinical Epidemiology, 48*, 61–66.

Sage, A., & Melsa, J. (1971). *Estimation theory with applications to communications and control*. New York: McGraw-Hill.

Samejima, F. (1969). Estimation of latent ability using a response pattern of graded scores. *Psychometrika Monographs*(17).

Saris, W. E. (1990). The choice of a model for evaluation of measurement instruments. In W. E. Saris & A. Van Meurs (Eds.), *Evaluation of measurement instruments by meta-analysis of multitrait-multimethod studies* (pp. 118–129). Amsterdam, The Netherlands: Koninklijke Nederlandse Akademie van Wetenschappen.

Saris, W. E. (1996). Integration of data and theory: a mixed model of satisfaction . In W. E. Saris, R. Veenhoven, A. C. Scherpenzeel, & B. Bunting (Eds.), *A comparative study of Life satisfaction in Europe* (p. 281 -299). Budapest: Eötvös University Press.

Saris, W. E., & Andrews, F. (1991). Evaluation of measurement instruments using a structural modeling approach. In P. P. Biemer, R. M. Groves, L. E. Lyberg, N. A. Matheowetz, & S. Sudman (Eds.), *Measurement errors in surveys* (pp. 575–579). New York: Wiley.

Saris, W. E., & Münnich, A. (Eds.). (1995). *The multitrait Multimethod approach to evaluate measurement instruments*. Budapest: Eötvös University Press.

Saris, W. E., & Stronkhorst, H. (1984). *Causal modelling in nonexperimental research: An introduction to the Lisrel approach*. Amsterdam: SRF.

Saris, W. E., & Van Meurs, A. (Eds.). (1990). *Evaluation of measurement instruments by meta-analysis of Multitrait multimethod studies*. Amsterdam: North Holland.

Saris, W. E., Veenhoven, R., Scherpenzeel, A. C., & Bunting, B. (Eds.). (1996). *A comparative study of Life satisfaction in Europe*. Budapest: Eötvös University Press.

Särndal, C. E., Swensson, B., & Wretman, J. (1992). *Model Assisted Survey Sampling*. New York: Springer Verlag.

Scherpenzeel, A. C., & Saris, W. E. (1993). The evaluation of measurement instruments by meta-analysis of multitrait-multimethod studies . *Bulletin de Methodologie Sociologique, 39*, 3–19.

Schmid, C. H., Lau, J., McIntosh, M. W., & Cappelleri, J. C. (1998). *An empirical study of the effect of the control rate as a predictor of treatment efficacy in meta-analysis of clinical trials*. (In press)

Schreiber, A. T., Wielinga, B. J., & Breuker, J. A. (Eds.). (1993). *KADS: A principled approach to knowledge-based system development* (Vol. 11). London: Academic Press. (ISBN 0-12-629040-7)

Schulz, K. F., Chalmers, I., Grimes, D. A., & Altman, D. G. (1994). Assessing the quality of randomization from reports of controlled trials published in obstetrics and gynecology journals. *Journal of the American Medical Association, 272*, 125- 128.

Schulz, K. F., Chalmers, I., Hayes, R. J., & Altman, D. G. (1995). Empirical evidence of bias: Dimensions of methodological quality associated with estimates of treatment effects in controlled trials. *Journal of the American Medical Association , 273*, 408–412.

Schuman, H., & Presser, S. (1981). *Questions and answers in attitude surveys: experiments on question form, wording and context* . New York: Academic Press.

Schwartz, D., & Lellouch, J. (1967). Explanatory and pragmatic attitudes in therapeutic trials. *Journal of Chronic Disease, 20*, 637–648.

Sculpher, M. J., Seed, P., Henderson, R. A., Buxton, M. J., Pocock, S. J., Parker, J., Joy, M. D., Sowton, E., & Hampton, J. R. (1994). Health service costs of coronary angioplasty and coronary artery bypass surgery: the Randomised Intervention Treatment of Angina RITA trial. *Lancet, 344*, 927–930.

Searle, S. R., Casella, G., & McCulloch, C. E. (1992). *Variance Components*. New York: Wiley.

Senn, S. (1994). Importance of trends in the interpretation of an overall odds ratio in the meta-analysis of clinical trials. *Statistics in Medicine, 13*, 293–296.

Shafer, G. (1996). *The art of causal conjecture*. Cambridge: MIT Press.

Sharp, S. J., Thompson, S. G., & Altman, D. G. (1996). The relationship between treatment benefit and underlying risk in meta-analysis. *British Medical Journal, 313*, 735–738.

Shavelson, R. J., Webb, N. M., & Rowley, G. L. (1989). Generalizability theory. *American Psychologist*(44), 922–932.

Shipley, B. (1997). *An inferential test for structural equation models based on directed acyclic graphs and its nonparametric equivalents* (Tech. Rep.). Canada: Department of Biology, University of Sherbrooke.

Simes, R. J. (1986). Publication bias: the case for an international registry of clinical trials. *Journal of Clinical Oncology, 4*, 1529–1541.

Simon, H. A. (1953). Causal ordering and identifiability. In W. C. Hood & T. C. Koopmans (Eds.), *Studies in econometric method* (pp. 49–74). Wiley and Sons, Inc.

Simon, H. A. (1954). Spurious correlation: a causal interpretation . *Journal of the American Statistical Association, 49*, 467–479.

Simpson, C. H. (1951). The interpretation of interaction in contingency tables. *J. Roy. Statist. Soc. B, 13*, 238–241.

Sinclair, J. C., & Bracken, M. B. (1994). Clinically useful measured of effect in binary analyses of randomized trials. *Journal of Clinical Epidemiology, 47*, 881–889.

Sjöstrom, H., & Nilsson, R. (1972). *Thalidomide and the Power of the Drug Companies*. Harmondsworth: Penguin.

Slavin, R. E. (1995). Best evidence synthesis: An intelligent alternative to meta-analysis . *Journal of Clinical Epidemiology, 48*, 9–18.

Smith, T. C., Spiegelhalter, D. J., & Thomas, A. (1995). Bayesian approaches to random-effects meta-analysis: A comparative study. *Statistics in Medicine, 14*, 2685–2699.

Snee, R. D. (1985). Computer-Aided Design of Experiments — Some Practical Experiences. *Journal of Quality Technology, 17*, 222–236.

Snyder, D. L. (1975). *Random point processes*. New York: Wiley.

Sobel, M. E. (1990). Effect analysis and causation in linear structural equation models. *Psychometrika, 55*(3), 495–515.

Sobel, M. E. (1995). Handbook of statistical modeling for the social and behavioral sciences. In G. Arminger, C. Clogg, & M. E. Sobel (Eds.), (pp. 1–37). New York: Plenum Press.

Somsen, R. J. M., Molenaar, P. C. M., Van der Molen, M. W., & Jennings, J. R. (1991). Behavioral modulation patterns fit an animal model of vagus-cardiac pacemaker interactions. *Psychophysiology, 28*, 383–399.

Sowa, J. F. (1984). *Conceptual Structures*. Reading, MA: Addison-Wesley.

Spiegelhalter, D. J. (1998). Bayesian graphical modelling, a case-study in monitoring health outcomes. *Appl. Statist, 47*, 115–133.

Spiegelhalter, D. J., Freedman, L. S., & Parmar, M. K. B. (1994). Bayesian approaches to randomized trials. *Statistics in Society, 157*, 357–416.

Spirtes, P., Glymour, C., & Scheines, R. (1993). *Causation, prediction, and search*. New York: Springer-Verlag.

Spirtes, P., & Richardson, T. (1996). *A polynomial time algorithm for determinant DAG equivalence in the presence of latent variables and selection bias. Proceedings of the 6th International Workshop on Artificial Intelligence and Statistics*.

Spirtes, P., Richardson, T., Meek, C., Scheines, R., & Glymour, C. (1996). *Using d-separation to calculate zero partial correlations in linear models with correlated errors* (Tech. Rep. No. CMU-PHIL-72). Pittsburg, PA: Carnegie-Mellon University, Department of Philosophy.

Spirtes, P., Richardson, T., Meek, C., Scheines, R., & Glymour, C. (1997). Using path diagrams as a structural equation modeling tool. *Sociological Methods and Research, 27*(2), 182–225.

Spirtes, P., & Verma, T. (1992). *Equivalence of causal models with latent variables* (Tech. Rep. No. CMU-PHIL-33). Pittsburgh, Pennsylvania: Carnegie Mellon University.

Standards of Reporting Trials Group. (1994). A proposal for structured reporting of randomized controlled trials. *Journal of the American Medical Association, 24,* 1926–1931.

Stelzl, I. (1986). Changing a causal hypothesis without changing the fit: Some rules for generating equivalent path models. *Multivariate Behavioral Research, 21,* 309–331.

Stern, J. M., & Simes, R. J. (1997). Publication bias: Evidence of delayed publication in a cohort study of clinical research projects. *British Medical Journal, 315,* 640–645.

Stewart, L. A., & Clarke, M. J. (1995). Practical methodology of meta-analyses (overviews) using updated individual patient data. *Statistics in Medicine, 14,* 2057–2079.

Steyer, R., Gabler, S., & Rucai, A. A. (1996). Individual causal effects, average causal effects, and unconfoundedness in regression models. In F. Faulbaum & W. Bandilla (Eds.), *SoftStat'95, advances in statistical software 5* (pp. 203–210). Stuttgart: Lucius & Lucius.

Stigler, S. M. (1985). *The history of Statistics.* Cambridge, Mass.: The Belknap Press of Harvard University Press.

Strotz, R. H., & Wold, H. O. (1960). Causal models in the social sciences. *Econometrica, 28,* 417–427.

Taves, D. R. (1974). Minimization: a new method of assigning patients to treatment and control groups. *Clinical Pharmacology and Therapeutics, 15,* 443 453.

Thissen, D., & Steinberg, L. (1986). A taxonomy of item response models. *Psychometrika*(51), 567–577.

Thomas, L. C., Crook, J. N., & Edelman, D. B. (Eds.). (1992). *Credit Scoring and Credit Control.* Oxford: Clarendon Press.

Thompson, S. G. (1994). Why sources of heterogeneity in meta-analysis should be investigated. *British Medical Journal, 309,* 1351–1355.

Thompson, S. G., & Sharp, S. J. (1998). *Explaining heterogeneity in meta-analysis: A comparison of methods.* (In press)

Tippett, L. H. C. (1931). *The methods of statistics.* London: Williams and Norgate.

RESEARCH METHODOLOGY

Tukey, J. W. (1977). *Exploratory Data Analysis*. Reading, Massachusetts: Addison-Wesley.

Van Benthem, J. (1991). *The Logic of Time: A Model-Theoretic Investigation into the Varieties of Temporal Ontology and Temporal Discourse* (2nd ed.). Dordrecht/Boston/London: Kluwer Academic Publishers.

Van den Berg, G. M., De Feber, E., & De Greef, P. (1992). Analysing statistical data processing. In K. Weichselberger & W. Kloesgen (Eds.), *New techniques and technologies for statistics* (pp. 91–100). Bonn, Germany.

Van den Brink, W. P. (1982). Binomial test models for domain-referenced testing. *Evaluation in education: An international review series*(5), 165–176.

Van der Linden, W. J. (1991). Applications of decision theory to test-based decision making. In R. K. Hambleton & J. N. Zaal (Eds.), *Advances in educational and psychological testing: Theory and applications* (pp. 129–156). Boston: Kluwer.

Van der Linden, W. J., & Hambleton, R. K. (1997). *Handbook of modern item response theory*. New York: Springer.

Veenhoven, R. (1996). The study of life satisfaction. In W. E. Saris, R. Veenhoven, A. C. Scherpenzeel, & B. Bunting (Eds.), *A comparative study of Life satisfaction in Europe* (pp. 11–49). Budapest: Eötvös University Press.

Verbeke, G., & Molenberghs, G. (Eds.). (1997). *Linear Mixed Models in Practice*. New York: Springer.

Verma, T., & Pearl, J. (1988). Causal networks: Semantics and expressiveness. In *Proceedings of the 4th workshop on uncertainty in artificial intelligence* (pp. 352–359). Mountain View, CA. (Also in R. Shachter, T. S. Levitt, and L. N. Kanal , *Uncertainty in AI 4*, Elesevier Science Publishers, 69–76, 1990)

Verma, T., & Pearl, J. (1990). Equivalence and synthesis of causal models. In P. B. et al. (Ed.), *Uncertainty in artificial intelligence 6* (pp. 220–227). Cambridge, MA: Elsevier Science.

Vickers, S. (1989). *Topology via logic*. Cambridge: Cambridge University Press.

Vonesh, E. F., & Chinchilli. (1997). *Linear and nonlinear models for the analysis of repeated measurements*. New York: Marcel Dekker.

Wainer, H. (1991). Adjusting for differential base-rates: Lord's paradox again. *Psychological Bulletin, 109*, 147–151.

Wald, A. (1947). *Sequential Analysis*. New York: Wiley.

Ware, J. H. (1989). Investigating therapies of potentially great benefit: ECMO (with Comments). *Statistical Science, 4*, 298–340.

Webb, E. J., Campbell, D. T., Schwartz, R. D., & Sechrest, L. (1966). *Unobtrusive measures: Non-reactive research in the social sciences*. Rand McNally.

Weinberg, C. R. (1993). Toward a clearer definition of confounding. *American Journal of Epidemiology, 137*, 1–8.

Wermuth, N. (1992). On block-recursive regression equations. *Brazilian Journal of Probability and Statistics, 6*, 1–56. ((with discussion))

Whitehead, A., & Jones, N. M. B. (1994). A meta-analysis of clinical trials involving different classifications of response into ordered categories. *Statistics in Medicine, 13*, 2503–2515.

Whitehead, J. (1992). *The Design and Analysis of Sequential Clinical Trials.* Chichester: Ellis Horwood.

Whittaker, J. (1990). *Graphical Models in Applied Multivariate Statistics.* Chichester, New York, Brisbane, Toronto, Singapore: John Wiley and Sons.

Whittaker, J., & Sewart, P. (1998). Graphical models in credit scoring. *IMA J. Math. Appl. Bus. Ind., 9*, 241–266.

Whittle, P. (1990). *Risk-sensitive optimal control.* Chichester: Wiley.

WHO European Collaborative Group. (1986). European collaborative trial of multifactorial prevention of coronary heart disease: final report on the 6-year results. *Lancet, 1*, 869–872.

Willems, M. (1993). *Chemistry of Language, a graph-theoretical study of linguistic semantics.* Phd thesis, University Twente.

Wittes, J., & Brittain, E. (1990). The role of internal pilot studies in increasing the efficiency of clinical trials. *Statistics in Medicine, 9*, 65–72.

Wolf, F. M. (1986). *Meta-analysis: Quantitative methods for research synthesis.* Newbury Park, CA: SAGE Publications.

Wolstenholme, D. E., & Nelder, J. A. (1986). A front end for GLIM. In R. Haux (Ed.), *Expert systems in statistics* (pp. 155–177). Stuttgart: Fisher.

Wright, S. (1921). Correlation and causation. *Journal of Agricultural Research, 20*, 557–585.

Wright, S. (1923). The theory of path coefficients: A reply to Niles' criticism. *Genetics, 8*, 239–255.

Wright, S. (1934). The Method of Path Coefficients. *Annals of Mathematical Statistics, 5*, 161–215.

Yampratoom, E., & Allen, J. F. (1993). Temporal Reasoning for Planning and Scheduling. *SIGART Bulletin, 4*(3), 26–29.

Yang Jonsson, F. (1997). Non-linear structural equation models: simulation studies of the Kenny-Judd model. *Stia Statistica Ulsaliensis*(4).

Yusuf, S., Collins, R., & Peto, R. (1984). Why do we need some large, simple randomized trials? *Statistics in Medicine, 3*, 409 420.

Yusuf, S., Peto, R., Lewis, J., Collins, R., & Sleight, P. (1985). Beta blockade during and after myocardial infarction: An overview of the randomized trials. *Progress in Cardiovascular Diseases, 27*, 335–371.

Zeh, H. D. (1992). *The physical basis of the direction of time* (2nd ed.). Berlin: Springer-Verlag.

Zelen, M. (1969). Play the winner rule and the controlled clinical trial. *Journal of the American Statistical Association, 64*, 130–146.

Index